ALSO BY ROBERT D. KAPLAN

The Coming Anarchy: Shattering the Dreams of the Post Cold War

An Empire Wilderness: Travels into America's Future

The Ends of the Earth: A Journey at the Dawn of the 21st Century

The Arabists: The Romance of an American Elite

Balkan Ghosts: A Journey Through History

Soldiers of God: With the Mujahidin in Afghanistan

Surrender or Starve: The Wars Behind the Famine

EASTWARD
TO
TARTARY

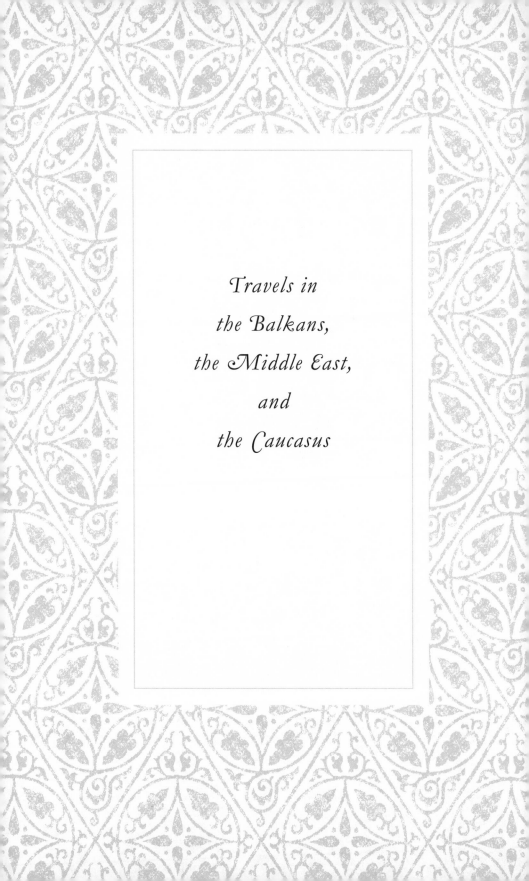

*Travels in
the Balkans,
the Middle East,
and
the Caucasus*

Eastward to Tartary

Robert D. Kaplan

RANDOM HOUSE

NEW YORK

All rights reserved under International and
Pan-American Copyright Conventions. Published in the
United States by Random House, Inc., New York,
and simultaneously in Canada by Random House of
Canada Limited, Toronto.

RANDOM HOUSE and colophon are registered
trademarks of Random House, Inc.

Library of Congress Cataloging-in-Publication data is available

ISBN 0-375-50272-6

Random House website address: www.atrandom.com

Printed in the United States of America on acid-free paper

4 6 8 9 7 5

Book design by Caroline Cunningham

To Allen Pizzey and Dee Hemmings

... it appears to me more appropriate to follow up the real truth of a matter than the imagination of it; for many have pictured republics and principalities which in fact have never been seen and known, because how one lives is so far distant from how one ought to live . . .

—NICCOLÒ MACHIAVELLI, *The Prince*

To know the worst is not always to be liberated from its consequences; nevertheless it is preferable to ignorance.

—ISAIAH BERLIN, "The Originality of Machiavelli"

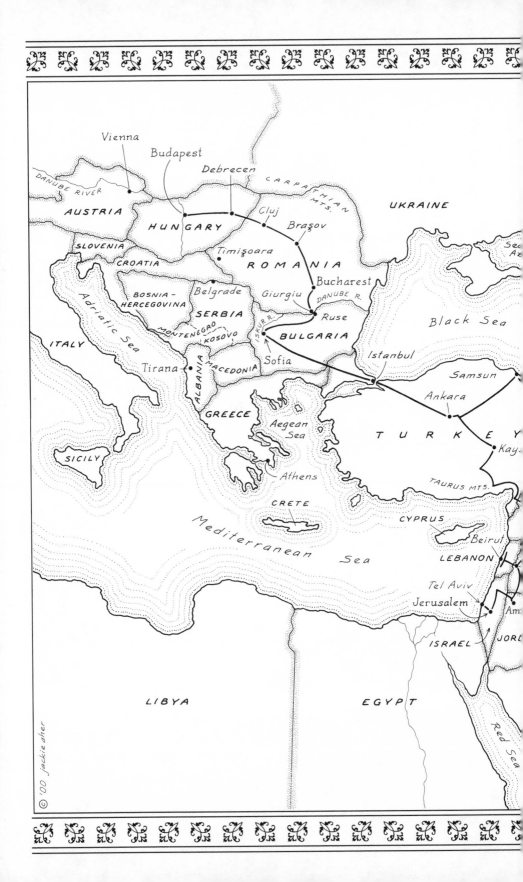

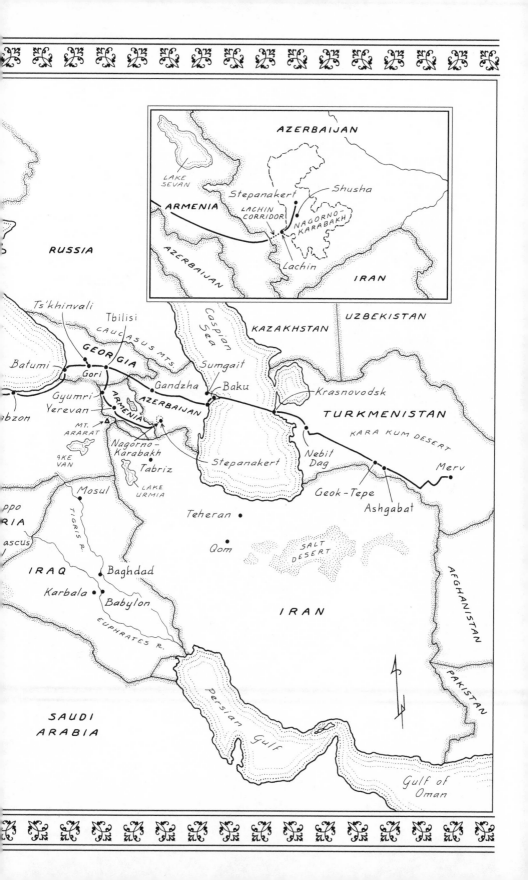

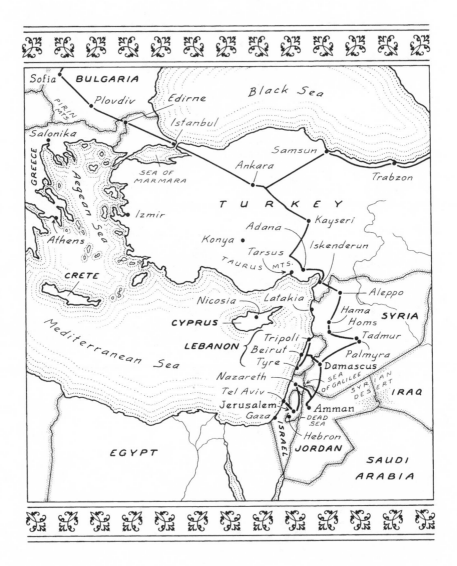

AUTHOR'S NOTE

Balkan Ghosts, to which the first part of this book is a sequel, was a portrait of the Balkans at the end of the 1980s that tried to anticipate the problems there in the 1990s. Likewise, *Eastward to Tartary* portrays the Greater Near East at the turn of the twenty-first century, and looks forward to the next decade or so in that region.

"Should we intervene?" That is the question often asked in crisis situations. This book, like *Balkan Ghosts,* offers no answers, but describes the lay of the land. Because foreign policy, when it is serious, is guided by necessity and not by sympathy, a landscape, however grim, will never deter the seasoned policy maker from intervention if an abiding national interest coincides with a moral one. Indeed, it is only the grimmest human landscapes that demand interventions in the first place.

Frederick the Great used to tell his generals, "He who defends everything defends nothing."[1] Likewise, he who writes about every place in a vast region writes about no place. A book that dealt with every country from Morocco to India—the extent of the Near East, according to some definitions—would be unwieldy. My aim here is to record a journey, not to write a comprehensive survey. Some readers will be surprised not to find Iran and Iraq in this book. I wrote about Iran at length in *The Ends of the Earth* and about Iraq in *The Arabists,* and felt it would be more useful to introduce Americans to countries like

Syria, Georgia, Azerbaijan, and Turkmenistan—countries that have received relatively little attention but whose future may define tomorrow's news, as old-style leaders pass from the scene.

April 2000

CONTENTS

Part I

THE
BALKANS

1

RUDOLF FISCHER,

COSMOPOLITAN

The scent of plum brandy and red wine mixed with the mildew and dust from old books and maps. It was ten in the morning, February 17, 1998. I was in an apartment in the drab eastern outskirts of Budapest. My host, Rudolf Fischer, suggested that we start drinking. "The slivovitz is kosher—look at the Hebrew label! And the wine is young—from a barrel in Villányi, in southern Hungary. It will rest easy in your stomach and loosen our tongues."

Peasant rugs, folkloric weavings, and other Balkan bric-a-brac filled Fischer's small living room, which also functioned as his library: early-twentieth-century volumes, in several languages, on Balkan nationalism, the Persian and Ottoman empires, the Byzantine heritage of Greece, and other subjects having to do with Europe's back-of-beyond. Fischer, with thick white hair, a mustache, and a wistful expression, wore suede trousers and a sleeveless sheepskin shepherd's vest. His rakish appearance and the backdrop of maps and trinkets reminded me of the Victorian explorer, linguist, and secret agent Sir Richard Francis Burton in old age, in his library in Trieste.[1] It was to Fischer that I had come for advice before beginning my journey through the Near East, from the Balkans to Central Asia, what the Elizabethans called Tartary.

"I was born in 1923," Fischer told me, "in Kronstadt, in Transylvania, a mainly German city, which is now called Braşov in Romania. My father was a Hungarian Jew from a strictly Orthodox family. My mother was a Saxon German and a Lutheran. She was among the Nazis' favored *Volksdeutsche*"—a term laden with racial implications, reserved for ethnic Germans in Eastern Europe and southern Russia. "My parents loved each other deeply. Does that surprise you? Before Hitler, relations between the ethnic groups were full of such irony and subtlety, you cannot imagine. My mother escaped from Communist Romania by pretending to be Jewish and going to Israel. My wife is also a Saxon Lutheran, from near Kronstadt. Of course," he added, smiling, "I was Jewish enough for the Nazis, but not enough to satisfy the Israeli rabbis of today." Fischer handed me his calling card. There was no telephone number or address on it, just two words:

RUDOLF FISCHER
χαλαμαρας

The Greek word, he explained, signified "a nineteenth-century writer of love letters" to women on behalf of their husbands, who were away in the Turkish army and did not know how to write their own.

We exchanged toasts, and Fischer unfurled his set of late-nineteenth-century Austrian army staff maps and a somewhat earlier German one. "These are the maps you must use at the start of your journey," he told me. "They are better than the Cold War–era maps. The maps before 1989 are, of course, useless. The Iron Curtain is still a social and cultural border. Do you know the real service provided by McDonald's in Hungary and the other formerly socialist countries? They are the only places where people—women, especially—can find a clean public lavatory."

Fischer washed down his second slivovitz with red wine. Pointing with his finger at the mid-nineteenth-century German map, he told me: "The Carpathian Mountains, which now run through Romania, mark the end of Europe and the beginning of the Near East. North and west of the Carpathians lay the old Austro-Hungarian empire. Here, the map is like a modern one—see how crowded it is with towns. But, look: To the south and east of the Carpathians, the map is virtually empty. That was the old Ottoman Turkish empire, where few surveys had been done and trade was not regulated—Walachia, Serbia, and Bulgaria. These places are still underdeveloped compared to Transylvania, Croatia, and Hungary."

Let me explain; it is less complicated than it sounds. Very simply put, the split running through the Balkans between the Austro-Hungarian and Ottoman empires to which Fischer referred reflects a much earlier division. In the fourth century A.D., the Roman empire divided into western and eastern halves. Rome remained the capital of the western empire, while Constantinople became the capital of the eastern one. Rome's western empire eventually gave way to Charlemagne's kingdom and to the Vatican: Western Europe, in other words. The eastern empire—Byzantium—was populated mainly by Greek-speaking Orthodox Christians, and later by Moslems, when the Ottoman Turks captured Constantinople in 1453. The border between the eastern and western empires ran through the middle of what after World War I became the multiethnic state of Yugoslavia. When that state broke apart violently in 1991, at least initially it echoed the division of Rome sixteen centuries earlier: The Slovenes and Croats were Roman Catholics, heirs to a tradition that went back from Austria-Hungary to Rome in the West; the Serbs, however, were Eastern Orthodox and heirs to the Ottoman-Byzantine legacy of Rome in the East.

The Carpathians, which run northeast of the former Yugoslavia and divide Romania into two parts, reinforced this boundary between Rome and Byzantium and, later, between the Habsburg emperors in Vienna and the Turkish sultans in Constantinople. Rudolf Fischer told me that the Carpathians, which were not easily traversed, halted the eastward spread of European culture, marked by Romanesque and Gothic architecture and by the Renaissance and the Reformation.[2] "This is why Greece, too, belongs to the East," Fischer said. He added that "Romania—because of the influence of the Renaissance and the Reformation in the northwest of the country—had been more developed than Greece before World War Two!" and waved his hand for emphasis. "It was only the Truman Doctrine—$10 billion in American aid, in 1940s dollars no less—that created today's westernized Greece.

"Let me go on in the same vein," Fischer continued. "The differences between the Hungarian Stalinist leader Mátyás Rákosi and the Romanian Stalinist leader Gheorghe Gheorghiu-Dej, and even more so between their successors, János Kádár and Nicolae Ceauşescu, were the differences—don't you see!—between Habsburg Austria-Hungary and Ottoman Turkey. Rákosi and Kádár may have been perverse Central Europeans, but as Hungarians, they were Central Europeans nonetheless. But Gheorghiu-Dej and Ceauşescu were Oriental despots, from a part of Europe influenced more by Ottoman Turkey than by Habsburg Austria. That's why communism did less damage to Hungary than to Romania."

Indeed, in Central Europe, communism claimed to be the cure for the economic inequalities and other cruelties wrought by bourgeois industrial development, a radical liberal populism of a sort, while in the former Byzantine-Ottoman empire, where there had never been such modern development, communism was simply a destructive force, a second Mongol invasion.

"Váci utca," exclaimed Fischer, referring to a fashionable shopping street in Budapest, "with its chandeliers and *Merry Widow* atmosphere—that is not a creation of postcommunism but of communism itself as Hungarians, with their Central European tradition, interpreted it in the 1970s and 1980s."[3]

❧ ❧

History and geography, of course, are only blueprints upon which humankind superimposes the details.[4] Take the Iron Curtain, a creature less of geographical and cultural patterns than of late–World War II power politics, which created another division to go alongside the one that separated the Habsburg and Ottoman empires. In one sense, the differences in development between ex-Communist countries affected by Habsburg rule—such as Hungary, the Czech Republic, and Poland—and those affected by Byzantium and Ottoman Turkey—such as Romania and Bulgaria—are profound. In another sense, however, Hungary shares more than it may like to admit with its former Warsaw Pact allies Romania and Bulgaria. Fischer explained that despite its economic progress, Hungary still cannot easily escape its past:

"Our whores in Budapest are Russian and Ukrainian; our money—though it floats freely—is still worthless in the West; our oil and gas are from Russia; and we have mafia murders and corruption just like in the countries to the south and east. Mafia shootings and the drug trade put pressure on the Hungarian government to make [entrance] visas compulsory for Romanians, Serbs, and Ukrainians, who are thought to be the culprits, but that will never happen, because it will separate us from the ethnic Hungarians just over the [Romanian] border. We are tied to the ex–Communist East, whether we like it or not."

He might have added that the hallway in his building was dark and untidy, like many that I had seen throughout the formerly Communist world, where decades of state ownership had given people no incentive to maintain property, an attitude that was changing slowly. There was, too, the building itself, and all the others in Fischer's neighborhood, whose unfinished look and poor construction—plate glass and mustard-colored cinder blocks—were more typical of buildings in formerly Communist Central Asia than those in Austria, just a two-hour ride away by train. The Berlin Wall may have fallen in November 1989, but for a traveler almost a decade later, its ghost was still present.

"What about NATO?" I asked. "Will its new eastern frontier—following the admission of Poland, the Czech Republic, and Hungary—mark the border of the Near East?"

"NATO doesn't matter," Fischer said, waving his hand dismissively. "Only the EU [European Union] is real." He explained that the European Union is about currency, border controls, passports, trade, interest rates, environmental and dietary regulations—the details of daily life—which will change Hungary. "For decades Austria was not part of NATO, but did you ever think of Austria as part of Eastern Europe or the Near East? Of course not." (Austria had not been part of the European Union, either, but its economy operated along the EU's free-market lines.)

Therefore, it appeared likely—at least if the EU expanded into Hungary, Slovenia, the Czech Republic, and Poland but took a decade to grant full membership to Romania, Bulgaria, Macedonia, Turkey, and Russia—that the Western alliance would be an eerie variation of the Holy Roman Empire at its zenith in the eleventh century, and the split between Western and Eastern Christianity would be institutionalized once more, as it had been during the divisions between Rome and Byzantium and the Habsburg and Ottoman empires. The Near East would then begin on the border of Hungary and Romania. Completing the reemergence of this older map, Russia was now returning to the dimensions of sixteenth-century Muscovy: a vibrant city-state within a chaotic hinterland.[5]

"Hungarians want to *spiritualize* the frontiers—that is the word that they use here," Fischer remarked.

"You mean they want the borders to be filters: to protect, but not to divide," I said.

"Perhaps," Fischer replied dryly. "What the Hungarians really want is to let ethnic Hungarians from the east into Hungary, but nobody else." Fischer then railed against the "modern age" in Europe, in which democratic stirrings in the late nineteenth and early twentieth centuries strengthened ethnic nationalism, while industrialization strengthened the power of states. The result was the collapse of multiethnic empires like Habsburg Austria-Hungary and Ottoman Turkey and the rise of uniethnic powers like Germany and of nasty tribal principalities in the post–World War I Balkans, though they were in some cases called parliamentary democracies. Even the 1848 democratic revolutions in Central Europe, it seemed, were not so pure; they were based on ethnicity as much as on liberal ideals, and in Hungarian (Magyar) areas, at least, were opposed by the minority Croats, Serbs, and Romanians.[6] For Fischer, with his background, the modern age had meant "Magyarization campaigns" and other forms of "ethnic cleansing," crucial to the establishment of petty states tyrannized by ethnic majorities. The modern age, he told me, was symbolized by what had happened on his twenty-first birthday, September 17, 1944:

"Because my father and I had fled Romania when World War Two broke out and managed to get visas to Australia, I was in the Australian army on my twenty-first birthday. My commanding officer had given me a short leave. Thus, I spent my birthday alone, walking in the Australian countryside and thinking about who among my family and friends back in Transylvania were alive or dead. What had happened to them?

"Soon after the war, I learned that on that very day, Hungarian soldiers shot the entire Jewish population of Sármás, a village east of Kolozsvár, in Transylvania.[7] Those poor people. They had thought of themselves as Hungarians. *They spoke Hungarian.* They had managed to survive five years of fascism without being deported to concentration camps. It was as if they had been miraculously forgotten while every kind of horror reigned around them. Then their *own* Hungarian soldiers appeared in Sármás, and what did they do? They herded all the Jews into pigsties for several days and then took them to a hill and massacred them. Within the Holocaust, there were many little pogroms."[8]

A week after Fischer told me this story, I would visit that same hill in Sărmaşu, Romania. It was a vast and sloping fold of grass surrounded by villages of rotting wood, where wild pigs scampered through the mud and peasants in black sheepskins worked with scythes. I saw three lines of graves, 126 in all, each with a Star of David and a Hebrew inscription. The graves were surrounded by an ugly cement barrier, a brutal box that might be called "modern history." I climbed over the barrier and read the Romanian inscription:

> . . . [Hungarian] fascist troops, the enemies of mankind, occupied the village of Sărmaşu, where they herded all the Jews—men, women, and children—inside pigsties, where they kept them without food and tortured and humiliated them in the most vicious manner for ten days, after which they were taken to this hill of weeping and killed in the most sadistic ways on the eve of the Jewish holiday Rosh Hashanah. . . .[9]

Of course, this monument in Romania made no mention of equally horrible atrocities perpetrated against Jews by the Romanians themselves during World War II.

"That is why I remember so vividly walking alone in Australia on my twenty-first birthday," Fischer continued. "Because the memory of it was preserved by what I later found out had occurred on that same day in Sărmaşu. You see, Robert, Hungarian nationalism, Romanian nationalism—they're all bad. The boundary formed by the Carpathians was benign compared to these modern nationalistic boundaries, because the Carpathians divided empires within which peoples and religions mixed. I am a cosmopolitan. That is what every civilized person must now try to be!"

I told him that cosmopolitanism must always be linked to memory. Without memory, there would be no possibility of irony—the very stuff of history. For, as Fischer said, Jews, Gypsies, Kurds, and other minorities were generally safe within autocratic regimes such as Habsburg Austria and Ottoman Turkey but were killed or oppressed when these autocracies began giving birth to independent states dominated by ethnic majorities, such as Austria, Hungary, Romania, Greece, and Turkey.

Fischer picked up his walking stick and told me to take my coat. "We're going for a walk. I have something to show you before you start your journey."

For thirty minutes, he led me briskly along dreary boulevards wheezing with traffic, through underpasses and an empty park, then along the tracks of a railway that wove through the foul backyards of old apartment buildings. We passed people wearing baggy clothes and soiled smocks, carrying battered briefcases. "You are now in what the early-twentieth-century Austrian writer Heimito von Doderer called 'the serious parts of a town,' where a city shows the ugly organs underneath its pretty skin," Fischer remarked. I thought of the necklace of diamond-and-tomato-colored lights along the streets by the Danube, with their smart shops and packs of Western tourists, several tram stops away to the west: Budapest's downtown was already in Western Europe and the twenty-first century, but this part of town was still in Eastern Europe and, as I soon learned, living in the time before the collapse of the Berlin Wall.

Near Orczy Square, in the far-off southeast corner of Budapest, we came to an immense hodgepodge of metal-framed stalls and greasy canteens set up in abandoned Russian railway cars. I saw Chinese-manufactured high-top running shoes on sale for the equivalent of ten dollars, sweaters for four dollars, socks, clocks, jackets, cell phones, shampoo, toys, and just about any other necessity—all cheap and made in either Asia or formerly Communist Europe. Many of the goods were Russian. The food at the canteens was Turkish. The merchants were Chinese, Kazakhs, Uzbeks, and other Central Asian nationalities, but mostly Chinese. I noticed bus stops for destinations in Romania and other points east, but never west. Hungarian policemen were ubiquitous, for there had been several murders here recently. Nobody was well dressed.

"People in Budapest call this place the Chinese market," Fischer told me. "It grew in the early 1990s, after the Soviet Union collapsed and China loosened travel restrictions on its own citizens. It is a real caravansary." Chinese families dominated a vast underground trading network that provided cheap goods for the overwhelming majority of people in Eastern Europe, who could not afford the new Western-style shops. Here, any language worked. Commerce was the great equalizer. "Yes, it is a bit violent, with gangland killings," Fischer said. "But is it any different from the backstreets of Odessa one or two hundred years ago, where my Jewish ancestors and yours were carrying on much as these people do now?

"This is all I have to show you, Robert," Fischer concluded. "Remember that the Iron Curtain still forms a community. Just look at this market. Over four decades of the most comprehensive repression cannot be wished away in a few years." Fischer guided me onto a tram and rode with me for a few stops. "It is good that you will be passing through Transylvania. Ah, so much to see there," he said, his voice full of longing. Then he stepped off the tram and waved good-bye by lifting his walking stick.

I left the tram near the Nyugati Pályaudvar, Budapest's soaring, iron-columned West Station, built by Alexandre-Gustave Eiffel in the 1870s, before he built his tower in Paris. From West Station, I began my journey east. Where I was going, and why, I shall now explain.

2

HEADING EAST

My plan was to cross what I shall call the New Near East, that part of Eurasia which lies east of the European Union and the newly expanded boundaries of NATO, west of China, and south of Russia. This is a volatile region where the cultural legacies of the Byzantine, Persian, and Turkish empires overlap. It contains 70 percent of the world's proven oil reserves and over 40 percent of its natural-gas reserves.[1] Just as the Austrian empire was "the seismograph of Europe" in the nineteenth century, the New Near East—stretching from the Balkans eastward to "Tartary"—might become the seismograph of world politics and the site of a ruthless struggle for natural resources in the twenty-first.[2] Indeed, the United States military's Central Command, which has responsibility for the Near East and is the closest thing the U.S. has to a colonial-style expeditionary force, recently added the formerly Soviet Caucasus and Central Asia to its area of responsibility.

Specifically, I decided to travel southeast from Hungary through Romania and Bulgaria to Turkey, then south through Syria, Lebanon, Jordan, and Israel. After returning to Turkey from Israel, I would strike east across Anatolia into the Caucasus and Central Asia. Because the former Yugoslavia has been written about at such length, I decided to bypass it. The destruction wrought by ethnic war there was obvious—the result of history, of the evil leaders who manipulated its memory, of

1998 trip

the ruin of the Yugoslav economy in the 1980s, which I had witnessed personally, the collapse of the Cold War security structure, and the West's failure to intervene in timely fashion. But what was happening elsewhere in the Balkans was not obvious.

I wanted to see firsthand the future borders of Europe, the underpinnings of the coming meltdown of Arab dictatorships, and the social and political effects of new Caspian Sea energy pipelines. (While the recent oil discoveries in the Caspian were initially exaggerated, the region will constitute the equivalent of another North Sea in terms of oil production in the next decade, in addition to being a transport hub for some of the world's largest natural-gas reserves.) But the fate of particular political systems in the region also preoccupied me, for I knew that in almost every country through which I would pass, governing institutions were flimsy. True, many states would call themselves democracies—but the actual power relationships in many places showed that the military, security services, and business oligarchies all played an important, if unacknowledged, role.

I wondered, too, how people saw themselves. Were national or ethnic loyalties giving way to new forms of cosmopolitanism, through globalization? If so, what did that mean for the future of authoritarian regimes? If dictatorships gave way to more democratic rule, would that mean more stability or less—more civility or less—in the countries through which I would pass? Even in Israel, the only place along my route where democratic rule had long been institutionalized, democracy may not necessarily remain enlightened, or civil, in the decades to come.

※ ※

I headed first for Debrecen, a Hungarian city three hours away to the east. The frontier between Europe and the Near East that I would cross did not begin and end in a certain place but fell away in a series of gradients. The first gradient was the Chinese market on the eastern outskirts of Budapest, more Oriental and less developed than Budapest's touristy downtown by the Danube. I would see more gradients in the weeks ahead.

From the train, I saw a flat and threadbare landscape of muddy roads, lonely copses of poplars, houses with peeling walls, and rotting chicken coops. After ninety minutes the train crossed the Tisza River and the flat landscape became emptier and more panoramic, with rich, coal-black soil and oceans of lemon-green grass shimmering in the late-winter sunlight of an unseasonably warm day. This was the Puszta or Alföld, Hungary's "Great Plain," the westernmost Asian steppe. It was through this plain that the seven Magyar tribes, the forebears of the modern Hungarians, had entered Hungary under Prince Árpád in A.D. 896, having spent nearly a thousand years migrating westward from the Ural Mountains, on the western edge of Siberia, and passing through the northern Caucasus, where they encountered Bulgars and Turks. Hungary's Finno-Ugric language, with its many words of Turkish origin, attests to this nomadic ancestry.[3]

In addition to the Magyars, other Central Asian peoples also reached this plain in the early Middle Ages: Scythians, Huns, Avars, Tartars, Kumyks, Petchenegs, and others who left their genetic imprint, then receded and disappeared.[4] Before that, this plain was a northeastern frontier region of Rome, where the relative order and prosperity of the imperial provinces of Pannonia, Upper Moesia, and Dacia gave way by the sixth century to the chaotic rule of such tribes as the Gothic Gepidae and the Indo-Iranian Sarmatians.[5] Its utter flatness and empty vistas lent the Hungarian Plain the look of a frontier. But it was no frontier that I had crossed. Debrecen, near the Puszta's eastern edge, turned out to be a small replica of Budapest.

❧ ❧

I had last been to this agricultural trading city of over 200,000 in 1973, when I hitchhiked through Eastern Europe. I remembered sleepy sidewalks, few wares for sale, yellow Gothic buildings with flourishes that made them look like fancy pastries, and greenish domes that hinted of the Orient. Now, there was much to buy. The area by the train station was the local equivalent of Budapest's Chinese market, with throngs of people dressed in cheap tracksuits, selling and buying a vast variety of low-end goods from Asia and the ex-Communist world. An entire hall in the station was filled with rows of inexpensive black shoes. But downtown Debrecen resembled downtown Budapest. Here were ATM machines and chrome-alloy shop signs with fancy lettering. Foreign banks with marble facades were as numerous as the Protestant churches, which give Debrecen the sobriquet the "Calvinist Rome." Many fitness stores and boutiques, with names like Yellow Cab 2nd Avenue 48th Street New York, sold modish hiking shoes, and "info boards" advertised lessons in "Taekwondo, rugby, hip-hop techno rap dancing . . ." A quiet and dilapidated Baroque courtyard that I remembered from a quarter century ago was now freshly painted in pastels and dominated by a sign advertising MICROSOFT SOLUTION PROVIDER. Traffic and crowds were dense, with packs of teenagers, in tight jeans, nestled around shop windows. The kiosks were filled with Western entertainment and computer magazines. The most ubiquitous images in Debrecen in February 1998 were of Leonardo DiCaprio and of an 1890 map of Hungary that included Transylvania (which became part of Romania in 1918).

The business activity surprised me: Debrecen was known for its religious conservatism, and I was far from Budapest, in one of the poorest parts of Hungary. In the mid-sixteenth century Debrecen was a hotbed of the Reformation, and Catholics were forbidden to settle. Here, a Calvinist college was established and local Calvinists made a pact with the ruling Moslem Turks to provide for the town's security. But the so-called Protestant work ethic did not invigorate the Calvinists of Debrecen. "In eastern Hungary, Calvinism has been mere conservatism and fatalism, yet another element of ethnicity surrounded by religious walls, proscribing innovation," László Csaba, a Hungarian economist and social critic, had told me in Budapest. It has always been the Catholic areas of Hungary that displayed economic dynamism. (Csaba had added that the "Prussian work ethic," based partly on Protestantism, was also misunderstood. "The Prussian work ethic was not entrepreneurial, but fitted to bureaucracy and mass industrialization. It functioned only if someone else supplied the jobs and told people what to do. In a postindustrial entrepreneurial age," he continued, "don't expect the formerly Prussian parts of Germany to be economically impressive. Budapest and the rest of Hungary are closer to Catholic Munich than to Prussian-Protestant Berlin, and in a new Europe of region-states, the region oriented toward Munich may be stronger.")

Another reason I was surprised by Debrecen's dynamism was because Hungary's economy was weakest east of the Tisza River, where unemployment in 1997 reached 20 percent compared to a national average of 8.7 percent. But such weakness was relative in a "tiger" economy, in which exports had risen from $5.5 billion annually in the late 1980s to $20 billion in the late 1990s. Hungary exported more engineering products to Western Europe than did Spain and Portugal: Nearly half of Hungary's exports were high-tech.[6] In fact, Hungary exhibited what economists call a normal development pattern, where a third of the country (the region around Budapest) was somewhat ahead of the national growth average and a third (the region east of the Tisza) was somewhat behind. Hungary's small size and flat topography, and the central location of the capital city, made it easier for the effects of Western investment in Budapest to seep out to other regions. I would travel southeast 750 miles to Turkey before I found another economy like Hungary's, where expansion was not limited to a few urban areas.

I spent the night at the Aranybika (Golden Bull), an old-fashioned European hotel built in 1914 in Secessionist style, with faded grandeur, moderate prices, and good service—the last of its kind that I would encounter on my journey.

Early the next morning I left Debrecen. The bus station, a clean, grim, Communist-era edifice of gray cement and plate glass, with a shiny new PEPSI sign, had an electronic timetable. My bus to Biharkeresztes, thirty-eight miles to the southeast, on the Hungarian-Romanian border, was packed with prosperous-looking provincials and smelled, wonderfully, of cheese and sausages. Because of the many detours and stops the driver made, the trip took two hours. Here the Puszta at its eastern edge, before the foothills of the Carpathians came into view, was truly majestic: a paneled vastness of black earth and green grass and, here and there, crumbling collective farms, thatched roofs, mules drawing water from wells, and the occasional Gothic steeple. New shop displays and Opel taxis were signs of expansion even here. When the driver reached the train station at Biharkeresztes, I was the only passenger left on the bus.

Now I sensed another frontier gradient. The nearly deserted train station consisted of a few rooms of cheap plywood and a ticket counter under a dim lightbulb. Though the Romanian border was only a mile or so away, a woman in a blue smock took twenty minutes to work out the details of selling me an international ticket to "Kolozsvár," the city that Romanians call Cluj (though its name was officially changed to Cluj-Napoca in the early 1970s). As I walked toward the train, a Hungarian border guard looked at my passport for a moment, then let me pass. On board, I pried open the door of one of the carriages and entered. I was alone in the compartment. The train began to move; my face was glued to the window. An elevated hot water pipe caught my eye. Where the pipe's shiny new metal and fiberglass insulation ended and rusted metal and rags began—the same point where mounds of trash and corrugated shacks began to appear, where cratered dirt roads suddenly replaced paved ones—marked Romania.

3

THE WIDENING

CHASM

More shacks and trash appeared, along with deserted factories surrounded by cement walls and rusted barbed-wire fences. The train halted at Episcopia Bihorului, just inside Romania. Several officials boarded my car. I saw one of them dart into the lavatory and slip the toilet paper into his battered briefcase. Another asked for my passport, inspected it closely, and took it away, returning it with an entry stamp ten minutes later. A third asked what my "purpose" was in Romania; I told him I was visiting old friends. As I exchanged $80 for an inch-thick stack of inflated local currency with a fourth official, a fifth man, with a long, dark coat and black fedora, peeked into my compartment and stared at me hard before moving on to the next compartment.

The experience was an improvement over what Romanian border controls had been like in the Communist era, when visas were required for Americans and when traveling with a typewriter was forbidden (without a bribe). In Hungary, the border was now seamless; my passport had not been stamped when I entered the country, only glanced at. No one had bothered about my "purpose." The process lasted not minutes but seconds. Positive change there was in Romania, but it was happening at a slower pace, and starting from farther back, than in Hungary. And relative change, more than absolute change, is what history is often about.

When the train pulled into Oradea a little while later, I saw slick bill-boards, a few people with cell phones, a well-dressed woman with an expensive leather attaché case and another with a laptop computer—stagy improvements from the dreary 1980s landscape in Romania. But there was more. As the train continued southeast through pali-saded, fir-mantled slopes that signaled the beginning of the Carpa-thians and Transylvania, I saw hordes of Gypsies washing clothes on rocks along ash-blue streams; peasants in sheepskin vests cultivating fields with pitchforks; women, draped in black, riding in horse-drawn wooden carts; dome-shaped hayricks alongside rusted methane-gas tanks; chickens running out of the path of the train on the diesel-soaked ground; wildflowers blooming beside piles of twisted and charred metal; abandoned railway cars beside industrial complexes black with rust, pebbly concrete; and chemical pollutants beside the grinding reality of subsistence agriculture: the residue of dictator Nico-lae Ceauşescu's Stalinist regime. Here was a primitive, tragically beauti-ful corner of Europe where the residual culture of the High Middle Ages had been brought low by communism's pseudomoderniza-tion, with a suffering late-twentieth-century peasantry and with Gothic churches, graveyards, and stone fortifications atop many a hillock that overlooked winding streams in broad valleys, now defaced by cement-and-iron skeletons of rotting factories.

In the late afternoon I reached Cluj, where I found a few decrepit taxis at the station. I gave one of the drivers the address of my friend, who lived at the outskirts of town. As the driver looked at his map, the frames of his ancient eyeglasses literally fell apart. With a roll of black tape from the dashboard, he slowly bound together—as he must have done many times before—the plastic bridge, apologizing to me for the inconvenience. He charged me 30,000 lei (under $4) for the fifteen-minute journey. I learned later that I should have paid only $2.

The day had been a shock, more so than any I had experienced traveling this way during the Cold War. Because of Hungary's market-oriented reforms in the period from the late 1960s through the 1980s known as goulash communism, Communist Hungary had always been far more developed than Communist Romania. But now the gulf seemed permanent. Foreign investment in Hungary in the first decade after the collapse of the Berlin Wall totaled $18 billion, six times more than what Romania received, though Romania's population—23 million—is more than double Hungary's. And the divide was worsening between Hungary, a small Central European country, and Romania, the largest and most populous country in the Balkans. In 1997, for example, American companies invested twenty-four times more money in Hungary than in Romania: $6 billion versus $250 million.

Transylvania (*Ardeal* in Romanian and *Erdély* in Hungarian, meaning, as *Transylvania* itself does, "the land beyond the forest") is a multiethnic region fought over for centuries by Romanians and Hungarians. On my first night in Cluj, I listened to the conversation of a group of Westerners who had started small firms here. They compared, unfavorably, their Romanian employees with their Hungarian ones. The Romanians did not work as hard, they told me. Romanians were devious and suspicious of one another, they did not plan ahead, and they spent their money as soon as they got it—on clothes or an automobile down payment. One Westerner told me that "you can wait weeks here for a car permit. You may need to reexport your car in order to import it with the right papers unless you know the right Romanian official to bribe." These generalizations were, of course, made by people who lived and were risking their money in Romania. Yet for me, the evening exuded optimism: Reporting on Romania during the Communist era, when Cluj was virtually off-limits to foreigners because of the government's campaign of repression against the ethnic Hungarians who lived there, I could never have imagined that one day Westerners would be doing business here at all.

Walking to the mayor's office the next morning, I renewed my love affair with Cluj. Here was the Mitteleuropa that one associates with the birthplace of modernism, with Freud and Kafka and Kokoschka and Klimt: a mini-Prague, with steep, gabled roofs, leaden domes, cobblestone streets, and Baroque courtyards in shades of ocher and mint, all the more poignant because of the peeling walls and general dilapidation. I saw a sprinkling of satellite dishes, new boutiques, and private security guards, though no ATM machines or much else. The hotels had continued to deteriorate since I was last here in 1990, and no new ones had been built. Cluj was the historic capital of Transylvania—its population was 318,000, compared to Debrecen's 200,000—yet com- [*Hungary*] pared to Debrecen, it was an economic backwater.

But there was one important sign of renewal: *individuals*. Communism, by forbidding self-expression and by emphasizing the crowd and the mass, had unwittingly fortified the very national stereotypes it had claimed to erase, turning the faces one saw in Romanian streets into Byzantine icons with mad, suffering expressions. Now the Romanian population was less archetypal. I noticed would-be hippies with long hair and baggy jeans, café habitués in trendy black fashions and dangling cigarettes, nouveau riche climbers, sports enthusiasts, and so on, who, by choosing their own self-images, however derivative they may have seemed to me, were beginning an assault on national stereotypes. The women, with their innate fashion consciousness, seemed far ahead of the men. Perhaps Romanians did spend money irresponsibly on clothes, but after decades of living under Eastern Europe's most repressive Communist regime, their changing clothes and hairstyles seemed a quick and easy way to celebrate their freedom. Narcissism may be repugnant at advanced stages of capitalism as in the United States, but here it indicated progress. It seemed to me that *Romanian* signified less of a stereotype than it had a decade ago, and would signify even less of one in the future.

Soon I passed a long column of health workers on strike, who, I later learned, earned $50 per month; they were carrying placards that demanded higher pay. The strikers were silent, and their faces displayed forbearance: a Romanian national characteristic that had had negative repercussions during centuries of authoritarian misrule but which now might ease a difficult economic transition. Though I was pleased by the nascent individualism I had seen in the streets, it had to be considered alongside an imponderable degree of ethnic-national awareness among a people first mentioned by Herodotus: predominantly Eastern Orthodox Christians, they spoke a Latinate tongue and had for centuries been surrounded both by Slavic speakers and by Catholic and Protestant Hungarians.[1]

For example, there was Gheorghe Funar, the twice-elected "mad mayor" of Cluj, a self-declared Romanian nationalist, who had torn down Hungarian street signs, painted park benches in the blue, yellow, and red tricolor of the Romanian flag, and renamed Piaţa Libertăţii (Freedom Square) as Piaţa Unirii (Unification Square), celebrating the 1918 unification of Transylvania with Romania—and thus its separation from Hungary. In this square, Funar placed six Romanian flags by the statue of Matthias Corvinus, the fifteenth-century Renaissance ruler of Hungary and Transylvania, and changed the statue's lettering from HUNGARIAE MATTHIAS REX to simply MATTHIAS REX. When Hungary opened a consulate here in July 1997, Funar ordered municipal workers to steal its flag.

Funar greeted me in his office, wearing the pin of the ultranationalist organization Vatra Românească (Romanian Hearth). He was stocky, of average height, with black hair combed straight back and a dark suit. I guessed he was about fifty years old. His immobile expression was cold and wary. His eyes darted about as he clenched his fist repeatedly. He spoke in a measured, didactic whisper, as though trying to control his insecurity and rage. His style and ethnic nationalism reminded me of Slobodan Milosevic and Ratko Mladic, the Serbian political and military leaders who had prosecuted the brutal war against Bosnian Moslems. Funar's official résumé provided few insights: He had been a member of the Communist party who ran the cafeteria at the local university in the 1980s. That was all. Such monsters seem to come out of nowhere: Half-educated, nursing grudges from obscure wounds early in life, they slip upward through the cracks of opportunity at times of great social upheaval. As I sat there, I thought not only of Milosevic and Mladic but of Hitler, too.

"The Romanian people," Funar told me through a translator, "want political parties that defend their national interest, because we feel threatened. We require a military plan against the Russians, and therefore we must be protected by NATO. . . . We don't have any Hungarians in Transylvania; we have only 1.4 million Romanians who are confused about their loyalty. . . . The big church at Piaţa Unirii is not Hungarian. The Hungarians stole all the German churches and burnt ours. . . . Kolozsvár and Clausenburg are not the real names for Cluj. They were the names given under Hungarian-Nazi occupation and have no validity. . . . It will be unfortunate for everyone if Hungary gets into the European Union and Romania does not. . . . Organized crime is widespread in Hungary, but not here. Romania is a safer place for Western investment." The mayor ended by accusing Romania's democratically elected government of colluding with the Hungarians to reinstate dictatorship in Romania.

This was nonsense, of course. The "big church" at Piaţa Unirii, St. Michael's, with its magnificent Gothic vaulting, was built in the mid-fourteenth century by a prosperous German community that had employed Hungarian workmen. Notices in Hungarian filled the entranceway. Kolozsvár and Clausenburg are centuries-old historical names for Cluj, handed down by the local Hungarian and German communities. Criminal activity, according to Western businessmen and diplomats, was possibly more extreme in Romania than in Hungary.

But Funar was a sideshow. The crowd that had turned out to support the striking local health workers was larger than that for the nationalistic Avram Iancu Day, which Funar had helped organize, in honor of a local nineteenth-century hero who had fought the Hungarians.[2] Funar's political support came mainly from Walachian and Moldavian peasants who had been forcibly relocated to Cluj from southern and eastern Romania by Ceauşescu and felt threatened by the more sophisticated Transylvanians—both Romanian and Hungarian. Nationally, the popularity of Funar and that of his fellow extremist Corneliu Vadim Tudor, of the Greater Romania party, hovered around 10 percent. Funar would not be permitted to run for mayor a third time. Such careers flower only during times of economic or political catastrophe.

Still, the need to retain a strong national identity seemed to me greater here than in Hungary. Ioan-Aurel Pop is a medieval historian who heads the Center for Transylvanian Studies in Cluj, located in a derelict villa surrounded by weeds and unfinished apartment blocks. He told me that Romanians have "a particular personality shaped by history," but they have never had the luxury of experiencing a modern nation-state like other Europeans. And they yearn for that, he said, as much as many in the West now yearn to cast off nationalism altogether. "The Hungarians and the Austrians were masters here for seven hundred years. We [Romanians] have controlled Transylvania only since 1918. An equilibrium is required." But the people I saw in the street, I told him, were looking to Western—particularly American—models, not to Romania. Wouldn't new technologies and global capitalism deny Romania the chance of repeating the national experience of Western countries? Pop thought for a moment, then suggested that both of our observations might be true and that Europe's future could be quasi-medieval:

"Western European integration will change Eastern Europe. In twenty years, Europe could be a place of strong nationalisms but without strong borders, because of the global economy. That could mean a Hungarian economic takeover of Transylvania, which would then have a separate identity as a transnational, cosmopolitan region between Hungary and Romania. Whether that is good or bad could depend on the political model coming from Western Europe. If right-wing nationalism grew in France and Italy, or Germany, and separatist violence grew in Spain and elsewhere, that could have a nasty influence on new democracies in Eastern Europe."

Later that day I saw Pop again, along with some of his colleagues from Cluj's Babeş-Bolyai University and fifteen of their graduate students, who pummeled me with questions about America's intentions in the Balkans. One student, a woman with striking golden hair, sat at the rear of the small room. With nods from her professors and friends, she offered a harsh social critique of the type ignited in Romania by the rebirth of individual spirit following the collapse of communism, aroused by the perennial fear of Russia, and aggravated by the widening chasm between Romania and Central Europe.

"Romanians know that Russia will never really be democratic," she began. "We know that our enterprises are worth little and that our democracy, like in the 1920s and 1930s, is without ethics. We lack a modern middle class, and our new aristocracy is the *nomenbratura* [the spoiled children of the ex-Communist elite that stole state assets after 1989]. Our political establishment is incompetent and intractable. You Westerners will tire of us, you will see. You tell us we must privatize, but it is the mafia and the Russians who buy our companies. A major Romanian oil company was put on sale, but nobody in the West wanted it. It was sold to Lukoil, a Russian company. This is how the Russians will eventually own our country again. The Russians will operate through third parties in Europe, so your experts will be able to deny our fears. . . . Greece was poor and corrupt after World War Two, but the United States saved it from communism. The West now needs to save us from the Russians again."

In fact, Atlantic Richfield had bought an 8 percent share of Russia's Lukoil, an example of how the global economy dilutes the economic imperialism she feared. Moreover, hard evidence for Russian involvement in the Romanian economy and local crime was, thus far, meager. Nonetheless, as one Western executive would tell me in Bucharest: "No one really knows who owns the casinos, some of the hotels. . . . Too much is obscure, and that does not make for a good impression. When Romanians do sell an enterprise, they sell merely to the highest bidder, who meets the rate of extortion. They don't investigate the buyer's background. That adds another layer of uncertainty regarding who owns what. This is not how it was in the thirties, when the Jewish, German, and Greek business communities set some reasonable standards; they're all gone."

A foreign diplomat in Cluj summed up the situation: "There are few Western investors in Cluj, and more don't seem to be coming. The Romanian tax code changes all the time, and there is no predictability in investment laws. Also, Cluj is isolated, halfway between the capitals of Budapest and Bucharest. What potential investor wants to ride an entire day or night on an uncomfortable train or fly on an awful airline to get here? Cluj's only hope is a transnational future with weak state borders, as in the days of the Habsburg empire. . . . But the list of corporations in this city can fill a phone book, because any Romanian who forms his own corporation can import a car. Meanwhile, the few foreigners who are trying to start businesses have trouble getting their cars legalized. . . . And Funar is not the only problem. The ruling Peasant party in Bucharest can't even get its local wing in Cluj to implement an agreement that Romania signed with Hungary in 1997, which provides for the protection of minorities."

Both the students and professors I met in Cluj stressed that the main problem in this Eastern Orthodox country was "the absence of an Enlightenment, making Protestant values represented in Transylvania by Hungarian Calvinism their only defense." Transylvania, they told me, required a degree of autonomy from "the Gypsy rule of

Bucharest." While the students and professors were overwhelmingly Romanian of origin and Eastern Orthodox, the tradition of cosmopolitanism in Transylvania—with its mixed population of Romanians, Hungarians, Germans, and Jews prior to Hitler and Stalin—along with the new freedom of expression since 1989, had allowed them to compare their own Romanian culture severely with their Hungarian Calvinist neighbors'. Needless to say, they all hated and were embarrassed by Mayor Funar.

❧ ❧

From Cluj, I continued southeast toward Bucharest, first by car for an hour with a Romanian friend, when I stopped to visit the Jewish graves at Sărmaşu—then by train. Everywhere on the rolling Transylvanian heaths the soil was black and fertile, and yet the landscape was dotted with horse- and mule-drawn carts and mountains of stacked firewood. This potential European breadbasket was practicing a primitive agriculture. Despite the abundance of oil in southern Romania, forests were being felled here for firewood. There were few good roads.

Near Sărmaşu, I found a complex of large, deserted mansions that had been owned by nineteenth-century Hungarian nobles. They were surrounded by medieval walls with mottled stone arches and punctuated by Corinthian columns and towers that combined Byzantine and Gothic motifs. No attempt had been made to preserve or landscape these magnificent estates. They had simply fallen into ruin. There were deep gashes in their roofs. Windows and floors were broken or missing. Ducks and other birds drank from garbage-strewn puddles on the overgrown lawns amid stately poplars and willows. I found children in rags from a nearby village playing in one of the abandoned buildings. Except for the rusted telephone poles and mounds of tin cans, plastic wrappers, and other refuse, there were few signs of the twentieth century. The site reminded me of the medieval ruins of Angkor Wat, in the midst of the Cambodian jungle. The brutal legacy of Ceauşescu's communism—the application of a peasant mind to the Industrial Revolution—would endure far into the future.

The train I boarded near Sărmaşu was overheated. My seat was broken. The young man next to me was traveling from Baia Mare, in Romania's far north (near the Ukrainian border), to Bucharest to look for work. "You know what the problem is with this country," he told me in English. "Our mentality, our fatalism, the bribery and extortion. Nothing is happening in Bucharest except promises, stealing, and corruption. We are still waiting for real economic reform nine years after Ceauşescu was executed. And we have this danger if things go bad." He meant extreme nationalists like Funar.

As he spoke, I was again captivated by the landscape. Because of its Hungarian and German populations, Transylvania had been the extreme southeastern outpost of the culture of the Reformation and the Enlightenment, which did not advance beyond the Carpathians to what would later become Romania. The Romania that came into being in 1859 was a union only of the formerly Turkish-ruled provinces of Moldavia and Walachia.[3] Transylvania did not join these provinces until the defeat and disintegration of the Austro-Hungarian empire at the end of World War I. Near Rupea, several hours southeast of Cluj, on a rolling plateau formerly populated by German Saxons—who had come here in the twelfth century, and had left in the late twentieth, in flight from Ceauşescu—I beheld hills running with rich black mud in the rain and crowned with the ruined battlements, crumbling rooftops, and dagger-pointed steeples that the Saxons had left behind. In the background was a haze of industrial soot from belching, Communist-era factories.[4]

I got off the train at Braşov, where I spent the night. Formerly the medieval Saxon settlement of Kronstadt, Braşov was Rudolf Fischer's hometown, at the very southeastern tip of Central Europe. A few miles farther on—where the highest peaks of the Carpathians end abruptly at the entrance to the Walachian Plain—both the Renaissance kingdom of Hungary and the Habsburg empire had given way to Turkish rule. Before sunset, I easily climbed to the top of a small mountain in Rîşnov, a former German settlement near Braşov, where the ruins of a thirteenth-century citadel stood. For the next four centuries these ocher walls, now overgrown with grass and wildflowers, had withstood periodic Tartar and Turkish advances into the Carpathians. Under a crescent moon that had just risen and which the Romanians call "the new prince," I looked directly down upon the remnants of several German villages in the foothills, each a replica of the next, with steeply pitched red roofs in perfect rows, like trees in a forest, and highlighted by Gothic and Baroque churches. Along with the late-medieval district of Braşov, where I was staying, it would be the last architectural trace of Central Europe that I would see in my travels.

That evening, walking through Braşov's Baroque square, I saw young Romanians in leather jackets on motorbikes, women in striking black leotards, and others with fashionable blazers and glasses. The older people, all dressed in the same baggy clothes, looked upon the young in disoriented amazement. The television in my shabby, state-owned hotel offered German MTV, with heavy-metal music played by a group in futuristic military uniforms.

The next morning I boarded the train, headed south for Bucharest.

4

THIRD WORLD

EUROPE

Bucharest lay two hours south of Braşov. At first the train climbed through the high Carpathian passes. The granite, snow-flecked peaks were girdled in towering fir, oak, and beech forests, casting dark shadows. Pearly torrents tumbled from the snowmelt of an abnormally warm late February. Romanian soldiers in fur hats stood at attention as the train passed. Wood smoke and lignite fumes fouled the snow and pure mountain air. Then the train descended to a plain that seemed even more immense than the Hungarian Puszta. There were no trees in the distance, and the drab pigment of silt thickened the air, melding with the earth and obscuring the horizon. Ugly factories and towns with no architectural character littered the plain of Walachia, "the land of the Vlachs," the name that others had used for Romanians before the nineteenth century.

The train passed through Ploieşti, where the smell of oil filled the compartment and the yellow flares of vented gases appeared next to barrackslike apartment blocks devoid of greenery. Ploieşti had been the premier oil city of Romania, once as strategic as the Persian Gulf. During World War I, British agents bombed the ten refineries here to deny them to the Germans. In World War II, the Nazi-puppet govern-ment of Romanian general Ion Antonescu had one overriding objec-tive: keep order in Romania so that the Germans could pump Ploieşti's oil for their war machine. In 1944, Allied planes carpet-bombed

Ploieşti. At the turn of the twenty-first century, as I would learn later in Bucharest, Ploieşti's strategic importance loomed anew, but more subtly.

Suddenly, the featureless plain filled with cardboard and scrap-metal squatters' settlements as awful as many I had seen in Africa, Asia, and Latin America. Then I saw unpainted cement-block houses with laundry drying on lines and the occasional satellite dish: These were the northwest suburbs of Bucharest, Romania's capital. At the station, taxi drivers assaulted me. One had his arm on mine, another on my duffle bag. I knew that the proper fare to my friend's apartment downtown was 15,000 lei, about $2. I insisted that the driver use the meter. He did, but he had rigged it. The fare came to the equivalent of $5.50. I was fortunate to be able to stay with a friend. The least expensive of the city's main hotels now charged $156 per night. The Athenee Palace, refurbished by the Hilton and owned by a mysterious Romanian consortium, charged $300 and up. Diplomats and Western businesspeople I met called this extortion.

It was the gray dust, which had always reminded me of Damascus and Teheran, that I noticed first. Bucharest's weather usually comes neither from the north—where it is blocked by the Carpathians—nor from the south—where it is blocked by Bulgaria's Balkan Range—but from the east and northeast: Ukraine and Russia. Otherwise, the transformation of this formerly forbidden Cold War Stalinist city, which I had not seen since shortly after the Berlin Wall fell, amazed me. Now I knew why those Westerners who rarely ventured beyond the center of Bucharest were so upbeat about Romania. In place of the terrified urban peasantry I remembered from my visits in the 1980s, I found a downtown comprised of the latest Italian fashions and hairstyles, cell phones, casinos, private exchange dealers, and sidewalk stands selling books and compact disks—everything from *Mein Kampf* in Romanian to Israeli pop music, with an emphasis on computer and management books. I saw young couples embrace passionately on the sidewalks. Topless clubs were ubiquitous, and Mexican soap operas dominated the thirty television channels, including cable. As in Paris and New York, black apparel was chic. Some boutiques featured live models in the windows. Drafty restaurants offering the Communist-era fare of greasy pork cutlets and plum brandy still operated, but they had been surpassed in popularity by intimate establishments, often with only a few tables, run by young people and offering a more wholesome, international cuisine. There were cell phones everywhere, whose beeping filled the cafés: the perfect accessory item for hustler economies with weak hard-wired infrastructures. Western diplomats suspect that some of the casinos here launder money for organized crime and the drug trade.

"There are no limits with the nouveaux riches here," Ioana Ieronim, a poet and former diplomat, told me at dinner. "This is how we were in the interwar period, in the 1930s. We are resourceful, adaptable, exaggerated, pseudocosmopolitan émigrés in a new, global world. We are one-dimensional Latin-Oriental clones of the West. Because of an outburst of freedom, there is a crassness and directness here that you won't find among the French or Italians, whom we superficially resemble." Ioana told me how she had watched "a young, beautiful, revealingly dressed woman try to buy a young professional man" in one of Bucharest's new boutiques. The woman told the man how a sexual relationship with her would be worthwhile, because she could help him with "powerful connections." (The man did not accept.)

Romanians were adapting to global capitalism in the same aggressive manner that they had once adapted to fascism and, later, communism. In the past, Romanians had exhibited the most bestial anti-Semitism, but Jews now seemed in favor, because they symbolized the cosmopolitanism to which young Romanians aspired. Ladislau Gyemant, the vice-dean of Babeş-Bolyai University in Cluj, had told me that when Hebrew was offered as a foreign language, four hundred students, only a handful of whom were Jewish, registered. Bucharest's most popular actress and nightclub performer was a Romanian Jew, Maia Morgenstern. In December 1997, when municipal authorities put up Christmas lights for the first time since the 1930s, Hanukkah, too, was given terrific exposure in the local media. Walking by the Polish embassy in Bucharest one day, I noticed a billboard exhibit of Poland's "different cultures." Among the three photos the embassy displayed was one of Jews celebrating Rosh Hashanah.

But while its tiger economy was taking Hungary from the Communist "Second World" to the Western "First," Romania seemed to be drifting from the Second to the Third World: with squatter settlements, a mass of rural peasantry, and a new consumer class limited mainly to a few districts of Bucharest, a city of 2 million in a country of 23 million. Romania's annual per capita income in 1997 was $1,500; Hungary's was nearly $4,500.[1]

✸ ✸

"When we buy computers, compact disks, and clothes, we borrow the material consequences of the West without grasping the fundamental values that created such technologies in the first place," Horea-Roman Patapievici, a Romanian philosopher and historian, told me. My visit with Patapievici, on my second evening in Bucharest, condensed all that was ever intoxicating to me about Romania, a country like a sensual, macabre, perpetually fascinating, and occasionally brilliant film noir.

Patapievici lived on an upper floor of a badly lit apartment block, whose hallways were plagued by some of Bucharest's legions of stray dogs. He greeted me wearing blue jeans and a silk smoking jacket, an Orthodox cross dangling from his neck, and led me into a study filled with an eclectic assortment of books, icons, and classical compact disks. Friends had told me that Patapievici, in early middle age, with hard, graven features, was a physicist who had waded into philosophy and history and quickly became famous among Romanian intellectuals as an original thinker. "He is completely in his own realm," a Romanian journalist had told me. "He is thinking on a level much deeper than that of politicians and academics."

"Romanian culture is like an onion," Patapievici began with a shrug. "There is no core. There is a layer from the fascist era, from the Communist era, and from the present. The future, for the time being, belongs to this new American layer. And it *is* American, not Western European: fast food, rap music, MTV." I thought of how Romanian youth had flooded Orthodox churches for the first time in their lives in order to pray for Michael Jackson after he was reported ill in 1996. "True, the fashions are European," he continued, "but so are the fashions in New York. We will continue to superficially Americanize as long as Russia does not explode or expand, or as long as Ukraine does not collapse."

In other words, the widening gulf between the Balkans and Central Europe need not prove fatal so long as the former Soviet Union remains reasonably benign and the American version of democratic capitalism remains the model for the formerly Communist world.

Patapievici went on: "The task for Romania is to acquire a public style based on impersonal rules, otherwise business and politics will be full of intrigue, and I am afraid that our Eastern Orthodox tradition is not helpful in this regard. Romania, Bulgaria, Serbia, Macedonia, Russia, Greece—all the Orthodox nations of Europe—are characterized by weak institutions. That is because Orthodoxy is flexible and contemplative, based more on the oral traditions of peasants than on texts. Unlike Polish Catholicism, it never challenged the state. Orthodoxy is separated from, yet tolerant of, the world as it is: fascist, Communist, or democratic, because it has created an alternate world of its own based on the peasant village. In this way, Orthodoxy reconciles our ancient heritage with modern glitz."

Indeed, Teoctist, the last leader of a major institution to profess undying loyalty to Ceauşescu, only days before his execution, was still the Orthodox patriarch in 1998. The church here was continuing its oppression of Greek Catholic Uniates—Orthodox Christians who went over to the pope several hundred years ago. (Historically, Orthodox churches have often enjoyed better relations with Moslems than with Western Christians, seeing the latter as a greater threat.)

"Orthodoxy and Islam are both Oriental. And communism," Patapievici said, waving his hand, "was just a case of Orientals practicing a Western pseudoscience. Like Nazism, communism was a rebellion against modernity and bourgeois values. But Nazism and communism have not exhausted the possibilities for extremist ideologies, I think. That is because ideas are reflections of the reigning technology: Nazism and Stalinism required the tools of the industrial age to be what they were. So, with postindustrialization, we are in favorable times for dangerous cults and new ideologies."

※ ※

I had come to Romania during its first real cabinet crisis in over sixty years, the first test of the country's fledgling democracy. Patapievici told me if the Romanian cabinet was now stuck in directionless machinations, it was not accidental, or the result of this or that minister. "Again," he said, "there is this pattern of rumor, lack of information, conspiracy, and intrigue, which is similar to other Orthodox societies where institutions are weak and rules vague."

The thirties had seen royal dictatorship under King Carol II; the forties, General Antonescu's Nazi-backed military regime; the late forties through late eighties, Communist rule; and 1989 through 1996, a neo-Communist government that, while democratically elected, had not ruled very democratically.

The governing Peasant party was currently divided over implementing the historic reconciliation agreement with Hungary and much else. Prime Minister Victor Ciorbea's government had missed deadline after deadline for privatization and other reforms set by the International Monetary Fund. The prime minister's penchant for chairing cabinet meetings lasting as long as eighteen hours, in which nothing was decided, had heightened investors' fears. Inflation had soared and a budget was delayed. After nearly six months of such agony, Ciorbea finally resigned in April 1998, but his replacement, Radu Vasile, was also stymied by continuing party divisions and feuds across the political spectrum. Romania's president, Emil Constantinescu, whose election in 1996 had ended seven years of neo-Communist rule, was at the time interpreting his role strictly constitutionally and not forcing the cabinet to make decisions. Romanians openly feared *Bulgarizarea*— ungovernability of a kind that neighboring Bulgaria had briefly experienced in early 1997.

Romanian analysts and Western diplomats I met agreed with Patapievici that the crisis was tied to "national character." It wasn't, they said, that individuals did not matter. Of course, individuals were unpredictable, and so, likewise, was history. But as Rudolf Fischer had told me, concepts like "Habsburg Central Europe," of which Hungary had been a part, and the "former Byzantine and Ottoman empires," of which Romania had been a part, also meant something tangible, for what is the present if not the sum total of the past up through this moment?

For example, Romanians lived for centuries next to Russia and then the Soviet Union, suffering repeated Russian invasions. They adopted Eastern Orthodoxy from Greek Byzantium; they experienced the anarchy and underdevelopment of Turkish rule; they were misgoverned for decades by the Stalinist brand of Oriental despotism under Ceauşescu; yet they spoke a language with Latin roots, similar to Italian and Portuguese, and have always yearned to be part of the West. This historical and cultural experience is real, and, being real, it has consequences in terms of how both the people and their leaders behave. To ignore such consequences is to immobilize meaningful discussion, as well as to substitute illusions for reality. To tell Romanians, at least all the Romanians that I have known, that as a people they have no defining characteristics based on a common experience and are simply individuals who happen to speak the same language and have (for the most part) the same religion but who are otherwise unconnected to each other in a global meeting hall would be to dehumanize them.[2] When Patapievici told me that Romanian culture has no core, he implied it as a defining characteristic of Romanians rather than as a denial that they had a defining characteristic.

Romanians are among history's ultimate survivors. Traugott Tamm, a late-nineteenth-century German, wrote:

> The Rumanians are living to-day where fifteen centuries ago their ancestors were living. The possession of the regions of the Lower Danube passed from one nation to another, but none endangered the Rumanian nation as a national entity. "The water passes, the stones remain"; the hordes of the migration period, detached from their native soil, disappeared as mist before the sun. But the Roman element bent their heads while the storm passed over them . . .[3]

As to the passivity characteristic of Orthodoxy, Stelian Tănase, a local newspaper editor, concurred with Patapievici. "In our religion," Tănase told me, "only God takes risks; we don't. Here you are not supposed to stick your neck out, so ambition is associated with shame. Yet many of us, especially our politicians, are ambitious, because for the first time in decades we are allowed to express ourselves. But the need to deny this leads to duplicity and intrigue."[4]

Outside Tănase's office, I found a large anteroom filled with hangers-on, men in tight-fitting suits, smoking, with evidently little to do except bring Turkish coffee to visitors, escort them to and from the staircase, and answer the phone, a familiar scene in the Turkish, Arab, and Persian worlds. I would encounter it often in the course of my journey, but I saw it for the first time here in Bucharest.

The political crisis, however, had less to do with Romania's historical and geographical legacy than with the legacy of Ceauşescu's communism. Dorel Şandor, a hip new Bucharest policy wonk, with his own well-appointed research institute, told me that by not allowing a reform wing of the Communist party, or any dissent whatsoever—unlike Hungary and Poland—Ceauşescu had destroyed utterly the political elite, and even the evolutionary mechanism for one to emerge. The consequence, Şandor said, "is a nation of coffeehouse politicians, where, despite the names of the political parties, there are no ideas, just personalities. It's all vanity!" he exclaimed. "Romanian politics are defined by a high level of energy, with sterile results. We are Italy without Italy's middle class. Romanian liberals are not the center-right reformers that define liberal groups elsewhere in Europe. Here we have pocketbook liberals, concerned only with their own short-term profits, people who don't want foreign competition to threaten their new wealth. Because no idea unites them, they are fragmented. With fragmented parties and weak institutions, everyone fears a catastrophe if the prime minister resigns, but the downfall of a prime minister should be a normal occurrence in a parliamentary system."

With his well-tailored black clothes, clipped black beard, black desk, and black laptop computer with its high-resolution liquid crystal panel and other information-age paraphernalia, Şandor resembled a trendy Manhattan consultant. "Because Romanians adapt so well, we start at the top, with the latest styles and exotic technologies," he told me. However, Şandor's Western ways were evidence not only of his adaptability but also of his exposure to the West all along—even before the fall of communism—because of a job he had held in Ceauşescu's government. His sociopolitical commentary was, nevertheless, sharp. That was another dilemma of postcommunism: The very people who had the requisite analytical and bureaucratic skills had acquired them through membership in the former Communist elite (and were often using them outside or in opposition to the bureaucracy). Thus, the only ones who knew how to effect reform often lacked the motive to do so. Şandor—an adviser to a political party of ex-Communists now reborn as socialists—was cleverly lamenting a political stalemate that he and his ilk were partly responsible for.

The stalemate had cost Romania time that it didn't have. Whereas, by 1998, 70 percent of Hungary's banks had been sold to foreigners, so that their financial institutions would henceforth operate on international standards, bank sell-offs had barely begun in Romania. Romanian privatizations were repeatedly delayed, followed by demands that only minority shares be sold to foreigners. A Western privatization expert told me emphatically, "This is still a peasant society, with a peasant's suspicion about selling off what is conceived of as the national patrimony." Information in Romania was jealously guarded rather than disseminated. A fellow journalist told me that while his office in Budapest required a new roll of fax paper every other day because of the many reports sent to him by Hungarian state ministries, in Romania his fax roll lasted a month.

Underlying these problems, according to many a diplomat and foreign investor, was a brutal realization: *Beyond the president and a few ministers, there was nothing here but dead wood. Almost no one in the bureaucracy was remotely competent or potentially employable by a Western firm.* Romania's Levantine-Ottoman system discouraged the very investment that could transform the culture, because international corporate values are Western. Henk Mulder, president of the Dutch ABN-Amro Bank in Bucharest, told me: "We indoctrinate our Romanian staff with the company ideology—integrity, respect, teamwork, and professionalism. We tell them that our policy is to pay our taxes and not to make loans to our friends. Western managers are not aloof, but Romanians like to hide behind titles. I tell my staff not to call me Mister, and to confront me with problems. This is how you change Romania. Success depends on Western ownership and on real entrepreneurs displacing the *nomenbratura.*"

The foreign businesspeople I met in Bucharest admitted that their unofficial policy was to hire only Romanians under thirty. Anyone older was thought to be too influenced by "the local way of doing things" to be redeemable. Throughout the entire ex-Communist world, in fact, not just one but several generations had been wasted. A Romanian friend, holding his palms toward the sky in his squalid apartment, told me: "Even if you are thirty-five, your life is ruined. No one from the West will employ you, and it is only Western companies that have good jobs to offer."

5

BALKAN REALISTS

Sylviu Brucan looked up at me from the handwritten manuscript on his desk, his white hair almost invisible against his pallid skin, his icy blue eyes penetrating. I sensed an extraordinary intelligence. At eighty-two, Brucan seemed almost sexless, a brain without a body: the court eunuch, or a Balkan Richelieu in a baggy black tunic and white sneakers. Surrounding him was a room full of old newspapers and journals and hundreds of books, including those by and about Nixon, Kissinger, and other devotees of Realpolitik. His somewhat dilapidated house on the northern edge of Bucharest appeared forlorn. Through the open window I heard dogs bark, and I could smell lignite.

I had come to see this living icon of the Cold War because the legacy of communism in the Balkans seemed to me more pronounced than it had seemed the last time I visited the region, soon after the Berlin Wall fell: Now, nine years later, Romania's recovery was only beginning.

A Communist in his twenties who spent World War II imprisoned by General Antonescu's Nazi-backed regime, Brucan became a principal adviser to Gheorghe Gheorghiu-Dej, the Stalinist dictator of Romania from the late 1940s until his death in 1965. With his rabid denunciations of the United States in Romanian newspapers in the late 1940s, Brucan did his bit to start the Cold War. Later on, Brucan became the ghostwriter for Gheorghiu-Dej's protégé, Nicolae Ceaușescu. A Jew, Brucan survived Gheorghiu-Dej's purge of Ana Pauker's pro-

Moscow heavily minority wing of the Romanian Communist party. But when Ceauşescu acceded to the Party leadership in the late 1960s, the uneducated cobbler from Walachia kept his Jewish intellectual comrade at a cool, albeit respectful, distance. In 1987, after Ceauşescu had been in power for two decades, and with Romania in the grip of police state terror and economic collapse, Brucan, in a brave act, publicly criticized Ceauşescu for the brutal repression of a rebellion among workers in Braşov. In December 1989, when the military arrested Ceauşescu and his wife, Elena, following riots in Bucharest and Timişoara, in western Romania, it was Brucan and six others at the top of the Communist power structure who gave the order to have the couple killed, helping to ensure their own grip on power through 1996.[1]

"Illiteracy is reviving," Brucan began, as if he were lecturing a student. "When we were in power, a simple peasant could send his children to the university. Now, no," he said, waving his hand. "The price of economic reform is heavy. Historically, center-right governments, as in Poland and the Czech Republic, carry out post-Communist reform. But here the rightists are all extreme nationalists, like Funar and Vadim Tudor, who are the real inheritors of Ceauşescu's national communism. Vadim Tudor promises to end the chaos, yet he knows that anti-Semitism does not do well these days, but anti-Hungarianism, yes." Brucan smiled. In fact, it had been Brucan and his allies who fought the emergence of the center-right wing he now said was so necessary. Nevertheless, Brucan's analysis, like Dorel Şandor's, was acute.

Was Antonescu, whom the Communists executed in 1946, a tragic figure or a criminal one? I asked, steering the conversation toward history.

"He was both. On the one hand, Antonescu tried to restore Bessarabia [eastern Moldavia] to Romania. He destroyed the [fascist] Iron Guard. On the other, he brought German troops and the Gestapo into Romania. And," Brucan added, smiling, "what he did to the Jews in Trans-Dniestria was not so nice."[2]

"Why did you become a Communist?"

"I was not a Communist—I was a Stalinist. Stalin was a highly repressive, intolerant individual, one of the great killers of history. I was attracted to him. Stalin was my only hope against Hitler and the Gestapo torturers: Stalinism was the national opposition in Romania to dominance from Germany. *You* were nowhere," referring to the United States, which, Brucan noted, did not enter the war until the Nazis were at the gates of Moscow and Leningrad, and then only after Hitler had declared war on America. I thought of what Romania's late ambassador in Washington, Corneliu Bogdan, had told his friends—"The West did not lose Eastern Europe at Yalta. It lost it at Munich."—when the West abdicated responsibility for Eastern European security to Hitler and Stalin.

"I would listen to Stalin over the radio from prison," Brucan continued. "My admiration for him was total, organic. Even when I first began to become aware of his crimes, I still admired him. He was efficient. In this part of the world, you admire someone who is able to get things done.[3] That's why at the beginning of my career I thought communism could do things. If it was cruel, I did not object, because I was one of the beneficiaries. It was convenient for me personally. I had all sorts of perks—villas on the Black Sea and in the Carpathians. Such benefits diminish critical thinking. Until the Khrushchev report [of Stalin's crimes in 1956], I was prepared to forgive Stalin anything. Because it offers freedom of thought, democracy with all its weaknesses, I now realize, prevents the abuse of power.

"Ceauşescu, of course, knew very little about Marxism. He could not even discuss *Kapital,*" Brucan said, sneering. "I wrote his articles for him. But Ceauşescu had memorized everything about Stalin. Like Stalin, Ceauşescu learned by rote. Both men had fantastic will and memory. Like Stalin, Ceauşescu was underestimated by his colleagues. I admit, I never thought he would rise to the top. Ceauşescu was a monster politically and a disaster economically, but in Eastern Europe during the Cold War, only Tito and Ceauşescu had great [independent] foreign policies, which gave Yugoslavia and Romania more status than their actual power justified."

"So why did Ceauşescu end up being so stupid?" I asked.

"He was shrewd. She was the stupid one, a real dumb peasant. You see, as Ceauşescu aged, he developed a bladder problem. It was the kind of personally embarrassing issue that forced him to rely on his wife, and that's how she became so politically powerful. In effect, she got them both killed."

"Was it necessary to execute them?"

"You have to understand the military situation on the night of December 24, 1989. The ministries were under fire, we knew that many generals still supported Ceauşescu, and we had information that they were planning an attack on the garrison in Tîrgovişte [an hour northwest of Bucharest], where he and Elena were being held. We needed to prevent more bloodshed. After a lot of discussion, there was decisive agreement among us that the two would be executed the next day, after a smooth trial. I was the most ardent that they must be killed. Iliescu," Brucan said, sneering again, "as usual, was unsure at first what to do." Ion Iliescu would follow Ceauşescu as president, remaining in the job until 1996.

"Was there any question about executing her?" I asked.

Brucan smiled dryly. "It was not even discussed. There was no question about that. She was worse than he was."

"Shouldn't they have been given a proper trial?"

Brucan gave a laugh and turned his icy eyes on me, as if stunned by my innocence. "A jury trial? There was no time. We had time for a short trial, so that's what we did. We wanted a political trial, to educate the population, but the military situation, as I said, was too dangerous."

Whereas in 1990 I had detected unease among Romanians over the execution, in 1998 none remained. As awareness has deepened of the long-term damage done by Ceauşescu's rule, even intellectuals here now showed no remorse, or any doubts whatsoever, about the use of a firing squad. As for Brucan, Iliescu, and the other Party members, the execution was certainly convenient: A proper, public trial in which the Ceauşescus could defend themselves would have revealed much damaging evidence about the men who decided their fate. When I asked a Romanian-speaking foreign diplomat in Bucharest why there had been no "truth and reconciliation" process in Romania, like ones in eastern Germany and South Africa, he snapped, "Truth and reconciliation is not a Latin-Oriental thing to do." But that explanation did not account for what had really happened. Let Brucan tell it:

"Elsewhere in Eastern Europe, peaceful transitions occurred because there was a reform wing of the Communist party that was able to ease the ruler out. Even in Bulgaria this was the case. Here, a reformed wing was outlawed by Ceauşescu, so instead of a negotiation, there was a popular explosion a few weeks after the Berlin Wall collapsed. And with no organized opposition, *we* were alone. We were the only ones in the chaos who knew how to rule. So, sure, we took advantage of the vacuum. The revolution was no mystery. Supremacy and power are more important than ideals. Iliescu was here, in place. The other candidates were exiles who had no idea what was going on." Brucan waved his hand in derision.

And because Iliescu and the other Gorbachev-style Communists were operating in a vacuum without credible, organized opponents, they took advantage of early elections to rule for seven years. Now many Romanians believe it is too late to commence a truth-and-reconciliation process, since so many records have likely been doctored or destroyed. So suspicion reigns, as if the Berlin Wall fell only yesterday. Had Gorbachev not been forced from power himself in 1991, it is possible that quasi-authoritarian, neo-Communist rule in Romania would obtain still.

Brucan then talked about the current security situation: "You have one superpower and four other significant powers: Western Europe, Russia, China, and Japan. Coalitions of three of these five will dominate world affairs. It's mathematical."

"What about the United Nations?"

He laughed as he had when I had asked him about a jury trial for the Ceauşescus. "The U.N. has nothing to do with anything.

"Russia is weak," he went on. "Yeltsin cannot pay pensions for six months. Chechnya showed a Russian military in shambles"—our conversation took place in early 1998—"nevertheless, Russia is an old empire and knows how to play a weak hand well. And," he added, smiling broadly, "Finkelstein is very clever." Brucan's use of Russia's then-foreign minister Yevgeny Primakov's original Jewish name demonstrated both his knowledge of Communist-era personnel files and his own cynical understanding, borne of life experience, that even when, as in Primakov's case, Jews learn Arabic and help Saddam Hussein evade U.N. inspections, they are still, in this part of the world, thought of as Jews. The issue, though, is subtler now, given the philo-Semitism begotten by global cosmopolitanism, plus the fact that so many members of the Russian oligarchal power structure—Primakov, business magnate Boris Berezovsky, reformer Grigory Yavlinsky, and so on—are Jewish.

Before leaving, I asked Brucan if Mircea Răceanu, a former, high-ranking Foreign Ministry official whom I had interviewed twice in the 1980s and who now lived in Washington, was among the handful of Communists, including Brucan himself, who had signed a letter in March 1989 protesting Ceauşescu's repression. "No," Brucan answered with disdainful condemnation. "Răceanu was CIA, an American spy, sir," a charge I later learned was true. Răceanu, without telling his wife—because it would have been more dangerous for her had she known—had decided to cooperate with the Central Intelligence Agency out of patriotic conviction for political change in Romania. Răceanu wanted to topple the system, whereas Brucan wanted to preserve it by forcing Ceauşescu out. Răceanu was a true hero of the Cold War. Brucan was more complicated, less worthy, but a more enduring type: a classic practitioner of power politics, fated to ply his craft in a place that the West had abandoned for half a century.

※ ※

"I am not a hero; I am an antihero. Democracies don't need heroes as much as dictatorships do," Romania's president, Emil Constantinescu, told me. "I didn't suffer like those who went through the Communist prison system. They're the moral leaders, not me. The members of the old regime stated that everyone in Romania collaborated, that we all lied. Well, I was a geology professor, a member of the Party, yes. But I never praised Ceauşescu during his dictatorship. What is more, millions of other Romanians were like me: They did not collaborate. I am a president who cannot be blackmailed, because I never compromised my soul. People need to know that we can have a democratic system based on truth, not lies; that not everyone can be bought and not every value is for sale. With truth, you can do unimaginable things—you can overturn a tragic legacy of history."

Constantinescu was the first morally legitimate Romanian ruler since the death of King Ferdinand in 1927. Ferdinand had been succeeded by his six-year-old grandson, Michael, but real power resided in

a regency council. That was followed by Carol II's corrupt and disastrous reign, which dominated the thirties prior to fascist and Communist rule. Ferdinand and his English wife, Queen Marie, had lived in the
Cotroceni Palace, where Constantinescu now received me. He was in
his early fifties, with gray hair, goatee, and fashionable glasses—a typical professor, I thought, but Constantinescu's most striking features
when he entered the room were his infectious smile and the bounce in
his gait. Romania's president exuded optimism. He was in the midst of
a cabinet crisis, and had been up since 1:00 A.M. the night before. But he
did not look tired. We talked for two and a half hours. "My job is to be
a modern democratic ruler—not a ruler from on high looking down on
the population, which has been the Balkan tradition, but someone who
is here today and back in private life tomorrow, someone who has to
beg the people for their vote."

"What is the hardest thing you've had to learn?" I asked him.

"That we are not all equal. The passage from dictatorship to democracy is a passage from the collectivist to the communal ideal.
Collectivism annihilates the individual, while community means an association of individuals. And in rediscovering our individuality, we find
that some are more intelligent than others, some work harder, some are
more innovative, some are luckier and in a better position to acquire
wealth. Competition means unsentimental selection of the best. This
was done with the utmost toughness in Britain and America. It is only
important that there be equality of opportunity, not equality of result.
To say to a people like the Romanians, whose individuality has been
crushed by communism, that they are all equal is an insult. Because this
was a hard truth to accept during the early phase of industrialization.
Communism seduced intellectuals with the lie of equality, which in
practice turned out to be rule by the lowest among us."

"What about the equality of nations? Is Romania equal to Hungary?"

"The West used to lump us together as 'Communist countries,' but
as time goes by, it is clear that each country carries its past with it. We
will overcome ours, but the West must be patient. We did not start
from the same level of development as Hungary; our problems are
deeper. For example, Ceauşescu decimated Romanian society by forc-

ing it to pay off the foreign debt ahead of schedule, so that we could be 'independent.'" Constantinescu laughed at the tragicomic absurdity of Ceauşescu's policies. "Meanwhile, Hungary and Poland kept borrowing from the West for development. Well, when the Wall fell, the West wrote off their debts! . . . Real democrats did not come to power here until 1996, but we couldn't govern even then, because we had no honest institutions. Only dictatorships are stable: They have no crises, just murders. Precisely because our situation is more fragile, we need NATO. . . ."

That was the heart of the president's message. In 1998, while analysts argued about how NATO's expansion into Central Europe would affect the West's relations with Russia, the more important NATO debate that nobody joined at the time had to do with the Balkans. The notion that NATO's expansion threatened the reconstitution of Russia as a benign democracy was absurd, because there was little chance of a truly democratic Russia in the first place. The German government, with its considerable financial resources, was having enough difficulty rehabilitating 17 million former East Germans, following four decades of Communist rule. The chance of democratizing 149 million Russians, spread over seven time zones and riven by conflicts between Orthodox Christians and Moslems—none of whom were heirs to the Enlightenment, and who had seven decades of communism behind them rather than four—was never very good. Just as the Soviet Union's collapse was mainly the result of internal factors, so too would Russia's future be determined by its own actions. The real significance of NATO's expansion into Hungary, the Czech Republic, and Poland had less to do with Russia per se and more to do with how the expansion institutionalized the divide between the Christian West and the Orthodox East— for it wasn't just Russia that was now cut off from the new Europe, but the Balkans, too. Rather than worry about Russia, which had little chance of conforming to NATO's membership standards, Western analysts should have been concerned with Orthodox countries like Romania and Bulgaria, which had a fighting chance.

Because the ex-Communist states of Central Europe will eventually be accepted into an expanded European Union, NATO membership is not critical to their success. In Hungary, for example, NATO membership meant, as a Budapest analyst had told me, mere "presentation," a seal of "product approval" that Hungary could use to lure further private investment. But for Romania and Bulgaria, NATO is their only hope, for their leaders knew very well that they had no chance of imminent and full European Union membership. In the poorer and more isolated Balkans—threatened by violence spilling over from the former Yugoslavia—NATO membership loomed as the ultimate, totemic symbol of Western civilization and American support, whose conferral, it was believed here, would secure local democracy.

Constantinescu told me: "We see NATO as representing a set of values characteristic of the West: high economic performance, democracy, civil society, values from which we had been separated brutally when the Americans failed to rescue us from the Red Army in the late 1940s. NATO is a national dream for Romanians."

Constantinescu's case boiled down to this: States, like individuals, were not equal, and democracy was slow and messy. Thus, unless America meant to redivide Europe along historical and religious lines, it would have to provide a security umbrella for Romania similar to Hungary's. Brucan, when I had asked him about NATO, said he was pleased with the Russian purchase of a Ploieşti refinery, because it would allow Romania to refine Russian oil and reexport it to the West. "The better our relationship with Russia, the stronger will be our relationship with the West. Otherwise, Europe and the United States will take us for granted." Constantinescu implicitly trusted the West; Brucan trusted nobody and preferred to play one power off against the other.

Brucan's strategy was historically legitimate: Medieval Walachian and Moldavian princes had also played outside powers off against each other, and Romania was the only nation whose army aligned itself actively with both sides during World War II, fighting with Hitler in the first half of the war and with the Allies in the second half. Ceauşescu, to the degree that he was able, given the strictures of the Warsaw Pact, played the Soviet Union off against the United States, winning Most Favored Nation trading status from the U.S. Congress.

It was clear that if Constantinescu's strategy of trusting the United States did not soon result in full NATO membership for Romania,

Brucan's strategy might replace it. And because of the new strategic reality emerging in both the Balkans and the Black Sea–Caspian Sea region, which I will now explore, that would harm the West. This was perhaps why some of my most interesting conversations in Bucharest were with the Romanian military.

6

PIVOT STATE

General (retired) Prof. Dr. Costache Codrescu and I sat talking in our overcoats in the basement of the military war college, built in the 1930s on the Calea Victoriei during Bucharest's era of bourgeois expansion. Surrounding us in the semidarkness were red Byzantine columns adorned with gold leaf. Cups of Turkish coffee lay on a table before us. The general's obsession with titles, the lack of heating, and the Oriental architecture and coffee were typical of the Near East, even as he and other Romanians insisted passionately in their Latinate language that they belonged to the West. Such poignant insistence was relevant, for it indicated in what direction Romanians saw their destiny. Because their culture was such a blend of the Latin West and Oriental East, Romanians worried about being left behind on the wrong side of a divide, a divide they knew was real because of their forty-four-year isolation from the West.

Codrescu, a seventy-two-year-old military historian, jerked his head and threw his hands about theatrically while joking about his stature. "I am from Moldova [Moldavia], and Moldovans are short but smart"— he tapped his head with his finger—"like Ştefan cel Mare"—Stephen the Great, the short fifteenth-century prince who had built a strong Moldavian principality to thwart the Ottoman Turkish advance. Then Codrescu spoke about the military's role during the December 1989 revolution that toppled Ceauşescu:[1]

"We in the army had always known that Romania would be isolated and defenseless in the event of an East-West confrontation that might descend into local wars. We would be isolated because of our difficult history with Hungary over Transylvania and Russia over Bessarabia [eastern Moldavia]. We would be defenseless because we had been discharging soldiers to work in the fields during the hard economic times of the 1980s. When the Berlin Wall fell in November 1989, we felt even more vulnerable. The end of communism in Hungary and Bulgaria suddenly meant national regimes on our borders.

"Ceauşescu didn't trust the army. He kept us in the dark, secluded within our worst assumptions. So when we received the news on December 16, 1989, that antiregime riots had broken out in Timişoara following the arrest of a Hungarian priest, we became suspicious. We immediately saw a connection with a recent Hungarian demand for Transylvanian autonomy.[2] We knew that as a result of an Austrian-Hungarian agreement the previous July, Hungarian troops were shifted to our border. [The Austrian-Hungarian agreement had allowed citizens of Hungary and other Warsaw Pact states to cross freely into Austria. This precipitated a flood of East Germans to the West via Hungary, which in turn led to the collapse of the Berlin Wall four months later.] The Bulgarians and Russians were also moving troops close to us. I know how paranoid this sounds. We read too much into these troop movements. But we didn't know then that the protests in Timişoara were genuine.

"So we waited for the signal to advance to the Hungarian border to defend our homeland. Instead, we were ordered into the streets of Timişoara to defend Ceauşescu. Only then did it dawn on the general staff that Ceauşescu—not the Hungarians or the Russians—was the enemy.

"The Romanian army has always thought in terms of the national patrimony, particularly in the matter of Transylvania and Bessarabia. It was the hope of recovering Bessarabia from Stalin that led Antonescu into an alliance with Hitler against Russia. But after Antonescu came to power, no more territory was lost. I am not defending what Antonescu did to the Jews. But he kept the state together, so we must forgive him his sins."

A Romanian general who forgives Antonescu the murder of 185,000 Jews because he kept Romania united suggests the deep insecurity and brutality that run throughout this society. Another army officer close to Ceauşescu told me that in the six-week period after the Berlin Wall fell and before he was overthrown, Ceauşescu was planning to "rehabilitate" Antonescu as a Romanian national hero, as part of a last-ditch effort to keep himself and his wife in power. Slobodan Milosevic had recently done likewise in neighboring Serbia when he converted the Communist party into a nationalist-fascist one. Thus far in Romania, only President Constantinescu himself had publicly repudiated Antonescu.

Because Romania teetered between a civil society and a descent back into fiery nationalism, Constantinescu and a group of young English-speaking generals he had recently appointed were trying to make the Pentagon happy with the Romanian military, hoping that Romania would be "locked" into NATO before it was too late. Romania was transforming its military from a large, badly educated force—more suited for manual labor than for fighting—into a smaller, better-trained service organized along flexible Western command lines. A Balkan expert for the U.S. Army described the Romanian military to me this way:

"They are ahead of other armies in the region in terms of efficiency. Their top guys assume the blame and don't punish officers below them. It's partly a factor of Latin honor. The civilians say we need the military to run things, but the Romanian armed forces say, 'No way.' The Romanian army's desire to stay clear of politics is purer than in [the armies of] Greece or, certainly, Turkey. Romanian officers are forbidden to belong to political parties. In reality, democracy survives in Romania only because of the restraint of the military."

The Romanian military also had a good fighting reputation. The Nazis considered Romanian soldiers among their fiercest Axis troops. It was only because the Romanians had been forced-marched while underfed that the Russians were able to break through their lines at Stalingrad. When the journalist C. L. Sulzberger asked the Nazi general Hans Speidel to name the best non-German troops in the Axis alliance, Speidel responded, "The Romanians. Give them good leadership and they are as good as any you'll find."[3] When Romania switched sides in August 1944, Allied commanders were equally satisfied with the aggression of the Romanians. The Romanian military's attitude toward America was now no less enthusiastic than it had been toward the two sides it fought for in World War II. During the Iraq crisis in March 1998, the chief of the Romanian General Staff, division general Constantin Degeratu, told me that "we have given the U.S. overfly rights and the use of several air bases. We stand by the U.S. We are ready to take part in any operation. I gave [chairman of the Joint Chiefs of Staff, General Hugh] Shelton full assurances, backed by our president and the cabinet. We understand exactly your problem with Iraq."

The Defense Ministry was among the many monstrously ugly structures built by Ceauşescu that had required the leveling of historic nineteenth-century Bucharest. Here, plied with Turkish coffee, I met the Romanian chief of staff, a short, wiry man in his late forties with dark hair and a warm smile. Degeratu explained Romania's strategic position. "Before World War Two, we tried to stay neutral and make deals with everyone. That proved impossible. So we had to fight with the Germans against the Russians, then with the Russians against the Germans. Still, we came under Russian domination. Later we tried to play the Chinese—and the Americans to a small extent—against the Russians. But that failed, too. We ended up isolated, with low-quality equipment and a military that was best suited for slave labor." He disagreed with Brucan. "Neutrality does not work. We are not a great power, and our position is too vulnerable. Romania is the only country in Europe between the two great regions of instability and uncertainty, the former Yugoslavia and the former Soviet Union. For the sake of ourselves and Europe, we require stability. No other country in Europe needs NATO as much as we do."

Colonel Mihai Ionescu, a military historian and strategist, elaborated on General Degeratu's points:

"In this era of imperial recuperation, Russia will employ subtler means to retake us: organized crime, intelligence operations, and corrupting our elites. But for the time being, we have room to maneuver. Russia doesn't touch our borders anymore, but must work through Ukraine and Moldova. And with the breakup of the Soviet Union, the

Black Sea is no longer a Russian lake. But it is dangerous to think that this ambiguous situation will last. That is why the West must enlarge eastward!"

The Romanians were terrified by what they saw in the former Soviet Union. The dramatic plunge in development that I had seen when I crossed from Hungary into Romania was duplicated when one crossed from Romania into Moldova and Ukraine: netherworlds of awful roads, where, if you left your car unattended, it would likely be stolen. In the past, it had been the Russian army that frightened Romanians. Now it was the social anarchy breeding a tyrannical reaction in Moscow. Not only was the Iron Curtain still real in a sense, so was the "second Iron Curtain," between Eastern Europe and the former Soviet Union.

Iulian Fota, a slickly dressed engineer whom Constantinescu had made an assistant secretary of defense, told me: "Russia's strategy is to re-create its sphere of influence throughout the former Soviet Union and Bulgaria, then work with France and Greece, and Syria and Iran, perhaps, to limit U.S. power in the Near East. Opposing that configuration will be a Turkic alliance of Turkey and Azerbaijan with Israel. We can help the Turks and Israelis. Once Caspian Sea oil starts flowing to Europe across the Black Sea, Romania's international security profile will grow. Romania is no longer on the periphery of Europe. With our refining capabilities at Constanţa [on the Black Sea] and Ploieşti, we will be on the new pipeline network. We're in the middle of a new, volatile region between Europe and the Caspian."

This analysis, while self-serving, was keen. Greece may be part of NATO, but the Bosnian Serb leader Radovan Karadzic—an indicted war criminal—was given a hero's welcome in Athens in 1992: this suggests a deeper historic and religious attachment alongside the official post–Cold War alliance structure.[4] But Romania was a potential strategic Western asset for a reason that nobody in the Defense Ministry had mentioned:

In a stable democracy, which Romania was struggling to become, security policy is ultimately tied to public opinion. Because of their experience of living under Ceauşescu's Stalinism and the uncertainty that went with being on the eastern fringe of the Western world, Romanians—

civilians as well as the military—were as passionately pro-American as the English and French after V-E Day, in May 1945. While Western Europeans decried the U.S. for its "warmongering" in Iraq, Romanians unabashedly supported us. In many a crisis—Kosovo excepted— the French, the Italians, and other Western Europeans looked for the slightest inconsistency in U.S. policy to deny its validity. As cultural resentment of America's loud materialism intensified, along with the unifying effect of a single currency, a neutral, perhaps even hostile, Western-Central European power bloc might form. Thus, it was crucial for the U.S. to have friends in southeastern Europe whose military bases it could use. In the 1973 Middle East war, the U.S. had relied on Portugal as a base to resupply Israel when traditional European allies— England, France, and West Germany—refused to help. Romania could become a new Portugal at the other end of the Continent.

Because the Near East was a region of major oil reserves, aging dictators, high unemployment among young males, high absolute growth in both population and urbanization, and dwindling water supplies, the West's problems with Saddam Hussein might foreshadow other military emergencies there in the twenty-first century. Romania, on the northwestern fringe of the greater Near East, was a natural forward base—especially as oil power moved north from the Arabian peninsula to the Caspian and nearby Turkey's political power increased as huge water reserves gave it increasing leverage over water-poor Arab states.

But if Romania should not become a forward base for the West, the military feared the country would fall into the abyss. At a late-night dinner at the officers' club, after much plum brandy and wine, I brought up Harvard professor Samuel Huntington's "Clash of Civilizations" thesis.[5] Colonel Ionescu, a tall, avuncular man, responded with some anger: "Huntington is dangerous, especially in connection with NATO enlargement." But Ionescu did not mean to attack the validity of Huntington's thesis. Quite the opposite. He, like every other Romanian officer I met, was terrified of a civilizational boundary in Europe in which NATO expansion ended at the Hungarian-Romanian border and the multiethnic region of Transylvania became a battleground between Western and Eastern Christianity.

Romania was Europe's true pivot state, big enough to affect the cultural face of the Western alliance were it accepted as a full-fledged member yet compact enough for its membership to be viable, unlike sprawling Russia.[6] With Romania's 20 million Orthodox Christians joined to NATO, a civilizational divide at Hungary's eastern border would be unlikely; with Romania outside, such a divide could emerge as the Continent's overriding fact. With Romania absorbed into the West, Europe stretches to the Black Sea; with Romania estranged, Europe becomes a variation of the Holy Roman Empire, while the Balkans rejoin the Near East.

Thus, the turn of the twenty-first century offered a rare and fleeting moment for bold statesmanship in the Balkans. At the outbreak of World War II, Bucharest was wealthier and more cosmopolitan than Athens. With all its problems, Romania at the end of the Second World War, as Rudolf Fischer had told me, was more salvageable than Greece had been, as the latter was both riven by conflict and lacking a modern bourgeoisie. Nevertheless, the Truman administration acted boldly, yanking Greece into NATO. Whatever problems Greece has caused the Western alliance, they are minimal compared to what they would have been had Greece been excluded from NATO. Would Clinton or his successor do for Romania what Truman had done for Greece?

For the moment, the Romanian military was pro-American. At a time of civilian political turmoil, the officers saw NATO as a source of good careers and decent salaries, improved training and equipment, and access to international networks, including seminars and frequent trips abroad. But if NATO expansion beyond Central Europe were to flag, even as EU expansion into Central Europe did not—two trends that looked obvious at the time of my visit—then the Romanian military might turn narrowly nationalistic and politically active again, as it had been under General Antonescu, and as his revived public reputation now suggested.

※ ※

"Romania is a country that has almost never known normality," Mihai Oroveanu, the director-general of the Ministry of Culture, told me one day near the end of my visit to Bucharest. I had sought out Oroveanu because a friend had described him to me as "an old-bourgeoisie type who has inexplicably survived communism." I found him in a room at the rear of the National Theater building, surrounded by books and photographs of Romanian cultural icons, such as the playwright Eugène Ionesco and the sculptor Constantin Brancusi. With high leather boots, khaki pants, and a sleeveless leather jacket, Oroveanu, a huge, gray-haired man, looked like an aging Hells Angel. "I'm moving paintings around, so I'm in work clothes," he explained.

"In almost every century," Oroveanu told me, "we have been a battle zone and a disaster area. The Romanian state that came into existence in 1859 with the unification of Walachia and Moldavia was essentially a medieval one. It was a German, Carol the First of Hohenzollern-Sigmaringen, who first created modern institutions here between 1866 and World War One. But too many of the best officers and professors were killed in the First World War. The interwar period saw the rise of many peasants to the middle class, but they had no moral leadership. Then the Communists destroyed our most energetic peasants, the *chiabur,* the equivalent of the kulaks. I now fear a return to intolerance and superstition, helped by computers. Here you could easily have slick materialism without morality. The new capitalists are only imitators of the Western bourgeoisie."

At the opera house on my next to last night in Bucharest, all that I had experienced in Romania was summed up with heartbreaking clarity. Packs of stray dogs prowled and children in tattered clothes played soccer on the scraggly entrance lawn in the early evening as couples, young and old, looking like a down-at-the-heels 1930s bourgeoisie, waited with their seventy-five-cent tickets to enter the hall. Then, for two hours, I listened to Puccini and Verdi sung brilliantly by soloists in worn shoes and tuxedos on a scuffed and gloomy stage, battling scratchy acoustics. The audience was wildly enthusiastic. They were crying to twenty-first century Europe from the sepia-toned early half of the twentieth. *Don't forget us,* they said.

⁂

I left Bucharest for Sofia in early March 1998. The train compartment was freezing, filthy, rust-stained, and filled at seven-thirty in the morning with unwashed laborers in overalls, shouting and drinking brandy out of crude jugs. A well-dressed middle-aged couple entered, clutching their seat-reservation stubs. The laborers would not move. Finally, a conductor ordered two of them out to make room for the couple.

The train headed south, entering the flat plain of the Danube, like an African savanna with its thatched huts, dirt paths, and mule-drawn carts. At Giurgiu, on the Romanian side of the Danube, the laborers left our compartment. Officials stamped our passports. Then they and the Romanian conductors deserted the train, which filled immediately with an army of smugglers, their bags and suitcases stuffed with canned food, cigarettes, produce, and who knows what else. The compartment was now jammed with people standing in the aisles: men with outlandish clothes, shaven heads and unshaven faces, and the most violent of expressions, spitting, coughing in my face, and stepping on my feet as ashes fell from their cigarettes. Profanity ruled. The middle-aged couple across from me cowered in fear as the train slowly crossed the wide Danube into Bulgaria.

7

"CIVILIZATIONAL

CHOICE"

A few minutes later the train stopped at Ruse, on the Bulgarian side of the Danube, where the smugglers poured out. On a platform teeming with Gypsy peddlers, I exchanged my remaining Romanian lei for Bulgarian levas and paid $22 to an old woman behind a rusty metal grille for a Bulgarian visa. Returning to my compartment, I saw another old woman sweep out the mess made by the smugglers as a new conductor checked our tickets. At the beginning of the twentieth century, when the future Nobel Prize–winning author Elias Canetti was born here to a Sephardic Jewish family, Ruse had been a cosmopolitan, multiethnic outpost of Central Europe. Now it belonged to a rootless, urbanized peasantry. The modern states that formed after the collapse of Ottoman Turkey—states that, while sometimes democratic, were monoethnic—expelled some minorities; then Nazism drove out others. Communism followed, which, in the guise of social justice, destroyed what remained of a middle class. The illusion that human progress is inexorable arises from the accident of one's historical and geographical good fortune. Canetti was aware of this and spent much of his life analyzing the human proclivity for mass violence and hysteria.[1]

The train headed south across the Danube plain, then west along the northern face of what Bulgarians call the Stara Planina, the Old Mountains, known to outsiders as the Balkan Range. We passed green and brown fields threaded by hauntingly beautiful rivers; many shacks, horse-drawn carts, and roofs with missing terra-cotta tiles; and a handful of cars and satellite dishes. Once, when the train slowed, I observed a crowded village market with cinder-block stalls filled with old clothes and other drab necessities, which reminded me of markets I had seen in Central Asia. Bulgaria looked to me like another Romania, an ex-Communist Eastern Orthodox country drifting from the Second to the Third World, though its countryside appeared less ravaged than Romania's, with fewer hideous factories and scars of pollution.

There was no food or water on the train, but a fellow passenger made me a gift of hard-boiled eggs. At the end of the day, the train entered a steep and winding canyon as the mountain scenery escalated in magnificence. An hour later, when the train emerged on a cold plateau, I could see Sofia, Bulgaria's capital, on the horizon.

※ ※

Sofia's train station was a product of 1970s, late–Zhivkov era gigantism: As Bulgaria's Communist boss Todor Zhivkov became increasingly vain and insecure, architecture here became increasingly inhuman in scale. The freezing station hall, about one and a half football fields in length, was made of rough gray stone and dirt-brown concrete and was dominated by a concrete carving on the wall of industrial gears and pulleys. Making the hall appear even more vast were tiny food stalls and a handful of broken wooden benches, the only places to sit. In a dirt lot beyond the station was a city of homeless youth and impoverished Gypsies. The landscape of the station district showed how tyranny creates a social vacuum.

As in Romania, in Bulgaria I found a depressed countryside surrounding a booming capital city, where construction projects, traffic jams, new shops and restaurants, and streets crowded with beggars and smartly dressed men and women had erased the ghost of communism. My hotel room overlooked a statue of the Czar Alexander II, "the Czar Liberator," whose declaration of war on Ottoman Turkey in April 1877 ended in March 1878 with the Treaty of San Stefano, which recognized an independent Bulgaria incorporating much of Macedonia and Thrace. The one-hundred-twentieth anniversary of the treaty had been celebrated the day before my arrival, March 3, 1998. The statue was covered in wreaths. I noticed that men and women in the streets, both old and young, whether in suits, casual café attire, or even punk outfits, all wore red and white strings on their coats and sweaters. These were *Martinitsa*s, from the Bulgarian word for the month of March. In March A.D. 680, when Khan Asparuh, the founder of the first Bulgarian kingdom, was losing a battle against the Byzantine emperor Constantine IV, he tied a white thread around the leg of a dove as a sign to his mother that he was still alive. The dove bled slightly from the tightness of the thread, making a red-and-white tribute to what would prove to be Khan Asparuh's victory. Bulgarians wear Martinitsas the entire month, or until the first stork appears from the south. For the pagan, Martinitsas are also a symbol of regeneration at springtime, with red symbolizing fertility, and white, purity.

Thus, in the midst of a global economic transition that was leading to the gradual erosion of nation-states and national characteristics, here, as in Romania, I found another ancient people little known outside its borders yet united by a common historical experience and a unique ethnicity, for Khan Asparuh's Bulgars were a Turkic people from the north Caucasus who, after having arrived in the Balkans, intermarried with the Slavs. The Martinitsas recalled this pre-Christian, pre-Slav heritage, as did many of the dark, angular faces of people in the streets, which reminded me of the bas-reliefs I had seen of Thracian warriors, yet another ancient Balkan people who had enriched Bulgarian bloodlines.

Because the Bulgarians and the Romanians focused on their own histories and their mutual enmity—Bulgaria had lost the southern Dobruja to Romania after the Second Balkan War of 1913 but gained it back through Nazi pressure in 1940—each evinced little concern for the other, despite their common fate as they awaited the second round of NATO expansion. On my last night in Bucharest, a group of Romanian friends at dinner had wondered why I was even bothering to visit Bulgaria. None of them had ever been there. "You'll be back in Romania in a few days," one warned. I found the same attitude in Sofia. Few here were even faintly curious about Romania. Except for the smugglers and Gypsies, the Danube might as well have been the edge of the known world.

Rather than look to each other, at the end of the twentieth century—as at the beginning—each national group in the Balkans looked to the Great Powers for solace. (Polls conducted by the Center for the Study of Democracy in Sofia and the Lambrakis Organization in Athens, under the aegis of the Helsinki Commission, found that among Albanians, 86 percent hated Serbs, 59 percent hated Greeks, 58 percent hated Macedonians, and 47 percent hated Bulgarians; among Bulgarians, 23 percent hated Turks and 51 percent hated Gypsies ["Roma"]; among Greeks, 38 percent hated all Slavs, 55 percent hated Gypsies, 62 percent hated all Moslems, and 75 percent hated Albanians.)[2]

※ ※

"The Bulgarian public is absolutely desperate for NATO membership," Solomon Passy, president of the Atlantic Club in Sofia, told me. "If Romania and Slovenia are accepted and we are not, it will be a second Yalta. All in-between mechanisms are exhausted. We are dissatisfied with the 'Partnership for Peace.'[3] Another ersatz group like that will not work. Our only option will be national suicide. It wasn't just Romania that wanted to help you. We too offered air corridors for U.S. bombing of Iraq [and Serbia], where we know radical military action is needed." Passy's remarks were a mild exaggeration of what I was to hear often in Sofia. For Bulgaria, a small nation that was once much larger—all its neighbors having helped themselves at one time or another to its territory—America had now assumed the former Soviet Union's role in the geopolitical firmament: the big bear protecting it against the surrounding wolves. Though at the time of my visit Bulgaria's democratic government was proving far more effective than the one in Romania, impressing even the International Monetary Fund, Bulgarians felt themselves far more vulnerable than Romanians. There were many reasons.

As I had seen at the train station, social anarchy was never far from the surface here. An agrarian country, where Ottoman occupation had lasted longer and was more severe than in Greece or Serbia, Bulgaria had even less of a historical bourgeoisie than Romania. Bulgaria is surrounded by Orthodox nations and Moslem Turkey, all latecomers to modern development; it lacks the open window to the Central Euro-

pean Enlightenment that Hungary has always offered Romania—
however much Romanians have resented it. At Europe's southeastern
tip, bordering Asia Minor, Bulgaria has often been destabilized by migration and invasion. Of its 8.8 million people, as many as 600,000 are
Gypsies, or Roma, as they are called here.[4]

The Gypsies, poor and abused, foreshadowed the anarchy that Bulgarians feared if their new and advancing democratic institutions were
to stumble. Eighty-five percent of Bulgaria's Gypsies are unemployed.
The crime rate among Gypsies is high. So is the birth rate, with four to
five children per family. Gypsies are referred to as "a ticking time
bomb." Only 60 percent of Gypsy children attend school. The rest do
not learn Bulgarian. "Under Zhivkov, the Roma had jobs provided
them by the Party, thus they mixed with Bulgarians. Now they are isolated," an official told me. In Budapest, Rudolf Fischer had described
the Gypsies as "a social problem" rather than just another case of ethnic intolerance (though it is that, too). Antonina Zhelyazkova, president of the Institute for Minority Studies in Sofia, told me that "all
Bulgarians aspire to be middle-class, but the Roma do not aspire to
that, and that is the root of the hatred toward them."

"Our big worry is that, yet again, no one in the West will pay
attention to us and we will be forgotten at the far end of the Balkans," Atanas Paparizov, a former minister of trade, told me. Sufficiently small as to approach invisibility—and separated from Central
Europe by hundreds of miles of often mountainous terrain, yet tied
to the former Yugoslavia by a long border and the complex issue of
Macedonia—Bulgaria, too, seemed trapped far beyond the Western security umbrella.

The distance between Washington, D.C., and Sofia became clear to
me when after a long day of interviews, in which I had listened to Bulgarian worries about Gypsies, NATO, the conflicts in Bosnia and
Kosovo, and Russian infiltration through organized crime, I returned
to my hotel room and turned on the television at the moment when
Washington commentator Chris Matthews was shouting on *Larry King
Live* about Monica Lewinsky and how "Clinton is like O.J. in the
Bronco . . ." Despite the illusion of proximity created by satellite television, the problems of 8.8 million people here might have been a fig-

ment of my imagination given what the Washington media felt was important. Even in the spring of 1998, at the height of the debate regarding the first round of NATO expansion, Romania and Bulgaria were absent from news about the subject. Consequently, any American journalist who bothered to come here was likely to enjoy endless and undeserved attention. During a meeting I had with a dozen Bulgarian political experts at the home of U.S. ambassador Avis Bohlen, one of them said, "So what are your real opinions about Bulgaria, Mr. Kaplan? Because we in this room are not kidding ourselves. What you write could very well affect U.S. policy here."

Bulgaria's head of state, President Petar Stoyanov, actually thanked me for taking the time to write about his country. Having been to many countries whose rulers wished that I had stayed away, I was struck by the president's certainty that almost any kind of publicity would be good for Bulgaria. The fear here was of being forgotten.

I met Stoyanov amid the funereal surroundings of the former Communist party headquarters, with its maroon carpets and ashen marble. In his mid-forties, dark, wearing a well-cut suit, Stoyanov, with his wire-rim glasses, looked exactly like the aggressive lawyer he had been before being elected president in December 1996. The difference between him and President Constantinescu of Romania was fundamental. Whereas Constantinescu, a university professor, made his points eloquently and circuitously, Stoyanov, who strode quickly into the room, greeted me with no introduction or formality, took his jacket off, and came right to the point:

"We have made a civilizational choice in our desire to join NATO. We don't want to fall victim to a political trade-off as happened at Yalta. For forty years we were like someone who had undergone an operation and never had the bandage removed from his eyes. Under communism we lived with perennial-deficit technology, no access to modern goods and travel, not to mention the psychological devastation. Communism was a bad religion with a modern security apparatus. Because of the Iron Curtain, investors knew more about Sri Lanka than about Central and Eastern Europe."

"Are you worried about Kosovo?" I asked.

"*Worried* is a mild word to use. I am very tense and anxious. If things were to take a bad turn in Kosovo, we would be the hardest hit. A new embargo against Serbia would be detrimental to the Bulgarian economy. We are the only Balkan country with no outlet to Central Europe except through Yugoslavia. We would be geographically stranded if the West adopts a weak policy in Kosovo."

Bulgaria, unlike Romania, was deeply and tragically implicated in the historical problems of the former Yugoslavia. The 1878 Treaty of San Stefano that arose from the Russian victory against the Turks in the Balkans had awarded what is today the former Yugoslav Republic of Macedonia to Bulgaria. Though that treaty was abrogated by the Congress of Berlin a few months later, Bulgarians have always believed that the Macedonian Slavs are really western Bulgarians who speak a dialect of their language. Because historic Macedonia overlaps Bulgaria, southwestern Bulgaria is also known as Pirin Macedonia. Were unrest in Kosovo ever to destabilize neighboring Macedonia, then the century-old conundrum that arose with the breakup of the Ottoman empire in the Balkans—over the questions of Macedonia's borders and whether Macedonia is, in fact, a real country—might be rekindled, undermining the Bulgarian state.

Following the breakup of Yugoslavia in 1991, sovereignty for Macedonia sparked large, angry protests in Greece, whose territory historic Macedonia also overlaps. Bulgarians, by contrast, overwhelmed by an economic collapse wrought by decades of communism, remained apathetic, as though they had left their historical grudges behind them. Unfortunately, that was not entirely so:

"The Albanians will take over Macedonia in twenty years. You will see, it will be merely a matter of demographics. It is a principle of nature that the animals on the lowest stage of evolution give birth to more," Stoyan Boyadjiev, the president of the Macedonian Cultural Union in Bulgaria, told me. I had entered a nondescript building and taken an elevator to a glitzy and spacious office, cluttered with cell phones, where a group of half a dozen old men placed themselves in a semicircle around me and began talking about their homeland—which, by their lights, should have been "the Bulgarian province of Macedonia," stolen from them by the Serbs and Tito, and incorporated into Yugoslavia. After Yugoslavia disintegrated, this part of Macedonia became independent. But they thought it should have been returned to Bulgaria. Their claims poured out as they ordered me to take notes. They described the current Macedonian president, Kiro Gligorov—an eighty-one-year-old man who had braved an assassination attempt in his struggle to maintain peace in a poor, ethnically divided land where Albanian Moslems were pitted against Macedonian Slavs—as "an absolute Stalinist and the biggest enemy of the USA."

"You must tell the highest decision makers in your country to get rid of that Stalinist, Gligorov, and his Bolshevik state, Macedonia, because there are true democrats ready to assume power," Boyadjiev told me. He referred to members of the Internal Macedonian Revolutionary Organization (IMRO), in whose Bulgarian office I was now sitting.

IMRO had produced the twentieth century's first terrorists when, with Bulgarian support, its assassins sought to undermine the parts of Macedonia "stolen" from Bulgaria by Serbia and Greece after the Second Balkan War of 1913. IMRO resurfaced after the collapse of Communist Yugoslavia and was now a fairly moderate political party in Skopje, the Macedonian capital. Its extremists, though, were here in Sofia, old men with bitter memories:

"I was three times in a Titoist concentration camp in Bitola [in southern Macedonia] because I dared to say, 'I am a proud Bulgarian.' How can anyone be an individual without first having pride in his nationhood? . . ."

"My father and I spent twelve years in a Serbian prison because we fought for a free and democratic Macedonian Bulgaria. You want me to forget that? Never! . . ."

"There is no Macedonian language. What they speak in Skopje is just a Comintern dialect of Serbian. Macedonia's real language is Bulgarian. . . ."

As they talked on, young, tough-looking men wearing blazers hovered about, making phone calls, serving Turkish coffee, and listening intently. The old ones were full of hate, but the young ones just wanted a fight, it seemed to me. It was a combustible mix: bitter old men and impressionable young thugs, the mix from which Romanian fascism had emerged. In 1923, A. C. Cuza, an elderly professor at the university in Iaşi, in the Romanian province of Moldova, had founded the anti-

Semitic League of National Christian Defense. Cuza's protégé was a young student, Corneliu Zelea Codreanu, who in 1927 founded the fascist Legion of the Archangel Michael. Isaiah Berlin has suggested that the worst violence of this century began with dangerous ideas in people's heads. I saw it in this room, in the worshipful way these young thugs gazed at their aged mentors.

I left the building at dusk, just as the loudspeaker from a nearby mosque was calling Sofia's Moslem minority to prayer. The mosque's call and the view of snow-capped Mount Vitosha rising above the narrow streets made Sofia momentarily appear to me like the small Balkan village it once was, when the violence of the twentieth century had begun. IMRO, of course, was a minority party and was not at all about to gain power in Bulgaria. But like the social problems of the Gypsies, it gave a face to a lurking fear here should a fragile economy falter. As President Stoyanov had told me, "Only solid institutions and a competent class of middle-level bureaucrats can lock in stability." Neither existed so far.

Bulgarians were worried by the taste of anarchy they had experienced the year before my visit. The newly coined Romanian word for ungovernability, *Bulgarizarea,* stemmed from that period. In early 1997, street demonstrations against a corrupt and ineffective government of former Communists had led to violence, with the looting of parliament. IMRO thugs beat up both student demonstrators and innocent Gypsies, the latter simply because of their race. The people hoarded basic commodities and prepared for the worst, which did not occur. Rather, new elections brought the non-Communist Union of Democratic Forces (UDF) back to power. Because UDF rule from 1991 through 1994 had been neither competent nor orderly, divided as the coalition was into fourteen factions, analysts were pessimistic, and I could see why. This time, however, the UDF had united all factions into one party and organized a cabinet of young technocrats, who, helped by President Stoyanov, seemed to have put the country on the road to stability and true reform.

"After the Zhivkov regime fell in November 1989, we went through a period of post-Communist euphoria," Stoyanov told me. "People expected that overnight we would become like Switzerland. When that didn't happen, there was a period of attempted reform by the UDF, which only made people nostalgic for communism as it became clear that we had no experience with capitalist competition. Then came three wasted years under neo-Communist lethargy. But the poverty during that period forced the population to break with these neo-Communist illusions. Everyone knew that there was no going back to the past: That psychology accounts for the quick reversal from anarchy to stability in 1997."

But this was not the whole story. Ognyan Minchev, the executive director of the Institute for Regional and International Studies in Sofia, told me: "There is official democracy. The question is, what lies behind it?" For the crisis in the former Yugoslavia, the uncertainty of NATO membership, and the problem of the Gypsies were magnified by something else that was happening around me at the time of my visit.

8

WRESTLERS

VERSUS DEMOCRATS

Within twenty-four hours of crossing into Bulgaria by train from Romania, I had begun hearing two words over and over again: *wrestlers* and *groupings,* with an emphasis on Multigroup, the Orion Group, and the Tron Group. "They run the country," I was told, or at the least were as palpable a presence in people's lives as the elected government. In early May 1998, a few weeks after I left Bulgaria, Anna Zarkova, a local journalist who had exposed these groups in her articles for the daily *Trud,* was doused with sulfuric acid hurled at her face at a bus stop. Zarkova, the mother of two children, lost her left ear and the sight in one eye as a result of the attack. For this reason, I cannot name the private citizens who gave me the following information without endangering their lives.

In the Communist era, Bulgaria had a great Olympic wrestling tradition. When the regime favorites lost their subsidies, many of them went into racketeering—with the help of their friends from the security services—and amassed tremendous wealth during the power vacuum that followed the regime's collapse. A close friend, a Bulgarian woman in her mid-twenties who specializes in human-rights cases, told me:

"The wrestlers are all big and tough, with cell phones, fancy cars, Versace suits, and young girls on their arms. All their girlfriends look alike: thin, with blond hair and vacuous expressions, and adorned with gold. At a restaurant where a meal cost more than most Bulgarians make in a month, I heard one of these girls repeat over and over to her wrestler boyfriend, 'This is so cheap. I can't believe how cheap this is. . . .' The wrestlers and their girls go to expensive nightclubs with loud music, where go-go dancers sing cheesy lyrics, like 'I love *shopska* [peasant's] salad.' We all know that our cars will be stolen if they are not 'insured' with one of the wrestlers' insurance companies. Another name for the wrestlers is the *moutras*—the 'scary faces.' We are all repulsed by their behavior, but we have to deal with them. This is a country where people have put their life savings into sugar and flour because of inflation [and where the monthly salary is $140], yet there is a criminal class with stolen Audis and Mercedes."

I saw the wrestlers frequently in Sofia. A late-model high-performance car would screech to a halt, muscular men in fashionable clothes would emerge with cell phones, wearing enough cologne to be noticeable from fifteen feet away. The boss would occasionally have two beautiful women with him, one on each arm. It was both frightening and pathetic. Their expensive homes, on the slopes of Mount Vitosha, above the haze of pollution that hovers over Sofia, were surrounded by two-story-high brick walls and punctuated with satellite dishes. Nearby sprawled a vast Gypsy settlement of muddy shacks, growling dogs milling about.

※ ※

"One of the reasons our criminal groups became so powerful is that they were organized by the state itself. This is something unique to Bulgaria. The other important factor was the embargo against Serbia: Violating the embargo was a catalyst for organized crime in the Balkans, like Prohibition in the United States," Bogomil Bonev, Bulgaria's interior minister, told me. Bonev, a towering, thickset man with wavy black hair, spoke in a tense voice in his vast, gloomy World War II–era office, in the same building where security officials of the former Communist regime may have worked out details for the 1981 assassination attempt on Pope John Paul II. The situation was now reversed: The Communist-era security service, Darzhavna Sigurnost, along with former Olympic wrestlers, had formed various criminal "groupings," which Bonev was hunting down. "My biggest problem has been that our policemen do not look at the wrestlers as criminals. Our moral values have been impaired. To young Bulgarian girls, the wrestlers became sex symbols. There is evidence that our criminal groups have links to Russia. We need urgent judiciary reform. Our criminal-justice system has elements of the Soviet one under Vyshinsky." Andrei Yanuarievich Vyshinsky was Stalin's chief prosecutor during the 1930s purge trials.

Organized crime is, of course, a common feature of former Soviet Bloc societies. By the 1980s, Communist parties had evolved into large-scale mafias, which, when the system collapsed, simply divided into smaller mafias that purchased politicians in new and weak democracies. Common, too, are allegations of a new Russian imperialism by way of European-wide crime connections and energy monopolies like Gazprom. Nowhere, however, were such phenomena so transparent as in Bulgaria in 1998, a poor, small country in which democratic institutions have been fighting valiantly against Russian attempts at "resatellitization" by criminal stealth. Bulgaria illustrates how the potential evils of the new century are ominous precisely because of their ambiguity, for it is no accident that the word *groupings* is used instead of *mafias*. These networks include legitimate enterprises—audited by Western accountants and, increasingly, linked to Western multinationals—as well as legitimate entities which engage in activities such as compact-disk pirating, illicit-drug activity, money laundering, and extortion. One foreign diplomat told me, "These groupings engage in violent intimidation and corrupt politicians, yet their genius is to cover their tracks to an extent that they are quasilegitimate."

The groupings in Bulgaria indicate how global capitalism does not necessarily promote civil society: It all depends upon the nature of capitalism in each locale. What may appear as a legitimate enterprise could be a netherworld of thuggery when the doors close. A few years ago, the owner of a well-known bank in Sofia beat up his chief foreign currency trader in front of the staff. The boss was enraged because the dealer had lost $1.2 million in a transaction. The boss forced the dealer to sign a document stating that he would work for a paltry wage until the losses were restored. The boss, a former wrestler, is now an influential member of several "economic groups" here.[1] The story was reported by Jovo Nikolov, a flinty crime reporter for the Sofia weekly *Kapital,* the nation's most respected news publication, whose old clothes, unshaven face, and chain-smoking were a throwback to a bygone era in American journalism. Nikolov, along with Bulgarian officials, foreign diplomats, and others, told me how Bulgaria's crime groupings evolved, what they have done, and how they may illuminate Russia's new imperial strategy.

※ ※

Bulgarian crime has no centuries-old tradition like Italy's, or even one of heroic thieves and warrior clans as in Russia, Serbia, or Albania. Nor is there the colorful ethnic ingredient here that distinguishes criminal circles in the Caucasus, particularly in Georgia and Chechnya, with their family mafias and highwaymen. The Bulgarian groupings are the result of the transition from Communist totalitarianism to parliamentary democracy. Because such a transition is unique to history, so are these groups. Zhelyu Zhelev, Bulgaria's first post-Communist president and the author of a 1982 dissident work, *What Is Fascism?* (in which he actually describes communism), told me that a totalitarian state should normally be followed by a military regime, as in Spain, where Francisco Franco converted his fascist regime to a military dictatorship bolstered by the Church, which set the stage for a peaceful, relatively civil, and slow transition to democracy.[2] "The West's victory in the Cold War and its support for democracy worldwide made a direct transition to democracy possible in Eastern Europe," Zhelev explained, but the new democracies, weak and lacking institutions, created power vacuums filled by organized crime.

Bulgaria's criminal empire arose in the late 1980s, before the fall of the Berlin Wall, when a middle-aged Bulgarian apparatchik, Andrei Lukanov, who had spent many years in the Soviet Union and had numerous Party contacts there, realized that the Communist system was dying. So Lukanov developed a plan to turn local Bulgarian party leaders into businessmen. Todor Zhivkov, the aging Communist party boss of Bulgaria since 1954, believed that Lukanov was a radical reformer and hated him. But Lukanov understood the future. Just as another middle-aged apparatchik in Serbia, Slobodan Milosevic, realized that his generation of Communists could preserve their villas and hunting lodges following the collapse of communism by promoting ethnic nationalism, Lukanov saw that Bulgarian Communists could remain in power through economic "reform." Lukanov, who in the early 1990s was twice prime minister of democratically elected, neo-Communist governments here, used privatization to help found Multigroup—the most powerful of the oligarchal "groupings"—by transferring state assets to his friends.

On October 2, 1996, the fifty-six-year-old Lukanov, then an ex–prime minister, was gunned down in front of his house in Sofia. Nobody was arrested, but it is assumed that Lukanov was murdered by the beast he had created. His views had become too conservative for Multigroup's new regime, headed by an ex–Olympic wrestler and former son-in-law of one of the bosses of the security services during the Communist era. Another theory is that the assassination was ordered by erstwhile allies in the Bulgarian socialist regime whose corruption Lukanov had threatened to expose. A Western executive here told me: "Lukanov knew that his friends were sucking so much milk off the state that the supply would soon run out. He knew that they would eventually have to compromise with the democratic authorities in order to satisfy the IMF and international investors," which, in fact, was what started to happen in 1999 and 2000. Still others believe that the killing was the work of the Russian mafia. Yet in the shady world where Lukanov garnered both power and money, these suspects converge as foes of democratic reform. Some of Lukanov's former associates may have killed him for the same reason that Zhivkov hated him: Lukanov had always been the messenger of a future that none of these people liked.

Of course, the groupings did not arise simply because Lukanov had an idea. The breakdown of the Communist state provided numerous opportunities for people close to power to cash in. Some Olympic wrestlers gained control of motels along Bulgaria's international highways and at border checkpoints, which provided revenues from prostitution and currency dealing and helped give them access to the car-theft business. This involved the theft of both local vehicles and those stolen in Western Europe, which passed through Bulgaria to the former Soviet Union by ship across the Black Sea. In 1989, the last year of Eastern European communism, 4,318 cars were stolen in Bulgaria. In 1991, the number was 12,873, and it has remained close to that level ever since. The groupings then formed car-insurance companies, offering guarantees against car thefts in return for hefty premiums. Throughout Bulgaria, I saw stickers affixed to cars and houses with the name of a security agency, particularly VIS-2, run by another ex-wrestler. These stickers were often not accompanied by alarm systems: The owners had paid protection money for them and were safe from break-ins. (In the summer of 1998, the state began cracking down on these stickers and eventually ended the practice.)

The groupings also own energy firms, sports and tourist facilities, and food-processing companies, among other enterprises, often purchased with government loans from corrupt state officials; they will never be paid back, according to diplomats and other experts. (The failure to repay such large loans helped fuel inflation.) The groupings' control of Bulgaria's agricultural import-export market was accomplished through "beatings, kidnappings, and assassinations," according to the journalist Jovo Nikolov. He noted that "the largest 'economic groups' sometimes bear an uncanny resemblance to the state itself: They maintain giant security, intelligence, and data processing departments. . . ." So, just as increasingly powerful multinational corporations may be a new and evolving political form, crime-based oligarchies in the former-Communist world may be another—all under the triumphant rubric of "global capitalism."

A dispute between Bulgaria and Russia at the time of my visit revealed how the Kremlin was using the groupings as a lever against the Bulgarian state. Bulgaria depends upon natural gas from Russia via a pipeline whose ownership is evenly divided between Russia and Bulgaria. Gazprom, a Russian energy monopoly, however, controlled not only the Russian half but the Bulgarian half, through shadow companies under the groupings' command. In the late 1990s, when the Bulgarian government began demanding control of the Bulgarian share of the pipeline, the Kremlin, backing Multigroup and its allies, objected, and threatened to curtail Bulgaria's energy supplies if the Sofia government did not yield to the groupings. Foreign diplomats told me that this

Russian threat to deny Bulgaria natural gas commenced after Bulgaria formally applied for membership in NATO in March 1997.

The bond between Bulgaria's groupings and Russia existed on three levels: strong party connections that evolved into economic connections, forged in the Communist era, when Bulgaria was the most subservient satellite state; strong links between the KGB and Bulgaria's Communist-era security service that became crime connections; and general social connections among criminals nourished by the similarities between the two countries' Slavic languages. This is most apparent at the Bulgarian Black Sea port of Varna, a hangout and transportation hub for Russian criminals. What makes Bulgaria particularly vulnerable to Russian organized crime is that unlike such other formerly Communist states as Hungary and Romania, here—for linguistic and historical reasons—Russians as a people are very much liked, even if Russian communism was not.

Thus, even with stable democracy, Bulgaria may not become a civil society if it continues to be undermined by this new and subtle Russian imperialism. "The biggest danger here is a mixed regime of official democracy while real power is held by semilegal groupings," former president Zhelev told me. "The political parties could easily evolve into masks for mafia structures, with crime groups financing election campaigns." The West could then leave Bulgaria to its fate by declaring it a "democratic success story." Since the Washington establishment prefers to simplify its problems by accepting official truths, this seemed a possibility. Bulgarians are right: They are in danger of being forgotten.

Like Romanian president Constantinescu, Zhelev, with his gray hair and a sad, friendly face, was his country's first moral leader in many decades. He told me that "communism was the perfect form of fascism," because it controlled totally not just political structures but economic ones, too.[3] "That's why communism had a longer life than fascism: It was born in 1917 and died in 1989, while fascism was mainly a phenomenon of the 1920s through the 1940s." Communism and fascism are also alike in that they are both extreme and perverse results of the centralization of state power made possible by the Industrial Revolution.

But the new evils are less monumental than the old ones. Zhelev's

Communist predecessor, Todor Zhivkov, had ruled Bulgaria like a Roman emperor, with an array of palaces and bodyguards and retainers, not to mention lethal security services, and an arrogant expression stamped permanently on his face. Zhelev, when he was president, had always been approachable. Nor did he enrich himself during seven years in office, unlike almost every other ruler in his country's long history. He received me over instant coffee in his dim walk-up apartment. Democracy, even if somewhat dysfunctional, was a vast improvement over what had been. But the issue here was whether democracy would become a convenient mechanism for criminal oligarchy. Political systems are not defined by their labels but by the actual workings of the power relationships within them.

※ ※

Near the end of my stay in Sofia, I saw two examples of American influence here: a shelter for homeless children and a university for students from throughout the Balkans and the former Soviet Union.

The shelter, on the outskirts of the capital, was run by the Free and Democratic Bulgaria Foundation, founded in 1991 by Yvonne and John Dimitri Panitza, both of whom worked for *Reader's Digest* throughout much of the Cold War. After the fall of communism, John ("Dimi") Panitza returned to his homeland, armed with American values. The Faith, Hope, and Love Center serves mainly Gypsy children who otherwise would live on the street, where many such youngsters are beaten by Bulgarian skinheads. Like many such places, the center manifested an institutional grimness, manically relieved by the colorful and happy designs on the walls. What I remember most is how each child desperately grasped my hand—refusing to let it go—while leading me proudly to his or her dormitory bed. The beds were the only possessions that these children had ever had and a semblance of stability that their lives otherwise lacked.

Another day, I drove two hours south of Sofia to Blagoevgrad, in the majestic, snowy wastes of Pirin Macedonia, the site of the newly established American University of Bulgaria, housed in the town's former Communist party headquarters. The university is the latest addition to a string of American liberal arts colleges in the Near East, first established by New England Protestant missionaries in the mid-nineteenth century to spread their ideals. They include the American universities of Beirut and of Cairo. (The one here is administered by the University of Maine.) In the cafeteria, overlooking the town square and the mountains beyond, I sat down to lunch with a group of eighteen- and nineteen-year-old students from Serbia, Albania, and the ethnic-Albanian region of Kosovo. Each spoke impeccable English and had scored high on American SATs. They were part of a new global elite, comfortable in various languages and cultural settings. Yet because they had grown up in countries wracked by Communist-inflicted poverty and ethnic divides, they evinced a realism that even the most seasoned of their American counterparts often lacked.

When I was there, small-scale fighting between Serbian security forces and the ethnic-Albanian Kosovo Liberation Army had begun. A student from Serbia felt that Milosevic knew he could not hold on to Kosovo indefinitely, but could grant autonomy to the Albanians only after bloodily internationalizing the crisis to a point where he could blame the West for the loss. "Unless the U.S. intervenes soon, many more Albanians may have to be killed before Milosevic reaches that point," he said (which is what basically happened the following year). An Albanian from Kosovo added, "The new criminal elite in Serbia may actually need the West to impose more sanctions so it can make more money through sanctions-busting." The discussion continued at this level of sophistication. Though they they were not in full agreement, the Serbian and Albanian students left the table arm in arm, literally. The genius of American democracy and free intellectual inquiry had subtly worked their magic with these kids.

American and Russian values in Eastern Europe were still at war: the humanism demonstrated by a homeless shelter for an abused minority and a university to foster tolerance pitted against the absolutism and thuggery of criminal oligarchies. Bulgaria was a poignant, if obscure, battleground in this struggle.

Two years later, in mid-2000, the situation in Bulgaria had subtly changed. Rather than bad wrestlers versus good democrats, the lines had become less clear. The wrestlers had been both weakened and forced to make clean, productive investments. Meanwhile, the honesty of Bulgaria's new political establishment was increasingly in doubt. At the same time, trade and other links between the European Union and Bulgaria were deepening. In other words, formerly Communist Bulgaria was evolving into a typically weak and corrupt democracy that, while closer to the West, could not yet depend on it. Nevertheless, Bulgaria was physically closer to the newly enlarged NATO than any nation in the Middle East or the Caucasus. Its democracy, while weak, was certainly salvageable. Bulgaria's destiny might well depend on how much shrewdness and courage the next U.S. president and secretary of state have at their disposal, in order to lock Bulgaria permanently into the Western alliance.

9

THE LEGACY OF

ORTHODOXY

Toncho Zhechev, Bulgaria's best-known living writer, was typical of Balkan intellectuals in that religion was central to his thoughts. He lived in a large, dimly lit apartment overlooking a forest near the Russian embassy. The author of thirty-two books, all but three of them novels, the sixty-eight-year-old Zhechev, in his pricy sport shirt, could have passed for a banker. Reflecting the obscurity of his language and country, none of his works has been translated into English.

Zhechev's most famous novel is *Bulgarian Easter,* which demonstrates how the spiritual battles within the Bulgarian Orthodox Church were never spiritual at all, but political. "There has never really been spiritual opposition to tyranny here," Zhelev told me, "because we never had deep Christian values in the first place, only pagan ones. The Bulgarian church continued the Byzantine tradition in which the church and state were synonymous. In the West, the church could be a corrective to the state, but Orthodox churches are historically ill equipped to supply moral values when the state has none. The Bulgarian church, for instance, was always closer to Croatian Catholics than to its brother Orthodox Church in Serbia." This was because Bulgaria and Serbia were at odds over Macedonia.

"I don't believe we can save the Bulgarian Orthodox Church," Zhechev went on. "Under communism, no other sphere of life had so many state security agents. Most Bulgarians will remain religiously in-different; some will join Protestant sects. But I'm not sure if Protestant rationalism can work in a place so geographically separated from the Reformation. The better choice would be a resurrection of true Ortho-doxy. The Orthodox world needs a Reformation of its own. We need a Luther, because in Bulgaria now it is just naked politics."

He spoke about the schism between the aged patriarch Maxim and the priests who opposed his collaboration with the Communists. Maxim had said the dissenters would have to pray for repentance. The dissenters replied that Maxim's "gang of cops" needed to be "replaced by real Christians, not slaves of the Socialists."[1] President Stoyanov threatened not to attend the services of either faction, or even to allow military flags to be consecrated on St. George's Day, as long as the schism persisted.

"I so much like your Melville," Zhechev remarked suddenly, out of context, as though rebuking his own culture. "*Moby-Dick* is such an ex-pression of America's strong energy and effort to defeat nature, yet the story has such lovely ambiguity. In the Orthodox world, only Russia has had great religious thinkers opposed to the church establishment—Berdyaev, for example," he said, referring to the early-twentieth-century Russian intellectual who, in *The Origin of Russian Communism*, explained how Lenin's and Stalin's totalitarian state owed as much to the Orthodox Church as to Karl Marx.

Zhechev was the third Bulgarian who had mentioned Nicolas Berdyaev to me; all three were frustrated by the Western belief that Russian communism was Marxist. Playwright Georgi Danailov told me: "Russian communism is only from Russia. It is not from Marx and the other Germans! You must read what Berdyaev has to say about the Orthodox Church!" And so I did.

Berdyaev writes that Lenin's regime was "the third appearance of Russian autocratic imperialism," following Peter the Great's early-eighteenth-century empire and the earlier, medieval czarist state, which had as its principal tenet "the doctrine of Moscow the Third Rome" (after Rome itself and Constantinople). Lenin's theocratic imperium was, despite its professed atheism, culturally immersed in this czarist Byzantine theocracy, from which he and Stalin had emerged. (Stalin had studied to be an Orthodox priest, and his speeches reflected the hypnotic, repetitive quality of Orthodox hymns.) It was not only the Russian masses—the serfs—who lived within the mental confines of Orthodoxy but the intellectual and political class, too. Berdyaev explains:

> Russians were true to type, both in the seventeenth century as Dissenters and Old-ritualists, and in the nineteenth century as revolutionaries, nihilists, and communists. The structure of spirit remained the same. . . . There always remains as the chief thing the profession of some orthodox faith. . . .[2]

Russian nihilism derived from Orthodoxy and reflected Orthodox aesthetic withdrawal from society—the notion that "the whole world lieth in wickedness." Bolshevism was an Orthodox form of Marxism, according to Berdyaev. It underscored *"totality."* "The wholeness of the Christian East is set in opposition to the rationalist fragmentariness of the West," he wrote, and reached an apotheosis with Stalin's totalitarianism. Because Orthodoxy was a total system, doctrinal disagreements could not be tolerated and led, therefore, to schisms, mirrored in the split between Bolsheviks and Mensheviks.

The Orthodox Church, moreover, as many Romanians had told me, was inherently collectivist and anti-Western, emphasizing the primacy of the nation over individuals, as in the writings of Dostoyevsky and Solzhenitsyn.[3] This was contrary to Western humanism. The Bulgarian church, like its Romanian counterpart, opposed both the Vatican and Protestant sectarianism, as well as capitalist reforms. The crisis of the Orthodox churches in Romania and Bulgaria may have been a delayed reaction to the fall of communism, a system in which the church was deeply implicated.

According to Berdyaev, Russians "did not believe in the stability of civilization, in the stability of those principles upon which the [bourgeois] world rests . . ." Toncho Zhechev and other Bulgarians shared that belief in upheaval, perhaps because the Bulgarian bourgeoisie had never been large or permanent.

As I prepared to leave his apartment, Zhechev remarked, "A spiritual vacuum never lasts indefinitely. Something new will replace it. The situation now is unbearable. I don't know where we are headed. At some point the people will realize that God is within us, not within the church."

❧ ❧

The unusual warm weather that had graced my journey broke suddenly with a mid-March snowfall as I departed for Plovdiv, to the southeast. As the train threaded through the Plain of Thrace, with the enchanting Sredna Gora Mountains to the north and the rugged Rila and Rhodope Ranges to the south, I could imagine the progression of medieval armies and caravans that had traveled this route to and from Constantinople: Hun, Bulgar, Slav, Byzantine Greek, medieval Bulgarian, Crusader, and Turkish. I noticed, too, the squalor of the drab towns through which the train passed. This, as in Romania, was an Oriental and medieval pattern of development: The new wealth created in the cities—the glitzy downtown restaurants and shops I had seen in Bucharest and Sofia—was being invested abroad rather than in the nearby countryside, which looked just as it had under communism. One Bulgarian politician I met called it "a Mercedes-through-mudhole style of city-state growth."

The journey to Plovdiv took two hours. Had the Great Powers at the Congress of Berlin in 1878 not negated the Treaty of San Stefano, Plovdiv might have become Bulgaria's capital. As it happened, the Congress truncated the Bulgarian state envisaged by the treaty, stranding Plovdiv in the Ottoman province of eastern Rumelia, which rejoined Bulgaria only in 1885, after Sofia's primacy was already established. Plovdiv had been the Philippopolis of the classical age, built in 342 B.C. on an earlier Thracian site by Philip II of Macedon, the father of Alexander the Great. A frontier town near the edge of Constantinople's domain, it was sacked by Huns, Bulgars, Slavs, Byzantines, and medieval Bulgarian czars. Under Turkish rule, it became a prosperous Moslem market town with a class of rich Christian merchants. Plovdiv is still known for its trade fairs. With the end of the Cold War, it is well placed geographically to benefit from Bulgaria's increased commerce with Greece and Turkey, whose borders are nearby.

In the underground passageway leading from the platform to the station hall—bare when I was last here, in 1990—I saw kiosks well stocked with bras, panty hose, perfume, and Western computer books translated into Bulgarian. I checked into the Trimontsium, the Stalinist gray pile where I had stayed eight years before; it had not changed. There was little heat or hot water, the cheap plywood doors and their flimsy handles were broken, the furniture was old, the fax machine was turned off at night, and the female receptionists smoked. Some of them looked like prizefighters. But outside this 1980s time warp of a building, the new Plovdiv beckoned.

Along the main shopping street, bright facades had been grafted onto old buildings: REEBOK: THIS IS MY PLANET; HAIR SCULPTURES 98; and so on. Everywhere, it was crowded and noisy. As in Bucharest and Sofia, the fashions were from Paris and New York, with an accent on magenta lipstick and black attire. Again, it was the women, with their fashion consciousness, who appeared far more modern than the men. (Bulgaria had historically been a pagan, matriarchal society.) I bought a greasy, spicy sausage from a sidewalk stand, sat down at a café, and ordered a raki, the anise-flavored liqueur of the old Turkish empire, and watched the passersby.

There are two kinds of shops and restaurants in the ex-Communist world: the Plexiglas, marble, and chrome alloy–constructed shop or café-restaurant, with fine whiskies and wines and an international cuisine featuring excellent salads, fish, and other wholesome selections—places frequented by the nouveaux riches—and the drafty eateries with grimy windows, zinc countertops, and cigarette ashes ground into the tablecloths, where poor Communist-era food is served on cheap crockery—frequented by the rest of the population. Though in the past few weeks I had seen many seemingly modest families splurging at McDonald's, the benefits of consumer capitalism seemed mainly for the former Communist elite. Many children begged on the streets, most of them Gypsies.

At the Plovdiv journalists' club I met Ivan Bedrov, executive director of the Journalists for Tolerance Foundation, and the foundation's editor, Yordan Danchev, both in their early twenties. Over Coca-Cola, with soft rock music playing in the background, the pair complained bitterly about their society.

Jewish graves had recently been vandalized in Kyustendil, in Pirin Macedonia, they told me. Bulgarian television reported that "Gypsies or Turks must have committed the crime." The Bulgarian media refer to Protestant Pentecostals as "sects composed of drug addicts." A poll in Plovdiv had shown that 32 percent of the people backed IMRO, the Internal Macedonian Revolutionary Organization. Only the ruling Union of Democratic Forces was more popular. IMRO thugs in Plovdiv had attacked Gypsy settlements and called for the exile of Jehovah's Witnesses. "If there are problems in Macedonia caused by Albanian Moslems," Bedrov said, "then IMRO will launch a campaign against Moslems here.[4] IMRO has credibility because it was the first group to demonstrate against the neo-Communist government in 1996, before it fell."

In other words, if the economy collapses, if Macedonia erupts, or if the government was further infiltrated by criminals, the result could be a mess. But the odds that nothing terrible will happen were also good. Weren't these two young journalists themselves a sign of hope? I had never encountered such independent-minded social critics in Communist Bulgaria.

I had a few hours to spare before boarding the train southeast to Istanbul. Walking about the old quarter of Plovdiv, I mounted a staircase to a small park of rich green grass as dark as moss, which afforded a prospect of the entire city. Directly below me was a precious cobblestone maze of eighteenth- and nineteenth-century houses built in what Bulgarians call "national Revival style," with hand-carved oriels, decorative wooden balconies, and roofs with terra-cotta tiles, mottled and discolored, like dying leaves. But stretching far into the Thracian Plain and utterly dwarfing this handful of traditional houses were ranks of concrete-and-cinder-block apartment houses without a hint of a garden or a playground. From this vantage point, the eighteenth and nineteenth centuries appeared marginal compared to the dehumanizing twentieth. From such Communist decades, Bulgarian politics now had to evolve. Behind me, on the highest hill overlooking Plovdiv, was a gigantic sculpture of a Soviet soldier with an AK-47 assault rifle. The sculpture would probably have to remain. To remove it would threaten the foundation of the houses below.

I descended the staircase and entered a nearby church, where I felt the pagan mystery beneath the surface of Eastern Orthodoxy, with its heavenly chants, ethereal smell of beeswax, and disembodied faces staring at me from gold-leaf icons amid an aura of dusky sensuality. This was another level of existence that competed successfully with the physical one, and even embraced it, for all its corruption. But perhaps only from such a world, with its power and magic and treasure trove of national tradition, could a better society be created. Perhaps from such beauty, morality could issue.

10

"TO THE CITY"

I arrived at the Plovdiv train station early for the 10:55 P.M. train to Istanbul, only to learn that the train would be departing more than two hours late, at about 1 A.M. The kiosks were closed. There was a single café open, with foldout chairs outside in the freezing March night, serving only stale wafers and instant coffee in thin paper cups. Rock music blared from a transistor radio by an old cash register. I retreated into the drafty station hall, where homeless Gypsies had also taken refuge, and seated myself atop a peeling radiator that provided a little heat.

A Japanese backpacker and a young Irishman soon arrived. Each of us took turns sitting on the radiator, the only one that worked. The backpacker had recently finished university in Japan and was about to start work in a bank in Tokyo. This winter journey through the Balkans was his adventure before settling into a regimented life. The Irishman was a composer who had been visiting a Bulgarian woman he had met at a concert. The Istanbul train finally arrived at 1:20, and the backpacker and I said good-bye to the Irishman, who was waiting for a train to the Black Sea. Our train had no tap water or heating, and I fell into a fitful sleep as we rattled southeast into the night. Finally, a Bulgarian immigration official knocked on the door of the compartment to stamp passports. Then the train pulled out of the little border town of Kapitan Andreevo, named for a Bulgarian hero of the Balkan Wars, whose outcome had created this frontier with Turkey.

As the train crossed the Turkish border, invisible in the blackness, I thought about how the essence of travel was to slow the passage of time. One could fly from Sofia to Istanbul in an hour, rather than break the journey in Plovdiv, as I did, and then spend an uncomfortable twelve hours getting from Plovdiv to Istanbul. But how else could one truly grasp the distance between Bulgaria's capital and Turkey's largest city? What would better reveal the geographical and historical relationship between Bulgaria, once a vassal state of Ottoman Turkey, and the Turkey of today? Flying from place to place encourages abstractions, whereas land travel brings one face-to-face with basic, sometimes unpleasant truths. I preferred to travel by second-class car and stay in cheap hotels. This was how I had lived and traveled in my twenties, when I had little money, but then I had no way to meet heads of state, diplomats, businesspeople, and intellectuals. Now that I had such contacts, and a bit more money, I still preferred the train or bus over the plane; it allowed me to go on learning.

The idea that the Internet and other new technologies annihilate distances is a half-truth. Americans and Bulgarians might send E-mail to each other, but once they leave their computer screens, they face two vastly different societies: one in which you had to pay protection money to keep your car from being stolen, and one in which you didn't; one in which your currency is worth something, and one in which it isn't; one where World War II ended in 1945, and one where it lasted until 1989 . . .

Because of the precipitous decline in foreign-news coverage in America, it was harder now than in the 1980s to know what to expect in a place like Bulgaria. Thus, I often felt like an explorer. In Romania, I had happened upon a society that was falling dangerously behind its fellow ex-Communist neighbors in Central Europe; in Bulgaria, I found a society that was regarded as a democratic success abroad but was under siege from criminal clans. What would I find in Turkey, a country that, for all its size, NATO affiliation, and critical geopolitical position linking Europe and the Middle East, was too easily taken for granted? I had no idea.

The train halted at Kapıkule, where a Turkish official brusquely ordered us outside. It was 4:30 A.M. In a freezing downpour, he told us to walk fifty yards in the dark to a ramshackle building to have our passports stamped. As I ran through the rain, I heard the call of the Moslem faithful to prayer from a nearby mosque. I noticed the red flag with the star and crescent, and the stern picture of Mustafa Kemal Atatürk, the founder of the Turkish Republic following the collapse of the Ottoman empire after World War I.

"No visa!" the mustachioed policeman said unhappily after leafing through my passport.

"But I never needed a visa to visit Turkey in the past," I replied.

Pointing behind him, he said, "You must go there, to that building."

I walked out into the rainy night, my belongings still on the train, which threatened to leave momentarily. In the other building, I found a single uniformed official snoring, his head thrown back and his feet up on an old desk.

"Visa!" I yelled, holding up my American passport.

"Forty-five dollars," he answered, as though talking in his sleep.

"That's an outrage!" I replied angrily.

He shrugged, "Forty-five dollars or no visa."

I gave him the money, which he dropped into a desk drawer before sending me back with a chit to the first building to have my passport stamped.

I have found that countries often show their true faces at remote border posts, where the patina of modernity created by an airport is absent. Kapıkule had a particularly mean reputation and a tradition of drug smuggling, aggravated by a historic relationship of mistrust between Bulgaria and Turkey: Turkey's brutal five-hundred-year-long occupation of Bulgaria had been repaid by Communist Bulgaria's equally brutal repression of ethnic Turks. Only recently had relations between the two countries improved. Had I judged solely by my experiences with border officials, I would have thought that Romania and Bulgaria, not Turkey, were members of NATO. But the extortionist cost of a single-entry visa was, I would soon learn, part of a larger political story in Turkey that had not quite made it through the world media filter. As in Romania and Bulgaria, what would turn out to be the most surprising aspects of Turkey would also be the most obvious.

I slept for an hour and woke as dawn was breaking over the Plain of Thrace between Edirne and Istanbul, cities that until the early twentieth century were called Adrianople and Constantinople. Adrianople had been the original capital of the Ottoman Turks, the city from which Mehmet II Fatih (the Conqueror) had marched on Constantinople and defeated the Byzantine Greeks in 1453. Through the morning fog, I could see bare branches on a bleak and bony earth. I sensed the legacy of wildness and impermanence left by the movement of armies through this continental gateway.

As the train neared Istanbul, I saw an explosion of construction and mounds of lignite everywhere, evidence of a city far more populous than any I had encountered so far on this journey. On the fringes of the city, the construction was cheap, no better than what I had seen in Bulgaria and Romania. But then came the great highways; gleaming, upscale apartment houses; and innumerable late-model foreign cars parked in the quiet Sunday dawn beside villas of real brick, each with a mature garden—something missing from the homes in Sofia and Bucharest, with their legacy of Communist poverty and ugly functionalism. We passed a complex of tennis courts and a modern racetrack, followed by brand-new auto showrooms. Clearly, we were approaching a fulcrum of economic and social power. The Balkans, with their tragic history of Communist underdevelopment and Ottoman oppression, seemed suddenly far behind me.

I pulled down the window and breathed sea air for the first time on this journey. In the Sea of Marmara, which separates the Balkan Peninsula from Asia Minor, I saw oil tankers and masses of pigeons pivoting alongside the train. Then came Constantinople's old Byzantine walls, named for Emperor Theodosius II, even though he was only twelve when building began in A.D. 413. I thought of how Justinian, born seventy years later near present-day Sofia, must have felt on first approaching this city, whose great monuments, such as the Church of Divine Wisdom (Hagia Sophia), he would soon erect. Justinian had arrived along the same route, and his times were oddly like my own. "The subjects of Justinian were dissatisfied with the times and with the government," Gibbon writes in *The Decline and Fall.* "Europe was overrun by the barbarians and Asia by the monks"; or, as we might say, by immigrants and fundamentalists.[1]

Like so many travelers before me, I was coming "to the city" from the provinces, a phrase that in Greek is *I-stin poli,* corrupted by the Turks to "Istanbul." The statues of Süleyman the Magnificent and Kemal Atatürk, who in the sixteenth and twentieth centuries, respectively, approximated the greatness of Justinian in the early sixth, towered over the dancing, windswept waters as the train made a sweeping curve along the Sea of Marmara into the Golden Horn, as broad gray domes and pencil-thin minarets began appearing through the early-morning mist.

The spice bazaar, the aggressive hawkers by the Galata Bridge, the Ottoman-era Yeni Cami, and the crowds jamming the ferry boats for points up the Golden Horn and nearby Bosporus lent the environs of Istanbul's Sirkeci train station the exotic confusion of the Orient. But such was the decrepitude of the Soviet inheritance in Romania and Bulgaria that this train station gave the impression that I had returned to the West. Unlike the grim, filthy stations in Romania and Bulgaria, the station and its adjacent restaurants were clean, and decorated with fine blue tiles. There were helpful guidebooks on sale, and the information booth was manned by smiling attendants. Many of the waiting taxis looked new, and the drivers were polishing them as they awaited customers. Here was a level of energy that even the most modernizing parts of Bucharest and Sofia lacked. Though it was Sunday, a holiday in this officially secular Moslem society, I heard the vibrating roar of jackhammers as workers dug up a street.

At the foreign-currency counter I was told that my Bulgarian levas were worthless and could not be exchanged for Turkish liras, so I gave them to the Japanese backpacker as a souvenir. After saying good-bye to him, I bought a local newspaper and sat down for an early lunch of grilled meat, yogurt, and syrupy Turkish tea. It was 11 A.M. and I had not eaten since the evening before, in Plovdiv.

The local newspapers were full of stories about the military's silent, unofficial takeover of the government. What was this? I had seen noth-

ing about it in the international newspapers I had found in Bucharest
and Sofia, nor had I heard anything about it on the BBC World Service.
After finishing my lunch and finding a room for $30 a night at a hotel
frequented by Middle Eastern businessmen, I set out to discover the
obvious.

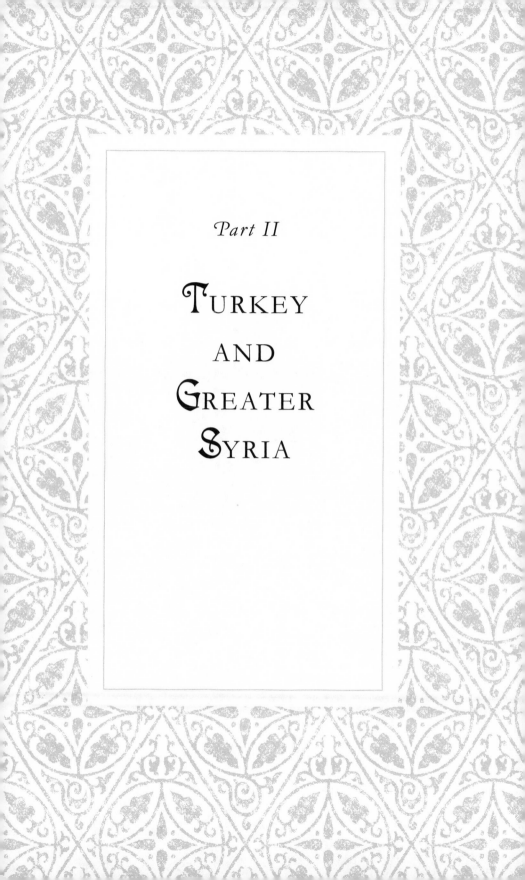

Part II

Turkey
and
Greater
Syria

11

THE "DEEP STATE"

Istanbul's İstiklal Caddesi was jammed with Sunday shoppers. Empty seats were scarce at a row of noisy fast-food restaurants serving grilled meat and gooey desserts, each with second- and third-floor dining rooms. At every corner people were lined up at ATM machines. Brightly lit shop windows displayed luxury goods, from fresh figs to diamonds. In an art nouveau pavilion, stores selling compact disks blared the melodramatic drumroll of Turkish popular music. I smelled roasting chestnuts and frying fish from a nearby restaurant. Café-bookstores with stacks of literary journals stood adjacent to kiosks selling amulets, protection against the "evil eye."

Yet it was the exquisitely cluttered art and antique shops that finally overwhelmed me, each with a jumble of perfectly arranged treasures—lithographs, carpets, lamps, handsomely bound books, and so on—as though the owner had spent part of a lifetime placing each object. It would take years for the antique shops in Bucharest, Sofia, and Plovdiv to amass such harmonious luxury. I bought a *simit* (a bread ring flavored with sesame seeds) and had my shoes shined by a man who kept his brushes and polishes in a magnificent box of hammered brass, bedecked with turbanlike domes. The ritual took almost ten minutes. Commonplace but elaborate traditions such as baking bread and shoe maintenance—the substance of material culture—have been preserved here intact, allowing Turks to enjoy the benefits of global materialism without losing their identity. Turkey's dynamism—the economy was growing by 7 percent yearly—underlined for me the damage done to the Balkans by communism.

In 1993, when I had last visited Istanbul, the population was 10 million. Now, the city has grown to 12 million, in a nation of 68 million. The masses of shoppers were as varied as the goods on sale. Men with beards and women with head scarfs proclaimed their faith, yet they too were laden with shopping bags amid a pageant that included even more men and women in tight jeans and fashionable capes, who filled the café-bookstores and boutiques. Islamization here was simply one aspect among many of a society that was growing increasingly complex at warp speed. Turkey, like Egypt, Iran, and India, sucks you in with the immense depth of its civilization and issues, as if the world outside its borders were not quite real.

From İstiklal Caddesi I walked downhill to the Golden Horn, crossed the Galata Bridge on foot back to the train station, then took the ferry north up the Bosporus to the seaside village of Yeniköy, on the European side of the straits. As the sun descended on the water, I thrilled to the smell of gasoline, salt water, and strong tobacco, a magical blend. By the time I reached the flat of my friend, the Turkish writer and sociologist Nilüfer Göle, the electricity had gone out because of a sudden storm. In her candlelit drawing room, filled with rugs, art books, and smoky, gilded mirrors, where the balcony curtains trembled in the winds off the Bosporus, she spoke of the military as another civic pressure group in a society of dense, associational links.

"The military is just like the lawyers' and women's organizations," she said. "It uses the media and briefs politicians. But as the country becomes increasingly democratic and complicated in its own way, the military gets scared. It overreacts to global social forces beyond its control."

Later, Nilüfer and I drove north to Tarabya, where we met her husband, Asaf, at a seaside restaurant. Yachts and sailboats cluttered the moonlit harbor. The restaurant was crowded with wealthy Turks with cell phones, who reminded me of the wealthy Latinos one sees in trendy Californian restaurants: fellow members of a global civilization.

A waiter emerged to tell Nilüfer that her car had been sideswiped.

She went outside, where a policeman chided her for not having an insurance document. She rebuked the policeman for blaming her when she was the victim. "Why don't you get out of your police car and stop cleaning your teeth," she told the officer, who quickly apologized, along with the other driver. Within a minute the issue was resolved. Bribes were out of the question. This was Turkey, where crises dissolved almost immediately into compromises—to the dismay of foreign correspondents.

※ ※

Chronic intrigue and crisis girded by an underlying equilibrium have characterized Constantinople, now Istanbul, for two millennia. However high-pitched the political drama here, the lands surrounding Constantinople were usually weaker and less stable. At the close of the twentieth century, notwithstanding a dispute between secularists and Islamists and a protracted Kurdish insurgency in Turkey's southeast that has claimed nearly forty thousand lives since 1984, Turkey represents the most stable governmental dynasty in world history, with the Turkish soldiery able to trace the roots of its power to the Roman emperors.

In the fourth century, when the Roman empire split into western and eastern halves, Constantinople became the eastern capital. A century later, the western empire was overrun by Visigoths, and the Byzantine Greeks of Constantinople became the sole heirs to imperial Rome. Byzantine emperors then succeeded one another for a thousand years, until the Ottoman Turks captured Constantinople in 1453. But the Ottoman victory merely completed an ongoing process of migration and cultural infiltration as Turkish nomads from Central Asia moved into Asia Minor and merged Byzantine culture with their own. The Ottoman sultans, with their elaborate imperial court system and reliance on eunuchs, were in effect latter-day Byzantine emperors, whose mosques imitated the architectural style of early Byzantine churches. These sultans ruled for over 450 years, until the final collapse of their empire in World War I. The English historian Arnold Toynbee called the Ottoman sultanate "truly the . . . revival of the Roman Empire in the Near and Middle East."[1]

Kemal Atatürk's Turkish Republic, which succeeded the Ottoman sultanate following World War I, was a creation of the military: the sole surviving institution of the Ottoman state and the core of its elite. In the Ottoman empire, the state and the military had been inseparable. The Janissaries—the professional infantry—were "slaves of the sultan." Atatürk, an Ottoman war hero who had commanded Turkish troops in their defeat of Allied forces at Gallipoli in 1915, ruled Turkey as a benevolent military dictator. After World War II, an ongoing experiment with democracy commenced, with periodic military interventions.

In 1960, the military staged a traditional coup against the civilian government, executing the prime minister, Adnan Menderes, in a show trial for corruption and conspiring with Islamists. Since then, the military has tried to behave more subtly. Mounting terrorism in 1971 led to a "coup by memorandum," which forced the resignation of civilian prime minister Süleyman Demirel. The military replaced him with civilians unaffiliated with existing parties.[2] In 1980, more terrorism and the threat of civil war between right- and left-wing guerrilla groups led to a military intervention in which, again, the structure of civilian government was maintained.

Turgut Özal, Turkey's prime minister from 1983 until 1989 and then its president until his death in 1993, became the first civilian leader to chart a bold policy course without the military's consent. He privatized the statist economy, creating an entrepreneurial middle class, composed mainly of devout Moslems. Though this troubled the military, the West's victory in the Cold War and its subsequent insistence on democratic regimes discouraged further coups.

But rather than bring Western-style democracy to Turkey, Washington's proscription against overt military takeovers in this NATO-member state has had the ironic result of permitting the military a greater, more permanent role in government. Coups, like wars, signify limits—with beginnings and ends. In the past, when a Turkish general announced a coup, he also promised to hold elections and return the army to its barracks after a designated period. Now the military's role is more insidious, and it is more likely to become a permanent presence in Turkish politics.

Turks I met had various names for what had happened: "a soft coup," "a pashas' coup," a "coup by media," and "history's first postmodern coup," in which "the deep state" surfaced to resume control over the "official-but-superficial" state.

Each description was accurate. Here are the facts:

In 1996, Necmettin Erbakan became Turkey's first Islamist prime minister after an election divided the secular parties. Erbakan formed a minority government and flew off to sign agreements with Libya and Iran, even as the Turkish military strengthened its links with Israel. A power struggle was on. In early 1997, Turkey's National Security Council, dominated by the military, intimidated Erbakan's already-weak government into signing a series of laws which, in effect, led to the closure of many businesses owned by Erbakan's fundamentalist supporters. Both the military and the majority of secular, middle-class Turks were incensed over Erbakan's visits to Iran and Libya after coming to office, his establishment of a religious school system to turn out Islamic firebrands, his plans to build mosques in Istanbul's central Taksim Square and near the presidential residence in Ankara, his infiltration of religious types into the civil and provincial administrations, and the presence of Islamists at state dinners. After all, Erbakan had been elected with only 22 percent of the vote, and was only able to form a government because of what many considered a malodorous deal with another party, in which he agreed not to prosecute a former prime minister for alleged corruption. Media articles reflected the public's disquiet over Erbakan's bold actions, and pressure built on the military to do something. In a town near Ankara controlled by Erbakan's party, a "Jerusalem Night" was proclaimed, in which Yasser Arafat was denounced for selling out to the Israelis, and the guest of honor, the Iranian ambassador to Turkey, called on Turkey's young people to take up arms against Israel and the United States. Meanwhile, a nationwide poll showed that 60 percent of Turks opposed Erbakan's government, and 30 percent wanted him removed by whatever means necessary. For Turks, who define secularism not as opposition to Islam but as the separation of church and state, Erbakan had clearly gone too far. As the poll indicated, in this particular crisis, secularism was more sacred for many Turks than democracy. By mid-1997, as the military continually briefed the media on the iniquities of the government and warned of action against religious Moslems, Erbakan resigned, replaced by Mesut Yılmaz, an uninspiring centrist who did not please the military, either. When he hesitated to crack down on female students at Istanbul University who wore a specific kind of head scarf, called a *türban,* which had become an inflammatory Islamic symbol, the military held more briefings and convened the National Security Council, which demanded tough action against "extremists." Yılmaz balked, warning publicly that the civilian government and not the military would determine the pace of de-Islamization. Then in late March 1998, the National Security Council convened again, and announced that the government had agreed that religion could play no role in a secular state and that crackdowns would ensue on mosque construction and Islamic business enterprises.

As one Turkish analyst told me, "At National Security Council meetings, the generals bring thick dossiers from which to lecture, and the civilian cabinet ministers come as tourists." Without actually doing anything official, through a "soft," "postmodern" process in which one kind of power hid behind the white-lie facade of another, the "deep" military state lying beneath the civilian surface had reasserted itself. It was not deep in a conspiratorial sense but deep in the sense that it was firmly grounded. To middle-class Turks, the generals were not so much generals as Ottoman "pashas," well-meaning and paternalistic notables. Even more so than in Romania, opinion polls here repeatedly demonstrated that the military was the most trusted institution among middle-class voters.

The Americans made no serious objection to this "soft," "pashas' takeover," though NATO had declared civilian control a prerequisite of membership, and at the same moment President Clinton was in Africa, preaching the benefits of civilian parliamentary democracy.

In Turkey, I realized that the Clinton administration demanded democracy in places that were strategically and economically marginal and where all other alternatives had failed, such as in sub-Saharan Africa. It also recommended democracy in places where a middle-class economy was already highly developed and further growth required more freedom, as in the Pacific Rim. But in places that were both vital for U.S. energy interests and potentially explosive, like most of the Moslem Middle East, one high-ranking American official told me, "We don't mention the word *democracy*."

Turkey was a case in point. Here democracy was officially proclaimed, but the reality was more complex and the West held its tongue. The military's slow-motion intervention against Erbakan had the overwhelming support of secular Turks, who saw the generals as their most effective pressure group. Whereas power in the United States is divided among the president, the Congress, and the Supreme Court, in Turkey it is divided between generals and politicians, with similar results: relative stability and moderate policies, despite constant low-level turbulence. Only, the Turkish military is not a branch of government; it operates more like a powerful lobby that has managed to run government from within.

※ ※

Like many of the high-ranking Turkish officers I had met over the years, retired Lieutenant General İhsan Gürkan, eighty-two, looked like a banker or corporate executive with his receding hairline, glasses, and commanding expression. He entered the dark lobby of my hotel carrying a briefcase; his pinstripe suit might as well have been a uniform. "I was one of Atatürk's lower-middle-class smart boys," he explained.[3] "My family had little money, so a military education was a good opportunity for me. Turkish officers are not wealthy and property-conscious but duty- and mission-conscious. We intervene in politics when necessary, but unlike generals in Latin America, we never stay long in power. Our job is to defend democracy and secularism, and Atatürk's ideology of dynamic change and common sense. The military is an elite, the first Turkish institution to come into contact with Western ideas. At the beginning of the eighteenth century, Sultan Selim III forbade the study of maps, but he made an exception for us."

Given his stodgy demeanor and boilerplate defense of military intervention, I might have dismissed General Gürkan as a reactionary. But what makes the Turkish military unique is that it is in fact revolutionary. "The generals are Jacobins," İlkay Sunar, a political-science professor at Bosporus University in Istanbul, told me. "Atatürk's revolution might have been secular, but it was a revolution nonetheless—just like Islamic ones—and the generals believe the revolutionary flame must be kept burning. What they may not realize is that Turkish society has already internalized the revolution. In their own way, even the Islamists here have been secularized." What he meant was that they operate within the system and do not engage in terrorism.

The generals have never forgotten that the Ottoman empire was destroyed by factionalism, ethnic separatism, and foreign intervention, and they want to prevent this from happening again through political fragmentation, Kurdish guerrilla activity, and Islamic and global forces from outside Turkey's borders. "That is Turkey's dilemma," another professor, Mim Kemal Öke, told me. "The state cannot resist dilution by world economic forces, but in the eyes of the military, a strong state and their own revolutionary ideology are inseparable."

The split between the military and the society is reflected in the division between the traditional bourgeoisie in Istanbul and the Moslem nouveaux riches in the heartland of Anatolia. Among the military-backed old bourgeoisie in Istanbul are Jewish families, wealthy for generations, who have countered the influence of Greek and Armenian merchants who are considered "anti-Turkish" by the military. Together, the Jews, Greeks, and Armenians comprise a Byzantine-style elite centered in Istanbul that had no competition until Özal's economic reforms in 1983 created Moslem nouveaux riches in the rest of the country. Erbakan represented the Islamic nouveaux riches, while the military identified with the old Istanbulis. That many generals have family roots in the old Ottoman empire, particularly in the Balkans and the Caucasus, whereas religious Moslems are from Anatolia, widens this divide. In order to compete with the military, Özal's new Moslem middle class in Anatolia needed the political stability and predictability that the military offered. Still, the divide in Turkey was real, and Israel was at the center of it.

※ ※

Though the new Turkish-Israeli strategic alliance was reported in the West, it was not given nearly enough emphasis at the time. Rather than a fleeting arrangement of diplomatic niceties that would unravel the moment Israel next attacked the Palestinians, this was a seismic shift. By Near Eastern standards, its importance rivaled the Sino-Soviet split.

In 1996, the two countries signed thirteen military accords.[4] In early 1997, nearly all the ranking officers of the two militaries met each other as large, uniformed delegations exchanged visits. Israel agreed to upgrade Turkey's Phantom jet fleet and to train Turkish pilots in electronic warfare. The two sides also agreed to coproduce missiles and to share intelligence about Iran and hostile Arab states, and concluded a free-trade agreement.

The alliance was formed under unpromising political conditions—between a Likud government in Israel and Erbakan's fundamentalist government in Turkey. Among the Turkish intellectuals I met—usually the very people who would be pro-Palestinian because of their traditionally leftist views—none opposed an alliance driven by overwhelming national interest.

Turkish-Jewish relations, like Iranian-Jewish relations until the Iranian revolution, have been historically friendly. In 1492, when the Jews were expelled from Spain, the Turks welcomed them to the Ottoman empire. Before World War I, the Young Turk revolutionaries invited more Jews to immigrate to Ottoman lands as a hedge against the Arabs. Partly because of the anti-Semitism of Russian czars, world Jewry has traditionally been pro-Turkish. In 1949, Turkey recognized the fledgling state of Israel, though relations until recently were more symbolic than substantive.

By the end of the twentieth century, Israel's need for a close ally in the Moslem world was obvious. Turkey's more friendly position toward Israel was the result of several factors. As a number of Turks told me, they simply became tired of diplomatic initiatives that failed to induce the Arabs to end their support of the Kurdish Workers' party, which was responsible for the insurgency in southeastern Turkey. Turkey's relations with Syria—the Workers' party's chief sponsor—have been further aggravated by Syria's insistence that the Hatay region, in southern Turkey, is really Syrian. In the case of Iraq, Turkey has not entirely given up its claim on the oil-rich Mosul province. An entente with Israel, the Turks felt, would add an unbeatable military alliance to their diplomatic efforts.

The Turks felt, too, that the Jews could help them with their Greek problem. A diplomat here told me: "The Turks are pro-Israel because they can use the Jewish lobby in America as a silver bullet against the Greek and Armenian lobbies, which deny them high-tech military equipment from the U.S. If that sounds convoluted, welcome to Byzantium." Nor were the Israelis averse to such an arrangement, as Greek Cyprus had long been a reputed base for Palestinian terrorists.

The determining factor for the Turks may have been the realization that because of their quasi-military regime, their Kurdish guerrilla insurgency and unstable borders with Near Eastern states, and an anti-Moslem bias in the West, they might never gain full admittance to the European Union. Thus, they required another alliance. Distrusted by the Arabs because of the Ottoman colonial past and kept at arm's length for so long by the European Union, Turks shared with Israelis a sense of being outsiders. As General Gürkan told me in the lobby of my hotel, Arab businessmen sitting on sofas next to us, "Israel is the only country in the Middle East that we understand. This is a permanent relationship." Permanent from the military's viewpoint, at any rate. Religious Moslems, whose numbers were steadily increasing in this society, felt differently.

As the twentieth century drew to a close, Turkey was flexing its muscles as a regional power rather than as a member of the Western alliance. Turkish naval vessels were active off the Albanian coast. Turkish businessmen were ubiquitous throughout the Balkans and, as I would soon see, in the Arab world, the Caucasus, and Central Asia. Turkey was competing with Greece to organize a Balkan security pact on its terms. Now, with Israel's help, it was projecting power throughout the modern Middle East, shepherded by its ability to cut off water supplies to Syria and Iraq. Even as the Turks maneuvered closer to the European Union, Turkey had begun to exhibit a certain indifference toward the West.

To say that a new Byzantine-Ottoman imperium was emerging would surely be an exaggeration. But it was true that Turkey was a keystone of power and stability in the Near East, the unspoken organizational fact of the region's geography and politics. Though Turkey's subtle authoritarianism was far more stable than the one-man thugocracies with narrow power in Arab countries to the south, its ongoing social evolution was unpredictable, in part because of the country's economic dynamism.

I was about to strike out for the Anatolian hinterland, en route to the historic lands of "Greater Syria," which would take me through present-day Syria, Lebanon, Jordan, and Israel. I would then return to Turkey again as a base for further travels into the Caucasus and Central Asia.

12

THE "CORPSE IN

ARMOUR"

I stumbled with my backpack over broken pavements on narrow, twisting streets leading to Istanbul's Karaköy dock, across the Golden Horn from the train station where I had arrived. I was headed first by ferry, and then by train, bus, and service taxi, for Israel—by way of Syria, Lebanon, and Jordan. As radically different as all these countries were, much of the territory through which I would pass had been united for two thousand years under Romans, Byzantines, Arabs, Mamluks, and Seljuk and Ottoman Turks. It would be rash to assume that current divisions are permanent.

At the dock, crowds of commuters poured on and off the ferries. I purchased a token for the equivalent of forty-five cents and boarded. The engine started up and the boat slapped over the choppy waters of the Bosporus, from the European to the Asian shore of Istanbul. The crenellated walls of the Topkapı Palace, ashen pink at this early hour, receded on the European side, along with the rest of the Balkan peninsula. I warmed my hands over a glass of apple tea, slurping the delicious *çay* before it spilled as the ferry trembled. Twenty minutes later, we pulled up to the dock of the Haydarpaşa railway station, graced by a pavilion of luscious blue ceramic tiles and a fanlike wrought-iron awning. Behind the pavilion was the station building: a grand mustard-colored Baroque edifice that conjured up the fading glory of the late Ottoman empire. While workers scrubbed the floors and windows of the express train that would take me to Ankara, Turkey's capital, over two hundred miles to the southeast, I sat on a bench and watched as ships passed from the narrow Bosporus into the Sea of Marmara. I was full of anticipation.

It was October 1998. Over the next few days I would cross the mountains of Anatolia into Syria, where, according to the current Turkish prime minister, Mesut Yılmaz, "dark conspiracies" were being hatched against Turkey and, in fact, war between Turkey and Syria appeared imminent. Turkey was staging military exercises on the border. Only the day before, Turkish officials had accused Syria of waging a fourteen-year undeclared war against Turkey by supporting the Kurdish Workers' party (Partiya Karkeran-e Kurdistan, or PKK), a leftist guerrilla organization that had been battling the Turkish military near Turkey's southeastern border with Syria.

The 25 million Kurds in the border regions of Turkey, Syria, Iraq, Iran, and Armenia were the only major Middle Eastern ethnic group left stateless following the World War I peace treaties.[1] More than half the Kurds live in Turkey, where until recently they were forbidden from speaking or broadcasting news in Kurdish and from learning about Kurdish history in school. Having lived for decades under military siege, the Kurds have been demanding more rights. For years, Syria had used Kurdish guerrillas to harass Turkey, just as it had used the Shi'ites in southern Lebanon to harass Israeli occupation forces there. One Turkish general remarked publicly that Turkey's army would "drive through one end of Syria and out through the other" unless Syria ceased all support for the Kurdish rebels and ejected its leader, Abdullah Öcalan, from Damascus, a city that Western intelligence specialists called "the Vatican of the PKK guerrillas."[2]

Syria denied all links to Öcalan and the PKK, claiming that Turkey had provoked an artificial crisis on behalf of its new ally, Israel. It also charged that Turkey was starving Syria of water and occupying historic Syrian land in the Arabic-speaking region of the Hatay. To all this, Turkish foreign minister İsmail Cem replied: "There is only one problem to sort out: Syria must end its support for terrorism."

The Turkish-Syrian dispute was not a passing news story but a curtain-raiser for the twenty-first-century Near East. By supporting

Kurdish terrorism, Syria was punishing Turkey for damming Euphrates River water—through a network of twenty-two dams—that would otherwise flow south into Syria. Water had publicly emerged as the issue that nearly brought the two countries to war. Ottoman ghosts, dormant for most of the twentieth century, had rematerialized in the hostilities between Turks and their former Arab subjects. For the first time in living memory, Turkey was seen as part of the heartland of the Middle East rather than of Europe, linked with Israel in a dispute with Syria. American embassy officials in Turkey told me that while they had had little business with their State Department colleagues in Damascus and Tel Aviv, this would now have to change.

In a country where street dogs are sometimes referred to as "Arabs," anti-Arab hysteria against Syria was easy to whip up, and it displaced for the moment Turkey's dispute with Greece over Cyprus and the Aegean Islands in the Turkish media. Ironically, Turks often seemed more forgiving toward the Orthodox Christian Greeks, Bulgarians, and Serbs than toward the Arabs, who were fellow Moslems. While all these peoples had revolted against Ottoman rule, the World War I "Arab Revolt" against the Turks is still seen in Turkey as the great betrayal of the Ottoman empire, precisely because the Arabs were coreligionists. Indeed, the more deeply Islamic a Turk is, the more he dislikes the Syrians and other Arabs. For example, the most virulent anti-Syrian statement came from Recai Kutan, the chairman of the new Islamic Virtue (Fazilet) party, which had replaced Erbakan's Welfare party after the latter was disbanded by the military. Kutan, in an oblique reference to the religion of Syrian president Hafez al-Assad, said Syria was ruled by "Nusairis, a perverted branch of the Alawite sect."[3]

Let me explain. Turkey's religious fundamentalists, like Syria's, belong to the dominant Sunni branch of Islam; and both hate the Alawite minorities in their respective countries. The Alawites are a branch of Shi'ism whose members have for decades taken refuge in secular Turkish and Syrian nationalism as a defense against Sunni Moslem fundamentalism. Thus, Turkey's religious Moslems hate Syria for two reasons: because the Syrians are Arabs, "mere dust," as the Turkish saying goes, and because the regime in Damascus is dominated by Moslems who are both heretical and secularized. Such hatred has long been reciprocated by Syrian president Assad. In a meeting with Soviet leader Leonid Brezhnev in the late 1960s, after Brezhnev had made the mistake of asking Assad why Syria felt threatened by Turkey, Assad launched into a tirade against Ottoman imperialism.

While Turkey's motives for provoking Syria were understood—they were the same ones that had produced its strategic alliance with Israel—the timing seemed a mystery. Why now? According to a foreign diplomat I spoke to it was simple: The 800,000-man military really ran Turkey, and a new chief of staff, Hüseyin Kivrikoğlu, had been appointed on August 30. The new man wanted a more aggressive policy toward the PKK. The Turkish General Staff, this diplomat told me, was where Turkey's real foreign policy was made, not at the Foreign Ministry. The General Staff was studying the war between the military and Islamists in Algeria (in case of a similar conflict in Turkey), as well as post-Assad scenarios in Syria and even post-Syria scenarios for the Middle East in the event of Syria's demise after Assad.

Israeli officials were impressed by how Turkey bullied Syria in this crisis, even if publicly the Israelis took pains to distance themselves from Turkish policy (to the extent of canceling military exercises on the Golan Heights lest Assad feel squeezed simultaneously by Israel and Turkey). "Did you see the way Assad collapsed?" an Israeli intelligence official would say to me me enthusiastically later in Tel Aviv. "He expelled Öcalan. He stopped assistance to the PKK. Okay, he'll start helping the Kurds again, but for now Assad has crumbled."[4] Israel respected a military power that was willing to snub regional public opinion in defense of its own interests—something that Israel itself often did.

🐾 🐾

It was time to board the train to Ankara on the way to Damascus and beyond. Twenty-four hours earlier, I had not been sure I would be allowed to visit Syria. For two months I had tried to obtain a visa through the Syrian embassy in Washington. But the embassy would issue me neither a journalist's visa nor a tourist visa, perhaps because of the highly critical articles I had published about Syria in years past. The *Lonely Planet* travel guide said that the Syrian consulate in Istanbul issued tourist visas immediately, so I assumed it didn't bother to check the names of visa applicants with Damascus.

The consulate was on an upper floor of an old building. Though banner headlines in the Turkish press had proclaimed imminent war with Syria that morning, a policeman with an assault rifle at the building's entrance waved me through without checking my backpack. It was 9:45 A.M. Consulate hours were "9:30 A.M. to 11 A.M.," but when I emerged from the elevator, the door to the consulate was locked. A Spanish tourist waiting in the hallway told me he was bicycling from Spain to the Holy Land. We were about to leave, when at 9:55 a window slid open and a man silently handed us visa forms. The application asked: "Have you ever visited Occupied Palestine?" I lied and wrote, "No." In five minutes, after paying $65, I had a Syrian visa, and arranged to leave Istanbul the next day.

The spotless, air-conditioned train that pulled out of Haydarpaşa station for Ankara was as comfortable as the train I had taken at the start of my journey from Budapest to Debrecen. Looking at the passengers, I noticed many fine leather attaché cases, cell phones, and Moslem head scarves. Some of the women with head scarves also carried attaché cases and cell phones: Again, it was the spectacle of modernity amid tradition that made Turkey appear so dynamic.

For the first ninety minutes of the journey, the Sea of Marmara lay off to my right, alternating in color between corrugated iron and smoky blue as the sun slipped in and out of the clouds. The sea was dotted with oil tankers and small islands encrusted with red-roofed houses. This was the area of northwestern Anatolia where the Ottoman Turks had emerged in the late thirteenth century under Ertugrul, a nomad chieftain, and his son, Osman. They would ultimately replace the Seljuks, another Turkic dynasty. Here, too, on the southern shore of the Sea of Marmara and on the nearby islands, was where both Byzantine and Ottoman emperors had spent their summers. (It was also the site of a tragic earthquake in 1999, after my journey.)

I entered the dining car and ate a three-course lunch with wine, served on a white tablecloth, as I watched women picking onions in the fields and loading them into red sacks. Eventually, the Sea of Marmara disappeared from view as we entered a lush green river valley, at the end of which was a gorge followed by a dry and horrifyingly beautiful landscape. This was the Anatolian steppe, the land bridge a thousand miles long and three hundred miles wide known also as Asia Minor, connecting Europe with the heart of Asia.

The steppe was a geologic tapestry of upheaval and impermanence, a cake-swirl pattern of yellow-and-black hills created by water and wind over eons. Anatolia's landscape was like the process of history itself— a process that would preoccupy my thoughts as I traveled throughout Greater Syria—a continuing pattern of destruction as old forms imperceptibly give way to the new. Fields were literally on fire, burned by farmers to increase fertility the following spring. New mosques and apartment blocks heralded Ankara in the early evening.

Ankara was barely recognizable to me. When I had first come in 1983, the city was typical of the Communist-era Balkans nearby, a seedy, hilly town that stank of lignite. Now it had evolved into a blazing labyrinth of nonstop traffic jams, boutiques, interior-decorating centers opened late into the night, French restaurants, and prosperous suburbs with polished-stone buildings and tinted windows that trailed high into the hills and onto the steppe. In 1993, when I last visited, I had been struck by a new mall near the Sheraton Hotel. Now, five years later, such malls were everywhere. That evening and the next day, I spotted many smartly dressed women dining alone at cafés and restaurants, a rarity in Moslem societies; the percentage of women lawyers, physicians, and stockbrokers is higher in Ankara than in many Western countries.[5] It reminded me of China, with tens of millions of newly urbanized people prying their way into the middle class, as formerly middle-class people entered a more sophisticated global class.

The next morning I visited the Museum of Anatolian Civilizations, housed in an old Ottoman covered market, or *bedesten*—what would be called a souk in Arab countries. I inspected the cuneiform tablets that traveling merchants had brought here almost four thousand years ago from Mesopotamia, in present-day Iraq, introducing writing, and thus history, to Anatolia. Later, in the second millennium B.C., the Hittites, an Indo-European people, united the rudimentary city-states of Anatolia into a confederation with its capital at Hattusas, one hundred miles east of Ankara. I saw Hittite stelae with hieroglyphs asking the gods for good grape harvests, and terra-cotta vessels, and sculptures of horned animals with bulging eyes. In 1190 B.C., the Hittite confederation broke up under the invasions of Thracians, Phrygians, proto-Armenians, and Assyrians. The Hittite cuneiform script fell into disuse and the population fled from northern to southern Anatolia, forming a new group of city-states along the current Turkish-Syrian and Turkish-Iraqi borders, which in 700 B.C. succumbed to the rising Assyrian empire. In the museum's display cabinets, these cataclysms are marked by the shift from the crude terra-cotta of the Hittites to the intricate hammered wood and metal of the Phrygians. I also noticed the massive basalt from Carchemish, the greatest of the southern Anatolian cities that replaced the Hittite confederation. Carchemish was where T. E. Lawrence ("of Arabia"), the British fomenter of the Arab Revolt against the Ottoman Turks, began his Middle East career during an archaeological excavation in the summer of 1910.

Sitting on a bench, I studied the basalt and limestone relief sculptures from the ninth and eighth centuries B.C., depicting a procession of warriors from Carchemish with spears and plumed helmets, a procession which, like the Anatolian landscape itself, mirrored the march of history, with its unending formation, flowering, and passing of states and empires. I thought, too, of Arnold Toynbee's rumination about the collapse of Assyria, which foreshadows the political eruptions that may occur in the region in the early twenty-first century.[6]

Toynbee writes: "The disaster in which the Assyrian military power met its end in 614–610 B.C. was one of the completest yet known to history.... A community which had been in existence for over two thousand years and had been playing an ever more dominant part in South-Western Asia for a period of some two-and-a-half centuries, was blotted out almost completely." Indeed, only two hundred years after Assyria's collapse, Xenophon's Greek mercenaries, retreating from Persia and passing the Assyrian sites of Calah and Nineveh, "were struck," writes Toynbee, "with astonishment, not so much at the massiveness of the fortifications . . . as at the spectacle of such vast works of man lying uninhabited."[7] What is even more astonishing is that while Assyria had dominated the Near East for ages, Xenophon, an educated Greek general, knew almost nothing about it: "The very name of Assyria is unknown to him," Toynbee writes.

How was that possible?

Assyria was rediscovered only through archaeology and epigraphy. The Assyrian war machine was one of history's most terrifying, "continuously overhauled, renovated and reinforced right down to the day of its destruction," in Toynbee's words. It had collided bloodily with Babylon (in Iraq), Elam (in Iran), and Egypt, and produced some of history's first megalomaniacs in the persons of Ashurnasirpal II, the ninth century B.C. tyrant whose statues reveal "no smile, no piety, almost no humanity"; Tiglath-Pileser III, the eighth century B.C. father of mass deportations; and Sennacherib, who in 689 B.C. destroyed Babylon, comparing himself to a "hurricane."[8] Assyria's rulers razed Damascus and Samaria (in the West Bank), Sidon in Lebanon, Susa in Iran, and Memphis and Thebes in Egypt. They filled the pages of the Old Testament's book of Prophets with terror. By the time the Assyrian capital of Nineveh (near Mosul, in northern Iraq) was conquered by a coalition of Babylonians, Medes, and Scythians in 612 B.C., only Tyre, in Lebanon, and Jerusalem remained unscathed. Yet when Nineveh fell, Assyria disintegrated into dust; almost nothing of its civilization remained. Even its language, Akkadian, was swiftly replaced by Aramaic. Toynbee calls Assyria " 'a corpse in armour,' whose frame was held erect only by the massiveness of the military accoutrements" that smothered and killed the body of the Assyrian state.

History is replete with "corpses in armour": Sparta, Alexander's Macedonia, the Ottoman empire, and, of course, Nazi Germany, to name a few, even if none of them and their languages were so thoroughly obliterated as Assyria. Toynbee notes that Alexander's conquest of the Near East was repeated almost a thousand years later by that of the Moslem Arab armies after the Prophet Mohammed's death. "In this Arab act of brigandage . . . twelve years of conquest were followed by twenty-four years of fratricidal strife," leaving the Arabs forever bedeviled by divisions. The theme is always the same: Highly militarized and centralized states and empires, so indomitable in one decade or generation, hack themselves to pieces or are themselves conquered in another.

The story of Assyria, which bestrode present-day Syria and Iraq, is hauntingly appropriate to the dilemma of the early-twenty-first-century Middle East. Assyrian militarism grew out of the need to protect the inhabitants of the Syrian desert and Mesopotamia from the hostile mountain people in Anatolia and Kurdistan to the north and Iran to the east, and from the pharaohs of Egypt to the southwest. But such extensive militarization created a brittle Assyrian political culture, not unlike the heavily mobilized, dictatorial states now occupying the Syrian desert and Mesopotamia, as well as elsewhere in the Arab world where institutions, except for the military and security services, are weak or nonexistent.

From previous visits, I knew that Iraq, and to a lesser extent Syria, were places where beneath the barren carapace of the regime every associational link except the extended family and clan had been brutally eliminated, leaving precarious voids. Would Syria and Iraq disintegrate given enough hammer blows? Would even Turkey—despite its vibrancy, and with a seemingly stable blend of democracy and military dictatorship—devolve into something unrecognizable? Turkish flags flew outside the Museum of Anatolian Civilizations as if the Turkish Republic drew legitimacy from the record of great empires on its soil.[9] But the objects inside told another lesson: that no system of states is secure, and that ancient history may be as good a guide to the destiny of the Middle East as current media reports. Perhaps more so.

※ ※

"Atatürkism, Ba'athism, and Zionism are standardized ideologies. They're like 1950s chain stores that no longer cater to the specific tastes of increasingly varied and complex populations," said Doğu Ergil, a social scientist at Ankara University, whose office was decorated with Kurdish rugs, Ottoman-era furniture, African masks, and beer coasters from Holland and Germany. Ergil runs a human-rights foundation that helps Turkish Kurds. There was no sign outside the door, and I had had trouble finding it in the dark. "We've had threats, so we don't announce ourselves," he told me.

Ergil did not imply a moral or institutional equivalence among the three ideologies—Atatürkism, the fierce secularism that had created a

Turkish state from the carcass of the multinational Ottoman empire; Zionism, which advocated a Jewish national home in Palestine because in Europe and czarist Russia life for Jews had become intolerable, even before Hitler; and Ba'athism, a woolly Soviet-style socialism that was the founding ideal of the dictatorships in Syria and Iraq. He meant only that the three movements, all variants of twentieth-century state building, were blunt, ideological instruments of liberation for whole peoples—Turks, Jews, and Arabs—in which "freedom, especially for individual Arabs, was often mistaken for independence." Such ideologies, Ergil told me, "will become more repressive, each in its own way, as the crisis of identity in Turkey, Israel, and the Arab states deepens and the system is increasingly less capable of satisfying its people."

Ergil explained that in Turkey, political parties are not like parties in the West. Internally, they do not practice democracy; rather, they are chieftaincies run by one or two men. Parliament is almost always in stasis to a degree that Americans cannot imagine. Islamic fundamentalism grows—though in Turkey it is not so much theological as an assertion of traditional rural values—as migrants turn the poor outskirts of Turkish cities into big villages. Because many of these migrants are Kurds, according to Ergil, "there is a growing convergence between Fazilet [the Islamic Virtue party] and the Kurdish movement, though neither is comfortable admitting it." Meanwhile, "the military provides order, if not stability."

The solution, Ergil told me, will not be federalism, since Kurds now live everywhere in Turkey, but decentralization. "Right now, the relationship between Ankara and the smaller towns is like that between the sun and the planets. The system is antiquated. The political chieftains merely distribute spoils. There is enormous pressure in Turkey for real democracy and the rule of law. The economy, already dynamic, can explode upward once the state devolves. In Turkey, Moslem head scarves on women in universities or in parliament are like computers—they are a postmodern weapon against stasis and the immorality of the conventional political parties. Here, when you see a head scarf on a woman, think of it as the hippie peace symbol."

For decades, Ergil said, Turkey's oldest political party, the Republican People's party, spoke of "republicanism, secularism, nationalism, statism, and populism" but never of "democracy." That came much later, and even now, "Westernization here is interpreted as secularization, not as democratization." The only major political force advocating real democratization and decentralization for Turkey was the Islamists, who sought to overthrow Atatürk's secular republic.

13

THE NEW CALIPHATE

From Ankara, I had planned to travel by bus 175 miles southeast to Kayseri, a town in the middle of Anatolia that first became important under the Phrygians in the early years of the first millennium B.C. But a friend told me that the Islamic Fazilet (Virtue) party was holding a rally in Kayseri and that it had organized a special bus for journalists from Ankara. So at seven-thirty the next morning, I walked to the Ankara headquarters of the party, where the bus was waiting.

The Virtue party's headquarters were new, with computers and stylish furniture. Well-dressed men with meticulously trimmed beards milled about, bringing around fresh bread and coffee. Among the gathered journalists, there were a few fashionably dressed women wearing head scarves. Wherever I had encountered Islamic movements in the Middle East, certain features rarely varied: a heightened organization and fastidiousness among the adherents that created its own peculiar energy. The Islamists were often the first groups in the region to have Web sites, E-mail, cell phones, and other accessories of the modern world. Whereas the secular parties in Turkey were well established, with long experience in government, the Virtue party was still in the process of *becoming,* and thus seemed to be a real movement. Because its members were the educated sons of working-class families, there was an emphasis on scientific and technical training rather than on the liberal arts, the domain of wealthy Turks, who could afford an education with no practical end. Many Islamists were engineers. Murat Mercan, who headed the Center for Policy Research, an Ankara think tank associated with the Virtue party, gave me a business card, then briefed me on the political situation in central and southeastern Turkey. "In the southeast, the secular parties are dead. There are only two parties left, us [Virtue] and the Kurdish one. Kayseri is a business center with a lot of new money created by Özal. The nouveaux riches there are heavily Islamic."

The bus left Ankara, and soon we were traveling through the lonely vastness of baked, yellow hillsides that sloped and twisted gently mile after mile, with a silence and clarity bequeathed by the dryness and absence of trees. Later came a green, poplar-lined river valley with silvery blue water, then mountains, then more bleached hills. A steward passed by with scented water, cakes, and Pepsi. I talked with a woman, wearing a head scarf, who wrote for an Islamic newspaper. She spoke easily about the Islamic extremism of the Taliban in Afghanistan, and about the unspoken competition between the new Islamic nouveaux riches in Anatolia and the Jewish businesspeople in Istanbul. She became my de facto translator for the day. There was little unusual about this woman, who was at once assertive and religious. *Islam,* like *Christianity* and *Judaism,* can be a crude, generic term. Just as Christians in Lebanon during the war-torn 1970s and 1980s acted differently from evangelical Christians in the American Midwest, Turkish Islamists were very different from Islamists in Algeria, Egypt, or Iran. Here, women had achieved far more freedom than in most Arab societies, and spoke freely. Because Turkey's religious revival followed industrial and political modernization that in turn produced an authentic middle class— rather than an artificial one created by overnight oil wealth, and with a tyrant in charge, as in Iran—Turkey's Islamists differed from their Iranian counterparts. (Because Afghanistan had experienced very little modernization at all, its Islamic movement, a creature of overcrowded refugee camps in Pakistan, was even more primitive.)

We came to a rest stop, a modern supermarket stocked with a large variety of gifts, food, and drinks. The other journalists, all Turkish, took out their microrecorders and surrounded a man with a dark suit who had been on the bus with us and who now delivered a loud speech. He was a religious businessman who owned a tour company, one of whose buses had been involved in a fatal accident. He was blaming the bus's manufacturer for it, and the Virtue party rally gave him an opportunity to get his message out to the media.

The bus ride continued past several mountain ranges across the bleached, yellow steppe. Four hours after leaving Ankara, we arrived on the outskirts of Kayseri and pulled into a slick car dealership called Toyota Plaza. Upstairs was a restaurant, where we ate on a terrace overlooking a parking lot filled with new cars. The owner of the dealership, a supporter of the Virtue party, hosted the lavish luncheon. His assistants passed around sweets and cell phones on trays, in case any of us had calls to make.

Kayseri, Turkey's ninth-largest city, seemed endless, with drab industrial quarters, unfinished cement apartment blocks, and noisy construction sites. After lunch we were taken to a factory that manufactured bath towels, and another that made pastrami. They were both ugly and impressive: dark, sharp-angled buildings crowded together on the dusty steppe. I thought of what a diplomat in Ankara had told me, comparing Turkey and Greece, two historic rivals: "Greece already is a middle-class country with ten million people and a low birthrate. It has nowhere else to go. But Turkey's middle class and industrial power are still emerging, while the Islamists and the military both grow in significance."

I left the bus to find a hotel, then walked back to Kayseri's central square for the Virtue party rally. I heard the chants half a mile away. Against the backdrop of an Ottoman-era mosque and the black basalt walls of the Citadel, built by the Seljuks in the thirteenth century, a speaker was addressing thousands of people, packed so closely together that I had difficulty making my way to the podium. In the crowd, men wore beards, knit skullcaps, baggy work clothes, and worn, dark sport jackets. Most were fingering prayer beads. The women, heavily outnumbered, wore head scarves and black coats, and stood apart. There were many children at play and old people, chatting and drinking Pepsi. A folkloric dance group performed for the appreciative crowd. People gripped each other's hands and then hugged; there were real bonds here.

I knew these people—not personally, but I knew them. These were the inhabitants of the *gecekondus,* poor settlements surrounding Turkish cities that are literally "built by night" and filled with migrants from the countryside—a lumpen proletariat that was overwhelming Turkey as people poured into the cities to take factory jobs. But it was a peculiarly Turkish proletariat. Because many were in the process of joining the middle class, they did not feel disenfranchised, and a portion of them supported established secular parties. Nor was the Islam that attracted this underclass as harsh as the fundamentalism that attracted the proletariats of Algeria and Iran. When the French scholar Olivier Roy describes "Islamic spaces," he writes about bleak spheres without conviviality or leisure activities or culture of any kind: only ideology, along with business and social service networks. "The neofundamentalism of today," writes Roy, "is but a lumpen-Islamism."[1] Yet, in this "Islamic space" in Kayseri's main square, there was singing and dancing.

The largest exhibit, visible from afar, were the scales of justice made of colorful streamers, in which democracy was weighted down by a black question mark. The speakers kept repeating that Virtue was the only party that represented real democracy, while the military and the secular parties wanted autocracy. They linked the West with autocracy, since it was behind the current power structure.

The theme was reprised at dinner. The party faithful were staying at a new hotel on the slopes of Mount Erciyes, a 12,000-foot extinct volcano. I had gone there after dark in the hope of interviewing Abdullah Gül, the Virtue party's shadow foreign minister. Gül was busy, but dinner was starting and I was invited to take a seat. In the vast hall, I noticed only a few women. Bearded men sat around the tables, ordering Pepsi and orange soda instead of alcohol and dining on soup and grilled meats.

"When will the United States support democracy in Turkey?" the man next to me asked. "Because until now it has been supporting the military." Before waiting for an answer, he added: "I have been to Israel, and there, democracy is more developed than in Turkey. The Virtue party needs to bring Turkey to the level of Israel."

I was not surprised by the statement. The Israeli-Turkish strategic alliance had encouraged many Turks from all political parties, including

Virtue, to visit Israel. The Israelis knew that the Turkish Islamists had a bright future and that their hostility toward Judaism was mild compared to that of Islamic movements elsewhere, so the Israelis saw them as open to influence. The Islamists knew that if Turkey ever became as democratic as Israel, the Virtue party would have much more political power than it did now, and would adapt the West's democratic principles against the West's own strategic interests. The West, the French scholar Roy wrote, "remain[s] a prisoner of the old schema of the Enlightenment whereby there is only one form of Progress . . . embodied in parliamentary democracy, [which] goes hand and hand with . . . the easing of moral codes, and secularization."[2] But the West was now beginning to see that parliamentary democracy could bring profoundly puritanical and antisecular forces to power, forces that would inevitably be anti-Western.

For this reason I was ambivalent about the Islamic movement in Turkey. The Virtue party was a Tammany Hall system that provided a social welfare net to the working poor, somewhat like that of the Moslem Brotherhood (Ikhwan) in Egypt and Hamas in Gaza and the West Bank. There seemed to be two tendencies in the Virtue party: a moderate group drawn from the late-president Özal's Motherland party and a more extreme version, given to conspiracy theories against the West and Jews.

The dinner ended and the party members drifted to a television set in the lobby, where they cheered Turkey's soccer team against Germany. (The Turks won that night.) A tall and well-built man with graying black hair and mustache approached me and introduced himself as Abdullah Gül. Gül was considered a moderate and represented many people in this increasingly traditional—but by no means radicalized—country. Men gathered around as we talked.

"We are religious and nationalist, like the early German Christian Socialists. I mean, we are traditional conservatives. Religious tolerance is deeply rooted in our Ottoman tradition. The Christian church survived in Kayseri through the early twentieth century, though CNN was not here to cover it. What has fewer roots here is radical republicanism"—of the sort that led to the World War I massacres of Armenians. "We can never be fundamentalist and succeed to power, because there is too little cultural material for fundamentalism in Turkey. The Ottoman caliphate had enough confidence that it didn't mind Kurds and Christians. There was no religious hatred in Anatolia. All the violence was a problem of the republican period." His imprecise phrase "the republican period" linked Atatürk's secularism (with its emphasis on ethnic-Turkic nationalism and its massive program of deportation of Greeks) with the atrocities of the Young Turk modernizers during World War I.

"So, yes," Gül continued, "there is a convergence between the aspirations of the Kurds and us. We are the civil-society party in Turkey. The other parties exist only within the secular ideology and corrupt political machine of the state. Of course, our democracy is still better than elsewhere in the Moslem world. Turks have a certain level of freedom and openness. Thanks to Özal, there are hundreds of radio stations, fifteen television stations, and so on. No one can control information now. The military will be isolated if it tries to direct the future."

"What about Syria?" I asked.

"We must distinguish between the people and the governments in both Syria and Iraq. In those countries, the people are occupied by their own regimes. More democratization in Turkey, especially if it has religious and traditional elements, will have a great effect on Syria and Iraq. The biggest mistake Atatürk made was to give away the oil-rich north of Iraq to the British" in 1926.[3]

"And Israel?" I probed.

"We are not happy with the deals that the Turkish military has struck with Israel. But they are a reality. We recognize Israel and invite Israelis to our country. They invite us. But it is not good for Turkey or Israel if Turkey is seen as a follower in the relationship. . . ."

In other words, an Islamic government would adjust the atmospherics but not the fundamentals of the new strategic alliance. It would not challenge the military. For me, that symbolized the direction in which Turkey was going. The Islamists were implicitly rendering unto the military what was the military's: control over macropolitics, the strategic direction of the state, and the internal order which that necessitated. But neither could the military control micropolitics—daily political and cultural life—even if such politics led to a retreat into neo-

Ottoman religious traditionalism. For the moment, there was a split in Turkey between Islamists and a secular military. But this split was not inevitable. For instance, Gül, like the generals, was unhappy about the loss of northern Iraq and would not mind reoccupying it if the Iraqi state collapsed. Twenty-first-century Turkey might indeed be both more militaristic and more Islamic. For 850 years—from 1071, when the Seljuks defeated the Byzantines at Manzikert in eastern Anatolia, to the end of World War I—the House of Islam had drawn its direction and political legitimacy from Turkey, not from Arabia or Iran.[4] But a growing Islamic movement, a more powerful military, and a surging economy that would breed its own form of democratization; and dynamic change could restore the locus of Islamic legitimacy to Turkey.

It was after midnight when Gül's driver gave me a lift down the slope of the volcano to my hotel. We drove through the darkness, with a full moon hanging low over the deathly escarpments and minarets. There is no magic like traveling alone, without friends or colleagues to condition one's opinions. It is the very loneliness that makes travel worthwhile: to be in isolation with historical forces, with only landscapes and books as guides. I would be up at dawn. The journey south over the Taurus Mountains to Antioch would take over seven hours.

🎴 🎴

The bus swiftly entered another mountain range. We passed apartment houses and reforested slopes, along with lush valleys and new highways. But gradually, as the day wore on, the landscape became hotter and drier. The ridges were so desiccated and empty that the slightest indentations showed. We stopped for lunch at a supermarket-like caravansary, with restaurants, cafés, gift shops, and fruit stands: Turkish highways were full of them. A busload of American tourists took over the restaurant, the last large group of Americans I would see until Israel. After lunch we passed through another stormy sea of mountains. Then, in midafternoon, as we approached the Mediterranean, the world began to change.

I saw cacti, palm trees, banana groves, and olive trees for the first time on my journey, along with more cypresses than I had seen north of the Taurus Mountains. The temperature climbed and the dust became finer. Then I saw the Mediterranean, glassy and pearly in the gauzy light, along with rusty ships, grain elevators, and parking lots filled with military vehicles. The faces in the streets here were darker than elsewhere in Turkey, the features more pronounced. After much static the bus driver found a new radio station, playing Arabic instead of Turkish music. We were passing through Iskenderun, the port founded by Alexander the Great to commemorate his nearby victory over the Persians in 333 B.C. This was the northwestern outpost of Greater Syria.[5]

Syria is a Greek word derived from the Semitic *Siryon,* which appears in Deuteronomy in reference to Mount Hermon, straddling the borders of Syria, Lebanon, and Israel. Throughout the nineteenth century, until the collapse of the Ottoman empire after World War I, the region that travelers called Syria stretched from the southern slopes of the Taurus Mountains of Turkey in the north to Egypt and the Arabian Desert in the south, and from the Mediterranean eastward to Mesopotamia. It encompassed southern Turkey, Syria, Lebanon, Jordan, Israel, and western Iraq. After World War I, Atatürk annexed a sliver of northern Syria to his new Turkish state. That strip lies east of here in the desert and was never really contested. But as my bus headed southeast of Iskenderun across a dramatic series of mountains (the northern end of the Lebanon and Anti-Lebanon Ranges) to a sprawling, fertile panel of cultivation, we were in the heart of the Hatay: a two-thousand-square-mile panhandle between the Mediterranean and the Syrian border where Arabs and Armenians once outnumbered Turks. In July 1938, the Turkish army moved into this area, and many of the Arabs and Armenians fled. This led to a Turkish annexation that was not protested by France, which then held the mandate for Syria. But to this day, on Syrian government maps, Iskenderun (Alexandretta) and the rest of the Hatay are shown as part of Syria, like the Golan Heights.

At the foot of a mountain I saw a city, and soon the bus entered a dusty and chaotic jumble of streets noisy with cars and old motorbikes. This was Antioch, called Antakya by the Turks, the main city of the Hatay. Antioch was one of the great cities of the ancient world. It was founded in 300 B.C. by one of Alexander's Macedonian generals, Seleucus, and named for his father, Antiochus. In 64 B.C., Pompey annexed

Antioch to Rome, and the city, strategically situated on both the main trade route from Anatolia to Arabia and on a branch of the Silk Road to China, became a thriving military and commercial center, with a famed school of Greek philosophy. The emperors Julius Caesar and Diocletian visited Antioch, and Peter and Paul preached there. In Antioch the followers of Jesus were first called Christians. Antioch was one of the Church's three original patriarchates, along with Rome and Alexandria. In the fourth and fifth centuries, under Byzantine rule, Antioch's elite spent their money on mosaics, and the archaeological museum here has one of the world's finest collections. At the height of its glory in the Roman-Byzantine age, when it had an amphitheater, public baths, aqueducts, and sewage pipes, half a million people lived in Antioch. Today the population is only 125,000. With sour relations between Turkey and Syria, and unstable politics throughout the Middle East, Antioch is now a backwater—seedy and tumbledown, with relatively few tourists. I found it altogether charming.

It takes so little to create enchantment, I thought as I walked the streets of Antioch that night, and yet places with far more resources than this city lack it utterly. I wandered into a restaurant, where a few stray cats lay sleeping amid the smell of fresh bread and olive oil, and tables cluttered with white wine and Middle Eastern dishes. There was an old lemon tree in the corner, and a grapevine covering a rusted metal trellis. People talked and smoked cigarettes till near midnight, speaking Turkish and Arabic. In the city itself, men walked arm in arm in the Arab manner (Antioch's population was still mostly Arab). I passed grimy blacksmiths' sheds and dusty stores with old Formica furniture and black-and-white photographs on the walls. I saw more typewriters than computers, and entered simple mosques and ancient churches with icons, and watched men twirling car keys as they sipped coffee while sitting on 1,500-year-old capitals near the archaeology museum. Antioch was a place where the extraordinary was often constructed from the mundane.

"Is the border with Syria open?" I asked people.

"Of course," they said.

Turkey's military exercises were taking place much farther east, in the desert. A shopkeeper who was an Alawite, like Syrian president

Hafez al-Assad, told me: "The Syrian people are our brothers. We share the same language and religion. Only one man is a problem in Syria—Hafez al-Assad. He has made Syria the country of *mukhabarat*!" (the Arabic word for "intelligence services," which my acquaintance used as shorthand for a police state). Throughout my time in Antioch I heard similar comments. The Arabs of Antioch were not shy about their hatred for the Syrian regime. I had heard it all five years before, during my last visit here.[6] Assad refused to acknowledge Turkish sovereignty over the Hatay, but the region's Arabs saw a closer relationship with Syria only after the demise of his regime.

For the moment, the past and the future of Antioch seemed to me more promising than its present. Antioch's delicious mix of Turkish and Arabic still gives the city a cosmopolitan essence, but this ancient crossroads of the eastern Mediterranean, ruins of which lay beneath the modern concrete, could rise again if political change were to come to Syria.

❧ ❧

One afternoon just before leaving Antioch, I realized that among my papers was an air ticket from Tel Aviv to Boston, along with names and phone numbers of people in Israel I planned to see: friends, government officials, and military officers. It was not a good idea to travel through Syria with such documents, especially given my visa difficulties in Washington. I told the story to the DHL representative, an Arab, who smiled, took my documents, and over a cup of coffee lamented the lack of freedom in Syria—like everyone else I met here. Even by regional standards, the situation was a bit unreal. Nobody in the Balkans, Turkey, Lebanon, Jordan, or Israel cared enough about where I was going next, where I had been, or who I was, exactly, to the point of excluding me. I was issued visas to all these places on the spot, though occasionally at exorbitant rates. The drama in Washington over my Syrian visa reminded me of similar encounters I had had crossing borders in Eastern Europe before the Berlin Wall fell.

When I turned on the Syrian television news in my Turkish hotel room and saw a desultory cavalcade of unhappy-looking people at meetings, seated in uncomfortable chairs, with photos of the leader, Assad, behind them, I again thought of Communist Eastern Europe.

The 9 A.M. bus to the Syrian city of Aleppo was two thirds empty. I met a Jordanian metallurgy student traveling to Amman from Istanbul, a Dutch backpacker, an Italian woman with a poodle, and counted about a dozen local Arabs. For an hour we traveled through fields of cotton and grain, then through a narrow canyon with a few villages that led to a vast parking lot filled with trucks. This was the Turkish side of the border. I saw old railway tracks that had been part of the Hejaz Railway, a popular way to reach Arabia from Istanbul through World War II. In a run-down building, a Turkish official stamped our passports. I saw the red Turkish flag with the white star and crescent for the last time on my journey south.

14

THE SACRED

AND THE PROFANE

Our bus left the Turkish checkpoint and passed a graceful Roman arch in the desert, restored in Ottoman times and known as Bab al-Hawa, Arabic for "Gate of the Winds." Then came the Syrian border post, with stone buildings and curbstones painted white and black: the same austere architecture, blending Crusader and Ottoman styles, appropriate to the desert landscape, that I would see throughout Syria, Jordan, and the West Bank. Above these buildings the Syrian flag flew, with its red, white, and black horizontal bars and two green stars representing Syria and Egypt, which from 1958 to 1961 formed the United Arab Republic, a failed attempt at Arab unity. The Turkish flag, with its star and crescent over a bloodred background, contained martial and religious themes, but the Syrian flag was emphatically post-colonial: a copy of the secular banners of European nations, revealing the Arab desire for the unity that the French and British had denied them when they carved up the Middle East. Syria's flag reflected its recent independence. It was a mid-twentieth-century flag. The flag of Turkey—a country never colonized—was timeless.

We left the bus and entered the Syrian immigration hall, huge and almost deserted, where a single official sat in a corner stamping passports. Except for a shipment of bananas from Turkey that a Syrian customs officer refused to let through, the border formalities were uneventful. While the customs officer haggled for two hours with the hopeful Arab importer of bananas, we waited in the hot sun. Because I knew that the Syrians were strict about admitting journalists and since I had only a tourist visa, I restricted myself to taking notes only in hotel rooms and other private places. In Syria, I resigned myself to being a tourist. It didn't bother me. The most insightful people I have met on the road have often been tourists and backpackers.

The landscape as we traveled east toward Aleppo was sharply different from what I had seen in Anatolia. The mountains and dramatic vistas were gone, replaced by a severe monotony of sandy, reddish soil and barren limestone hills. Pine and olive trees provided the only green in the landscape. Everything built by humankind here, including the endless boundary walls demarcating one plot of land from another, was made of stone. I saw no corrugated iron or barbed wire. This parched, rolling plateau between the Taurus Mountains to the north and the treeless Arabian wastes to the south made Greater Syria easy to define, even if the borders within it sparked controversy. I understood why the great English travelers of the early twentieth century, T. E. Lawrence, Gertrude Bell, and Freya Stark, loved this place: The Syrian landscape was like good poetry, beautiful in its spareness.

Villages appeared, and the bus stopped occasionally to discharge a few passengers. I saw lots of garbage and broken curbstones. I saw quarries everywhere and much new construction, but maintenance was lacking and storefronts were corroded.

It was early afternoon and young schoolchildren flooded the streets, all in green military uniforms, white scarves covering the heads of the girls. Many of the men in the road also wore military outfits, either brown or dark green. I noticed young women and old ladies in black Islamic coverings, many with veils, and other women in colorful traditional costumes. The post-modernity of Turkey and the newly democratic Balkan states, with the flagrant individualism of clothing styles, was nowhere apparent. Even the Islamists of the Virtue party, with their proletarian clothes, were far ahead of the traditionalism I saw in Syrian villages. Then there were the photos, in every shop window and on every car windshield we passed, of President Assad, with his dark mustache, intense eyes, and large head, along with photos of his sons, Bashar and Basil, in military uniforms and aviator sunglasses. Basil, the heir apparent, had been killed while speeding in his Mercedes outside Damascus in 1994; now Bashar was the presumed successor. Syria, unlike every other place I had visited since leaving Budapest, was a mobilized society: Everyone was in some sort of uniform—soldier, peasant, religious Moslem—while the eyes of the leader watched over all. The only spark of change I saw was the ubiquitous satellite dishes, which allowed Syrians to watch Jezzira television, an Arabic equivalent of CNN broadcast from the Gulf and respected for its objectivity: Syrians now knew what was going on around them.

With two border posts to negotiate and the delay over the bananas, the seventy-mile journey east from Antioch to Aleppo had taken five and a half hours. I had last visited Aleppo in 1976. The changes were overwhelming. The bus entered Aleppo from the west, where suburbs had shot up in the early 1990s during a wave of economic liberalization now at a standstill as regime cronies negotiated their next move.[1] The suburbs, with row after row of identical stone villas and comprising an area larger than Aleppo's old downtown, were mostly deserted. There were few trees or green spaces, but many new mosques: a way for the Alawite president to placate the Sunni fundamentalists he had crushed in the early 1980s. There was also a new traffic circle filled with a massive bronze statue of a leaping horse and rider representing Basil Assad, the president's late son, an equestrian. As we approached the city center, I noticed one giant poster of President Assad after another. In the 1970s and the early 1980s, during my previous trips to Syria, pictures of Assad were less obtrusive, but now the atmosphere of Aleppo's new western suburbs reminded me of Ceauşescu's Civic Center in Bucharest, the forbidden city of Stalinist architecture that the Romanian dictator had built before he and his wife were overthrown and executed.

Another shock came when I left the bus at the corner of Baron and Al-Maari streets downtown. The clean and modern avenues I recalled from 1976 were now a jumble of run-down buildings and signs, surrounded by mounds of trash and puddles. Once more I was struck by the poor maintenance and squalor, even compared to Antioch.

I walked down Baron Street to the Baron Hotel, a handsome stone building, an oasis amid the grimness. In the lobby, with its old piano, inlaid stone archway, giant gilded chandelier, lithographs in mossy gold frames, and Art Deco posters from the golden age of travel, I noticed immediately the smell of insecticide.

Was there a room available? I inquired.

A short, squat woman asked me if I had a reservation. "No," I said. "It doesn't matter," she said, "but it will cost you twenty-eight dollars a night, in cash."

"Fine," I said. When I asked if I could exchange some dollars for Syrian money, she whispered frantically, "Quick, give me your dollars before that man sees us," and pointed to someone lurking in a corner.

My room had a single, bare lightbulb, leprous walls, a ratty bed, an old phone with a frayed cord, and a broken plywood door hiding a hideous bathroom. There was a desk lamp but no outlet for it. Walking back to the lobby, I encountered the person who had been lurking in the corner whom the woman had warned me against. He too asked if I wanted to change money—competition for her, I supposed. Early the next morning at the Baron, yet another man would approach me furtively and ask if I wanted to exchange traveler's checks for 70 Syrian pounds to the dollar, an astounding rate given that dollar bills fetched only 44 pounds. I did not understand this convoluted system. I knew only that while the black market was illegal, everyone used it. In Syria, I never went to the bank.

Thirsty from my journey, I entered the Baron's dark and cavernous bar, where an ancient bartender with a copper complexion, a perfectly trimmed white beard, and a starched white shirt and bow tie stood up and beckoned me forward amid the peeling pilasters toward the rack of whiskeys, as if I had been wearing tails rather than jeans and a T-shirt. He was disappointed when I ordered soda water. Again, I thought of the Romania of the Ceauşescu era, where I had seen other bartenders trying to preserve an atmosphere of Old World civility amid decay.

Back in the lobby, I noticed a vitrine displaying some ancient pottery and a room receipt signed by Lawrence of Arabia, who had stayed at the Baron. So had Freya Stark, Kemal Atatürk, Charles Lindbergh, Theodore Roosevelt, Doris Duke, Agatha Christie, Lady Louis Mountbatten, the prizefighter Gene Tunney, Yuri Gagarin, David Rockefeller, and other luminaries. Of course, that was back in the days when the Baron, built in 1909, was a first-class watering hole on the edge of a town surrounded by gardens, and Aleppo was a stopover on the London-to-Baghdad Railway. The Armenian family that had owned the hotel had been forced to cede it to the Syrian government, and the service had deteriorated. You could make long-distance calls only from the lobby. Every other day, there was a twelve-hour water cut. When I paid the room bill, I had to beg the manager repeatedly to give me a receipt. The eerie hallways seemed populated by the ghosts of former guests and intimacies. I paused every time I passed the yellowing BOAC poster (the British Overseas Air Company, since replaced by British Airways). The Baron would turn out to be a microcosm of Syria itself.

※ ※

Aleppo, with a population of almost 1.5 million, is Syria's second-largest city after Damascus and, like Damascus, it is considered one of the oldest cities in the world, continuously inhabited for five thousand years. Aleppo appears in the Eblaite texts of the third millennium B.C. as *Hal-pa-pa,* meaning "milky white," a reference to the region's white limestone.[2] There is also a legend that Abraham, on his way to Canaan from Mesopotamia, stopped here to milk his cow. Aleppo, on the Silk Road, linking the Mediterranean with the Euphrates, was a main caravan city under the Hittites, Amorites, Assyrians, Babylonians, and Persians. Its importance rose further with the founding of Antioch, in the late Hellenistic period. Under the Romans and Byzantines, Aleppo was the urban jewel of inland Syria, declining only in the seventh century A.D. with the rise of the first Islamic dynasty, the Omayyads, who shifted political and economic power from nearby Antioch to faraway Damascus. But when Damascus's fortunes declined with the rise of Baghdad to the east, Aleppo recovered its greatness. The tenth century saw a brilliant new dynasty in Aleppo, under the Hamdanids, a clan from northern Iraq. The Mongols, under Hulagu in 1260 and Tamerlane in 1400, utterly destroyed Aleppo, slaughtering its citizens and exiling others to the badlands of Central Asia. Aleppo revived, though, despite the discovery of sea routes to Asia, which competed with the Silk Road. With the rise of colonial mandates and nation-states after the fall of the Ottoman empire in World War I, power again shifted to Damascus, and Aleppo declined once more. Aleppo's strategic position as the northernmost city of the Syrian Desert—the gateway to Anatolia, with a polyglot population of Arabs, Turks, Armenians, Kurds, Circassians, and so on—ensured its greatness as long as the rule of Arab Damascus did not suffocate it. But Aleppo seemed to be suffocating as rarely before.

Aleppo was a Middle Eastern version of a Communist Eastern European city, with broken windowsills, rotting doors, peeling paint, and polite, seemingly exhausted people with unkempt hair and worn, baggy clothes pushing dusty brown carts, though there were a few new Toyotas and Mercedes amid thousands of old, battered vehicles. The flashy signs of Turkish cities were, with few exceptions, absent. By Turkish standards, Antioch was a backwater; but traveling from Antioch to Aleppo was like switching from Technicolor to black and white. I saw long rows of busy sewing machines in the street and shoe-repair shops. The streets teemed with small children and teenagers. For years, Syria has had one of the world's highest birthrates; its population has been growing by an average of more than 3 percent annually since 1980, thus doubling about every twenty years.[3] People seemed reserved and eaten with worries. The middle class here is shrinking as the lower-middle sinks into poverty and an upper-middle, with connections to the regime, gets richer, a Damascus-based economist told me.

I wandered through the miles of vaulted medieval souks and khans, with their striped masonry and stalactite tiers dating from the Mamluk and Ottoman periods, for which this caravan city is renowned. In the busy shopping hours of early evening, I saw Syrian peasant women lining up to buy wool for carpets, and scores of busy shops selling fabrics, soaps, spices, and meat. The crumbling walls and abundance of cheap brown socks and burlap sacks lent an air of penury to these soot-layered markets illuminated by sulfurous lamps, making old Aleppo seem like a vast, breathing daguerreotype. The rich aroma of cardamom-spiced coffee was ever present. I heard the halting croon of the imam—louder than ever as the regime makes concessions to Islamists after murdering so many—his voice rising and falling like the swallows swirling above the silver cupola of the Gregorian Armenian church. The mosques were packed, but few men wore beards. A diplomat would tell me that any fundamentalists left after Assad's massacres of the 1980s did not announce themselves by dress. If there is a fundamentalist movement in Syria, it will remain concealed until the regime itself shows signs of weakening. But Aleppo may be ripe for the spread of radical Islam. The Christians were far less noticeable now, because of emigration and the higher Moslem birthrate.[4] I also heard less Kurdish and Turkish than I had remembered, as Aleppo loses its distinctiveness and is transformed into a northern version of Sunni-Arab Damascus, Homs, and Hama. I left the souk by the western entrance, near the luxurious new Amir Palace Hotel, whose tinted one-way mirrors kept the throngs of passersby from peering into the lobby and restaurant.

The streets were dark now, and I nearly lost my footing in places where there were no streetlamps. The only well-lit objects were the billboards showing Assad's portrait. I remembered Aleppo as beautiful, but the uncontrolled spread of cement unrelieved by trees or green spaces, along with the lack of renovation and maintenance, now gave the city a brutish, concrete ghastliness that reflected the aesthetic values of the insecure, vindictive peasants who for decades had run the regime. I saw only one shop in all of Aleppo without a picture of Assad; it displayed the late Princess Diana instead. Unlike in Istanbul or Ankara or Antioch, few people here were reading newspapers, and none talked politics. There were comparatively few computers in the shops: Both the Internet and cell phones were banned at the time. Bookshops were rare, and the ones I saw were empty. ATM machines did not exist. Tradition, repression, and economic stagnation fused together in Aleppo. Couples did not laugh together and hold hands, and I saw no women with attaché cases or sitting alone at cafés. The working class all dressed alike, and as I would find out, so did the rich.

The next night I went for dinner in the Armenian quarter, northeast of downtown and the souk. Like a diplomatic compound, the district was isolated from the rest of Aleppo. Everything reeked of cleanliness and money. There was no dust. The stones looked new and sandblasted, the restaurant windows polished and adorned with credit-card stickers. Amid the marble fountains, the exquisite relief and tracery work, the shiny marble floors, the arabesque woodwork of the overhanging balconies, and the jasmine and lemon trees, there were handsome men and lovely women in designer fashions, makeup, and eyeglasses. The shoes, the handbags, and the other details of their apparel were perfect. These men and women were dazzling, but they, too, all dressed alike. Unlike in Turkey or Bulgaria or Romania, I would not see anyone in Syria with unusually long hair, baggy jeans and a T-shirt, or anything else of fashion, tasteful or not, expensive or not, that signified creativity or *revolt*.

The wealthy diners in the Armenian restaurant were not all from established Christian merchant families. Some were Moslems who had quickly amassed money through political connections, in an economy where the laws on foreign currency, repatriation of wealth, business licenses, and so on were a murky labyrinth in which business acumen was a matter of knowing whom and how much to bribe. A foreign economist called it "a system that produced the worst of capitalism and the worst of socialism."

Over dinner, a businessman told me about a historian he knew in Damascus who claimed that the Kurdish guerrilla leader Abdullah Öcalan had never been to Syria or the Bekaa Valley in Lebanon and that Turkish claims that Syria backed Öcalan were a myth. I was stunned. The Western press had been writing for years about Öcalan's base in Syria and Syrian-controlled Lebanon, and about his Syrian residency permit. Öcalan had even given press conferences from the Bekaa Valley.[5] His presence on Syrian-controlled territory was not in dispute. There are uninformed people everywhere, but for a historian to believe so completely the lies of his unelected government troubled me. It reminded me of a visit to Syria in 1983, when I had scandalized a philosophy professor at Damascus University by asking him why there was no official display of grief at the funerals of Syrian pilots shot down over Lebanon—as there was at the funerals of Israeli pilots. The professor said he "couldn't even think about" such a question, and complained to the Ministry of Information (which had set up the interview) that I had provoked him. Syrians for decades were so fearful of criticizing the regime that many journalists traveled to Damascus merely to interview the foreign diplomats stationed there. Because tough reporting could get you banned from Syria, the media generally restricted their coverage of Damascus to bland reports about the Syrian government confirming this or denying that, about Syrian-staged releases of Western hostages from war-torn Lebanon, and so on.

"No Syrian will ever say anything critical of the regime in the presence of another Syrian outside his or her immediate family," a Damascus-based American diplomat once told me, a habit intensified by a latent reserve in the Syrian character. Said the same diplomat: "The threshold of hospitality is different here. People don't slap you on the back and befriend you immediately as in Egypt. Here all the humor and outgoingness happen behind closed doors."

Syria was a tragedy of twentieth-century politics.

※ ※

While Greater Syria is geographically definable, the territory of the "Syrian Arab Republic" is not; nor has the present Syrian state ever been linked to a specific national sentiment. Like Lebanon, Syria is a hodgepodge of ethnic and religious groups historically at odds.

The only patriotism that ever existed here was pan-Arab, but the collapse of the Ottoman empire, rather than liberating local Arabs, saddled them with political contradictions. Anglo-French rivalry for spoils resulted in a six-way division of Greater Syria.[6] The Turks regained the north; the British established the mandates of Palestine, Transjordan, and Iraq; and the French divided their zone into what became Lebanon and Syria.

But the French then enlarged the historic borders of Mount Lebanon to include a large population of Sunni Moslems under the domination of Maronite Christians, the latter allied with France, speaking French, and boasting a concordat with the Vatican. The "Syria" that was left was the writhing ghost of a would-be nation. Although territory had been cut away on all sides, Syria still contained not only warring sects, religions, and parochial tribal interests but also the historic nineteenth-century headquarters in Damascus of the pan-Arab movement, whose aim was to erase all the borders that the Europeans had just created. So, while much smaller than Greater Syria, this new Syria had fewer unifying threads.

Worse, each sect and religion was specific to a geographical area, making the new Syria a Levantine version of Yugoslavia: Aleppo, in the north, was a multinational bazaar city with greater historical links to Mosul and Baghdad (both now in Iraq) than to Damascus; south of Aleppo was the Sunni Moslem heartland of Hama, Homs, and Damascus; and the area south of Damascus was occupied by the Druze, another Moslem sect. In the West, contiguous to the newly enlarged Lebanon, was the mountain stronghold of the Alawites, who would one day rule in Damascus under Hafez al-Assad.

Both the Alawites and the Druze are remnants of a wave of Shi'ism from Persia and Mesopotamia that a thousand years ago swept over Greater Syria. The term *Alawite* means "follower of Ali," the martyred son-in-law of Mohammed, venerated by millions of Shi'ites in Iran and elsewhere. Yet the Alawites' resemblance to the Shi'ites is the least of their heresies in the eyes of Sunni Moslems. More serious is the Alawites' affinity with Phoenician paganism and Christianity. Alawites celebrate variations of Christmas, Easter, and Palm Sunday, and their ceremonies make use of bread and wine.

In an attempt to forestall Sunni Arab nationalism here, the French deliberately encouraged minority self-determination, granting regional autonomy and lower taxes to the Alawites and Druze and recruiting them into their colonial occupation force. The Sunni Arabs of Damascus—under the guns of Alawites, Druze, Kurds, and tough troops that the French had brought in from Senegal—felt occupied to a degree that they never did under the Ottoman Turks. Sunni paramilitary groups responded with street brawls and uprisings. The divisions in Syria in the 1930s were as bloody as those between the Arabs and Jews of British-controlled Palestine. After independence in 1946, the situation was exacerbated when the new Syrian state held free and fair elections.

Because so many votes went to regional, sectarian interests, only an ineffectual minority government could be formed following the July 1947 elections.[7] So when the chief of staff, General Husni az-Zaim, staged a coup in March 1949, crowds danced in the streets of Damascus. But Zaim, unable to placate the various nationalisms that plagued Syria, was soon overthrown and executed. A new military regime held fresh elections, but the vote was just as fractured as in 1947, and the country slipped into anarchy, saved only by Colonel Adib ash-Shishakli's December 1949 coup. Shishakli was hailed by foreign observers as the Syrian Atatürk, but by 1953 he was admitting that Syria was merely "the current official name for that country which lies within the artificial frontiers drawn up by imperialism."[8] In 1954, Shishakli was overthrown by sectarian elements both within and outside the military. In the fall of that year, Syria held elections once again, and again the largest number of parliamentary seats went to tribal and sectarian independents. The biggest gains went to the Ba'ath party (Arabic for "renaissance," a movement founded by Arab intellectuals, both Christian and Moslem), which sought to bridge sectarian differences by an appeal to secular Arab nationalism and East Bloc–style socialism. In 1958, defeated by its attempts at democratic self-rule, Syria joined itself to Gamal Abdel Nasser's Egypt. But the new state, the United Arab Republic, fell apart in 1961, partly because non-Sunni Syrians such as the Alawites resented the rule of the Sunni Egyptians. In 1963, the now heavily Alawite military came to power in Damascus in a Ba'athist coup. The Alawites, who comprised only 12 percent of the population, saw Ba'ath socialism as a secular counterweight to Sunni Islam. Another coup followed in 1966, and another in 1970, which brought Hafez al-Assad to power.

Assad did not suffocate Syrian democracy. He is the force of nature that filled the vacuum after democracy's failure and twenty-one changes of government in Syria's first twenty-four years of independence. His long tenure is particularly impressive given his ethnicity. "An Alawi ruling Syria is like . . . a Jew becoming tsar in Russia," writes the scholar Daniel Pipes.[9] Assad was helped by modern technology, such as state-of-the-art electronic surveillance systems and Soviet-bloc security advisers, giving him more control than any medieval tyrant ever held. But the Assad era, like the rule of Communists in Eastern Europe, may be only a historical intermission rather than a sign of enduring unity in Syria.

Because Islam was born as an ideal community without a clerisy or other legitimating institutions—with only the prophet Mohammed as a guide[10]—the House of Islam has been intermittently at war against itself since the seventh century A.D. Such a vacuum of legitimacy has allowed various mafia-style clans—helped by technology and the model of the modern European state—to enforce brutal, central control.[11] Take the case of Hama, a Sunni bastion in central Syria.

In February 1982, the Sunni Moslem Brotherhood took control of Hama and murdered Alawite officials, having previously massacred Alawite soldiers in Aleppo. Assad reacted by sending twelve thousand Alawite soldiers into Hama and killing as many as thirty thousand Sunni civilians, while leveling the town. Beneath the sterile carapace of Assad's rule lay a seething region that was no closer to nationhood in the 1980s than it had been after the Turks left. Syria, after all, is part of the same ex–Ottoman world as the Balkans—a world still coming to terms with the collapse of the Turkish empire and the boundary disputes it generated.

But Syria, unlike the Balkans before the fall of the Berlin Wall, has no real intellectual class to serve as dissidents or transition figures. Such people long ago fled or were eliminated. As for Assad himself, he is an Arab version of Mario Puzo's fictionalized mafia leader Vito Corleone, a courtly, self-educated gentleman of steely ruthlessness who can lecture his visitors for hours about the most obscure details of Byzantine, Crusader, Ottoman, and European colonial history, while his thuggish retainers hover around him. And like Brezhnev, Tito, and Ceauşescu, he staves off the future of Greater Syria's largest country, and thus defines the current era in the Middle East.

※ ※

A driver soon arrived to take me to Qala'at Samaan, the ruins of the basilica of St. Simeon, northwest of Aleppo near the Turkish border. Decals picturing Assad and Assad's sons were plastered on the windshield of the driver's mint-green 1955 Studebaker. "Those are nice decals you have," I told the driver, whose name was Walid. He smiled and later pulled over at a grocery stand in a village and bought several more stickers of Assad, giving them to me as a gift. He seemed genuinely enthusiastic. To him, the personality cult appeared natural, as though Syria were not a country but a tribal assemblage, and Assad the headman.

We left the main road and drove uphill into the high desert. At Qala'at Samaan, Walid let me wander alone for an hour while he chatted with a local farmer. The basilica here was completed in A.D. 490. It was built around a pillar atop which Saint Simeon Stylites is supposed to have spent the last thirty years of his life, from A.D. 429 to 459, an iron collar around his neck to keep him from falling off in his sleep. Before that, Saint Simeon, a shepherd boy from northern Syria who had found even the life of an anchorite monk insufficiently ascetic, spent six years atop smaller pillars. Referring to Saint Simeon, Gibbon writes: "This voluntary martyrdom must have gradually destroyed the sensibility both of the mind and body; nor can it be presumed that the fanatics who torment themselves are susceptible of any lively affection for the rest of mankind . . . inflamed," as they are, "by religious hatred . . ."[12] Indeed, Saint Simeon was known to be a reactionary who opposed compromise with other faiths and other forms of Christianity. Such extreme monasticism had its roots a century earlier in Egypt, when Saint Anthony, an illiterate youth, gave away all that he owned and walked into the desert to live by himself. His example spread throughout the Near East at a time of political and spiritual turmoil, when imperial Rome was collapsing, Christianity was spreading, and paganism would soon give way to Islam.

I approached the ruins of the church, the largest in the ancient world, covering five thousand square meters on a great hill overlooking the Syrian Desert and the Taurus Mountains in Turkey. I was alone. The silence and color and monumentality were magical. The towering Romanesque facade, its three levels of arches adorned with veiny Corinthian capitals, had turned salmon and charcoal, with tinges of yellow, in the late-morning sun. The intricate floral relief balanced the austerity of the stone ashlars and columns. Greek, Roman, and Byzantine aesthetics came together here in the Middle Eastern desert, invoking the cosmopolitanism of a lost Syria, a borderless stew of cultures under the weak imperial umbrella of Rome and Constantinople.

Through each arch I saw a separate maze of smaller walls, archways, and rows of broken columns and pilasters etched with Byzantine crosses and pagan suns. Through the silky haze and dust I saw cypresses and gnarled olive trees against bleak hillsides seared with stone walls. I recalled Freya Stark's comment that it is in the nature of "the Syrian landscape to renounce all but the essential, so that the essential may speak."[13]

I rejoined Walid and we drove a few minutes to Deir Samaan, a Greek town from the fifth century that had been a center for Christian monks and tax evaders of the era. Now it was a plain littered with ruins, where cattle and donkeys wandered. We stopped next at Wadi al-Qatura, where Walid laid out a picnic lunch of pita bread, goat cheese, and olives. We could see for miles over the dry plain, but detected no one. There had been a Roman cemetery here, and the carved faces of the dead emerged from the canyon's soft volcanic rock in all the earthen tones of a rich palette. These places had been abandoned when trade routes moved and water ran out.

Qala'at Samaan and the surrounding desert remain the traveler's Syria of the nineteenth and early twentieth centuries. But as we approached Aleppo and began once again to see the barracks-style uniformity of bare concrete and Assad's coercive billboards, erected in the mid-1980s in the wake of the massacre at Hama, I wondered how Freya Stark would react to the city now. Perhaps she would have ignored the brutishness of Syrian politics in favor of the dusty souks and the inspiring glacis of the medieval citadel. She was a gifted writer but a poor political observer, who anticipated unity in the Arab world, democracy in Iraq, peaceful political consensus in Syria, and the expulsion of Jews from Palestine if the Zionists ever tried to defend themselves.[14] This is why I have never been entirely comfortable with her books. Homeless peasants occupied the ruins of sixth-century Byzantine sites, to the dismay of archaeologists.[15] As political decay set in, as it had in fourth- and fifth-century Rome during the time of saints Anthony and Simeon, I worried that an extreme religion might again fill the vacuum.

* *

The next morning, I left the Baron and took a taxi to the bus station. I was headed south to Homs, then east to the ruins of Palmyra, deep in the Syrian Desert. It was early, and the air was tangy and fresh. The bus station smelled of lemons, grapefruits, baked bread, dust, and diesel fuel. Before I could board the bus, I had to go to a police outpost, where my passport was inspected. On the bus, my documents were inspected once again, and the other passengers had to show their identity cards. This was a change from the 1970s and 1980s in Syria, when I traveled with no official oversight. Later I learned that in December 1996, a bus had been bombed in Damascus. From then on, the authorities checked the documents of all long-distance travelers. I noticed two slovenly male passengers with handguns sticking out of their shopping bags: plainclothesmen of some sort. Homs lay more than a hundred miles south of Aleppo, halfway to Damascus. The bus was grimy. In the 1970s, buses in Turkey were awful, but in Syria they were cheerful and new. Now the situation was reversed. I looked out the window at a reddish limestone plain nearly filled with concrete houses. At the station in Homs there were no buses to Palmyra, so I took an old and battered taxi to another station across town, through a netherworld of gray buildings that were either old and collapsing, or new and half finished, with no sign of future construction. Garbage was everywhere.

Soon a bus left the second station for Palmyra, a hundred miles to the east. There were fewer than a dozen passengers, mainly laborers traveling beyond Palmyra to the Deir Ez-Zur oil fields. The driver's radio blasted a scratchy tribal rhythm that repeated the phrase *Baladna Suriye, Hafez Assad* ("The Nation of Syria, Hafez Assad"). As we left Homs, I saw ranks of tattered, dull buildings, two or three stories high, with balconies. Then came newer flats, hundreds upon hundreds of them packed tightly, without a tree or a blade of grass in sight: a Communist Eastern European sort of development again. Once more there was garbage. It was ghastly. But as Homs receded I saw groves of new olive and pine trees, then the desert inched up and romantic Syria reappeared.

It began with the same rolling limestone plain that I had seen between Aleppo and Homs, here stubbled with greenery. Then the greenery thinned and the soft red earth turned into a hard, flat expanse of ocher desert, strewn with black gravel. Finally, the desert turned brown and the gravel deteriorated into fine silt, forming small hills of hard-packed sand. The view was broken only by the flat tents of Bedouins and herds of sheep so large that at first I mistook them for dark rock formations in the distance. Occasionally, we passed a Bedouin walking along the road, dressed in a black blazer and a red-checkered kaffi-yeh. This was the waterless emptiness through which British officials such as Winston Churchill and Gertrude Bell drew arbitrary lines on a map creating "Syria," "Iraq," and "Transjordan" where earlier there had been only the Syrian Desert between the Mediterranean and the densely populated river valleys of Mesopotamia.[16]

After two hours, a multitude of date palms signaled an oasis—with a police post and a bust of Assad painted gold—where we stopped briefly. Then, as if a curtain had lifted on a Hollywood biblical pageant, I saw a peach-colored sea of sand and, in its midst, the monumental ruins of the ancient city of Palmyra. The driver left me on the archaeo-logical site, from where I walked a hundred yards to the Hotel Zenobia, a small, neo-Classical building of brilliant yellow, with a graceful balustrade and a trickling fountain, where I was given a bare room suf-fused with light, with a high ceiling and a view from my bed of the wind-ransacked ancient city of Palmyra.

Few stories from classical antiquity are so alive with beauty, ro-mance, gory spectacle, and power politics as that of the fall of Palmyra in A.D. 271–273.

When the Roman empire expanded eastward at the end of the first and the beginning of the second centuries, the oasis here rose in im-portance as a caravan center and buffer between Rome and Persia. The Romans called the oasis Palmyra, "the City of Palms"; the local Arabs called it Tadmor, "the City of Dates." Conveniently situated between the Mediterranean and the Persian Gulf, and benefiting from Rome's earlier conquest, in A.D. 106, of the Nabatean caravan cities to the south (including Petra), this favored political satellite of Rome, with its splen-did temples, palaces, villas, and colonnaded avenues, profited from the commodity trade with India as it adopted the manners of Rome, the ar-chitecture of Greece, and the ostentation and ceremony of the East. In A.D. 256, the Roman emperor Valerian conferred upon Palmyra's King Odenathus the title Corrector of the East, placing him in charge of the border area with Persia. Then in 267, Odenathus was assassinated and his Macedonian wife, Zenobia, took his place.

Zenobia was said to rival Cleopatra in beauty. She spoke Latin, Greek, Syriac, and Egyptian, and was learned in Oriental history and

Greek philosophy. She was an accomplished hunter and rider and could also march miles on foot.[17] More important, she was an astute and, if necessary, ruthless monarch, who may have been the power behind the throne when her husband was alive. Following her husband's assassination, Zenobia declared complete independence from Rome, had coins of herself minted in Alexandria, and solicited Arabia, Armenia, and Persia as allies.

Aurelian, who had succeeded Valerian as emperor, found such defiance from this self-styled "Queen of the East" unacceptable. The new emperor, who had risen through the ranks and whose defeat of the Goths and consolidation of the Danubian provinces had begun Rome's territorial rehabilitation, now turned his attention to the Orient. Marching from the Balkans into Anatolia, he subdued Bithynia (between Istanbul and Ankara) before defeating Zenobia's forces in two great battles: at Antioch and Emesa (Homs). Zenobia had bravely fought alongside her soldiers in each battle, but she could not raise another army, and barricaded herself inside Palmyra's walls, hoping that famine and Bedouin raids would weaken Aurelian's army or that her eastern allies would rescue her. Indeed, Aurelian's march across the desert from Emesa to Palmyra (the same route my bus had taken) was plagued by Bedouin attacks on his men and supplies. To end what had become a costly campaign, he offered Zenobia generous terms of surrender, but she refused. Aurelian had little political support at home. In a letter replete with frustration, Aurelian writes: "The Roman people speak with contempt of the war which I am waging against a woman. They are ignorant both of the character and of the power of Zenobia. It is impossible to enumerate her warlike preparations . . ."[18]

As Aurelian encircled Palmyra, Zenobia fled northeast on a dromedary. She was captured near the Euphrates, bound in chains, and taken to Rome, where she was paraded in the streets. Palmyra was spared, but after another rebellion the next year, 273, Aurelian burned the city and slaughtered the inhabitants.

At sunset I went out for a drink and early dinner in the garden of my hotel. Oleanders and palm leaves crackled in the wind and the voice of Nat King Cole singing "Mona Lisa" issued from a stereo inside. Two colorfully saddled dromedaries stood nearby, alongside a Victorian-era

carriage. Behind them, in three directions, were ruins of the city conquered by Aurelian: the slender columns, capitals, and cornices all stun-
ningly encrusted with sand and worn by the wind. In the distance was
the curry-yellow Temple of Ba'al, whose immensity reminded me of
Karnak in Egypt. In the ancient agora, I spotted a boulder awkwardly
perched atop a Corinthian capital, like a story from the past stopped
in midsentence. There were relatively few tourists, a consequence of
Syria's perverse politics: Civil society here would mean mass tourism
and the end of the golden age of travel, which limps along in places like
the Baron and the Hotel Zenobia. Because Assad's infamous Tadmor
prison lay close by, where East Bloc–style electric shock therapy was
still being employed and where five hundred Islamic prisoners had
been massacred in their cells in a single morning, I could not ignore this
irony.[19] Travel in Syria was a mixture of the sacred and the profane. Enjoying one reality meant ignoring the other. Syrian politics, with its cruel
and total reliance on physical power, was not wholly distinguishable
from the politics of Rome under Aurelian.

⁂

The breeze-block buildings and giant likenesses of Assad resumed
when I entered Damascus, three hours by bus southwest across the
desert from Palmyra. The suffocating ubiquity of posters of the leader
in shop windows and on walls and billboards reduced the city to two dimensions. Personality cults and the violence they imply are obscene. In
such a circumstance, a population can maintain its dignity only through
pessimism, cynicism, or laughter. I detected little laughter in Syria, but
the subdued atmosphere of the streets suggested plenty of pessimism
and cynicism.

Few of the Syrians I phoned returned my calls, and those who did
said they had no time to see me. The only journalists I knew with useful Syrian contacts came here repeatedly, and that sometimes meant
muting their criticism of the regime in order to be allowed to return.
One of the diplomats I saw told me that his office was probably bugged
and that the guards at the entrance passed on a list of all of his visitors
to Syrian intelligence.

In 1983 I had been here twice as a reporter, after earlier visits in the

1970s. Now, at first I was shocked by the deterioration in the urban core. Like Aleppo, downtown Damascus was rotting, filled with old cars, gritty facades, cracked windows, broken signs, and mounds of garbage, even as swanky new buildings and overpasses went up. The Hejaz Railway Station, with its wooden lattice ceiling, was trashed and deserted, filled with propaganda streamers. Martyrs' Square, where the Israeli spy Elie Cohen had been hung in 1965 after penetrating the inner circles of Syrian power, was a construction site. I peered over the outer walls surrounding many apartment blocks to see only broken glass and piles of waste. The maintenance of public space was, with the exception of a few pleasant parks, absent. Downtown Damascus looked as crowded and poor as the cities in Egypt that I remembered from the mid-1970s, on my first visit there: filled with hordes of young, bored men dressed in old polyester shirts and hovering around movie houses that showed karate films. Yet, as in every Arab city I have ever visited, people were polite and honest, running after you to return a loose coin you might have left at a soft-drinks stand. Arab society was a conundrum: Among themselves, and in the privacy of their own homes, honesty, civility, and cleanliness reigned, yet none of these attributes overflowed into public life and spaces. Of course, the mosques were spotless. But that may help explain the problem: The very perfection of the Islamic belief system begot a naive absolutism that made the compromises of normal political life impossible. Only some of the monarchies, as in Morocco and Jordan, could maintain political legitimacy without resorting to ideology.

※ ※

In 1976, the Shi'ite Mausoleum of Saida Zeinab (the granddaughter of Mohammed) lay at the southern edge of Damascus in a rural setting and was jammed with Bedouin as well as pilgrims from Iran and Afghanistan dressed in traditional tribal clothes, making the burial complex, with its golden dome and dazzling minarets of blue and turquoise faience, a grand, exotic spectacle. Now, the mausoleum lay in the midst of a concrete sprawl teeming with newly urbanized peasants and a market selling household items, while the mausoleum, decorated with pictures of Ayatollah Ruhollah Khomeini (who had come to power in Iran in 1979), was packed with men dressed in cheaply made Western clothing and women hidden beneath curtains of black. Since I had last seen this mausoleum twenty-two years ago, Islam had strayed farther from the timeless rhythms of the desert and village and had merged with the politicized environment of the proletarian masses, who required an inflexible armor of beliefs to stave off the demons of urban life.

Later, in the Damascus bazaar, I stopped for tea in a quiet alley, where I chatted with a graybeard, who told me he was an artist. "Everyone complains now," he said, "about the bad smell of gasoline, about the traffic, about the water shortages, and [by Syrian standards] the growing impoliteness. People are more tired and rushed, more materialistic and religious. Religion used to be natural. Now it is hard." On a wall above us hovered a poster of Assad. The man would not be drawn further into a discussion about politics.

As I walked farther into the bazaar, I found an older, Ottoman Syria of cafés and quiet streets and shaded pergolas, and beautiful fountains of white and black marble. Cardamom-scented coffee was being served on hammered-copper tables, and I watched a work crew busy with historical reconstruction. I climbed a steep street with lovely balconies overhung with flowers and saw the bare, roseate mountains surrounding Damascus and had a sense of continuity fighting a perverted modernity.

The next day, I wandered north beyond the bazaar and downtown, where I saw the quarters of wealthier Damascenes.

Near the Cham Palace Hotel were a few pizza and pastry shops— well lit, cheerfully modern, and with few or no photos of the president— filled with young people dressed in tight jeans, the women also wearing Gucci shoes and Islamic head scarves. Outside, on the street, I noticed a Mercedes pull over for two expensively dressed women, their necks rimmed with gold, and then drive off in the direction of the suburbs.

I followed on foot into the section of town called Abu Roumaneh, where the sidewalks were not broken and there was less trash. There were more women on the street, and many shops selling international clothes and perfume. It was nighttime, yet the streets were well lit. Farther north and uphill, the sidewalks were perfect and there was no trash at all. There were also more trees, and I picked up the luscious smell of jasmine. There were many late-model cars and Art Deco buildings. The children I noticed were well dressed, and seemed shy, unlike the noisier children in the poorer quarters of Damascus. I could have been in Rehavia or Talbiyeh, the exclusive neighborhoods of Jewish West Jerusalem. Then I came upon young men in civilian clothes bearing assault rifles. They were guarding the offices and residences of important figures in the regime. The streets were quiet and empty.

Damascus was more religious than it had been in the 1970s and 1980s, both more run-down and wealthier, with the social classes farther apart, like cities in the West. From the ever-present satellite dishes, I could tell that people were more politically aware. Yet whenever I talked to foreign diplomats about the regime, all I heard were rumor and speculation. I was eager to reach Lebanon.

15

THE CORPORATE SATELLITE

From Damascus, the bus climbed westward up the bare, scrappy hills of the Anti-Lebanon Range on yet another road lined with faded billboard posters of Assad. In an hour we reached the Syrian border post. Because I was the only passenger who was neither Syrian nor Lebanese, my passport was stamped immediately. I waited while the Syrian authorities took their time with everyone else. Then the bus continued to the Lebanese border station, a chaotic bazaar with money changers everywhere. Now everyone else got through the border formalities instantly, while I waited for a Lebanese visa.

"Eighteen dollars," the official told me, smiling. Talking with someone over coffee, he took my money and absentmindedly stamped my passport. The degree of personal freedom in Lebanon struck me at once. I took out my notebook in public for the first time since leaving Turkey. I changed some money and ran back to the bus, which had begun to move. The driver shouting at me for having taken so long, I jumped aboard. The whole procedure had taken five minutes.

Quickly, we descended the other side of the Anti-Lebanon and crossed the midsection of the Bekaa Valley, a green floor with olive trees interspersed with vineyards, and ascended the rocky, barren slopes of the Lebanon Range to the town of Chtaura. Chtaura isn't much unless you are coming from Syria, in which case you notice the slicker signs, the high-quality construction, and the credit-card stickers plastered to shop windows. Yet here too were posters of Assad, with his two sons—"the Holy Trinity," as one of my fellow passengers, a Lebanese, joked after we had crossed the border. But now there was a fourth figure sharing billboard space with Assad when Assad's sons were absent: a black-haired military man with an oily complexion, a stern gaze, a white uniform, and lots of decorations on his chest. This was Emile Lahoud, Lebanon's new president. He looked like a 1950s South American dictator.

In Chtaura we stopped for coffee at a general store. There was nothing special about the place except that, after a sojourn in Syria, I was overwhelmed by the bright lights, the abundance of products, the tasteful decor, the snappy service, and the smiling faces behind the counter, where there were separate cash registers for different currencies. The difference between real capitalism and Syria's pseudocapitalism was dramatic. The clearest expression of freedom, however, was that as we left Chtaura, the political figures on the billboards now shared space with singers and film stars.

As we reached the top of the Lebanon Range and began our descent to the other side and Beirut, the mountains suddenly turned green and the shadows softened. Birches, evergreens, and bougainvillea were abundant and lovely, dark stone walls appeared, mottled with age and salt winds from the Mediterranean, which met the sky near the horizon. The road swirled sharply downhill; every vista was dramatic. There were clothes drying in the sun and houses with red-tiled roofs, as in Turkey. It was Sunday and I saw a group of children surrounding a clown selling cotton candy. I also saw a bullet-riddled building squeezed between a row of new construction.

A few more westering switchbacks, then a vast panorama of rosy-white buildings at the edge of a headland embraced by a misty blue sea: Beirut. The view was soft and peaceful—not at all like the harsh silhouettes of the desert. But I was seeing the landscape of war and anarchy in the 1970s and 1980s, a place where Christians had fought Palestinians and Druze; where rival Christian militias had fought each other, and where Palestinian factions had done the same; where few bothered to count the number of cease-fires; where hundreds of Christians and Moslems had had their throats slit at roadblocks that divided the city along religious lines; where armed robbery and kidnaping had become inseparable from war; where Israelis had invaded and carpet-bombed; where two presidents, one prime minister, and several communal leaders had been assassinated.[1] And because it all happened in such a lovely setting, within driving distance of luxury hotels and fine restaurants, many of which continued to function, it was a war that journalists had reported in minute detail, turning Beirut into a mythic landscape of conflict.

Now the roadside exploded with advertisements, new glass-and-marble constructions, and buildings so tattered from bullet and mortar shells that they resembled lace. Then came a crowded, breeze-block slum with posters featuring a bearded Shi'ite cleric, the late Musa al-Sadr: Suddenly, there was no sign of Assad or Lahoud.[2] It was an urban landscape that spoke of compression, of a half-century's worth of events happening in a decade. The bus journey ended beneath a new highway overpass, with taxis and vendors all around. For the first time since Turkey, I saw people crowding around newspaper stands.

The taxi I took to my hotel in West Beirut passed through the city center, destroyed in the war, leveled as West Berlin was in the years of reconstruction following World War II: an enormous emptiness—a mile long and three quarters of a mile wide—in the middle of a metropolitan area, punctuated here and there by mortar-riddled buildings and new, futuristic steel, marble, and tinted-glass structures. A forest of towering, swiveling cranes dominated the skyline and the racket of jackhammers rarely ceased. It was eerie. The past was being erased; the future was a traditionless mystery.

My hotel room was two thirds the price of the one in Damascus, yet the service was more efficient and the room better maintained. I phoned some news sources, and my calls were returned immediately: What a change from Syria! I went for a walk along Rue Hamra, the main shopping street of Moslem West Beirut. There were fast-food joints, offering beer and sandwiches; trendy cafés; photocopy centers, with the latest Xerox machines, open until late at night; designer-clothing stores, and many hair salons and shops selling expensive eyeglasses. Women wore head scarves and modest dresses, but also tight jeans and tank tops, their belly buttons showing. And they walked and sat at cafés alone, using cell phones like the men. In one store, a woman with a tank top was talking to her assistant—from the Indian subcontinent—in English, with a customer in French, and with another customer in Arabic. Sri Lankan servants were everywhere in Beirut, it turned out. Lebanese, I was told, refused such lowly jobs. But in Israel, where per capita income was more than four times that of Lebanon, I would learn that many of the hotel maids in the Galilee were Lebanese.[3]

The Corniche was a rosy amphitheater huddled around a hypnotic stretch of ballpoint-blue sea. I saw children on Rollerblades, a new Hard Rock Café whose sign, in gold lettering on black marble, said THE TIME WILL COME WHEN YOU SEE WE ARE ONE, and many logos advertising new restaurants and boutiques. People picnicked on the rocks and men in tapered suits twirled car keys. Beirut was jammed with new Audis, BMWs, Mercedeses, Jeeps, and Ford Explorers. The high-quality stone buildings with flowers overhanging the balconies reminded me of the seaside suburb of Athens where I used to live: Beirut was generic Mediterranean, where Arabic was just another Mediterranean language, like Greek or Italian. Car horns blared, tires screeched, materialism and machismo reigned. Lebanon's civil war, with its blow-dried gunmen, was part of the past. I would have thought it was Syria that had been recovering from war, not Lebanon.

I picked up a glossy business magazine and learned that gated communities and a "water-leisure complex" were being built in the mountain suburbs, though a third of the population lived in poverty.[4] I walked into the Commodore Hotel, where the war correspondents had stayed in the 1980s—now just another insipid white-marble luxury hotel under new ownership. Traveling from Syria to Lebanon was like going from East to West Germany during the Cold War: same language, same country for so long, yet so different. Nevertheless, along with the posters featuring President Lahoud, the Iranian-style clerics, and Nabih Berri (the speaker of the Lebanese parliament and head of the local Shi'ite Moslem community), I also saw posters of Assad, indicating Syria's political influence here.

※ ※

The American University of Beirut, located on a hill near the Corniche and Hamra, may constitute the most romantic setting anywhere for a college campus, with stately stone buildings amid lofty cypresses and shaved lawns, all with sweeping views of the Mediterranean. Founded by American missionaries in 1866 as the Syrian Protestant College, the AUB became a monument to Wilsonian idealism—teaching the principles of democracy, self-determination, and free inquiry—long before Woodrow Wilson became U.S. president and the phrase was coined. Because of its openness to new ideas and its situation in the heart of Moslem Beirut, the AUB also evolved into a hotbed of Sunni Moslem–dominated Arab nationalism.[5] The AUB's American faculty and their friends became a pro-Arab communal counterpoint to the pro-Israel sentiments of American Jews—emotional commitment masquerading as objectivity in both subcultures. Now, in the civil war's wake, with secular Arab nationalism a void of misplaced hopes and more of the AUB's students coming from Lebanon and fewer from the Arab world at large, materialism was starting to vanquish politics at the AUB, and business and computer courses were on the rise.[6]

The morning after my arrival, I visited Farid el-Khazen, a young and earnest-looking associate professor of political studies at the AUB. Like every other Arab expert I saw in Lebanon (and, afterward, in Jordan), el-Khazen nodded sadly when I told him my impressions of Syria.

"Let me start with Lebanon," he said.

"Lebanon did not have a classic civil war," el-Khazen explained, "because foreigners and foreign invasions were inseparable from the intercommunal violence." In 1975, Palestinian refugees, backed by Lebanese Moslems, fought the Lebanese Christians. Then the Syrians fought the Palestinians, because the Syrians feared that a radicalized and uncontrollable Lebanon would draw them into a war with Israel. But the Israelis invaded Lebanon anyway in 1978, and again in 1982, siding with the Christians against the Palestinians, the Druze, and the Sunni Moslems. In 1982, an American-led multinational force arrived to keep the peace. But after Shi'ite terrorists backed by Iran and Syria drove out both the Americans and the Israelis, the Syrians inherited the power vacuum. The fighting finally began to die down in 1990 as the Syrians disarmed their erstwhile Christian allies. "There was never really a peace conference," el-Khazen told me, "but a diplomatic agreement, which merely ratified Syria's military solution." Thus, by patient trial and error over sixteen years of war, Assad had won for himself the role of de facto military overlord in Lebanon, effectively undoing the French crime of separating Lebanon from the Syrian motherland.

"There is now direct Syrian control here," el-Khazen said. "It is no exaggeration to say that Syria runs Lebanon with the consent of the international community. The Syrians must approve all major decisions. Nothing significant can take place without Syria's agreement. In domestic policy, their influence is decisive. In foreign policy, our leeway is zero. The international community considers Lebanon democratic and unoccupied; in practice, we are occupied. There is no other country in the post–Cold War world like Lebanon. We are a satellite, like the countries of Eastern Europe before 1989—not a colony or a mandate, since the Syrians let us run our sewage systems, our traffic, and hold local elections."

"But Lebanon is free compared to the countries of Eastern Europe before the Berlin Wall fell," I said.

"Lebanon is drawing on a reserve of freedom from the period through the civil war. But this reserve is being depleted. The press is coming under more pressure from the Syrians, and the judiciary is increasingly politicized. Lebanon never had political prisoners. Now we do."

"It's a bit like Hong Kong being taken over by China," I said

"In a way," he said. "But let's not flatter ourselves. Syria is no China, and Lebanon is no Hong Kong." Also, Lebanon is nearly one fourth the population of Syria: "a potential political cancer for Syria, not just a purse," as another scholar would tell me.

As for Syria itself, el-Khazen called it "a police state," where "the political class has been totally destroyed" and "where every corner of freedom has been smashed. It's a Cold War regime," he went on. "Ba'athism, like all ideologies, is expansionist. So the more stable the Syrian regime is, the more problems Lebanon will have. If political instability returns to Syria, then Lebanon will breathe again, as in the 1950s, when Lebanon was freer and Syria was unstable."

"What about the new president, Lahoud?" I asked.

"He's an apolitical strongman—just what the Syrians need. He is concerned with fighting corruption, with preserving the environment—these are safe issues. He talks about everything except politics." The

Lebanese presidency is reserved for a Christian Maronite, just as the prime ministership is reserved for a Sunni Moslem, and the speakership of the parliament for a Shi'ite Moslem. A respected figure in the Christian establishment would tell me that Syria had the choice of several Maronite candidates, who were civilians, before deciding on Lahoud. "But with Israel and Turkey now formally allied, Syria is feeling squeezed and feels safer with a pro-Syrian military man in power here. The Lebanese army is becoming Syria's army to help Syria against Turkey and Israel." Indeed, if Syria ever signs a peace treaty with Israel, it will be because Assad feels checkmated by the Israeli-Turkish alliance.

El-Khazen saw Lebanon's prime minister at the time, Rafiq Hariri, in a similar light: another apolitical strongman acceptable to Syria. Hariri, a Lebanese multibillionaire who made his fortune in Saudi Arabia and the Persian Gulf, was a controversial figure. He may be one of the few figures in history who, essentially, bought a country when he became prime minister after Lebanon's civil war. His money and power were everywhere: in rock quarries, media outlets, universities, downtown reconstruction, and so on. The term *conflict of interest* fails to capture the way Hariri operated as prime minister. Lebanon was his very own business venture. "Hariri's is not a Western but a Saudi way of doing business," el-Khazen explained. "There are no formal tenders, no transparency, or competition for projects."

"But isn't there another way of looking at Lebanon?" I asked el-Khazen. Hariri, like many a bullying, fabulously successful businessman, *made things happen*. The reconstruction of downtown Beirut, costing billions, was an astounding feat of dynamism and know-how. In other countries, the reconstruction would have languished for years in a morass of paperwork. Moreover, wasn't Syrian overlordship—at least in the first years following the civil war—rather convenient? Didn't it provide a cushion of stability, which, combined with Hariri's "can-do" style, allowed for a transformation that was almost beyond belief? Hadn't history already failed the Lebanese? Hadn't Lebanon's pre–civil war democracy turned modern class conflict and social grievance into old tribal-religious feuds? Hadn't democracy been a mask for rule by tribal mafiosi and warlords—the Gemayals, the Chamouns, the Jumblatts, and so on?[7] Wasn't Lebanon lucky to have even a partial democracy, in which Assad watched over Lebanese politics in roughly the same manner that the Turkish generals now watched over their own country's? What, after all, given all that had happened here, did the Lebanese expect?

"What about civil society?" el-Khazen asked me in return, ever so softly yet forcefully, raising his eyebrows. "Look at what's happening in Central Europe. Shouldn't we also struggle for the rule of law?" It was a powerful statement. For Arab intellectuals like el-Khazen, the old rules and standards of the Middle East no longer applied. El-Khazen concluded: "The income gap is widening. There is the poverty of Shi'ite South Beirut and the new gated luxury communities built in the mountains overlooking the sea, all within a Syrian-controlled oligarchy," in which Hariri ran the economy and Lahoud managed security.

The apolitical drift of the population—partly a worldwide trend, partly a fatigue syndrome after sixteen years of civil war—was making it easier for Syria to tighten its grip, el-Khazen's friends in the Lebanese human-rights community told me. According to them and others, Syria had unhindered access to all intelligence and security files; the Syrians could arrest anyone they wanted. The Lebanese cabinet was loaded with "constants"—direct Syrian appointees, that is. Few big projects could proceed without Syrian connivance, which often required a payoff. Journalists were threatened by Lebanese military intelligence, which the Syrians dominated. The press was being "suffocated" by the withdrawal of print subsidies and was banned from writing about certain topics, such as Assad.

The intellectuals I met in Beirut complained that "Syria was like Cuba," an anachronism that the fall of communism should have ended. Lebanon's municipal elections of October 1998 had brought into government educated people who raised new issues, such as the environment, but the elections were also devoid of real politics, and were a venue for mere "clan and local rivalries." Of course, this was not peculiar to Lebanon—the intellectuals wanting a debate over ideas, the rest of the population wanting only peace and more effective government, even if here it meant control by "Stalinist Damascus." Yet these Arab intellectuals were becoming part of the worldwide movement for civil society and human rights, unlike in previous decades, when their calls for secular Arab nationalism had been merely a catchphrase for what, in effect, meant dominance by the Sunni Moslem majority over the various Christian and Shia sects.[8]

※ ※

Farid el-Khazen, in his small office covered with stacks of monographs, was very much the academic intellectual. Gebran Tueni, the publisher of *An-Nahar,* Lebanon's most prestigious and venerable Arabic newspaper, was the archetypal media baron: expensively dressed, with a slick office from which aides rushed in and out. Yet Tueni agreed with el-Khazen.

"Syria totally controls Lebanon. It imposes pressure on television and individual writers, though, as a major institution, *An-Nahar* has more freedom. The succession struggle is on in Syria. And Assad's Alawite minority regime needs the Maronite Christians here as allies." Tueni explained that President Lahoud, a Maronite strongman who had rebuilt the Lebanese army with Syria's help, may be part of the aging Assad's strategy for saving his regime after he dies.

The Shia-influenced Alawites who ran Syria and the Catholic-influenced Maronites of Lebanon each needed the other to survive against the numerically dominant Sunni Moslems in both of their countries. The secular patriotism that unites different groups in the West under one government did not exist here. In the Middle East, the "state" was a European-imposed mechanism that now allowed one tribe to dominate another to a degree impossible in the nineteenth century, when means of control such as electronic wiretaps and means of status such as a seat at the United Nations did not exist. Thus, the words *Lebanon* and *Syria* were little more than geographical references. Arabs understood this. In 1976, when Assad backed the Maronites in their war against the Palestinians in Lebanon, his move was not seen in his own country as the bold statesmanship that it actually was—necessary to reduce the risk of war with Israel—but as one heterodox minority, his own Alawites, supporting another, the Maronites. That perception helped ignite the Sunni Moslem campaign of terrorism inside Syria to topple Assad, which ended only in 1982, when Assad virtually exterminated a large percentage of the citizenry of Syria's fifth-largest city, Hama. These were not states but feudal assemblages.[9]

"We're on the brink of an earthquake," Tueni told me. "Anything can happen. The major political party in Turkey is the army, and the Arab world is filled with crumbling, one-man regimes. There could be a new map, with new countries to replace Sykes-Picot [the secret 1916 Anglo-French agreement, negotiated by Sir Mark Sykes and Georges Picot, for the dismemberment of the Ottoman empire that drew many of the current borders in the Middle East]. Lebanon has more freedom. Our problems are out in the open. We won't crack up like Syria."

But Elias Khoury, a columnist for *An-Nahar,* was skeptical about the widespread collapse of Arab regimes. With a wry wit, a plaid work shirt, and fashionable wire-rimmed glasses, he seemed a "generic" writer-intellectual, divorced from any ethnicity. When I asked him if Syria's regime had a future, he said: "I hope not. Unfortunately, though, such a regime might well have a future. These regimes have succeeded in destroying not only their societies but any alternatives to themselves. Because no alternative can survive, the choice may be between total control and total chaos."

❧ ❧

As these Lebanese intellectuals and journalists described Syrian domination of Lebanon, their very remarks indicated the fragile freedom that Lebanon, like Hong Kong, enjoyed. For me, following the loneliness of travel in Syria, Lebanon was a feast of good conversation in fine settings.

Coming from Damascus to the Hamra district of Moslem West Beirut was like returning to the West. Yet Hamra seemed Middle Eastern compared to Achrafiyeh, in Christian East Beirut, with its tinted-glass-and-steel office buildings, leafy marble balconies, and cobbled lanes with brooding trees, elegant women, and cafés. Some streets in Achrafiyeh were dead ringers for Rome or the south of France. At a French restaurant in Achrafiyeh, I listened to a Lebanese diplomat talk about the danger that Turkey, now allied with Israel, posed to the Arab world. We ended the meal with "café blanc" (*ma zahr,* or "rose water," in Arabic, served hot in an espresso cup). Then we walked back to the

Foreign Ministry, a large and sleepy villa, where I lost my way in the corridors. I wandered alone into offices strewn with documents; nobody cared, or even asked who I was. Such was the difference between Lebanon and Syria.

Since the end of the civil war, the Lebanese have gone on a car-buying spree. I spent much of my time in Beirut in motionless traffic, watching drivers in nearby cars talk on their cell phones. Again and again, I heard of this family of Lebanese with five children and that family with three, all of whom had cars. Beirut was one big garage, and there were no plans for mass transit. "That was not the Saudi-Hariri" style, I was told. I was also told that Lebanese are too individualistic for mass transit. As a result, I spent an hour getting from Hamra to the northern suburbs, where two Lebanese lawyers treated me to dinner. It was a weekday night, but the restaurant was packed. The music was loud, the prices were astronomical, and *mezzes* (appetizers) cluttered each table, so one could barely see the tablecloths. On the way to the restaurant I had passed a multistory McDonald's Playplace, the glitziest McDonald's I had ever seen. Everything in Lebanon was overdone: the war, the noise, the cars, the food, the conversation, the number of boutiques, the physical beauty—both of the people and of the pine- and cypress-clad mountains along the dazzling blue seaboard. The desert determined Syria's personality, but the Mediterranean determined Lebanon's, rendering one landscape austere and the other Baroque—in war as well as in peace. (Compare the icy calculation of Assad's elimination of the Sunni Moslem Brotherhood in Hama in 1982 with the ad hoc, operatic barbarity of the militia battles in Beirut.) Still, Lebanon was, essentially, part of Syria, and that historical reality was central to future politics.

Over dinner with the two lawyers, I heard more about the iniquities of the Turks. "The Turks were here for four hundred years, yet they did not build one road! What infrastructure we inherited was from the French Mandate. . . . Anyone can make peace with Israel and we don't care, except for the Turks: Turkey and Israel are a dangerous combination." The discussion wandered to geography. I was informed that because Lebanon is mountainous, the Maronites and other sects had been able to escape into redoubts when the medieval Moslem armies invaded, while the Jews in Palestine—where there were no mountains— had to flee. (Judaism had thrived in areas of Palestine for centuries after the Romans destroyed the Second Temple in A.D. 70. It was the Moslem invasion in the seventh century that largely ended Jewish life in Palestine.) But while geography created sectarianism here, it also led to personal freedoms: Because the various religions could not agree on marriage or dress codes, Lebanon offered civil marriages, and people dressed as they pleased—in veils or tank tops.

KENTUCKY FRIED CHICKEN, BASKIN-ROBBINS, TIMBERLAND COMING soon, announced the signs in Jounieh, my next destination: a dramatic array of mountains clustered around a sandy strip north of Beirut, where the Christians had decamped during the civil war and stayed to create an alternative capital-cum–beach resort. The sea was filled with motorboats and Jet Skis; the streets, with new cars and construction crews as green mountainsides disappeared under a blanket of concrete. Jounieh was an environmental nightmare: no sidewalks, no architectural unity between one gated luxury-apartment complex and another, and no real public spaces except for empty lots between villas, where garbage had been dumped, while yacht clubs and expensive late-night restaurants occupied what was supposed to have been public beaches. In the late afternoon in Jounieh, I saw many fashionably dressed women in high-performance cars driving their Sri Lankan maids home after a day's work. The only middle-class people I saw in this Christian enclave were a Moslem tour group at the entrance to the cable car, with their veils, modest polyester clothes, and picnic lunches. When they finished eating, they window-shopped at the boutiques.

Lebanon suggests that the "end of history" is not democracy or humanism but materialism. People wanted goods and the money with which to buy them more than they wanted the rule of law. Of course, the former usually requires the latter, but not always. Take Lebanon: "Hariri operates with Syria's consent and bypasses parliament, which is useless in any case," Jamil Mroue, the editor in chief of the English-language *Daily Star* told me. In an editorial entitled "Our Spineless Deputies," the *Daily Star* had said that the country's subjugation had less to do with the Syrians than with the irresponsibility of parliament, which foisted problems on the Syrians much as the Turkish parliament foisted problems on the Turkish military.[10]

"Hariri is self-made," Mroue went on. "He knows nothing except how to make money. He is not American nouveau riche but Saudi nouveau riche. In America, making money requires some intellectual ability, since you make calculated risks within the law, but in Saudi Arabia it's all through your connections with the royal family." Mroue's point was that nouveau riche values in the West are those of a civil society, whereas here they are not.

Booming Lebanon looked good not because public spaces were being created but because enough private, corporate space filled the landscape—with boutiques and villas and gated complexes and restaurants and yacht clubs—so that you didn't notice the poverty and filth. "We are going toward a total separation between rich and poor. That is why the company [what Hariri was turning Lebanon into] requires the army"—Lahoud and the Syrians, that is—the *An-Nahar* columnist Khoury told me.

The Lebanese state had, in fact, become identified with an actual firm, Solidere—Hariri's brainchild and the French acronym for the Lebanese Company for the Development and Reconstruction of the Beirut Central District. Solidere was rebuilding downtown Beirut much as Napoleon III had rebuilt nineteenth-century Paris and the Marshall Plan had rebuilt Germany. Because the civil war had destroyed real government as well as consensus, "corporate planning," in the words of one local architect, had taken over.[11] After anarchy, in other words, had come a company. Like Bulgaria with its groupings and Turkey with its military, Lebanon with its military-corporate overlordship—controlled by the Syrians and managed Saudi-style—constituted a hybrid regime: partly democratic, partly authoritarian.

The question for Lebanon when I visited was money more than sovereignty. Solidere's wherewithal was borrowed and now had to be paid back. So I went to see Riad Salami, the governor of the Lebanese Central Bank, to understand how that worked.

"Forty-five percent of our economy is remittances from abroad," he explained. "Small countries with no natural resources will always have big diasporas, since there is simply not enough opportunity in a small place to satisfy everyone. And with a wealthy diaspora and bank secrecy at home, money pours in from abroad." (Some new skyscrapers in West Beirut were being constructed with money from Lebanese Shi'ites in West Africa, who were investing their profits here, not there.) Because this investment, as the bank governor explained, was ethnically motivated, it was not necessarily affected by emerging market turmoil. With this money, bonds had been issued for national reconstruction. Thus, Lebanon, with a population of slightly over 3 million, had a $16 billion debt and a bad credit rating. Salami's hope was that now that roads and other infrastructure were being rebuilt, foreign investment and tourism would follow as Lebanon became a hub for regional finance, medical services, education, and the conference industry. "We Lebanese have always been good at finance and other services," Salami told me, lighting a cigar.

It was a big gamble, based largely on cultural assumptions, and the Syrian political succession hinged on it. Lebanon was Syria's cash cow and an outlet for its excess labor. Forty percent of the letters of credit opened here were for enterprises in Syria, according to Salami. Syria took $6 billion annually out of the economy of Lebanon, where thousands of Syrians worked at low-paying construction jobs. Because the per capita income in Lebanon is $3,750 and the per capita income in Syria is $900, Lebanon is to Syria what the American southwest is to Mexico: an economic lifeline. While a truly prosperous Lebanon in the twenty-first century could help reform Syria, a failed Lebanon could turn Syria into a version of what Lebanon had been in the war-torn 1970s and 1980s. What was Syria, after all, but a similar hodgepodge of sects held together by force?

※ ※

"Lebanon pays the rent for Syria," Walid Jumblatt, the Druze community leader, told me. Jumblatt, bald and lanky, with bulging eyes, and dressed in faded old jeans and a simple shirt—a dissenter from the Mediterranean obsession with appearances—was the most interesting person I met in Lebanon: a medieval warlord who had cruelly defended his mountain stronghold of the Chouf, southeast of Beirut, during some of the worst hours of the civil war. He was also a connoisseur of wine, music, and archaeology. Jumblatt was an aesthete who hovered between the cultures of East and West, mingling his despair with sarcasm. On this trip, I met him first in Beirut, in the yard of the villa he had bought, where he sat in a chair reading a newspaper. He was drinking Turkish coffee from a traditional brass beaker. His servants and retainers called him by the Ottoman honorific "Walid *bey.*" Turkey, however distrusted, was ever present in the Arab world, as it was in the Balkans.

"Hariri, like Soros, is part of a new phenomenon," Jumblatt told me unhappily. "These are wealthy entrepreneurs who fill gaps as government declines. Hariri likes big projects. Downtown will be monumental, inhuman, concrete: like Jiddah [in Saudi Arabia]," he said, raising his eyebrows in disdain. "Beirut is invading the country with its horrible buildings. The Chouf Mountains will eventually be a suburb of Beirut." That was another criticism I heard often about the new order in Lebanon: The one benefit of the civil war had been decentralization, but Beirut was taking over again.

"People are tired of war and suffering," Jumblatt continued. "They accept this Syrian-sponsored Latin American–style dictatorship of the 1950s that we have now. President Lahoud represents a backward form of Chehabism." This was a reference to the former president and army commander Fouad Chehab, who preserved the balance of power between Christians and Moslems in the late 1950s and early 1960s. "Poverty grows throughout the country, while here in a few sections of Beirut it's *la dolce vita,*" he added, shrugging.

Jumblatt hated Lahoud. For Jumblatt, who had been an able commander in a guerrilla war between his Druze followers and the Christian Maronites in the 1980s, Lahoud was a toy soldier who had the uniform but had never distinguished himself in battle. As for the Syrians, they had assassinated Jumblatt's father, Kamal, in 1977, after he refused to accept Syrian hegemony over the Maronites. That Walid had to accept Syrian overlordship now made him more bitter. But Lebanon was not a modern bureaucratic state, and Walid and the other communal leaders owned businesses acquired through their feudal positions, which compromised the noble ideas they espoused.

Machiavelli writes that "where there exists so much corrupt material that the laws are insufficient to restrain it, it is necessary to institute . . . an even greater force, that is, a royal hand with absolute and excessive power may impose a restraint on the excessive ambition and corruption of the mighty."[12] Assad's Syria was not the restraining force that a humanist like Machiavelli had in mind; but neither, I thought, was Syria unduly coercive here—at least not yet.

Jumblatt invited me for lunch the following Sunday at Moukhtara, his ancestral home deep in the Chouf Mountains. As my taxi made its way through the southern Shi'ite slums of West Beirut to the coastal road south, I mentioned to the driver that this was where Hezbollah had held its Western hostages during the 1980s. "Damascus held them," he said. "The Syrians always controlled Hezbollah. When it was convenient for Syria, the hostages were released. Look," the driver continued. "Here's a Lebanese army roadblock. The soldiers have nice uniforms, but it's all for show." He exaggerated Syria's influence over the hostages, but the only time I saw cars stopped and inspected at the many roadblocks in Lebanon, they were manned by Syrian plainclothesmen.

Twelve miles south of Beirut we turned inland, ascending into the rugged, reddish drifts of the Chouf in a series of long switchbacks, passing stone buildings with overhanging wooden balconies, replicas of the nineteenth-century Ottoman architecture I had seen in Plovdiv, Bulgaria. There were brooks, floating islands of mist, and thick warrens of pines and cypresses. We stopped at Beiteddine (House of Faith), a palace built in the nineteenth century by Emir Bechir el-Chehab II, one of a succession of hereditary sheikhs who ruled "Mount Lebanon," that spine of mountains, including the Chouf, covering much of the country which originally distinguished Lebanon from the rest of Syria. Beiteddine's rambling geometry represented the finest aspects of Turkish, Arabic, Persian, and Crusader architecture: with vaulted entranceways, blue faience, white-and-black marble fountains, colored-glass lamps, carved cypress walls, furniture painted in the richest reds and greens, and courtyards decorated with Byzantine mosaics, where bougainvillea overlooked terraced fields and mist-embraced forests so green that they seemed almost blue.

But history here was less grand than the landscape and architecture. It was Emir Bechir's failure to reconcile Christian Maronites and Moslem Druze that led to deeper French and British involvement in Lebanon: the French on the side of the Christians, and the British (along with American missionaries) on the side of the Druze. By 1845, there was open warfare between Christians and Druze here, and in 1860, the Druze massacred eleven thousand Christians in the Chouf. Beiteddine is also associated with a failed 1978 peace accord signed here that led to more sectarian violence. In 1982, the Israelis invaded Lebanon and installed the Maronite Phalange militia in the Chouf. This led to the sort of massacres that had not occurred in the area since 1860, with Maronite and Druze freelancers, some armed with butcher knives, dispatching civilian victims. Maronites abducted Druze motorists, knifing them before throwing them into a gorge. In a torture chamber at Beiteddine, Druze poured boiling water over naked Christians.[13] In 1983, the Israelis withdrew from the Chouf, leaving the two sides to fight it out. By 1985, Jumblatt's Druze had won, storming down to the coast at Jiyeh to destroy the last Maronite defenses. At the moment of victory, British journalist Robert Fisk found Jumblatt at Moukhtara, "lamenting the moral improprieties of war":

Walid promised that all displaced Christian civilians would be allowed to return to their homes with appropriate compensation. There was, of course, no such recompense, and I later watched those Christian homes—hundreds of them, even the local Maronite church at Jiyeh—being dynamited to the ground and bulldozed into the earth. As usual with the Druze, there were no prisoners.[14]

But Jumblatt hadn't destroyed everything at Jiyeh. He recovered some magnificent Byzantine mosaics from the fourth through sixth centuries, which are tastefully displayed in the underground vaulted stables at Beiteddine. As with the Canaanite, Phoenician, Greek, Roman, and Byzantine pottery and the Roman glass and gold jewelry that fill many of the rooms of Beiteddine, the mosaics are Jumblatt's personal property. In Lebanon, the idea that the state—or the Christian community from which some of it was captured—might own such items is simply not contemplated. Beside the pottery displays at Beiteddine was a sign that said ALL ARCHAEOLOGICAL ITEMS ARE THE PERSONAL PROPERTY OF WALID JUMBLATT. The mosaics were simply Jumblatt's war booty.

Beyond Beiteddine, higher and deeper in the Chouf, lay Jumblatt's palace at Moukhtara: a compact network of buildings girded by clouds and dreamy forested fastnesses and ringed by cypresses and geraniums. Water rushed everywhere through a series of marble fountains. The windows were highlighted by roseate triangular arches. There were Byzantine statues, huge clay jars, Roman-Byzantine sarcophagi, and chambers for storing meat and oil. I wandered through Ottoman-Syrian sitting rooms with inlaid cypress furniture but could not find Jumblatt. He was in the courtyard sipping white wine and Apollonaris water with a French consultant, who was helping him market the wine he produced in nearby vineyards. We soon went inside for lunch and more varieties of red and white wine. By the dining table was a wall-size cabinet filled with Phoenician pottery, including fertility symbols. I thought of a friend, an Israeli archaeologist, who had once gone to the home of the late Israeli minister, war hero, and amateur archaeologist Moshe Dayan to demand that Dayan give back some archaeological relics that rightfully belonged to the Israeli state. Dayan gracefully agreed. Here the state was not sufficiently legitimate for that kind of pressure to affect Jumblatt. The state in Lebanon was a mere assemblage of feuding personalities, of which Jumblatt was one.

As we ate, fighter jets roared overhead, shaking the windows. Pointing to the sky, Jumblatt said: "I apologize for my southern neighbors. They have no manners." He suggested that rather than intimidate the Lebanese, who have no power over their own foreign policy, Israeli planes should be buzzing Damascus. This led to the subject of Assad. "When I was younger," Jumblatt said, "my father took me to meet Nasser. That was an experience! Nasser dripped with humanity. Assad is different—all iron and steel. Assad will tire you for hours with minute details of history—Crusader, Turkish. He knows it all. Of course, his lectures are designed to wear you down so that you might forget the points you hoped to raise with him." Jumblatt then told me the well-known story of his meeting with Assad six weeks after Jumblatt's father's death, in 1977. Jumblatt knew that Assad had ordered his father's assassination, and Assad knew that Walid knew. Assad told the younger Jumblatt, "You look just like your father." For Assad, killing Kamal Jumblatt had been business, nothing personal. And Walid, now the new Druze chieftain, had to contain his personal feelings and develop a relationship with the Damascus overlord. I thought of what Jumblatt had told me in another context: about how the Ottoman Turks, rather than commit atrocities as they had in the Balkans, had in the Middle East merely left a legacy of feudal anarchy.

Jumblatt has commemorated his father with an exhibit at Beiteddine that reveals the older Jumblatt as the radical aesthete he was: a recipient of the Order of Lenin; a man who knew Tito, Zhou Enlai, Nehru, Algeria's Houari Boumedienne, and other leftist leaders; and who slept on the floor with a gun beside him, surrounded by books and Oriental carpets. When I mentioned that it was the Communists who had killed a million Moslems in Afghanistan, Jumblatt replied, "But they gave my people aid and weapons." I told him that Middle East politics are like those of the ancient world—a Greek or a Roman could understand them better than an American. Jumblatt nodded in agreement.

On the way back to Beirut, the driver stopped at Deir al-Qamar, a Maronite village in the Chouf with a private museum, the Musée Marc Baz, where for the equivalent of $4 one could see a tableau of wax figures of Lebanon's celebrities, including Kamal and Walid Jumblatt. The emphasis, however, was on the Christian notables: French president Jacques Chirac (France being the traditional supporter of the Maronites) and the old Maronite warlords and their sons—Camille Chamoun; his son Dany; Suleiman Franjieh; and Pierre Gemayal, and his sons Amin and Bashir. Next to the tableau was an expensive café and restaurant for tourists. Given how many of these people had died brutal deaths, I found the exhibit obscene: The wax figures were like movie stars.

Over a hundred thousand people had been killed in the civil war, yet there was no public demonstration of grief in Beirut except along communal lines.[15] Though Solidere's downtown plan included walking paths to highlight new archaeological discoveries, there were no plans for a war memorial. Nor, as in West Berlin and Dresden, was there any

intention to leave a few of the mortar-riddled buildings as they were—
a lesson for future generations. Rather than reform or soul-searching,
Lebanon had sunk into collective amnesia and rampant consumerism.

⁂

Tyre lay fifty miles south of Beirut, fifteen miles from the Israeli border.
Since Israel occupied a strip of southern Lebanon as a "security zone,"
Israeli forces were even closer. I took local buses that stopped everywhere, so the trip to Tyre took over two hours. The bus tickets cost
$2. The drivers carried wads of currency, both Lebanese pounds and
dollar bills. The Lebanese economy was being dollarized, as the Turkish economy already had been. The bus passed a succession of banana
groves beside a calm sea.

   Tyre, when I arrived, seemed to exist in a sleepy, bygone era, as if
drawn by the early-nineteenth-century British lithographer-explorer of
the Middle East David Roberts: a sepia world of rustic Ottoman
villages in the shadow of antiquity; of shepherds resting their flocks
beside columned temples. Roberts had depicted Tyre as a cluster of
charming buildings surrounded by great ruins against a magnificent
seascape. If one ignores recent history, and the filth and cars and high-
rises in the distance, this peninsula town still looks that way. The bus
left me at a meeting of tumbledown mosques, reeling red-roofed
houses, rickety cafés, and a quiet souk, all surrounded by vast archaeological ruins bleached white and gray by the sun; and rotting, it seemed,
in the heat and humid sea breezes. On three sides was the magnesium-
blue Mediterranean, where men and boys fished with long poles in the
shallows, amid rocking wooden boats. I could forgive Freya Stark her
romantic description:

> ... Tyre, on her headland, listens to the waves. Her columns are
> lost or carried away or lie in the sea where they fell broken, and the
> water, clearer than glass, lisps over them or under, singing an old
> song learned in the mornings of Time. . . .[16]

Stark, writing during World War II, says correctly that Tyre lies "along
the Syrian coast." For until 1946, when Lebanon and Syria were created

as independent states from the territory of the French Mandate, Lebanon was loosely defined as part of Syria. And Tyre has more or less remained so, since southern Lebanon was less Lebanon than an abused plaything over which the two regional hegemons, Israel and Syria, fought. For part of the civil war, Tyre was so divorced from Beirut that it was called the People's Republic of Tyre, ruled by a collection of Sunni Moslem leftists and Palestinians. But Tyre is mainly Shi'ite, and the poster of the Shi'ite cleric Abbas Musawi, martyred by the Israelis, dominated the northern entrance to town. Tyre had its own identity—that is, mainly within Syria's sphere of influence.

Tyre's history followed the same pattern as Beirut's and Aleppo's: Throughout antiquity, it had prospered when hegemonic states in the Syrian Desert and Mesopotamia—Assyria, Babylon, and the Omayyad caliphate—had been weak.[17] For nearly a thousand years, during the Phoenician era and again in the Roman-Byzantine one, Tyre was as important as New York, Paris, or London. It was Tyrean sailors who founded the Phoenician colonies around the Mediterranean, as far away as Spain and Morocco, and introduced the alphabet to Europe. Herodotus, writing in about 450 B.C., says that "Tyre had already stood for two thousand three hundred years," meaning it is at least 4,750 years old by his calculation.[18] Under King Hiram, who reigned for thirty-four years in the tenth century B.C., Tyre colonized Sicily and North Africa and traded with India. The Mediterranean was then called the Tyrean Sea. It was Hiram, a friend of the Hebrew kings David and Solomon, who sent cedar for the building of the First Temple in Jerusalem. The Bible is full of references to Tyre: Jezebel, the infamous wife of the ninth century B.C. Hebrew king Ahab, was a Tyrean princess. (Another Tyrean princess of the era, Dido, was the legendary founder of Carthage.) In the early sixth century, B.C., Tyreans withstood a thirteen-year siege by Babylonian king Nebuchadnezzar, which is described in the Old Testament book of Ezekiel.

In the biblical age, Phoenicia was like the Arab world today: an assemblage of independent polities, of which Tyre was the greatest, united by language—a cultural area more than a political reality. Phoenician Tyre came to an end in 332 B.C., after a seven-month siege by Alexander the Great, who sacked the city and massacred the population. It was the causeway built by Alexander in order to attack the local fortress, as well as the landfills made by King Hiram, that make Tyre a peninsula rather than an offshore island. In 64 B.C., Pompey captured Tyre (the same year he captured Aleppo), and a great Roman city was built here. In the second century A.D., Tyre was the capital of Roman Syria. In the Byzantine age, it was an archbishopric. During the Crusades, it was the only city that Saladin couldn't capture.

Everywhere I saw ruins. The excavation area totaled five hundred thousand square meters, according to Ali Badawi, the young archaeologist and AUB graduate who managed it all. "What you see is Roman and Byzantine," he told me. "The Phoenician layer is underground, waiting for future excavations." The ancient harbor was offshore, underwater. It had served Tyre for sixteen centuries, until it was destroyed in an earthquake in the sixth century A.D. There was no shade or guardrails to protect the mosaics, which formed an avenue lined by columns that led to the harbor. I stared down into the bony rubble, beneath which lay the world of Hiram and Alexander. Pottery shards cracked beneath my shoes. The Roman hippodrome, with its sharp turns, was nearly a third of a mile long and seated twenty thousand spectators. Because of the dust, I could barely see from one end to the other.

Moving on to a later chapter in history, I returned to the small and picturesque souk, stocked with fresh produce and household goods but no souvenirs for tourists. Here I saw Shi'ite mullahs, Arabs in kaffiyehs, and other Arabs in beach attire. It was both charming and seedy, as in nineteenth-century lithographs. Close by was a new highway that, people told me, would continue to Haifa if there is peace with Israel. Historically, Tyre had been oriented toward the Galilee, just as Aleppo had been oriented toward Mosul and Baghdad. Only with weak borders could Tyre be great again.

※ ※

A few days later, as I traveled north from Beirut to Tripoli, the coast was one unending construction site. Tripoli was clearly in the Syrian orbit, with pictures of Assad and taxi drivers advertising fares to Homs and other Syrian towns. Its winding souk, with its vaulted archways by the sea, evoked Crusader, Mamluk, and Ottoman times. I took a taxi to the University of Balamand, a private institution overlooking the Mediterranean, whose president, Elie Salem, had been Lebanon's foreign minister during the civil war–torn 1980s.

"These countries," Salem told me, "Lebanon, Syria, Jordan, they are becoming large city-states, like the Phoenician city-states. See how Beirut is spreading, see how Damascus dominates the rest of Syria, see the growth of Amman. So you will have big-city municipal politics inflamed by ideology: Ba'athism, fundamentalism. Syria is frozen in time. Only peace with Israel can demobilize Syria's society and its regime. So the Syrian leadership is terrified of peace, but it is also terrified of being left behind. Syria, Iraq—these regimes are so autonomous that they were not affected by the collapse of the Berlin Wall. They were born after the earthquake of World War I. The Ottoman empire had become so weak that, in fact, states already existed within it. Sure, such states are artificial. But they will continue until the next political earthquake. Lebanon's openness and immigrant mobility—a benefit of its diaspora— may give it the strength to survive the next cataclysm. We'll see."

16

THE CARAVAN STATE

From Beirut I returned by bus to Damascus and then headed south to Amman, the capital of Jordan, a nine-hour journey. On the map, the Syria-Jordan border looks artificial, though in fact it follows the Yarmuk River, where the Moslem armies defeated the Byzantines in A.D. 636, which, together with the fall of Ctesiphon, the Persian capital in Mesopotamia, the following year heralded the Islamic conquest in the Middle East. Almost immediately beyond the frontier into Jordan the earth heaves upward and the sienna hills become mountains separated by deep, majestic valleys patched with olive trees, young pines, and eucalyptus. The reforestation was on a much larger scale than what I had seen in Syria, though the outskirts of Amman emerged in a checkerboard of new construction on the hillsides an hour before we came to the city itself.

Amman had spread far beyond the boundaries I remembered from my last visit, in 1985. Whereas much of Damascus, including the downtown, was falling apart, with faded signs and storefronts, in the early evening when I arrived, Amman was pulsing with light. Plastic waste containers on wheels stood beside many houses, as in the U.S. Like the trip from Damascus to Beirut, the journey from Damascus to Amman was like going from Eastern to Western Europe during the Cold War. While Beirut's dynamism was a matter of Mediterranean exuberance, expressing itself through a freewheeling economy, Jordan's was a deliberate act of public policy and thus more impressive. "It is not the private good but the common good that makes cities great," said Machiavelli.[1]

Despite the neon, the new cars, and the ranks of slick steel-and-marble buildings advertising global chains and consultancies, Jordan was a conservative desert society, its hilly capital still dominated by intimate, quiet neighborhoods, little teahouses, and traditional restaurants. At night the prayer call echoed sharply against the stone buildings and steep, rocky hillsides. The next morning, downtown Amman was crowded with men in kaffiyehs and women in head scarves, who were shopping for traditional clothes and textiles, cooking pots, water pipes, and so on. Because of the economic troubles in Syria and Iraq and the spread of Amman itself (with special outlying shopping districts for the nouveaux riches), downtown Amman had become a regional lower-middle-class souk for Jordanians, Palestinians, Syrians, and Iraqis, who drove long distances to shop here.

I saw fewer uniforms in Jordan than in Syria. King Hussein's photograph (this was before he died), though ever-present, was not plastered all over shop windows and car windshields to nearly the degree that Assad's was in Syria. Nor were there squares dominated by statues and billboards of the head of state. Despite the warnings of academics and journalists about the fragility of Jordan's monarchy, what I saw was a dynasty far more certain of itself than the one in Syria.

※ ※

"What you see in Jordan is a system created by small-business people; what you saw in Syria is a system created by worse-than-third-rate intellectuals," explained Kamal Salibi, retired professor of history at the AUB and director of the Royal Institute for Interfaith Studies. Salibi, the author of numerous books on Arab history, was soft-spoken and introspective as he helped me understand what I had seen so far in my Turkish and Arab travels.

Jordan, Salibi said, had developed without recourse to ideology, because of the royal family's reliance on the Bedouin and the merchant community. Assad's Syria was the brainchild of the Ba'athist ideology that had been hammered out during World War II by two half-educated members of the Damascene lower middle class, one Christian and the other Moslem: Michel Aflaq and Salah al-Din Bitar. Ba'athist ideology was a concoction of Arab nationalism, the Marxism that Aflaq had picked up as a student in Paris, and "German theories of a romantic and idealistic nationalism" that he had embraced in the late 1930s, during the Nazi era.[2] By the 1960s, it was such people as Aflaq and Bitar, not the merchants or the Ottoman- and French Mandate–era notables, who were influencing military officers like Assad. What the French scholar Olivier Roy writes about educated Islamic fundamentalists applies as well to these secular Ba'athists: Because their own societies had ignored these bookish sons of the lower middle classes, they resented their proletarian status and dreamt of a revolution and a "new, strong, centralized state."[3]

Salibi believed that Moslem fundamentalism would eventually prove an even greater failure than secular Ba'athism. "Islam does not have the mass following that even Arab nationalism had, because it is less ambiguous," he explained. "The masses want something foggy. They don't want to be pinned down, and no one, ultimately, wants to be ruled by someone else speaking in the name of God. That is why throughout history so many dissident sects have sprouted in the Middle East."

Salibi did not believe that Assad's regime was sustainable. "The only long-term unity that Syria has known has come under the imperial rule of Persians, Seleucids, Mamluks, and Ottomans. Today's Syria had consisted of six Mamluk provinces and three Ottoman *wilayets*. Aleppo was always oriented toward Iraq, and Damascus toward Egypt and Arabia. These were the reasons for the failure of democratic elections and the military regimes in the 1940s and 1950s in Syria. Syria is ungovernable without coercion," Salibi went on. "It needs a god in the sense of an ideology that goes beyond its borders, like Arab nationalism or fundamentalism—ideas that have failed. But because Syria is undeveloped politically, its people are susceptible to such ideologies. Perhaps only the business community can provide an avenue for civil society in such a place, because it cuts across clan lines." Salibi said that civil society could develop in places like Syria and Iraq only through a new military regime, representing the bourgeoisie, which would hold the state together while beginning the process of reform. This is exactly what Zhelyu Zhelev, the first post-Communist president of Bulgaria, had told me should have happened in the former Warsaw Pact states after the collapse of communism had the West not won the clear victory that it did in the Cold War, with overnight parliamentary government the consequence.

Salibi called Jordan "a nice accident of history." Had the French not been given control of Syria following World War I, leaving the British in 1921 to give the desolate east bank of the Jordan River to their wartime ally, the emir Abdullah, as a consolation prize, this puzzle piece of a country would have been divided among Syria, Palestine, and Iraq. Jordan may have been artificial, but Abdullah's family was not without legitimacy. Abdullah was the son of Hussein ibn-Ali, the grand sharif of Mecca, the thirty-seventh in a direct line of descent from the prophet Mohammed and a member of the Hashemite family of western Arabia, an area known as the Hejaz. The Hashemites were the traditional keepers of the Moslem holy places in Mecca and Medina. Moreover, it was Hussein and his sons—Abdullah, Ali, Feisal, and Zaid—who, with the support of British officers, including Lawrence of Arabia, initiated the World War I Arab Revolt against the crumbling Ottoman Turkish empire. Hussein's family was ill rewarded for its efforts. Syria and Lebanon became French Mandates; Ibn Saud and his Wahabi warriors threw the Hashemites out of the Hejaz in 1926, in the process of creating Saudi Arabia; and most of Palestine became a Jewish state. While Abdullah's brother Feisal was made king of Iraq, the Hashemite dynasty there was toppled in 1958, in the first of three military coups that led to Saddam Hussein's dictatorship. Jordan is all that is left of the Hashemites' World War I patrimony. In 1951, on the Temple Mount in Jerusalem, an Arab extremist assassinated Abdullah in the presence of his fifteen-year-old grandson, Hussein, who two years later ascended to the throne when Hussein's father, Talal, was declared emotionally unfit for office.

"The Jordanian royals," Salibi told me, "have real discipline. They ruled Hejaz for centuries before ruling Jordan. Both King Abdullah and King Hussein have been wise enough to tolerate an opposition and a real parliament yet tough enough to use coercion periodically to reset the rules of the game when things get out of hand." Thus, King Hussein brutally suppressed the Palestine Liberation Organization in 1970 and 1971, when the PLO threatened to topple the monarchy. He limited parliament's power after Moslem fundamentalists won the 1989 elections. And in 1998 he prevented parliament from undoing the 1994 peace treaty with Israel.

"The state of Jordan as it exists today is the creation of King Hussein," Salibi explained. "He has nurtured the commercial classes and the professional associations, and created modern bureaucratic institutions. And because he never killed or jailed ex-ministers, as Assad and his predecessors did in Syria, there is a large community of ex-cabinet ministers—with their own businesses and think tanks, all a vital part of the governing elite—who have a vested interest in the survival of the monarchy." I told Salibi what Gaetano Mosca, the early-twentieth-century Italian political theorist, had said: that if "the ruling class is soundly organized" around "many material interests" and is not morally or intellectually "feeble," it can resist "becoming a plaything of some . . . universal religion or doctrine," such as Islamic fundamentalism or Arab nationalism.[4]

Salibi did not believe that either kind of universalism would succeed. He imagined instead something quite different: "World War I, the collapse of the Ottoman empire, the Holocaust—a whole string of extraordinary, unrepeatable events created Israel and the Arab state system. But the future might have more parallels to ancient and medieval history." The current state system, with its political nerve centers at Damascus, Baghdad, and Cairo, mirrored the competition among the medieval Omayyad, Abbasid, and Fatimid caliphates, based, respectively, in those cities—a network of city-states linked by trade routes. The passing of the Industrial Revolution and strong states could herald a period of smaller wars and migrations and cultural invasions typical of the ancient world. It was even possible, I supposed, that the disintegration of Iraq into something resembling the former Ottoman Turkish provinces of Kurdish Mosul in the north, Sunni Baghdad in the center, and Shi'ite Basra in the south, following Saddam Hussein's demise, could lead to the revival of strong Hashemite influence in Sunni Baghdad for the first time since 1958, when military officers toppled King Hussein's second cousin King Feisal II. As for Israel, it could play a role similar to that of Jewish communities in the Middle East in medieval times: economic mediator between rival tribes and moving centers of power.

I asked Salibi if there was a historical basis for Jordan's de facto alliance with Turkey and Israel against Syria. "In Jordan there is an inoperative nostalgia for the Ottomans," he said. Syria and Bulgaria shared long land borders with Ottoman Turkey, and felt the full weight of its oppression. But the Hashemites, as keepers of the holy places during the sultan's rule, had a more agreeable experience under the Ottomans. From 1893 to 1908, the emir Hussein and his sons, including Abdullah, lived pleasantly in a villa overlooking the Bosporus in Istanbul, in compulsory exile ordered by Sultan Abdul Hamid II. Because Hussein and his family had begun the Arab Revolt against the Turks and succeeded, they felt less insecure about Turkey than other Arabs. In 1926, when the last Ottoman sultan, Vahdettin, died destitute in his San Remo exile, the emir Hussein's family in Hejaz helped pay for his burial. Many prominent Jordanian families, including that of ex-prime minister Zaid Rifai, are descendants of Ottoman bureaucrats who were posted here. Prince Hassan, King Hussein's brother, spoke Turkish.

I left Salibi's office thinking that while the future is always unknowable, history is still the best guide to what lies ahead. But that evening as I walked in Amman, I sensed how unpredictable history could be. The day the twentieth century began, Amman had been a dusty village, without prospects, in the desert outback of the Ottoman empire, little different from other villages in the region. But now I was walking along streets lined with grand villas, embassies, and ambassadorial residences, alongside fine restaurants and flower shops. As I thought of the sequence of events that had created this situation, I was awestruck.

❧ ❧

Amman was once a caravan city, like ancient Palmyra and Petra, and now was one again. Syrians, Iraqis, and Saudis drive long distances or fly in to buy goods and to find consulting, public relations, insurance, and other services. Jordan flourishes as a middleman economy with few natural resources; its middle class is proportionately larger than that of any neighboring Arab state. Present-day Amman, as ancient Palmyra and Petra did, depends on trade routes and the conditions along them. The Jordanian economist Fahed Fanek told me that the lifting of sanctions on Iraq could boost Jordan's gross domestic product by as much as 10 percent—not just because of increased trade, but also because Iraq's 23 million people would need the know-how available in Amman to rebuild their shattered nation.

Jordan is essentially a city-state linked by trade routes to other commercial oases. Almost 40 percent of the population lives along the Irbid-Zarqa-Amman corridor, extending from the Syrian border south to the capital. But Irbid, along with such towns as Ma'an in southern Jordan, has been important only in the negative sense. Occasionally, riots erupt in these towns, tied to economic causes, rousing officials in Amman to action.

§§ §§

One hundred and twenty-five miles to the south of Amman lies Petra (a "rock" in Greek), which from the fourth century B.C. through the first century A.D. was the capital of the Nabateans, a western-Arabian tribe that controlled trade routes as far north as Syria and which succumbed to Rome only after an ill-fated alliance with Rome's local enemy, the Parthians. In 1976, I hired a horse for a fee of five dollars, and rode through a high, narrow gorge called the *siq,* at the end of which was a stunning view of the Khazneh, the Nabatean Treasury, its classical facade cut from solid rock in Hellenistic-Roman style. It was the most dramatic building in Petra, whose other rock-carved ruins beckoned nearby. I slept on the floor of the Khazneh that night, and will always remember the silence and the absence of other travelers. The 1994 peace treaty with Israel had brought mass tourism to Petra, with a Mövenpick hotel and entrance to the *siq* now costing $60, so on this visit I struck east from Amman, rather than south, into a desert littered with early-medieval Arab forts.

Amman had grown so much that the eastern suburbs seemed never to end. When they did, I saw nothing but endless, featureless horizons and hard-packed, grayish sand strewn with black basalt gravel and boulders. The Hashemite kingdom of Jordan had now been reduced to a road and the telephone and power lines running beside it. Forty miles east of Amman, we came to a square edifice with round buttresses at the corners and crude slits in the walls. Its stark design and lonely prospect gave it an aura of great strength. This was the Qasr (Fort) of al-Kharaneh. An inscription indicates it was built in A.D. 710, making it perhaps the earliest such fort of the Islamic era. Nothing grew on the flat, dry plain. The guard on duty pointed directly south and announced, "Hejaz," indicating a region deep in Saudi Arabia, three hundred miles away, with nothing but desert in between.

Continuing east, I passed a stream of trucks and orange-and-white taxis, all with Iraqi license plates, heading toward Amman from Baghdad. Jordan was the only legal outlet for sanction-starved Iraq.

Ten miles from Qasr al-Kharaneh we came upon another fort: a babel of conical roofs and turrets surrounding a small dome. This was Qasr Amra, a fort occupied by the Omayyads, history's first Islamic dynasty. In the mid-seventh century, Islam was just beginning to develop its own material culture. Instead of the austere, geometric abstractions that later became associated with Islamic art, the early Omayyad buildings such as Qasr Amra reflect the sensuous legacy of Greek, Roman-Byzantine, and Persian styles. The frescoed interior of the poorly lit Amra recalled a Byzantine church.

Mysterious faces seemed to emerge from the fog of time. During World War I, T. E. Lawrence came here with some fellow Englishmen. In *Seven Pillars of Wisdom,* he writes: "They asked me with astonishment who were these Kings of Ghassan with the unfamiliar halls and pictures. I could tell them vague tales of their poetry, and cruel wars: but it seemed so distant and tinselled an age."[5] Given the nude depictions and the portrait of a Byzantine emperor and Christ Pantocrator under the dome, this fort may have been built and painted by the Ghassanids, a pagan Arab dynasty and ally of Christian Byzantium against Persia that was later overthrown by the Omayyads, who seized the fort, using it as a pleasure palace for their hunting expeditions.

My ruminations were interrupted by two busloads of Italian tourists snapping flash pictures, too busy checking light meters and switching lenses to pay attention to their guide's lecture. In Tyre, I had been alone amid the ruins thanks to the war between Israel and Hezbollah, but here the peace treaty made contemplative travel much harder.

Azrak lay fifteen miles farther east, sixty-five miles from Amman, a sprawling, dusty oasis and truck stop at the northern entrance of Wadi

Sirhan, a main communications artery to the Arabian peninsula since the time of the Nabateans, two thousand years ago. The black basalt fort, now a jumble of massive stones felled by an earthquake in 1927, lies along the busy main road. Though the fort dates from the thirteenth century (built by Saladin's forces during the Crusades), the Greek and Latin inscriptions reveal that it had been a military site since the time of the Roman emperor Diocletian, around A.D. 300, and was used subsequently by the Byzantine-allied Ghassanids, Omayyads, and Ottoman Turks. Lawrence lived in the fort for a time during World War I, using it as a base for raids against the Turkish rail line to the west. He wrote of Azrak's "unfathomable silence" and "shining pools."[6] Now there was the rumble of trucks and cars beside the ragged palms, dull with soot and dust. But Azrak was still what it had been since the time of Diocletian: an important oasis that reflected the power relationships among the settlements situated along the arteries of trade, migration, and pilgrimage.

To wit: a mile from the fort stood a restaurant with the usual vinyl tablecloths, prints of alpine meadows, and Koranic inscriptions over the entrance to small prayer rooms alongside the dining hall. The onions, grilled meat, hummus, and cardamom-flavored coffee were excellent. The tables were crowded with Shi'ite pilgrims, who had arrived in buses and car caravans, the men in immaculate white robes, the women hidden beneath black tents, carrying plastic buckets for washing. These pilgrims were en route from eastern Saudi Arabia to Amman—a distance of nearly a thousand miles—seeking special entry permits from the Iraqi embassy in Jordan to drive back across the desert to the Shi'ite holy sites of Najaf and Kerbala in central Iraq. Azrak, in other words, was a booming gateway to Saddam's Iraq. Indeed, the rise and fall of Roman emperors, medieval caliphs, Turkish garrisons, and modern Arab dictators have all been registered by the amount and type of traffic through this desert, where, because of the relative absence of oil and people, the ground is merely strategic.

※ ※

In a few hours I was back in Amman, which I would leave again the next day by crowded minibus for Zarqa, half an hour northeast of the

Jordanian capital, through an endless stretch of new housing and construction. Zarqa was an army base, a parking lot for Iraq-bound trucks, a Palestinian refugee camp, and a charmless working-class city of half a million Arabs and Circassians (a Moslem people from the north Caucasus). I saw donkeys and sheep grazing alongside apartment buildings. Zarqa's downtown was packed with sweets shops, juice stands, and stores offering cheap polyester clothes, plastic combs and brushes, hardware equipment, shoe repair kits, and spare auto parts. I noticed many more beards and head scarves here than in Amman, and many men in shoes with missing laces. Everywhere along the endless and treeless concrete I saw groups of teenage boys hanging about. In the upscale section of Amman where I was staying, it was usual to see people count dinars; here, they counted fils, of which 1,000 equals a dinar, or $1.40. Zarqa, I thought, was a good place to think about the future of Jordan and Greater Syria.

Seventy-five percent of Jordanians live in places like Zarqa.[7] Since mounting water shortages will curtail irrigation for farming, these places will grow as rural migrants pour in. As the Jordanian economy has lagged behind population growth, per capita income here has dropped from $1,800 in 1982 to $1,650 in 1998. Unemployment has hovered around 20 percent for a decade. Still, relatives help each other to a degree uncommon in the West: three quarters of Jordanian households have family close by. Also, public services like health care and schooling are better in Jordan than elsewhere in the non–oil producing Arab world: 85 percent of government employees work in health or education.[8] But the monarchy will be unable to sustain this level of spending, or prevent more joblessness by employing half the workforce, as it does now.

"People are used to being bribed by the government, but the cash is running out," one Jordanian expert told me, so the divide between rich and poor deepens. Though per capita income in Israel is nearly ten times higher than in Jordan, I saw more Mercedeses and other high-performance cars in Amman than I would see in all of Israel. Jordan appeared stable only in comparison to Arab states such as Syria and Iraq. Throughout the Arab world, in fact, the warlords of demography and resource scarcity were on the march, with populations in the individual countries doubling about every generation—40 percent of all Arabs were fourteen years old or younger—while per capita water supply was projected to drop by half between 1995 and 2025.[9]

"Young people here are being exposed to new ideas and ideologies, good and bad, and they have no allegiances," Abdullah Hasanat, the executive editor of the English-language *Jordan Times,* told me. "There is a lot of grumbling, even among the children of the ruling families. It will take a great deal of acumen for regimes to handle such complex societies." In Zarqa, dense with young men who seemingly had little to do, I speculated that democratization might be inevitable, but rather than bring civil society, it could herald many disease variants of democracy in a part of the world where populations were not prepared for parliamentary systems, with the self-restraint that such systems demanded of the citizenry. Democratization in the former Yugoslavia in the early 1990s had led to tyrannical majorities preying upon minorities. In the Arab Middle East, democratization could lead to the ethnic cleansing of Christians, as it did of Moslems in Bosnia.[10] Jordan and the Arab world are demographically dominated by youth, for whom educational and employment opportunities are increasingly inadequate. For young people who live in these societies, where the marriage age is rising because money for dowries is short, a rigid interpretation of Islam justifies their sexual frustration.[11] In societies riven by extreme economic divides, where sexual pleasure is reserved for those with money, poor youth may be able to find gratification only within religion.

Religious tolerance and the protection of minorities, therefore, may fare better under continued dictatorship. Christians in Syria are probably safer with Assad's heterodox Alawite regime, however brutal, than under one dominated by the Sunni Moslem majority, whether elected or not. As for Jordan, Moslem fundamentalists are heavily represented in the democratic parliament, which is kept in check by the royal family.

The Palestinian issue illustrates the radicalizing effects of uneven economic development. The uprising against Israeli rule, or Intifada, that began in December 1987 and continued sporadically through the 1990s was a revolution of rising expectations. Palestinian youth who exploded into the streets of Gaza and the West Bank were not envious of their fellow Arabs in Jordan or Syria—who, in many cases, were

even poorer and less free than themselves—but of middle-class Israelis, whom they encountered en route to their jobs as manual laborers and whose lifestyle was known to them through television. When
Palestinian peasants left the land to enter the Israeli labor market in the
1970s and 1980s, they removed themselves from the control of the old
families and notables.[12] It was this newly freed and radicalized urban
lower middle class that generated the Intifada. Though Palestinians
comprise roughly half of Jordan's population, they have only fourteen
out of eighty seats in parliament and are represented in only a handful
of the thirty government ministries. Ninety percent of rural Bedouin
voted in Jordan's 1997 parliamentary elections, but only 25 percent
turned out in the cities, as urban Palestinians protested by not vot-
ing. Because of the higher Palestinian birthrate, Jordan's twenty-first-
century city-state could be 85 percent Palestinian, according to experts.
But less, not more, liberalization will prevent a Jordanian Intifada: Security services here operate with less media scrutiny than in Israel,
where the Intifada required a degree of freedom that is absent in Jordan.

A free labor market in a peaceful, borderless Middle East might
reduce such pent-up pressures on individual states. As a Palestinian
friend in Amman told me, "In the 1940s, whenever my parents got
bored, they would travel from Jaffa to Haifa, to Beirut, to Damascus,
or to Cairo. Afterward, the Arab nationalists created passports and
hard borders and new dialects of Arabic for each state, and now we are
all in our prisons." But there is something else to consider. An Israeli-
Palestinian peace treaty, by creating a new and volatile state on the West
Bank, could lead to the end of Hashemite Jordan if the West Bank
Palestinians were to combine with the urban Palestinians on the East
Bank to overwhelm Jordan's Bedouin monarchy. Peace treaties are
simply agreements among elites who, whether Israelis or Arabs, all
speak English and often belong to the same global aristocracy. The
problem is the political, demographic, and social forces that such
treaties set in motion, which take years to mature and which the masses
control.

※ ※

The Hashemite royal family has survived here since 1921, when Abdullah became ruler of Transjordan (later Jordan), making Jordan's the

longest surviving regime in the region. In 1998, almost 90 percent of Jordanians had been born during King Hussein's reign. Hashemite Jordan, like ancient Palmyra and Petra, is a place through which goods, services, and ideas pass. No individual symbolizes Jordan's cosmopolitanism better than Prince Hassan, the heir to the throne until he was replaced suddenly by King Hussein's eldest son, Abdullah (named after Hussein's grandfather), who became king when Hussein died of cancer in 1999.[13]

The palace in Amman is an understated affair: a series of venerable stone buildings adorned with royal emblems that seem like a British heirloom. Here there is an open reliance on tradition rather than ideology. "When my grandfather Abdullah became king here, we had already been ruling Hejaz for centuries," Prince Hassan told me. "I like to think we are a traditional totalitarian regime that is evolving toward democracy. But in the West, the definition of democracy is too legalistic. Tribes and clans can be democratic in their own ways. I believe in a shift of emphasis from *civitas*—political communities—to *humanitas*. Helping refugees and street children, that is *humanitas*. Working against anti-Semitism and western Islamophobia, that too is *humanitas*."

The prince had a booming voice that filled his modest office. He was a tense man, and gripped a nearby phone cord as we spoke. I told him that I had little interest in discussing current politics—the peace talks with Israel and so forth. Rather, I was interested in the past in relation to the future. "Who reads history nowadays!" Hassan exclaimed in frustration. "The media have amnesia. There is too little historical thinking, too much reliance on intellectual fads rather than on tradition." He went on: "Every night I try to read from the historical records of my family, and I am struck by the similarity between the late nineteenth and early twentieth centuries and now. Winston Churchill is discussing the Kurdish issue in northern Iraq. . . . Churchill and other colonial officials like Gertrude Bell are creating new states on the map the way oil company officials are now drawing new pipeline routes. The West still sees the Middle East in terms of strategy and energy resources. There is not the sense of selfless mission, based on Enlightenment principles, with which the West now approaches Eastern Europe. Yet Ba'athism has done to Syria and Iraq what communism did to those countries." Hassan called Ba'athism "an intellectual fad that evolved into Sunni Arab racism against Christians and Jews, leaving a dangerous void."

"How permanent are countries like Syria and Iraq?" I asked.

"Let's meet here in ten years and we'll see," the prince said, grimacing. "But I agree totally—it is an artificial situation. The state system could collapse and we'd have a balkanized Middle East with ethnic-sectarian conflict. We are still dealing with the breakup of the Ottoman empire without the merits of the Ottoman empire, such as the *millet* system," in which religious minorities were self-governing "nations" under the sultan's protection. Another merit of the Ottoman system the prince mentioned was the caliphate, the religious authority in which "all schools of *sunna* [tradition] were represented." Hassan explained that "the destruction of the caliphate upon the collapse of the Ottoman empire removed legitimacy from daily Moslem tradition, creating a vacuum, which extremists have filled. But centrist Islam is still in demand," he said, "and moderates must concentrate on the *fatwa* [formal legal opinions] in order to enter the debate. We, the Turks, and others can create a modern Islamic tradition similar in concept to that of the Christian Democrats in Europe."

Hassan said that the Middle East required a "breadth of freedom" that was a "pluralistic hybrid" between Western and Eastern regimes. He worried, though, that a new generation of Western leaders lacked both the interest and the historical wisdom to help his family achieve that aim.

17

CROSSING THE JORDAN

Leopold Weiss, the grandson of a rabbi, was born in Lvov, Poland, in 1900. In 1922, he went to Palestine to visit an uncle who was a psychiatrist at a Jewish hospital in Jerusalem. From Jerusalem, Weiss traveled through North Africa and Arabia, where he became attracted to the Arabs' desert life. He converted to Islam, changed his name to Muhammad Asad, married an Arab woman, and made the holy pilgrimage to Mecca. Besides being among the few Westerners to visit Mecca and Medina, Asad was also among the early-twentieth-century explorers of the Arabian and Libyan deserts. He was befriended by King Abdul Aziz Ibn Saud of Saudi Arabia, becoming one of the king's envoys and troubleshooters. Asad also helped set up the modern world's first Islamic state, Pakistan, which he represented as its minister plenipotentiary to the United Nations. For a decade after Asad had converted to Islam, his father refused contact with him. But in 1935 the two began exchanging letters. The correspondence continued until 1942, when the Nazis sent Asad's father and sister to a concentration camp, where they both perished.

In his autobiography, *The Road to Mecca,* Asad looks to Abraham, the forefather of the Jews, for understanding:

"That early ancestor of mine whom God had driven toward unknown spaces and so to a discovery of his own self, would have well understood why I am here [in Arabia]—for he also had to wander through many lands before he could build his life into something that you might grasp with your hands, and had to be a guest at many strange hearths before he was allowed to strike root. To his awe-commanding experience my puny perplexity would have been no riddle."[1]

Asad, who, looked back on his Jewish childhood as "happy" and "satisfying," was the ultimate free man, negating and reinventing himself, and thus full of contradictions. I was attracted to Asad's autobiography because of the contradictions in my own life.

In the 1970s, when I was in my twenties, I traveled throughout Islamic North Africa and the Middle East, settling in Israel, where I served in the military. In Israel, finding life among people of my own faith claustrophobic, I rediscovered my Americanness. What I took away from Israel was not Zionism so much as realism: While Israel's security phobia might at times seem extreme, life in Israel taught me that the liberal-humanist tendency to see politics predominantly in moral terms could be no less so. In Israel, I often met foreign journalists who demanded absolute justice for the Palestinians and talked constantly about morality in politics, which in practice meant that anyone who disagreed with them was "immoral." *You couldn't argue with these people.* Meanwhile, my right-wing neighbors in a poor, Oriental part of Jewish Jerusalem sought absolute security. You couldn't argue with them, either, but at least their arguments were grounded in concrete self-interest and not in absolute moral terms. (A confidant of King Hussein and Prince Hassan told me that the reason the two men had trusted Yitzhak Rabin so much was that he always framed his arguments for peace in terms of Israel's military self-interest rather than morality.) Self-interest at its healthiest implicitly recognizes the self-interest of others, and therein lies the possibility of compromise. A rigid moral position admits few compromises. This is some of what I took away from Israel.

Two days after finishing my military service in Israel, I flew to the Balkans to resume my career as a journalist. Within weeks I was back in the Arab world, traveling in Syria, Iraq, Algeria, and so forth throughout the 1980s, without revealing my Israeli experience. As I had learned from the foreign correspondents I met in Israel, being an outsider is easy and thus I enjoyed the Arab world, just as I did the Balkans. But in Israel, though my Hebrew was now very rusty, I would never be completely an outsider. And so my feelings were mixed on my last night in Amman before I would cross the border into Israel. There, I would be less a traveler than someone returning to a former home.

※ ※

To get from Jordan to Israel, I took an early-morning bus from Amman north to Irbid. The town of Irbid was a summation of what I had experienced the previous weeks in the Arab world. As in many places in Jordan, the sidewalks and other public spaces were clean. But there were few trees, the streets were dominated by men in drab clothes, boys carried trays of coffee and tea into offices, and the bus station was a jumble of produce stands amid lines of vehicles departing at no particular time—no disadvantage for me, since this was a traditional society, where strangers were immediately helped. Irbid lay almost twenty miles east of the Jordan River, the border with Israel. Though the bus station was busy, I was the only person traveling to the border, so I had to take a private taxi for the equivalent of $15.

The Jordan River Valley is part of a deep rift in the earth's surface that stretches from Syria to East Africa. The descent to the Jordan from the biscuit-brown tableland of Irbid was dramatic. The temperature rose steadily as we neared the hazy ribbon of green fields along the river, where, on the other side, the mountains rise just as steeply as they do in Jordan. Occasionally, I noticed a faded sign announcing JORDAN VALLEY CROSSING: There was never a mention of Israel. The road was lined, as roads so often were in the Arab world, with dusty garages, rickety fruit stands, and small groups of young men talking and smoking. The border post was a series of old cargo containers in an empty lot, housing offices for customs, passport inspection, currency exchange, and other formalities. Now four years old, it looked sleepy and temporary. My bags were not inspected, and it took a few seconds to have my passport stamped. The only official way of knowing that Israel lay about a hundred feet away was at the currency-exchange office, where I changed my dinars for Israeli shekels.

I was not allowed to cross by foot. I was told to enter an empty bus whose engine was running. Soon, two elderly Arabs in suits and ties took nearby seats. Then came another passenger, with dirty, baggy jeans, wearing a short beard and a yarmulke and carrying an old brief-case. He may have been coming from one of the Israeli factories that had opened recently in Irbid. A burly fellow, he was both brusque and alert and did not nod to me as the two Arabs had done. There were no other passengers. The driver took his seat, and the bus headed toward the bridge.

The Jordan River here is an immaculate blue, all the more precious because it is so narrow. On the opposite bank lies a landscaped park of grass and palms separating the traffic lanes—like a traffic island any-where in the West, but a small wonder after the bleak, dust-strewn public spaces of the Arab world and many parts of Turkey. The bus stopped beside two young men in Timberland shirts only partly tucked into their jeans, to make room for the handguns at their sides. Their bad crew cuts and roving eyes suggested that they didn't see themselves as heroes in an action movie playing inside their heads—as do so many se-curity men I have encountered in other countries. They boarded the bus and glanced at our passports, then asked me to step outside with them.

The awkward concision of Hebrew—a modern vernacular only a century old—struck me as poignant after the elaborate Turkish and Arabic I had grown used to. My conversation with the two security agents slipped between Hebrew and English. They had no interest in my whereabouts in the Arab world. They simply wanted to run a test on an immigration officer who had started work that day. They handed me the Israeli passport of an Arab—commonplace, since many Israeli Arabs live nearby in the Galilee. The passport was phony, they told me, but because the photograph in it vaguely resembled me, would I try to make it past immigration with this passport?

"Where will my American passport be?" I asked.

"In my back pocket," one of them said. "Don't worry. I'll be a few feet away from you. I will never be out of your sight."

"Fine," I said. Israelis often ran security checks.

The immigration hall, with a luggage X-ray machine, resembled any small air terminal in the U.S. I handed the passport to a uniformed officer, a woman in her early twenties. She looked at it for about ten seconds, then, without even glancing at my face or asking me a question, walked over to the security agent and slapped the passport reproachfully on his chest. They smiled at each other, and he gave me back my real passport.

Leaving the immigration building, I found a small bus-and-taxi terminal with a new sidewalk and benches, tourist maps, phone booths, and a bank. The bank teller looked up from her paperback book just long enough to change my money. When I asked her where I could purchase a long-distance phone card, she snapped, "There," motioning with her raised eyebrow at a modern kiosk across the paved road. Because nobody was hanging about, the public spaces around me seemed vast. Nobody here had time for strangers. In *East Is West*, Freya Stark quotes a British official in Transjordan as saying, "Years of Arab courtesy spoil us for the rough and tumble of the Western World." Though such a statement could mask an untoward political sympathy (as it did in her case), it was nevertheless true.

With the phone card, I called a friend who lived in the central Galilee. He told me to take a taxi to the bus station in Bet She'an, a few minutes away to the west, where he would pick me up. On the way to Bet She'an, I noticed signs facing the other direction, announcing the PEACE BRIDGE and JORDAN. The peace treaty and open border that Jordanian road signs try to conceal, Israel celebrates.

※ ※

Bet She'an is one of the few places in Israel that have not benefited from the massive Russian immigration, the liberalization of the economy, the computer software, and the cell phones that changed society here in the late 1980s and early 1990s. Bet She'an's bus station recalled the same depressing development town, inhabited largely by Moroccan Jews, that I had known in the 1970s. The problem was cronyism: Bet She'an was testimony to the political failure of David Levy, the town's favorite son and Israeli foreign minister in various governments. Levy's family-based political machine did not lure investors, who chose other towns, also with high percentages of Oriental (Sephardic) Jews, that have since boomed. The first test of politics is to help your constituents, but Bet She'an has little to show for Levy's presence in Israeli cabinets for two decades.

Inside the bus station, I seated myself in a crude plastic chair at a café in the shopping arcade to await my friend. The modern arcade was cheaply constructed, with bubble-gum dispensers, plastic garbage receptacles, and self-service food counters. Discarded machine-printed receipts littered the plastic tables. I saw many people walking alone, rushing somewhere. Several soldiers and civilians were sitting by themselves, reading newspapers. Unlike armed soldiers' in other Middle Eastern countries, their assault rifles were pointed downward, with the safety latches on. The soldiers seemed middle-class: like the quietly polite children I had seen in Damascus's prosperous Abu Roumaneh neighborhood. For all the blather about Israel's invincible military, the fact is that for years it had been evolving into an army of suburban kids who just wanted to get home safely, while the Palestinians who came with Yasser Arafat from abroad to the casbahs of Nablus and Hebron are often veterans of the Lebanese civil war. That's one reason why Israel will have to give up the West Bank: It can't win an urban war there.

Except for the soldiers—whose homes were located throughout Israel and who were merely changing buses here—the locals were a graceless working-class lot, not at all as sophisticated as the wealthier Arabs I had seen in Beirut and Amman or as dignified as the poorer ones in Amman's downtown souk. I saw men with ragged, long hair, earrings, and garish T-shirts and women in athletic shorts and hair rollers, who chewed gum and carried bags of food. People of both sexes wore baseball hats, some of them backward. As in Syria, Lebanon, and Jordan, falafel and pita-bread sandwiches were on sale. But here, there were few employees at the counters, and you helped yourself to the pickles, peppers, and other condiments: This was a Western economy, without the child labor and double-digit unemployment of the non–oil producing Arab world, and as Israelis never tired of telling me, "We are picky. We don't trust someone else to fill our falafel sandwiches."

While Americans who fly directly to Israel find a more cohesive, ethnic society than the one they know in the United States, I felt a certain loneliness and alienation here, compared to the traditional societies over the border. Even the most westernizing places in Turkey appeared less rootless than Bet She'an, whose bus station I could almost have mistaken for one in a fast-buck Mexican border town. Social and economic dynamism is often ugly; fine gardens and graceful speech require years of tradition and elaboration.

My friend Mitch arrived and led me to his car for the drive north along the Jordan River Valley to the Sea of Galilee, from where we would climb into the hills westward to his home in Zippori, a village halfway between the Sea of Galilee and the Mediterranean. Mitch, who had served in the paratroops and in the information office during his military service, had left Jerusalem some years ago to renovate an abandoned Arab house in the Galilee. He spoke Arabic, and had hired some Israeli Arabs from nearby Nazareth. Together, they fixed up the house, installed a well and septic system, landscaped several acres, then built four vacation homes for tourists—mainly, young Israeli couples from Tel Aviv seeking a romantic weekend in the countryside. Mitch's politics were right of center, yet he shopped and rented videos in Arab Nazareth, bought his construction materials there, and used a local Arab provider for Internet access. Mitch's children were born in Nazareth's Protestant hospital. He was one of my oldest friends, among the best-read, most perceptive people I know. He never went to college. Instead, he spent several years traveling.

I glimpsed a roadside landscape of bicycle paths, flower gardens, reforested hills, fish-breeding ponds, and prefabricated farm sheds and subdivisions, which seemed deserted during the middle of the workday. All the while, Mitch talked nonstop about Israel, revealing changes that the international media—concerned mainly with the peace process and Israeli party politics—had not prepared me for: Israel was no less an undiscovered country than the others in the region. Among the things Mitch told me were the following, confirmed by Israeli newspapers I read and interviews I later conducted:

- Israel's military reserve system was weakening. According to myth, Israel had a small regular army to hold off Arab invaders for forty-eight hours, enough time to mobilize its citizen army of reservists. But accounts of the 1973 war revealed that many reserve units had performed poorly. The 1973 war was followed by a mini-baby boom when the war's veterans returned home, so in the early 1990s, the military was overwhelmed not only with new immigrants from a collapsing Soviet Union but with a relatively large number of eighteen-year-old recruits. Thus the number of useful positions for older reservists decreased. Finally, there came the liberation of the Israeli economy from its socialist constraints, the result of pressure and advice from American secretary of state George Shultz, an economist by training. Until that time, the number of reservists who were private entrepreneurs—and whose businesses would consequently suffer in their absence—had been small enough so that they could work out their own arrangements with the military. Now, so many Israelis were entrepreneurs that missing reserve duty had become commonplace. However—in an age of high-tech warfare and relatively high population growth, because of Jewish immigration from the ex-Communist world—the military did not need many of these aging men. For example, though Mitch had just received a notice from the army spokesman's office to report for a day of reserve duty in southern Lebanon, his commander phoned to ask him not to appear: The bus seated only fifty-five reservists, and eighty had been called up—more than had been anticipated. The commander was trying to reduce the number. A former Israeli general told me that in the future, the military draft here would continue "for cultural reasons only," because Israel required a more cohesive society than America's. But in terms of protection from surrounding Moslem states, a high-tech, high-paid volunteer force may ultimately be more efficient.

• The number of combat officers who were religious Jews had increased significantly. Now there were whole military units composed of graduates of *yeshivot hesder*—religious seminaries where study is combined with athletic and military training in a youth culture all its own. Elite military units had also attracted Russian and Ethiopian immigrants, who, though not always religious, were—like the yeshiva students—not part of the country's founding, secular-Ashkenazi establishment. But the most vibrant, antiestablishment force in Israel was Shas, an openly ethnic and sectarian political party representing religious Jews, predominantly Moroccan. Shas (a Hebrew acronym for *shisha sedarim,* the "six orders" of the Mishnah) illustrates that what Western experts call "corruption" is sometimes just an alternative power network that emerges when the official bureaucracy is unyielding, or too infirm to help the downtrodden. Some Shas cabinet ministers had been indicted: They looked and operated like Iranian *bazaaris,* yet they had established an education and social welfare network as impressive as those run by Hamas in Gaza and the Moslem Brotherhood in Egypt. Shas's shadowy grassroots system was a rebuke to David Levy's old-fashioned machine politics, which had delivered insufficient benefits to the Sephardim. Nor was Shas closed-minded regarding peace. Shas was willing to be part of any coalition, however hawkish or dovish, provided it got money for its religious schools and day-care centers. Religious-schooling was increasingly in demand in Israel as Zionist ideology weakened as the nation-building mission of secular schools declined, and as they faced more problems with drugs and delinquency.

• Foreign workers were another sign of Israel's increasingly complex, postmodern society. A kind of caste system had emerged, with Thai farmhands, Romanian construction workers, and Nigerian laborers doing low-paying work as Israelis felt increasingly uncomfortable with Palestinian labor. There were also South Lebanese working as hotel maids, and thousands of Jordanians who overstayed their visas and took off-the-books jobs. The Israeli economy, though it had stalled recently after years of sustained growth, was now rich enough to draw outside labor, regardless of regional politics.

• While the outside world hoped for Arab-Jewish cooperation, the most obvious sign of it—and one that Israelis incessantly spoke about—was car theft. Everyone I met in Israel either had had a car stolen or knew someone who did. Almost every parked car I saw, except for the old ones, had The Club or some sort of electronic tracking system. The problem had become so much a part of every-day life that it wasn't much reported overseas. Yet when a leading rabbi had his car stolen, a call to Arafat got it back. The Israeli security services apparently do not try to stop the thefts. According to one prevalent theory, the security services saw the business as a political concession to the Palestinians that also stimulated the Israeli economy, since it forced theft victims to purchase new cars. A name that arises in discussions of the unpleasant side of Israeli-Palestinian cooperation is that of Jibril Rajoub, a ruthless security czar for Arafat, who is helping the Israelis enforce the interim peace agreements and fight terrorism. Rajoub is Israel's Somoza—the former Nicaraguan dictator who helped the United States in Central America. Though the international media rarely mentioned him, I heard Rajoub's name often in Israel. He had spent a decade and a half in Israeli prisons, spoke fluent Hebrew, and had more influence with Arafat than more quotable Palestinians such as Abu Mazen, Saeb Erekat, Nabil Shaath, and Hannan Ashrawi. When I asked an Israeli intelligence officer if Rajoub might eventually replace Arafat, he replied: "Someone like Abu Mazen could initially replace Arafat. But if Abu Mazen, say, were killed or assassinated and the cruder element took over, I would not be totally surprised."

• Arab towns in the Galilee were in turmoil. The local elections that took place during my visit demonstrated the primacy not of ideas or even issues but of the increasing power of the old clans, the *hamoulas*. Intercommunal violence between Moslems and Christians was on the rise. One night in Nazareth, I saw that next door to the Church of the Annunciation, the Moslems had set up a makeshift mosque, using carpets and overhead blankets, from where they were blasting the Moslem call to prayer over a loud-speaker. The Moslems, claiming that a mosque had been part of the old Turkish barracks on the site, were threatening to build a new mosque with a minaret higher than the church, a focal point of international Christian pilgrimage. Nazareth, 90 percent Christian several decades ago, was now more than 60 percent Moslem, and that percentage was rising. The Israeli government was not anxious to help the Arab Christians: Israel's ties with Moslems in the Galilee were more important, and Christian groups worldwide (evangelicals excepted) have never been particularly supportive of Israel.

Nearing Mitch's home we passed through Hosha'aya, which resembled an upscale community in Southern California, with bougainvillea, security gates, and winding streets with speed bumps, lined with identical houses with red-tiled roofs and neat lawns. A few days later, I found myself stranded in Hosha'aya without a car. There were few people on the street in midday. When I managed to find some residents, they were all busy. Nobody knew where a public phone was or invited me into his home to use one. Everyone looked at once shy, preoccupied, annoyed, and suspicious. Finally, I found an Arab watchman who loaned me his cell phone. At such times, I was reminded that Israel's culture is a drastic, tactless expression of concreteness: of facts to replace other facts. Here the unsparing, gruesome details of the Holocaust are commemorated not abstractly but by, among other things, a security service, a military machine, and settlements such as Hosha'aya, whose significance is not that they are alluring or friendly—they often are not—but that they are *there*.

It was only midafternoon when I arrived at Mitch's house. I had left Amman at nine that morning for Irbid. Yet it seemed like ages ago.

18

SEPPHORIS AND

THE RENEWAL OF JUDAISM

The balcony of Mitch's house offered a prospect of serene harmony. A softly contoured hill dominated the view to the northeast, a valley to the north, and more hills in the distance to the northwest. The valley was the Bet Netofa, mentioned in the Talmud, where I could discern the remains of the old Roman road to the Mediterranean, the Via Maris. The hill rising several hundred feet over the valley to the northeast was the site of ancient Zippori—from *zippor,* the Hebrew word for "bird," because the town had sat "at the top of the mountain like a bird," in the words of the Babylonian Talmud.[1]

Now a national park, the hill had been continuously inhabited from the fifth century B.C. through Israel's War of Independence in 1948, when the population of the Arab village of Saffuriyeh fled en masse as the newly created Israel Defense Forces invaded. Many of the ten thousand Arabs went north to what became the Palestinian refugee camp of Ein Helweh, near the Lebanese port of Sidon. Mitch showed me a black-and-white photograph of Arab Saffuriyeh taken in 1945. It resembled many of the dun-colored, dusty, and treeless towns that I had just seen throughout Syria and Jordan. At mid-century a regular bus service had connected Saffuriyeh to Irbid, from where I had come the day before.

The Arab flight in 1948 left the hill unoccupied for the first time in over two millennia. But the following year, a moshav, a Jewish cooperative settlement, which included Mitch's property, was established immediately to the south of the great hill. Known in Greek and English (and therefore to classical scholars) as Sepphoris, the hill is testimony to the repeated invasions, infiltrations, and displacements that have lent the entire Middle East—and geographical Palestine in particular—its distinctive discontinuity compared to such long-settled civilizations as India and China.[2]

I mean "discontinuity" only in the grand sense: of Hittites replaced by Phrygians and Assyrians; Assyrians, by Medes and Babylonians; Byzantine Greeks, by Arabs; and Arabs, by Jews. For there is also much continuity in the history of ancient Sepphoris. Indeed, Sepphoris is a story of political and cultural compromise that is pertinent to the challenges facing Judaism today in Israel.

While Jerusalem was destroyed many times, Sepphoris has been continuously inhabited by Jews from at least the first century B.C. For that reason—and also because of the role that Sepphoris would play in medieval Judaism and in the written version of the oral law, known as the Mishnah—Sepphoris is the most popular archaeological site in Israel among Israelis themselves, though it is ignored by tourists and foreign travel writers, who focus instead on such places as Caesarea and Masada, whose connections to Judaism are either marginal, in the case of Caesarea, or brief, in the case of Masada.

Sepphoris first emerged from obscurity when Herod the Great fortified it with a royal palace.[3] Though the Syrian legate Varus destroyed Sepphoris upon Herod's death in 4 B.C., Herod's son, Herod Antipas, soon rebuilt the town, making it, according to the historian Josephus Flavius, the "ornament of all Galilee."[4] Josephus also writes that

> . . . the greatest cities of Galilee . . . were Sepphoris and . . . Tiberias; but Sepphoris, situated in the very midst of Galilee, and having many villages about it, and able with ease to have been bold and troublesome to the Romans, if they had so pleased,—yet did it resolve to continue faithful to those their masters . . .[5]

Because the Jews of Sepphoris collaborated with Rome, Jewish life here prospered long beyond the first century, producing books, such as the

Mishnah, which give Judaism its current riches. The Jews of Yodefat, nearby in the Galilee; the Jews of Jerusalem; and the Jewish zealots atop the rock of Masada in the Judaean Desert—all of whom resisted Rome—were utterly destroyed during the rebellion of A.D. 66–73. But Sepphoris took a pagan name in A.D. 68: Irenopolis, "City of Peace." It was the Jews' collaboration in places like Sepphoris that kept Judaism alive.

As this prosperous Galilean capital was beginning its collaboration with Rome, Jesus was growing up in the village of Nazareth, three miles to the south. Jesus, like his father, Joseph, was a "carpenter." But the Greek for "carpenter," *tekton,* can also mean "builder." Whether or not Jesus and his father helped build Herod's fortress in Sepphoris, Jesus probably came here often, climbing the very hillside en route from Nazareth that is visible from my friend's balcony. Jesus' grandparents, Joachim and Anne, raised their daughter, Mary, in Sepphoris. The Virgin Mary, as Mitch nonchalantly put it, "was a Zippori girl."

The legendary site of the home of Joachim and Anne was also a Crusader church, amid whose ruins I found a reused stone from the second century A.D. with a Greek inscription, saying that it was from the synagogue of the "Jewish community of Tyre, Sidon, and Zippori." These ruins were beautiful and forlorn; entry required a key from the adjacent Christian Arab orphanage, with whose director I shared a Turkish coffee. The ruins and the orphanage—not Nazareth, debased by tacky tourist development—were the genuinely evocative holy places here.

Was Jesus influenced by the town? Unlike many Jews of his time, Jesus was not a zealot, but preached peace and universal love. He was also an accomplished public speaker. Could the atmosphere of Roman-Jewish conciliation in Sepphoris—a commercial town, whose inhabitants preferred trade to war—have influenced him? Could he have cultivated his gift for oratory in Sepphoris's sophisticated commercial environment rather than in small and rustic Nazareth?[6]

In A.D. 132, an irascible warrior, Simeon Bar Kokhba, gathered the descendants of those who had survived the destruction of Jewish Jerusalem sixty-two years earlier and launched an ill-fated revolt against the Roman authorities, which the emperor Hadrian crushed in A.D. 135.

The survivors of the Bar Kokhba rebellion fled north to Sepphoris, which by the mid-second century had become the center of Jewish learning in Palestine. Here, the Sanhedrin (both the Jewish court and the legislative body) was relocated. And here, at the beginning of the third century, Rabbi Judah Ha-Nasi (Judah the Prince), the patriarch of the Palestinian Jews and a descendant of the great sage Hillel, moved to Sepphoris, where he lived for seventeen years and completed the Mishnah, which forms the basis of the Talmud.[7] Unlike the zealots of Masada and Jerusalem and the warrior Bar Kokhba, Rabbi Judah was a diplomat. According to the Talmud, he befriended one of the Antonine emperors (either Antoninus Pius or Marcus Aurelius), with whom he discussed philosophy.

Acquiescence to the great powers paid dividends. Sepphoris remained an outpost of rabbinical scholarship and Jewish culture for almost four hundred years after Rabbi Judah's death, evinced by the remains of a sixth-century Byzantine-era synagogue with a magnificent mosaic floor. The Moslem conquest in the seventh century led to the town's decline, and many Jews probably converted to Islam. But it wasn't until the first Crusade, at the end of the eleventh century, that Jewish life ended here. So did the Crusades: In Sepphoris there is a citadel from which Christian soldiers departed in July 1187 for Karnei Hattim (the Horns of Hattim), two large hills overlooking the Sea of Galilee. There, Saladin's Moslem troops set the fields afire, roasting the Christian knights in their armor and virtually ending Crusader control of the Holy Land.

Sepphoris is a story of cultural osmosis, of Jews thriving even as they adopted pagan and Islamic mores. Among the vast remains of Roman-Byzantine Sepphoris is a theater, which assimilated Jews probably attended. But the most intriguing of the remains is a Roman villa dated to A.D. 205, which coincides with the life of Rabbi Judah Ha-Nasi. The villa includes a *triclinium* (reception hall) with a resplendent mosaic floor—a virtual postcard from the past—dedicated to Dionysius, the Greco-Roman god of wine and ecstasy, who, in the mosaic's central panel, is shown in a drinking contest with Hercules. Who lived in this villa? Probably, to judge by the mosaic, it was a pagan notable. "However, one cannot rule out the possibility that a wealthy Jew may have resided here," write Ehud Netzer and Zeev Weiss of the Hebrew University in Jerusalem.[8] Might Rabbi Judah himself have visited this villa, or lived here and sipped wine upon the mosaic of Dionysius? After all, he spoke Greek and was a friend of the emperor and the other pagan powers, with whom he felt comfortable.

Such a question is sensitive indeed, because it relates to a current quarrel among Jews in Israel—between extremists, on the one hand, and rabbis like Judah Ha-Nasi, on the other, who try to steer Jews away from political and cultural confrontation so that they might rediscover, according to their own needs, the riches of their religion.

※ ※

Just as in the Moslem world, where the rise of political Islam means the end of real devotion, in Israel the identification of Judaism with extreme nationalism has threatened a similar result. In Josephus' two-thousand-year-old account of the internecine conflicts that racked Jewish Jerusalem before the Roman destruction, the various zealot factions—which resented Rome's tolerant humanism as much as its paganism—eerily resemble the parties of the Israeli right today.[9]

"The tragedy," Rabbi Yehudah Gilad told me, "has been that because so many religious Jews are on the far right, secular Israelis say, 'If this is religion, we don't want it—so let's vacation in Sweden and eat pork.'" Gilad is a young rabbi, with a dark, closely cropped beard, a knitted yarmulke, and a relaxed manner, who lives at Kibbutz Lavi, a collective religious settlement near Sepphoris. Gilad's home, bare except for a few pieces of simple furniture and religious books, reminded me of the homes of Moslem clerics I had visited in the holy Shi'ite city of Qom in Iran some years before. But unlike Iranian Shi'ism, Judaism and Zionism had the good fortune to be influenced by the European Enlightenment.

Gilad was, at the time, associated with Meimad (the Hebrew acronym for *Medinat Yahudit, Medinat Demokratit,* "a Jewish state, a Democratic State"), a dovish offshoot of the National Religious party. Though politically marginal, Meimad interested me, because it occupies the space where many Israelis want to live their lives: away from the extremes of global universalism and narrow orthodoxy. "Israelis are still new to the global village," Gilad explained. "Suddenly they have dozens of television channels, and because Israel is less diplomatically isolated than in the past, they can travel all over. But such cosmopolitanism will ultimately not satisfy them. Israelis will need to be anchored, like other people, in their own religion. And because our neighbors, friendly or not, will always be of another faith, universalism will not work here. A new modern orthodoxy is needed," where, for example, people can be comfortable observing some aspects of the Sabbath without observing others and not feel like hypocrites.

"Religious Jews," Gilad told me, "have a duty to make secular Jews feel more comfortable with religion rather than intimidated by it. I think it has been a disaster to mix theology with nationalist politics. I also have a dream of Jews settling all of *Eretz Yisrael* [Israel and the West Bank], but I have to tackle reality, too."

Judaism in Israel has yet to respond to the challenge of modernity by seeking a renewed humanism and cultural identity, said Gilad. Instead, it has become synonymous with "the land" after the capture of the West Bank in the 1967 war, a blood-and-soil ideology like that of the Orthodox Christian churches in the Balkans. Now the task is to make Judaism constructively relevant, a challenge with which Rabbi Yehudah Hanassi successfully dealt when he sought compromise with pagan Rome while articulating a body of religious law that guides Jews to this day.

Adapting Judaism to new and more complex times will not be easy in Israel, where orthodox nationalist parties have built walls between Jews and Arabs and between Jews and Jews while turning religion into a patronage mill. Many Israelis have become cynical about Judaism. Because everyone here is Jewish and Hebrew is the vernacular, people can sunbathe topless on Yom Kippur and still be good Jews overall, something hard to imagine in the Diaspora. Moreover, "Conservative and Reform Judaism as practiced in the U.S. seem rather too thin and obviously American for Israeli tastes," says Yehudah Mirsky, a doctoral student at Harvard and a friend of Gilad's. "Some new religious expression is still fitfully struggling to be born."

19

THROBBING HEART

OF THE MIDDLE EAST

I drove to Jerusalem with Mitch's wife and two of their children: south through the Jordan River Valley to Jericho, then west, ascending through the hills of the Judaean Desert to the holy city. For much of the trip we were in the West Bank, but on main highways used by Israelis. Eleven miles from Jerusalem, a new highway branched off to the right, connecting the large West Bank Jewish settlement of Ma'ale Adummim directly to the Jewish part of Jerusalem. Night had fallen, but I decided to take an old road that I knew from the 1970s, which passed through the Arab town of Al-Ayzariyah, the Bethany of the New Testament, where Jesus is said to have raised Lazarus from the dead. This way, when we came around a bend at the edge of the Judaean Desert, suddenly the Temple Mount and the walls of the Old City would appear across the narrow Kidron Valley.

Al-Ayzariyah had grown considerably since I had last seen it; it was now a crowded jumble of concrete rather than the sleepy town I remembered from two decades before. Young Arab men crowded the streets beside our slow-moving car. But I knew the way, and farther on, as I had foreseen, the road curved and the stars seemed to touch the burnished-gold dome of the Mosque of Omar on the Temple Mount, and the floodlit Turkish walls of the Old City evoked a fairy tale in their perfection. We followed the Old City walls to a stoplight, where we made a left turn: Three quarters of a mile beyond, the Arab world disappeared as though it had been wished away, and a more familiar, down-at-the-heels Western world began, cold and damp in the winter at this altitude, where rain clouds smudged the sky like candle smoke on an icon. Here I had once lived, in a poor Sephardic neighborhood where Menachem Begin had, to all intents and purposes, been elected prime minister long before the rest of Israel chose him.

I left the car at the home of another friend, Edit, while Mitch's wife and children continued on to visit their relatives.

"What route did you take to Jerusalem?" Edit asked me.

"Through Al-Ayzariyah, so we could see the Temple Mount," I replied.

"You what?"

Edit told me that the Arabs of Al-Ayzariyah throw stones at cars with Israeli license plates. I called Mitch to apologize for putting his family in danger. "Forget it," he said. "It's not that it's so unsafe. It's just that nobody does it anymore." He meant that no Jews drove through Al-Ayzariyah since the new highway from Ma'ale Adummim to Jewish West Jerusalem had been built. Another new road, called Highway One, running north from the Damascus Gate, effectively sealed off Arab East Jerusalem from Jewish West Jerusalem.

Nor did Israelis hike anymore in Wadi Kelt, a scenic riverbed east of Jerusalem, the site of several beautiful Greek monasteries and the ruins of Herod's winter palace. My friends told me that hiking in Jordan was safer than hiking anywhere in the West Bank. In the 1970s, Israelis went almost everywhere in the West Bank; now they went almost nowhere. In the Galilee, Mitch had taken me to a large supermarket commonly used by both Jews and Arabs, but in Jerusalem you were on one side or the other. The soft, Italianate landscape of Galilee reduced tensions. The Tel Aviv–Haifa coastal strip—all Jewish, upscale, and hedonistic—was also peaceful. But the harsh desert surroundings of Jerusalem vibrated with the tensions and contradictions of the Middle East. There was a divide not only between Jewish West Jerusalem and Arab East Jerusalem but between Orthodox Jews in North Jerusalem and secular ones in South Jerusalem.

I spent the next day in Ramallah, Arafat's unofficial capital in the West Bank. From Edit's house, I took an Israeli bus filled with Jewish commuters to the old railway station, then walked a few hundred yards to the Old City's Jaffa Gate. Entering the Arab Old City early on that weekday morning, I had essentially left Israel. The few Israelis I saw—police, soldiers, and civilians—were all in groups. When I left the Old City at the Damascus Gate in Arab East Jerusalem, I noticed that Arabic newspapers had replaced Hebrew ones at the stands, and instead of the Israeli English-language *Jerusalem Post* there was the *Jerusalem Times,* a Palestinian weekly. From East Jerusalem, I took a minibus—I was the only Jew among the passengers—to Ramallah. In the 1970s, Ramallah had been a sleepy hilltop town, where secular Israelis drove on the Sabbath for ice cream, but I saw no Jews there this time. Ramallah was now bustling. Palestinians returning from abroad had built fancy new villas and malls, with shops selling designer clothes and the latest electronic gadgets. As I returned to Jerusalem, I overheard an angry conversation among the Arab passengers about Jews who were still grabbing territory in the West Bank. I left the bus at the Damascus Gate. A few moments later I was back in the Jewish half of the city.

When I told Israeli friends that they should visit Ramallah, they were skeptical. It wasn't the best advice. A few weeks later, in December 1998, an Israeli soldier was pulled from a car by university students in Ramallah and stoned nearly to death. The stoning was videotaped and shown on national television. Israelis would go trekking in the Himalayas, but they wouldn't venture into Ramallah, the most pleasant city in the West Bank.

Thus, without needing a passport, I had slipped back and forth between what were already two countries. Actually, a de facto Palestinian state had been in existence since December 1987, when the Intifada began and Israelis no longer felt safe in Gaza, the West Bank, and East Jerusalem. This Palestinian state, eleven years old at the time of my visit, was no strategic threat to Israel, because Israel controlled the airspace above it and the main highways through it, while the newly constituted Palestinian police had only small weapons. This de facto state was similar to the weak and indefensible Jewish state that Israel might have become had the Palestinians accepted the 1947 partition proposed by Zionist leader David Ben-Gurion.

In fact, as some experts have said, the peace process was a divorce process for a couple that had long been living apart, a messy and complex divorce that would take a while longer to settle. Water resources, like bank accounts, had to be apportioned. Jerusalem, like a child, could not be divided, but would require the equivalent of a joint-custody arrangement, with two flags and divided sovereignty. Since one spouse is financially dependent on the other, the Palestinians can't prosper without access to the Israeli economy, so there will be trade and labor agreements. Once the divorce is made final, the two parties might gradually treat each other civilly, and Israelis might once again go to Ramallah for ice cream on the Sabbath. The outcome of the Israeli-Palestinian peace talks—unlike the future of, say, Syria, Iraq, and Jordan—is predictable and therefore uninteresting: The result will be a legal expression of what already exists on the ground. Because little will change on the ground, Israeli-Palestinian talks give few insights into the geostrategic future of the early-twenty-first-century Middle East.

☒ ☒

Take the future status of the Temple Mount:

"Are you Jewish?" the Israeli security officer barked at me in Hebrew, eyeing my dark hair and complexion amid the blond Christian pilgrims at the entrance to the Temple Mount.

"Yes," I answered.

"Then don't pray inside!" he said, shaking his finger at me.

The Temple Mount was holy to Jews as the site of both the First and Second Temples. The western retaining wall of the Second Temple (the "Wailing Wall") is the only remnant of the Roman destruction in A.D. 70. The Temple Mount is holy to Christians because of its association with Jesus' preaching and holy to Moslems as the site of Mohammed's ascension to heaven, commemorated by the gold-domed Mosque of Omar and the adjacent silver-domed Mosque of al-Aksa. Because I did not look like a tourist, the Israeli security officer may have thought I was a Jewish extremist bent on provoking an incident. Despite the claims to ownership by religious Jewish nationalists, Jews rarely venture onto the Temple Mount except as tourists.

In a manner of speaking, I did go there to pray. It happened to be November 11, 1998, the eightieth anniversary of the end of World

War I, and I wanted to offer my respects at the tomb of Hussein ibn-Ali: grand sharif of Mecca, father of Emir Abdullah, and great-grandfather of the late King Hussein. In 1916, Sharif Hussein ignited the Arab Revolt against the Turks, setting in motion the collapse of Ottoman Turkey in the Middle East and creating a political riddle whose answer is still uncertain. Before the guns went silent on the western front, 8.5 million men had died. In Europe, the slaughter led only to a bitter peace and World War II; in the Middle East, President Woodrow Wilson's ill-conceived policy of national self-determination crumbled amid the realities of power politics. The Hashemite monarchy that still ruled Jordan was among the few graspable benefits of the Great War. I said a silent prayer for the survival of the family of Sharif Hussein, whose tomb lay inside a wall surrounded by white marble and rich carpets.

Finding the tomb on the thirty-six acres of the Temple Mount had taken time. The first Arab I asked snapped: "Give me twenty shekels and I'll show you." The Arabs on the Temple Mount revealed a certain arrogance. While the Christian and Jewish tourists were circumspect in their behavior, going about with their cameras in small, quiet groups, for the Arabs the Temple Mount was their home. They picnicked on tea, goat cheese, and olives in the cypress grove beside the seemingly Persian magnificence of the Mosque of Omar. Arab women passed through the Temple Mount with plastic bags full of groceries and stopped to gossip. Arab boys played a noisy game of soccer by the Herodian pavement near Sharif Hussein's tomb. Elderly Arab men washed their feet in the fountains before going into the Mosque of al-Aksa for prayer. This was an Arab place, and it would stay that way whatever the symbolic formalities of any future peace agreement.

I left the Temple Mount through the Moslem quarter, with its peeling walls and knots of street children. Then suddenly the stones became clean; there were new lights and guardrails for archaeological cutaways, revealing excavations from as long ago as the eighth century B.C., the time of the First Temple. Here, I found fancy tourist shops, Israeli flags, and hordes of Jewish tourists. This was the Jewish quarter, whose historic preservation was a tribute to the former mayor, Teddy Kollek, Jerusalem's greatest builder since Herod. At another point, the stones faded again, and on the walls I saw maps and grisly photos of the Turkish massacres of Armenians in 1915. Now I was in the Armenian quarter. The maps showed the cities where the murders took place and the route from Kayseri through Antioch to Aleppo on which the survivors had fled, the same route I had taken from Istanbul to Jerusalem. Such posters had not been here in the 1970s, when ethnic identity and remembrance were less strong.

The Old City's various ethnic and religious groups coexisted thanks to the Ottoman *wilayet* system of communal self-government, which the Israeli authorities had only modestly tampered with. I was sure that the *wilayet* system would survive longer than Israeli rule in the parts of Jerusalem where Jews did not live, and rarely visited.

※ ※

It was forty-five minutes by bus from Jerusalem to Tel Aviv, where I took a taxi to a northern seaside suburb to meet an official in Israeli intelligence. He looked the part, with thick wire-rimmed glasses, a nervous and somewhat emaciated look, and a jaded, world-weary manner. Over coffee and cake at a fashionable café, I tested one of many theories of Greater Syria's future.

"Syria following Assad and a comprehensive peace treaty might be a Yugoslavia in the making," I suggested. "If it breaks apart, the Druze region of southern Syria could amalgamate itself with Jordan, while an Alawite mini-state could be carved out of northwestern Syria, becoming a refuge for Assad's clan in the years following his death. Sunni fundamentalists would then rule a rump state from Damascus. The new Alawite warlordship would be supported by both the Lebanese and the Israelis, who would see no irony in supporting Assad's clan under the circumstances. Jordan, meanwhile, would become a nice memory, as an unruly Palestinian state expands eastward in the wake of a peace treaty with Israel."

The intelligence official nodded and smiled. "The problem is," he said, "that anything is possible. One thing is for sure: Syria's future will be determined by nature, and by the laws of nature. Assad will die, or first become senile. Then," he said, making a fist, "over time it will be a matter of natural selection—which faction of the military or the security services is the strongest." Biology—power—in other words, not ideas, will determine Syria's future. And Iraq's, too, as when Alexander the Great died and the generals fought over his empire.[1]

"As for Jordan," the intelligence official went on, "everyone has a use for it: none of the other Arabs wants a border with Israel. . . . A Palestinian state, as you say, already exists. But the West Bank and Gaza have no common frontier, no clans or families linking them. Before 1967, Gaza was ruled by Egypt; the West Bank, by Jordan. It could take maximum force for an Arab leader to keep the two places together after Arafat goes." The possibility of Syria, Jordan, Gaza, and the West Bank going through tribal and religious upheavals at a time of dramatic modernization and urbanization made me think of the late Omayyad period, in the early eighth century, when armies were the personal property of the ruler while the spread of commerce, the growth of cities, and the diversification of society subjected the empire to great strain and various sectarian movements and preachers backed by armed groups sprouted.[2]

This Israeli official, had, like many specialists, an affecting sympathy for his subject. When I mentioned Aleppo and Damascus, he responded reverentially. "*Ah,* Aleppo. You know what a great civilization you are talking about. . . ." But when I mentioned Jerusalem, he waved his hand dismissively, telling me he went there only on business: a real Tel Aviv attitude. This," he said, pointing to the shops around us, "is what you should really look at."

He was right.

This north Tel Aviv beach suburb didn't exist when I lived in Israel. It was now a cluster of tall, well-made apartment buildings, with rows of shops selling foreign-made luxury goods and expensive cafés like the one where we were having coffee. Well-groomed men and women prowled around with shopping bags. It was Israel's version of Silicon Valley. While Jerusalem and the West Bank settlements served up the politics, the Tel Aviv–Haifa coastal strip, with its multimillion-dollar software firms and hundreds of computer-related start-up companies, paid the country's bills, generating a per capita yearly income of $17,000: close to Great Britain's and almost eighteen times Syria's. As in America, a rampaging materialism fueled the economy. Eyeing the hard, good-looking women in their thirties and forties, with their revealing clothes and shopping bags, a cab driver told me: "You need three jobs here to satisfy your wife. The women here want and want. . . ."

Tel Aviv was loud, rude, pulsing: with Brazilian food; intense, stressed-out conversations at Italian coffee shops; airlines that connected Israelis with all the Moslem countries of ex-Soviet Central Asia; new malls by the dozen; armies of Romanian and Nigerian guest workers inhabiting the poor quarters around the old bus station; and high-pitched videos blasting at the new bus station. As I waited for the late-afternoon bus back to Jerusalem, a small religious Jew with a brimmed hat slipped quickly into line ahead of me when I wasn't looking, talking on his cell phone. In the bus, people weren't just talking on cell phones but writing in notebooks and business diaries, and using pocket calculators as they did so. Beirut was somnolent compared to this. Tel Aviv, with its modern middle class, would be the Tyre of the twenty-first century.

As in antiquity, power would again radiate inland from the Mediterranean as two replicas of former Phoenician city-states, Greater Tel Aviv and Greater Beirut, overwhelm the less-dynamic capitals of the desert, Damascus and Jerusalem. Syria's economy was pathetic compared to Lebanon's; Syria's political control over Lebanon was possible only so long as a dictator kept Syria itself in one piece. Tel Aviv— not the Jewish settlements on the West Bank—was ground zero for Greater Israel: an economic magnet that exported twice as much as Egypt, Jordan, and Syria combined, whose exports were mainly agricultural commodities, textiles, and natural resources while Israel's were, increasingly, software.[3]

For decades I have heard that there would either be a Greater Israel or a Palestinian state. It turns out that there will be both: a Palestinian mini-state—without control over its skies or main highways—situated within a dynamic Israel that will continue to attract workers from across the border, making it the stabilizing force of historic Greater Syria, even as the current Syrian state weakens after decades of Soviet-style calcification.

Israel will prosper, surrounded by weak Palestinian Bantustans that are kept quiescent by the thuggish tactics of its leaders. "The term *peace process* is really so American," Menachem Lorberbaum, a religious Jew at the Center for Jewish Political Thought in Jerusalem, told me. "Israelis often use another term—*tahalikh medini*—which means 'settling the affairs of state.' At the moment, we have an old imperial entity of rulers and slaves. That is morally wrong. Because the [Arab] enemy lies within, we require a clear legal separation from the Palestinians. Following that, we will play the normal power game, making alliances with Turkey, possibly Iran, and some Arab states against other Arab states. That is the best possible future.

"*Trust* is the wrong word," Lorberbaum continued. "It has no place in foreign policy. *Love, hate*—they are both wrong. That is why both Peace Now [a dovish group] and Gush Emmunim [a hawkish group of settlers] did a great disservice to the country. Peace Now and Gush Emmunim were both started by the same class of naive, highly educated Ashkenazis who were traumatized by Israel's experience in the 1973 war, and both groups emerged with conceptions that were untenable. Peace Now trusted the Arabs; the Gush hated them and wanted to keep the West Bank. But it's not a matter of trust but of self-interest, ours and the Arabs'!" Lorberbaum exclaimed, staring intently into the distance.

It was time to leave Israel and continue my journey through the Near East. In Tel Aviv, I met an Israeli expert on Central Asia, a political laboratory of pure, amoral self-interest, as he explained. "I can tell you stories that I did not believe myself until there was no other explanation. You can only describe these things in terms of 'the Great Game' "— the nineteenth-century cold war between Russia and Great Britain over Central Asia. He told me about men who had high positions in this or that weak government in this or that Central Asian country and who had been dormant for years, saying nothing at cabinet meetings. Suddenly, these men had become agents agitating for this or that Russian project on what seemed purely commercial grounds but that always benefited Russia's strategic position. "The Russians, the Iranians, and others are battling over Central Asia," he said. "In Turkmenistan, for example, both Russia and Iran have had agents placed as cabinet ministers. The only defense is the half-Armenian foreign minister, whom the Turkmen president calls 'my Jew.' This half-Armenian is brilliantly cynical and shrewd. You should meet him. His cynicism is holding Russia and Iran at bay and protecting this poor country. Yet it can't last."

The way he described the political landscapes of Central Asia and the Caucasus reminded me of antiquity, when the only value was survival. I did not believe everything my Israeli friend had told me, yet I was fascinated and curious enough to make a plan to return to Turkey, from where I would travel by land straight east—into the Caucasus and the lands of "Tartary."

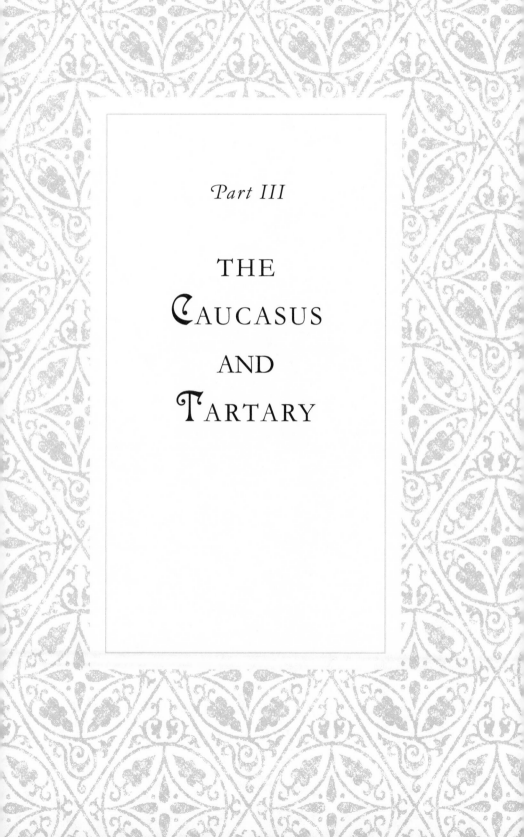

Part III

THE
CAUCASUS
AND
TARTARY

20

TO TURKEY'S

NORTHEASTERN BORDER

When I had arrived in Turkey from Bulgaria in the spring of 1998, I had discovered that a "soft" coup had taken place: By forcing the civilian prime minister to declare virtual war on the Islamists, Turkey's generals had dramatically increased their political power. By autumn 1998, the same generals were threatening Turkey's Arab neighbor to the south, Syria, with an invasion if Syria did not expel the Kurdish separatist leader Abdullah Öcalan. Syria quickly complied, and Öcalan was captured several months later by Turkey's security services in Kenya, where he had been hiding in the Greek embassy. Israel and the United States reportedly helped Turkey with the capture.

In the spring of 1999, I was back in Ankara to travel to the Caucasus. Öcalan was on trial for terrorism and murder. His capture had been a victory for the new pro-Turkish alliance of Turkey, Israel, Jordan, and Azerbaijan and a defeat for the anti-Turkish alliance of Syria, Greece, and Armenia. These were real historical fault lines. Jews, the Jordanian royal family, and the Azeri Turks of Azerbaijan had all had relatively good experiences during Ottoman rule, whereas Syrian Arabs, Greeks, and Armenians had been devastated by it.

The Turkish military's standing in Western defense ministries had rarely been higher, due in part to the realization that Turkey was a natural base for bombing both Serbia and Iraq and that Turkey could help prevent the Russian reconquest of the Caucasus. That spring Turkey had ground troops in Bosnia and fighter jets based in Italy bomb Serbia, and was regularly dispatching commandos into northern Iraq to contain Kurdish guerrillas. Yet the public mood was calm. The specter of casualties did not concern this phlegmatic nation, heir to an imperial mentality that stretched back a millennium.

In Ankara, the nearby war in Kosovo had to compete for news space with parliamentary elections that saw a dramatic rise in support for the ultranationalist National Action party (Milliyetçi Hareket Partisi, or MHP). The National Action party's success was only a superficial reversal of the religious trend I had observed the previous autumn—the Action party's nationalism was a secular form of fundamentalism. Both extreme nationalism and Islamism in Turkey had been born of a sense of frustration and historic grievance among Turkey's working poor. Both emphasized a lost golden age of Turkish Islam that could be recovered if only the moderates or secularists were purged from power.[1] And its brutality notwithstanding, the most credible force for defending the moderates and secularists in Turkey remained the military.

The election also reaffirmed Kurdish ethnic consciousness. While the pro-Kurd, pro-Öcalan People's Democracy party (Halkin Demokrasi Partisi, or HADEP) won only 4.5 percent of the vote nationwide and its candidates were outlawed from campaigning, it won a commanding majority throughout the Kurdish southeast. Once again in the Near East in the twentieth century, democracy was leading to separation, not reconciliation.

※ ※

I was on the road early one morning. The Black Sea port of Trabzon was 450 miles to the northeast—twelve and a half hours from Ankara by bus. The caressing rhythm of Turkish music on the driver's cassette heightened the drama of the landscape as we crossed a vast, rippling plateau sparsely covered in grass. Each undulation brought another hypnotic vista, beautiful and chilling in its loneliness. From the bus window I could see a dizzying swirl of plowed fields and new apartment blocks perched on naked hillsides. A uniformed attendant moved down the aisle serving tea and cake and, later, silently scrubbing the foldout tables. As the plateau broke into great mountains and deep valleys, perfect rectangular fields loomed below, bordered by young poplars and fruit trees. We alighted at a rest stop with clipped hedgerows and flower beds. The attendant hosed the bus down as we relaxed. The neatness was memorable because beyond Turkey's eastern border, there would be no more of it. Adjoining the rest stop was a military outpost with gendarmes standing at attention before more clipped hedgerows.

We passed through more mountain ranges, now dark with greenery as the proximity of the Black Sea and its wet climate became evident. The bus passed near Amasya, where the Greek geographer Strabo was born in 64 or 63 B.C. Strabo had traveled from Armenia in the east to Tuscany in the west, and from the Black Sea as far south as Ethiopia. His *Geography* is the only surviving work that documents the range of peoples and countries known to the Greeks and Romans during the reign of Augustus Caesar (27 B.C. to 14 A.D.). Strabo was alert to geopolitical change, for his youth here coincided with the decline of his own Pontic Greek civilization and the arrival of the Roman legions. The political geography of northeastern Turkey reads like an archaeological time line of civilizations: Hittites, Phrygians, Assyrians, Persians, Greeks, Romans, Byzantines, Seljuk Turks, Mongols, and so on. While a Westerner might see the present map—upon which Turkey occupies the whole of Anatolia—as both logical and permanent, Turkey's refusal to compromise with Kurds and Armenians showed how sensitive Turks were to the fact that it was not.

Indeed, for the Turks to acknowledge the truth of what the Young Turk regime perpetrated against the Armenians in 1915 (in which perhaps over a million civilians were murdered, or died in the course of forced expulsions) would be, in Turkish eyes, to expose themselves to claims for financial restitution, and—worse—to territorial claims, for much of eastern Anatolia had been part of a great Armenian civilization until this century. What at the end of the twentieth century was seen as a purely Turkish land mass had been for centuries a more eclectic mix of peoples. In fact, had it not been for one man, Mustafa Kemal "Atatürk," much of western Anatolia might still be Greek.

For three thousand years, until 1922, the western coast of Anatolia and the hinterland beyond had been part of the Greek world. But in 1921 a Greek army, taking advantage of the Ottoman empire's disintegration after its defeat in World War I, advanced deep into Anatolia against all military logic, creating weak or nonexistent supply lines. The next year, the ruthless and charismatic Mustafa Kemal, the only undefeated Ottoman general, drove the Greek army back to the Aegean, leaving 1.25 million ethnic Greeks exposed to the Turkish soldiery. Nearly the entire ethnic-Greek population fled or were subsequently forced into exile. The expulsion of the Greeks completed the radical transformation of Anatolia from the throbbing, multiethnic heart of a nineteenth-century empire to a uniethnic twentieth-century nation.

It was at Samsun, a dreary food-processing center of gray concrete, that my bus reached the brooding, navy-blue waters of the Black Sea. From Samsun we traveled eastward throughout the afternoon, the shoreline becoming more picturesque by stages. Approaching Trabzon, we entered a land of vine-swathed trees, weeping willows, and needlelike cypresses and ranks of thick, overgrown bluish-green brush on headlands shrouded in mist. The bus pulled into Trabzon during a golden sunset: exactly what this city had constituted in world history.

Trabzon is the Turkish-language corruption of the Greek *Trebizond,* which comes from the Greek word for "table"—*trapeza*—a reference to the flat promontory on which the city sits.[2] In 1204, Alexius and David Comnenus, scions of the Byzantine Greek royal family, escaped the Crusader conquest and looting of Constantinople and, with the help of an army provided by the Georgian queen Tamara, created a sovereign outpost of Byzantium here in eastern Anatolia. The new city-state of Trebizond got a boost in the mid-thirteenth century when the Mongol invasion of the Near East forced a diversion of trade routes north from Persia to Anatolia. Just as Dubrovnik's noble families were to play Ottomans off against Habsburgs to preserve the independence of their Adriatic city-state, the nobles and diplomats of Trebizond played Turkomans off against Mongols to survive, keeping this city and its sylvan environs as a cosmopolitan outpost amid the monochrome Turkic nomadism—for the goods that amassed at the docks here were transported to Europe by Genoese boats, bringing Latin civilization to this eastern port. And because the Ottoman Turks under Mehmet the

Conqueror did not subjugate Trebizond until 1461, eight years after Constantinople had fallen, history has conferred upon this place the aura of a last bastion of Greek Byzantium. In fact, a substantial Greek and Armenian population survived here through the centuries of Ottoman rule, until Atatürk's revolution took root; so here, too, modernity meant ethnic cleansing, though of a relatively benign and gradual kind.

My first night in Trabzon I was awakened by the blast of the Moslem call to prayer—louder, I recalled, than a few years earlier, when I had last visited. In the morning I noticed the ubiquity of head scarves. Trabzon had become a bastion of Fazilet, the Islamic Virtue party, whose vitality here was a backlash against the "Natashas"—Russian and Ukrainian prostitutes who had arrived in the 1990s from the nearby former Soviet states, threatening the stability of local family life. Reportedly, it was Turkish housewives—angered by what their husbands were doing at night—who brought Fazilet victory at the polls.

Trabzon represented historical discontinuity. The various artistic monuments of the Byzantine past notwithstanding, what I saw was a drab and dynamic, utilitarian parade of bustling kebab stands, cheap cafeteria-style restaurants, and shops selling crockery, auto parts, vacuum cleaners, kitchen and bathroom tiles, and so on, lining narrow, serpentine streets noisy and polluted with trucks and automobiles. The industrial uniformity wiped out any specific cultural trait or connection to the past.

Weary by afternoon, I slowed down. I listened more closely, and saw more minutely. I noticed the singing of the birds and the clink of tea glasses and smelled the fresh breezes amid diesel fumes, so that I could imagine, just barely, this once-and-perhaps-future kingdom by the sea. I took off my shoes and sat on the carpets inside the Fatih Cami (the Conqueror's Mosque), the perfect Byzantine basilica, with its dome and sloping roofs. Staring at the whitewashed walls, I imagined the frescoes smothered underneath, recalling the epoch when this building was called the Panagia Khrisokefalos, a reference to both the Virgin Mary and the "Golden-Headed" dome, for here had been the main cathedral of the Greek kingdom of Trebizond.

The next day I found what remained of the Armenian monastery of Kaymaklı, up a nearly impassable dirt road a few miles from the city center, amid a squatters' slum loud with children and roosters. A small boy led me into a destroyed building with a makeshift tin roof. The dirt floor, foul with excrement, was cluttered with hay, firewood, scraps of corrugated iron, and a set of barbells, which the boy proudly lifted to his waist. I looked at the stone walls, decorated with a turquoise-and-rosy-pink pageantry of Hell and the Apocalypse amid saints' portraits, all faded, defaced, and framed by fabulous filigree work, recalling the beauty of this fifteenth-century Armenian church. As the unknowing boy jumped up and down on the corrugated-iron pile, each rumble of the iron reminded me of another human displacement. I thought of the brutal ethnic expulsions that have pockmarked the history of the Near East, of which that of Kosovar Albanians taking place that same spring was merely the latest. The smell of earth, the reek of feces, and the artistic fragments of a past Armenian civilization conjured up for me yet another great crime. A monoethnic Turkish nation blanketing Anatolia with its cartographic imprint had not occurred naturally or peacefully, and was not therefore necessarily permanent.

For geography holds the key not only to the past but the future, too. The Black Sea, with its diverse civilizations, may transform this part of Turkey now that the Soviet Union and its formerly impenetrable borders are gone. The Natashas were only a part of what was happening here. Along Trabzon's harbor, there was now an endless market for goods from the former Soviet Union: fabrics, silverware, old war medals, cheap jewelry, tea services, and just about everything else, from socks to cell phones, was on sale. This was a working-class bazaar, like the Chinese market I had seen in Budapest. Trabzon was becoming more of a multiethnic Black Sea capital and less of a purely Turkish one. The kingdom of Trebizond could be reborn, I thought, in dreary, working-class hues.

※ ※

My last day in eastern Turkey was like my last day in eastern Hungary. In both places I was conscious of being near a great fault line, beyond which lay a starkly different world. Few people in eastern Turkey had any idea what was happening next door in Georgia. The large tourist office beside my hotel in Trabzon had no information about Batumi, the Georgian city on the other side of the border—not the names of hotels, the prices, not even the name of the Georgian currency. Batumi and Gürcistan (the Turkish name for Georgia) were terra incognita, and this heightened my sense of adventure.

East of Trabzon the coastline became more lush and rugged as I crossed raging rivers and terraced fields of tea and hazelnut. Mountains rose into white-granite cathedrals, their tops girded in clouds. It began to rain hard. I had entered the ancient land of Colchis, at the eastern end of the Black Sea, the destination of Jason and the Argonauts and the mythical home of the enchantress Medea, who helped Jason obtain the Golden Fleece. In the distance to the northeast, I saw another range of vine-shrouded subtropical mountains: my first view of the Caucasus. Trucks were everywhere, for the overland trade from Turkey was keeping Georgia alive. The last few kilometers to the border were bone-jarring. Though a new highway was being blasted out of the rock of this craggy headland, I was on the old, narrow track that during the Cold War was used only by Turkish military vehicles. The taxi stopped and I entered a derelict barracks-style building, where a lone Turkish official stamped my passport and wished me luck. I continued on foot across a dusty lot into Georgia and the former Soviet Union.

21

STALIN'S BEAUTIFUL

HOMELAND

The first structure I saw in Georgia was a building with a tall wire fence guarded by a Russian soldier, a Communist hammer-and-sickle on his cap, who screamed at me as he thrust a machine gun at my stomach. He wore cheap sunglasses and was sucking a lollipop. Though Georgia was a sovereign nation, Russian soldiers controlled the frontier with Turkey. The soldier looked at my passport, found the Georgian visa inside, and marched me, with his gun, to a kiosk with two-way mirrors. A slit opened in the kiosk and I saw the top of a bright red hairdo as a Russian woman examined my passport and stamped it. She directed me inside the building, where a steel cage closed around me and several Russian soldiers, also with lollipops, examined my possessions. Then they opened the cage and I walked toward another kiosk, this one without two-way mirrors, where a group of friendly Georgians glanced only casually at my passport and welcomed me to Georgia. They directed me to yet another caged enclosure, where a heavyset Georgian woman gave me a customs form—on which I lied, of course. Because of the absence of ATM machines throughout the southern part of the former Soviet Union, I was carrying $3,500, in twenty-dollar bills, in a pouch hidden under my trousers. But I declared only $400, fearful of being robbed by these officials. The woman directed me to another booth, the last, where a group of Georgian security police in tight shirts, and with muscular forearms and calculating expressions, looked over my passport and customs declaration.

"Give me twenty dollars," one of them said in a mixture of Georgian and broken English.

I played dumb and shrugged.

He smashed his fist on the table and repeated the demand.

I shrugged.

We stared at each other for a few seconds, then he let me through the gate. I was glad I had lied on the customs form, for I later learned that travelers had been relieved of as much as a hundred dollars here. Comparing the Russian soldiers to these Georgians, local criminality seemed at first sight more impulsive, less systematized than the Russian variety.

Actually, I hadn't entered Georgia so much as Ajaria, a small breakaway region of Georgia, where a Georgian dialect was spoken and the population was mainly Moslem. Using the religion issue to divide and conquer, Lenin had created Ajaria in July 1921. But differences in language and religion from central Georgia, which was Orthodox Christian, had little to do with Ajaria's present autonomy. Ajaria was a fairly benign criminal warlordship run by one Aslan Abashidze, whose power over Aslanistan, as it was called, was subsidized by the customs duties he extracted from legal and illegal goods entering by sea and over this land border with Turkey. People paid bribes to get jobs at the border posts—particularly at the port of Batumi—where they could shake others down to earn back their investment, and much more. It was like buying a taxi medallion and making the money back through fares.

Beyond the gate, I met a gang of taxi drivers. One grabbed my arm and my duffel bag, throwing it into his battered Lada. Unlike the comfortable Turkish taxis, manufactured to European standards and sprayed inside with freshener, the Lada had a cracked windshield and roof. The doors had no handles. Dark stains were everywhere, and onions rolled back and forth on the floor beneath my creaking seat as the vehicle lurched through deep potholes. The car gave off oil and diesel fumes.

"Georgia beautiful, yes!" the driver exclaimed.

"Yes," I replied.

It was indeed. Few places, with the possible exception of Romania, were to move me as deeply as Georgia. But like Romania, Georgia was an acquired taste.

The pinnacles of the Caucasus, capped with blue snow, hung like draperies above corrugated-tin huts and citrus orchards. Cattle reaching for eucalyptus leaves lined the road. Hideous apartment blocks of unfinished breeze block, splattered mortar, and makeshift corrugated-iron balconies—built in the Khrushchev era and prevalent throughout the former Soviet Union—announced Batumi. They were followed by a succession of Russian-provincial architecture: peeling white buildings, like rotting wedding cakes in Baroque, Empire, and neo-classical styles, with lead roofs and wrought-iron gates and balconies filled with flowers on wide, leafy streets, shaded by palms, cedars, cypresses, and fruit trees. Unlike the provincial towns of Turkish Anatolia, with their preponderance of men and with women in head scarves, here I saw women on the streets wearing short skirts and poorly made copies of European designs. Some carried umbrellas in the rain and walked like dancers, as though carrying in their genes the spirit of a struggling-to-be-born bourgeoisie that had, miraculously, managed to survive communism. Russians and Georgians all had wondrously sculpted faces. Here in mythical Greek Colchis, once a domain of wealth and sorcery, I had found a dilapidated and captivating Belle Epoque.

Batumi, a city of 136,000 that was named for the nearby Bat River, is situated where Anatolia meets the Caucasus. This ancient Roman, Byzantine, and Persian Black Sea port changed hands several times in the late nineteenth and early twentieth centuries. Russia captured Batumi from the Ottoman empire during the 1877–1878 Russo-Turkish War. The Turks, taking advantage of even greater chaos in Russia than in Turkey near the end of World War I, retook Batumi in 1918. After the armistice in which Germany, Turkey, and the other Central Powers conceded defeat to the Allies, fifteen thousand British troops replaced the Turks here. Within two years, though, the British left as the newly installed Bolsheviks reaffirmed their control over the czar's empire. Then the border was frozen shut for decades, with NATO-member Turkey on one side and the Soviet Union on the other. Thus, while the histories of Turkey and Georgia have been interwoven for millennia, the difference for someone walking across the border is vast. The time difference symbolized the depth of the transition I had experienced: I set my watch ahead not one but two hours on the Georgian side.

Yet a mingling of cultures would probably resume. Within a few months of my visit, the Russian border guards were to be withdrawn under a new treaty with Georgia, and the completion of the new road on the Turkish side of the border would dramatically increase links. And if the Georgian government in the capital of Tbilisi got its way, eventually all the border posts would be run by a private Western company, in order to eliminate corruption and thuggery. States throughout the former Soviet Union were so corrupt that the only way to bring honesty to—and earn public revenue from—their own frontiers was, literally, to sell them off.

The taxi ride cost 20 Georgian lari, or $10. As in most countries through which I had traveled, the dollar had become an unofficial, legal currency. The driver deposited me at the rear of the tenementlike Intourist Hotel. The cavernous, unlit lobby was covered in cheap plywood. An old woman in a smock was dusting the floor. Another one sat at the reception. Her transistor was playing beautiful, weepy hymns, an intoxicating blend of Greek and Russian music, my first introduction to the indefinable uniqueness of Georgian culture. Across the hall in the half darkness was a video-game machine, and, next to it, a souvenir shop, where another woman was writing in a ledger. One cabinet held pocketknives, sucking candies, and a book with diagrams of handguns. Another cabinet offered bras and ornamental daggers. In a store in Tbilisi a few days later, I would see beach balls sold alongside assault rifles. In a primitive capitalistic economy, storekeepers sold whatever they could get their hands on.

I used the hotel phone to call my translator, Eka Khvedelidze, whom I had hired beforehand through a friend. She appeared a short while later. "Don't stay here," she advised me. "There are rats in the rooms. Let's walk to the new private hotel." The private hotel had ugly furniture and dark brown carpeting, but it was well lit and clean, and the Russian blonde at the desk wore a fashionable black dress and smiled, unlike the ancient automatons behind the desks at the Intourist.

After depositing my duffel bag, I walked around Batumi with Eka.

A close inspection revealed barefoot children, garbage-strewn streets, cracked sidewalks, and potholes everywhere, along with Audis, BMWs, and Mercedes-Benzes: a typical African-style, post-Soviet economy fueled by corruption. There were shops, with gilded mirrors and magnificent chandeliers, that sold nothing but bubble gum and ice cream, and bars run by Russian women—one was drunk in the middle of the day—decorated with nothing but shower curtains and old Christmas ornaments. The market area was bursting with cans of paint and other goods from Turkey, and imported whiskeys and perfumes. Unlike the drab, convention-bound towns of Turkey, with their grilled-meats stalls and men in dark woollen caps sipping tea, here I found no evidence of tradition at all, as if everything—the interior decorating, the whole economy, in fact—had been improvised yesterday and might collapse tomorrow.

Aslan Abashidze had packed the local bureaucracy with Moslem officials and built several new mosques to institutionalize the difference between Ajaria (Aslanistan) and Orthodox Christian Georgia. In the ex-Soviet Caucasus, where religion was less a factor in ethnic identity than in the Balkans, this was a clear case of a modern politician inventing hatreds retrospectively. Abashidze was a small man with a large ego and a noble surname: his grandfather Mehmet had played a key role in brokering the agreement between Lenin and Atatürk that settled the border here. Aslan, as he was called, liked to receive visiting dignitaries in the new tennis courts he had built, which were the pride of his warlord fiefdom. I sought an interview with him several times, but was told he was busy and that I should wait another day. I never saw him. His offices were generic Communist style: massive white-marble hallways and dark red carpets that dwarfed a metal detector and a small cheap table. Around the latter stood a group of tough-looking young Georgians, who carried cell phones and sidearms and rubbed their unshaven cheeks as they inspected my *Atlantic Monthly* business card. Outside the office was a militiaman, also unshaven. His shoes were worn down to the soles, his uniform was missing buttons, and he was wearing one of those grandiose visored caps favored by the Soviet military. His breath stank, and he asked me for a cigarette. The official face of government here was uncivil, untamed.

Batumi was fascinatingly volatile, tacky and crumbling, nostalgically European and mock-Mediterranean, with an exotic hint of Tartary. But before I attempt to explain Georgia and its mini-empire of ethnicities and breakaway regions, I should try to describe the Caucasus as a whole, and the best place to start is with Georgia's, and the Caucasus's, most famous twentieth-century personage: Iosif Vissarionovich Dzhugashvili, better known as Stalin.

According to one noted writer, the difference between Aleksandr Kerensky, the enlightened social democrat who took power after Russia's February 1917 revolution, Vladimir Ilyich Lenin, and Joseph Stalin was the difference between the West, the semi-West, and the East.[1] Kerensky and the Menshevik social reformers were extreme westernizers; Lenin, a Great-Russian from the Middle Volga, was a "blend of Westernizer and Slavophile"; while Stalin was a Georgian from the Caucasus Mountains, where Russia ends and the Near East begins. In April 1941, when Stalin signed a nonaggression pact with Japan, freeing the Japanese to attack Pearl Harbor, foreign minister Yosuke Matsuoka raised his glass to the treaty's success, and, with the institution of hara-kiri in mind, declared that if the treaty were not kept, "I must give my life, for, you see, we are Asiatics."

"We are both Asiatics," Stalin replied.[2]

Of course, Stalin's despotism had many roots and cannot be reduced simply to the culture and geography of his birthplace. (Upon the death of his first wife, Ekaterina Svanidze, Stalin told a friend at the funeral, "She is dead and with her have died my last warm feelings for all human beings."[3]) But to say that the Oriental influence was merely incidental to his character is to ignore its essentials. The monumental use of terror, the very grandeur of his personality cult, and the use of prison labor for gigantic public works projects echo the ancient Assyrian and Mesopotamian tyrannies. The liturgical nature of Stalin's diatribes, which became the standard for official Communist discourse, bore the influence of the Eastern Orthodox Church, in one of whose Georgian seminaries Stalin studied as a youth.

Someone as evil as Stalin could have come from anywhere, but many of the methods he employed, such as playing one nationality off against the other until all were devastated, bore the influence of his early life in the Caucasus. What ultimately differentiated Stalin from the others among Lenin's inner circle (Trotsky, Bukharin, Zinoviev, and Kamenev), and what allowed him to destroy them all, was that they— all Jewish except for Bukharin; all from European Russia and the Ukraine—were cosmopolitan idealists and westernizers, however savage and cynical their methods, whereas Stalin saw the world anthropologically: For him, a Jew was a Jew; a Turk, a Turk; a Chechen, a Chechen; and so on. Such thinking was far more common to the Near East than to the West, for in the Caucasus the tribe and clan—not formal institutions—have always been the key to politics. That was, in part, an expression of Stalin's early life in the Caucasus: a Toynbean laboratory of history and ethnic identity that makes the Balkans look transparent by comparison. Trotsky writes:

> The frequent bloody raids into the Caucasus of Genghis Khan and Tamarlane left their traces upon the national epos of Georgia. If one can believe the unfortunate Bukharin, they left their traces likewise on the character of Stalin.[4]

While the cultures of Europe and Asia fuse along the shores of the Black Sea, the Caspian is all Asiatic, and between these two bodies of water is a land bridge where Europe gradually vanishes amid a six-hundred-mile chain of rugged mountains as high as 18,000 feet. These are the Caucasus, Russia's Wild West, though they lie to the south of Moscow and St. Petersburg. Here, since the seventeenth century, Russian colonialists have knocked their heads against the walls of steep gorges trying to subdue congeries of unruly peoples. To the west and southwest of the Caucasus lie the Black Sea and the most undeveloped part of Turkey; southeast lie the mountains and tablelands of Iran; east across the Caspian Sea are the desert wastes of Central Asia; and north lies Russia, shattered, like much of the Caucasus, by poverty and chaos following seven decades of communism. The Balkans border Central Europe. The Caucasus has no such luck.

The northern slopes of these mountains contain the various ethnic chieftaincies that are now part of the Russian Federation, and are properly called the North Caucasus, while the region to the south of the highest ridges is called the Transcaucasus, the land of Georgia, Armenia, and Azerbaijan (though the terms *Caucasia* or the *Caucasus* apply to the whole region). Because of abundant water and vegetation, allowing for domesticable animals and agriculture, it may be that civilization began in the Caucasus even before it did in Mesopotamia.[5] The very antiquity of the area, combined with the mountainous terrain, shelters miniature tribal worlds lost to time. Strabo noted that in the Greek Black Sea port of Dioscurias, now in the northwestern Georgian region of Abkhazia, seventy tribes gathered to trade. "All speak different languages because . . . by reason of their obstinacy and ferocity, they live in scattered groups and without intercourse with one another."[6]

Today, the Caucasus is shared by four countries and about a dozen autonomous regions, with as many as fifty ethnic groups, each with its own language or dialect. Some are well known and numerous, such as the Georgians, the Armenians, the Azeri Turks of Azerbaijan, and the Chechens; others are smaller and obscure, such as the Ingush, the Ossetes, the Avars, the Abkhaz, the Balkhars, the Kumyks, the Mingrelians, and the Meskhetian Turks.[7]

In 1991, the collapse of the Soviet Union (to which all of the Caucasus had belonged) set off a gruesomely violent pageant of warfare, anarchy, and ethnic cleansing that engulfed the region for years and simmers still, with 100,000 dead and 1.25 million refugees, as each armed ethnic group has tried to impose its version of the map on the other. No region of the Soviet Union equaled the Caucasus in proving how bloody and messy the death of a large empire can be.

In the 1990s, the American media and intellectual community embraced the causes of the Bosnian Moslems and the Kosovar Albanians, murdered and exiled in campaigns of terror directed mainly by ethnic Serbs, but they virtually ignored similar cases of ethnic killing in the Caucasian regions of Abkhazia, Ossetia, and Nagorno-Karabakh. And even as the problems of sub-Saharan Africa have become known through the coverage of a sympathetic global media, the infinitely complex and intractable Caucasus truly tests the limits of Western knowledge of the world—and the West's ability to manage it.

※ ※

Georgia is a small country by American standards. With 5.6 million people, it is comparable in size to West Virginia. But it is the most sprawling and ethnically variegated state in the Caucasus, with a history overwhelmingly complex and bloody. The Georgian capital, Tbilisi, has been destroyed twenty-nine times. It was on "Mount Caucasus" in Georgia that Prometheus was supposedly chained to a rock, an eagle continually pecking at his liver when he was punished by Zeus. The very antiquity of the Prometheus story—it is part of the creation myth of the Greek world—offers further evidence that the Caucasus was a cradle of civilization.

The Georgian word for Georgia is *Sakartvelo,* and Georgians call themselves *Kartvelebi,* or Kartvelians. All these names come from the pagan god Kartlos. In ancient times, eastern Georgia, known to Georgians as Kartli, was named Iberia by outsiders, leading to a confusion with Spain that persists to this day. One theory holds that the word *Georgia* comes from the Greek word *geo* ("earth"), for when the ancient Greeks first came to Georgia, they were struck by the many people working the land. Situated in the geographic and historic crucible where Russia meets the Turkic and Persian Near East, the various mountain ranges of the Caucasus have allowed the Georgians to remain linguistically intact over the millennia, a pocket people preserved in a dusty museum case, as it were.

Though comprising only one one-thousandth of humanity, the Georgians created one of the world's fourteen alphabets. Its crescent-shaped symbols emerged around the fifth century B.C., possibly from Aramaic, the Semitic dialect spoken by Jesus. Saint Nino, a slave woman from Cappodocia, in central Anatolia, brought Christianity to Georgia in A.D. 330, when she converted the Georgian queen Nana, after curing her of an illness. But the Greek colonies around Batumi may have been converted as early as the first century, making the form of Christianity practiced here among the world's oldest, combining with the Greek pantheon, Iranian Zoroastrianism, and various Anatolian cults.[8]

Like Anatolia, neighboring Georgia saw almost every ancient people occupy or pass through its territory and leave a genetic trace: Hittites, Phyrgians, and Assyrians from the south and west; the nomadic Cimmerians and Scythians from the northern shores of the Black Sea; and Medes and Persians from the south and east.[9] The Georgians were caught in that archetypal East-West conflagration between the Persian and Greek empires that forms the subject of Herodotus's *Histories.* Later, in the early-Christian centuries, Georgia became another East-West battleground, this time between Persia and Rome. A pattern emerged that continues to this day: While Georgia was superficially influenced by the West (Greece and Rome), its political culture became profoundly Eastern. The difference between Rome and Persia (and, later, between Byzantium and Persia) was that between semi-Western imperial officialdoms that were nonhereditary—and thus early prototypes of modern states and institutions—and a Persian society underpinned by tribal and clan relations.[10] In Georgia, it was the Persian clan system that proved more influential, and its remnants are visible today through the power of regional mafias and warlords; so despite the influence of European Russia in the nineteenth century, Georgia can be considered part of the Near East.

The other pattern that emerged in classical times and continues, even as it was obscured during seven decades of Soviet tyranny, is Georgia's internal disunity. Though there is one Kartvelian alphabet, there are three Kartvelian languages: Georgian; Mingrelian, in western Georgia; and Svan, in the mountainous north. Historic Georgia also included speakers of Abkhaz, a Caucasian language, in the northwest; Ossetian, an Iranian language, in the north; and Armenian and Turkic speakers in the south. In the tenth century A.D., despite three centuries of defeats at the hands of Islamic armies in Arabia and a weakening position in Anatolia, Byzantine armies were actually advancing in the Caucasus, because no Georgian or Armenian monarch could unite the squabbling principalities. It was only in the eleventh and twelfth centuries that a reasonably monolithic Georgian-Orthodox Christian culture emerged under King David "the Builder," which blended the mores and artistic values of Byzantium, Seljuk Turkey, and Persia. (It was King David's great-granddaughter, Queen Tamara, whose armies helped the Greeks establish the kingdom of Trebizond.) David was crowned the "King of the Abkhaz, the Kartvelians, the Ran, the Ka-khetians, and the Armenians," signifying Georgia's unwieldy diversity. Indeed, in the thirteenth century, Georgia divided again as the invading Mongols promoted provincial nobles over the king. In the fourteenth century came the Black Death and Tamerlane's conquest. Later, Georgia was divided between an Ottoman Turkish sphere of influence in the west and a Safavid Iranian one in the east, while the mountains to the north cut it off from fellow–Orthodox Christian Russia. Iranian oppression was so extreme that in the early seventeenth century, the population of Kakheti, in eastern Georgia, dropped by two thirds, because of killings and deportations.

By the late seventeenth century, though, Russia under Czar Peter (the Great) had begun its historic southern expansion to the Black and Caspian Seas, and by the late eighteenth century Russia was clashing with Persia over Georgia and the rest of the Caucasus. In 1801, Czar Alexander I forcibly incorporated Georgia into the Russian empire. What happened next was more dramatic than much of the preceding history taken together.

The nineteenth-century Russian czars quickly put Georgia on the road to modernity. Doubts about the benefits of czarist rule—compared with that of the Turks and Iranians—are put to rest when one notes that the population of Georgia rose from 500,000 to 2.5 million in the nineteenth and early twentieth centuries. There were costs, however. The Georgian church and nobility became subservient to Russian institutions, and Russian absolutism sparked peasant revolts. A case in point was the order from St. Petersburg in 1841 that western Georgian peasants cultivate only potatoes regardless of local conditions, which showed that the central planning of the Soviet era was rooted not just in Communist ideology but in the character of Russian imperialism.

In Georgia, the Armenians played the role that the Jews did elsewhere: that of the urban middleman minority of shopkeepers and entrepreneurs. Under Russia's modernizing rule, the clan difference between rural Georgians and urban Armenians was accentuated. That was why toward the turn of the twentieth century Marxism became so attractive to Georgians: It provided an analysis and a solution to their condition that was nonnationalist but opposed to czarist officialdom and the Armenian bourgeoisie.

Georgia—not Europe or Russia—was the real historical birthplace of mass-movement socialism, with large support not just from intellectuals and workers but from peasants, too.[11] But the utopian rhetoric of local Marxists notwithstanding, the weakening of czarist rule at the start of the twentieth century led immediately to ethnic conflict among Georgians, Armenians, and Azeri Turks: exactly what would occur here in the late twentieth century, when, despite universalist calls for democracy and human rights by dissident intellectuals, the collapse of the Soviet Union would lead to chaos and ethnic cleansing. And there is another frightening similarity between the start and the end of the twentieth century in the Caucasus: In 1918, a weakened and defeated Russia spawned three new states built on old ethnic identities in the Transcaucasus: Georgia, Armenia, and Azerbaijan. But all were destroyed in the 1920s as Russia reasserted itself under the Soviets. Were Russia to reassert itself again under a new autocracy, the West would have to prove as muscular here as in the Balkans if it chose to keep these states alive.

From the 1890s onward, Georgian social democrats struggled valiantly against ethnic disunity. In 1917, these Georgian "Mensheviks" took power in Tbilisi, disarmed soldiers, and worked together with Armenians and Azeri Turks in a losing battle against Lenin and his "People's Commissar of Nationalities," Stalin. Georgia had embraced Russia in 1801 because Russia offered a window to Europe as well as protection against Turkey and Iran. Had the czars and the Mensheviks (with all their flaws) been allowed to remain in power, the Caucasus today might be a model of civility. What Georgian would have thought in the nineteenth century that in the twentieth it would be the Turks and Iranians, however fundamentalist, who would prove less destructive to their interests than the Europeanized Russians!

Another lesson of this tragic story is that while history, culture, and geography are the only consistent guides to the future, they are not determinative—because of the influence of extraordinary individuals. Turkish influence would have been better for Georgia than Russian influence, because Atatürk took a backward Turkey and made it modern, while Lenin and Stalin took a directionless Russia and made it backward.

※ ※

I was walking in a park beside the Black Sea in Batumi with Eka, my translator, when a rainstorm forced us to take refuge in a café with blank walls, an old and wheezing refrigerator, loud electronic music, and a group of men in tight black jeans smoking and talking on cell phones. We sat as far from the stereo speakers as possible, and to pass the time, I asked Eka about the first democratically elected president of post-Soviet Georgia, Zviad Gamsakhurdia.

"The whole phenomenon with Gamsakhurdia was psychosexual," Eka began. "Zviad was like a rock star. You can almost see the psychological scars on the faces of his female followers. By their expressions, you know that these women are physically ruined, as though they were his concubines. Most are single or have unhappy marriages. They now expect Zviad to come back from the grave on a white horse. I'm not kidding."

I was reminded of the story of the Romanian fascist leader Corneliu Zelea Codreanu, whose return on a magnificent horse the peasants expected, even after he was killed in 1938 by King Carol II.[12]

This was the central narrative of Georgian politics in the years during and after the collapse of the Soviet Union: how the region's leading Communist-era dissident, "the Havel of the Caucasus," as Gamsakhurdia was sometimes known, led Georgia into bloodcurdling chaos, and how the ex-secret police chief and Communist party boss of Soviet Georgia, (and ex-foreign minister of the Soviet Union) Eduard Shevardnadze, brought Georgia out of that chaos and into a condition of semistable partial democracy. In Georgia, an idealistic dissident all but destroyed his country, while an old secret policeman rescued it—not because dissidents are bad and secret policemen are good, or because realism is better than idealism, but because of Georgia's particular circumstances and the personalities of the two men. There is no better example than the story of Zviad Gamsakhurdia to show that Shakespeare is a better guide to politics than political science. This is what happened, according to Eka and others I talked to, in Batumi and, later, in Tbilisi:

Zviad Gamsakhurdia was the son of the great twentieth-century Georgian writer Konstantine Gamsakhurdia. In the 1970s, the younger Gamsakhurdia, a lecturer in American literature at Tbilisi State University, led a protest movement against Soviet oppression that resulted in prison and exile. But his dissent was a matter of radical nationalism, not moral opposition to communism. His nationalism was inspired by his literary sensibilities and the peasant surroundings of his native Mingrelia, in western Georgia. Then there were personal circumstances. The weak son of a bullying and famous father, he was a national hero without confidence in himself. This vulnerability, combined with his good looks and romantic literary reputation, made him attractive to women. His jealous wife, Manana—described as "a low-class, awful, unattractive woman"—who dominated Zviad much as his father had, was enraged by this. Rarely had there been a political leader as susceptible to delusions of grandeur yet so easily manipulated.

Messianism, megalomania, and *infallibility* are the words applied to Gamsakhurdia.[13] "Gamsakhurdia never looked at you. He was comfortable only in front of crowds," Professor Levan Alexidze, a former adviser to Gamsakhurdia, later told me in Tbilisi. Alexidze said that Gamsakhurdia's wife "had something from the Devil. Once I came to Gamsakhurdia's office at two A.M. to suggest ways to stop the civil war that had erupted because of all his political arrests. The president told me, 'Okay.' But leaving his office, I met his wife on the stairs. She said, 'I didn't bring my husband and children to power for shit like you to ruin him.' The next morning at nine, the radio announced that there would be no negotiations with the opposition and that the president had declared emergency rule."

Gamsakhurdia rose to power when the Soviet Union began to collapse, which was, popular memory in the West aside, before the Berlin Wall fell, not a consequence of its fall. It was in the Caucasus, not Eastern Europe, that anti-Soviet protests began in unstoppable earnest. But the protests that rocked Eastern Europe in 1989 emphasized democratic freedoms; here in the Caucasus, they were purely nationalistic. In 1988, Armenians defied Soviet pleas and demonstrated for the return of their ethnic enclave, Nagorno-Karabakh, from Azerbaijan, sparking riots in the Azerbaijani cities of Baku and Sumgait. The next year, Georgians demonstrated against Abkhaz separatism in northwestern

Georgia. A massacre of Georgian protesters by Soviet troops in Tbilisi on April 9, 1989, led to Gamsakhurdia's nationalists taking local power away from the Kremlin. In 1990, Gamsakhurdia defeated the Communists in parliamentary elections, and the following year he was elected president. Surrounded by bodyguards and vicious dogs, having imprisoned his erstwhile nationalist allies while stoking the fires of ethnic hatred and increasingly relying on arson, mafiosi, and his wife, Gamsakhurdia had become Macbeth.[14] By late 1991, a few months after Gamsakhurdia's election, Georgia was engulfed in a civil war that destroyed the nation's cities, made internal travel impossible, and ruined the economy, such as it was.

In January 1992, a military council ousted Gamsakhurdia, who fled to nearby Chechnya. Pitched battles then followed in western Georgia between troops of the new military council and Gamsakhurdia's Mingrelian supporters, known as Zviadists, a term that suggested how little the civil war had to do with ideas and how much with personalities and linguistic-regional loyalties.

Lawrence Sheets, the Reuters bureau chief who lived in Tbilisi throughout the civil war, told me: "Every night downtown, macho men with grenade launchers fired into the air at nothing in particular. The road between Batumi and Tbilisi was blocked for months at a time by battles that had no military or political purpose. Mini-rebellions broke out based on nothing really except male testosterone." In fact, the civil war was as much a battle between rival mafias for criminal territory as it was for political control. "Georgian society had its own networks and codes," writes the scholar Ronald Grigor Suny in *The Making of the Georgian Nation;* it is "a society dominated by men" who perpetually view themselves as on display.[15] Anatol Lieven, a former Moscow-based correspondent for *The Times* (London) and the author of several books about the former Soviet Union, notes:

... the Georgians, with strong cultural traditions of individualism, machismo, and the cult of weapons, differ a great deal from the peaceable, gloomy, and obedient inhabitants of the cities of eastern and southern Ukraine. National character is not a concept much liked by contemporary political scientists, but it is necessary to explain why, all other things being equal, an ethnic dispute in Azerbaijan or Georgia would be much more likely to turn extreme and violent than would be one in Estonia or Ukraine.[16]

As I had found in Romania and elsewhere on my journey, the issue of national character again became unavoidable. To the average person, the idea that different national groups—Swedes and Iraqis, say—exhibit different characteristics is self-evident. Yet some intellectuals have trouble with such commonplaces, and for good reason: The acceptance of ingrained national characteristics can lead to stereotyping and the subsequent dehumanization of individuals. Moreover, the acceptance of national characteristics tempts pessimism, since if group traits are ingrained, then the optimistic notion that parliamentary democracy and free-market capitalism can transform societies is weakened. However, a viewpoint is not necessarily inaccurate because it happens to be morally risky and pessimistic, especially if it helps explain phenomena that are otherwise unexplainable.

"Georgians were passionate against the Soviets and passionate against each other," said Professor Alexidze. "Gamsakhurdia destroyed the Soviet spirit more than anyone, but in Georgia, a civil war was necessary because of the kind of people we are. The real cause of the war is our medievalness: Our knights of the round table simply quarreled and fought each other." These knights were Gamsakhurdia; his defense minister, Tengiz Kitovani, "a vulgar thug"; and the commander of the Mkhedrioni (Horsemen) paramilitaries, Dzhaba Ioseliani, a dapper professor and convicted bank robber, who promised to "blow out the brains" of anyone who opposed him. Kitovani and Ioseliani were part of the military council that toppled Gamsakhurdia.

From his exile in Chechnya, Gamsakhurdia maintained links with Zviadist troops in western Georgia. He also fell under the influence of the Chechen leader Dzhozkhar Dudayev, another deranged warlord, who in 1994 led Chechnya into a war with Russia that ended two years later with forty thousand dead, among them Dudayev himself. Step by step, the increasingly desperate Gamsakhurdia, the rabid, ethnocentric nationalist of the 1970s and 1980s, was allying himself with Georgia's historic rivals: Moslem Chechnya, Abashidze's Ajaria, and even Abkhazia, where a Russian-backed separatist rebellion caused ten thousand deaths and the cleansing of two hundred thousand ethnic Georgians from Abkhaz territory. Because Gamsakhurdia's forces blocked the main road out of Abkhazia into Georgia proper, half the refugees—Gamsakhurdia's own Georgians—had to detour through the mountains, where many died of starvation and exposure. This happened in 1993, when the West was preoccupied with Bosnia. But Abkhazia's wasn't the only separatist rebellion that led to ethnic cleansing in Georgia: At roughly the same time, South Ossetians were cleansing their region of thousands of ethnic Georgians.

Concurrently, Kitovani and Ioseliani had invited Eduard Shevardnadze back to Georgia from Moscow to provide international legitimacy for their hydra-headed gangland regime. Shevardnadze accepted. But rather than manipulate Shevardnadze, the opposite ensued. This former head of the secret police in Georgia played Kitovani, Ioseliani, and their associates off against each other until all were in jail. Then Shevardnadze brought reformers into government, while still keeping enough gangsters in power to prevent the formation of a unified opposition. Shevardnadze consolidated power by trial and error, and by surviving one assassination attempt after another.

By the end of 1993, Shevardnadze had surrounded the Zviadists' last stronghold in western Georgia in the town of Zugdidi, to which Gamsakhurdia had returned from Chechnya for a last stand. There, in late December, the fifty-eight-year-old Gamsakhurdia died. Either he committed suicide or was murdered; his death remains a mystery. Two months after his burial in Zugdidi, his wife exhumed his body for reburial in Chechnya. There was even a rumor that Gamsakhurdia had converted to the Islam of his Chechen allies as he lost all sense of who he was.

Professor Alexidze told me: "Our society is rotten, the mafiosi are strong, and while the West worships laws, we worship power. We leapt from the darkness in the late 1980s. We did not have the kind of social and economic development as in Central Europe. So our dissidents were never enlightened." By that definition, Havel, Sakharov, Walesa, and Djilas were real dissidents, but blood-and-soil nationalists such as Gamsakhurdia and even Solzhenitysn were not.

Back in Batumi, Eka finished her story just as the rain stopped, a condensed version of what I would hear throughout my travels in Georgia. Like others, she told me that she would put up with almost any kind of regime to prevent a recurrence of anarchy. She had her reasons. In 1993, the car that was taking her to the Tbilisi hospital where she would give birth to her son had to run the gauntlet of lethal roadblocks and mortar fire.

※ ※

It was a mystical landscape that I saw as we drove north in a taxi along the Black Sea coast from Batumi to Supsa, the terminal of a new oil pipeline from the Caspian. Alongside the brutish ugliness of concrete tenements and filthy black freight cars, we passed a succession of sublime, thickly forested hills, orchards, and gentle tea bushes on the terraced red earth, marked with cedars and cypresses. There was a stillness that reminded me of Africa as animals crossed the potholed road and young men hung about everywhere. Two roadblocks signaled the end of Abashidze's Ajaria and the beginning of Georgia proper. The taxi pulled over to a cluster of young men in tight black jeans with unshaven faces and predatory expressions, like switchblades ready to snap. Some had tattoos. One seemed drunk. The muzzle of his AK-47 assault rifle rested on his toe, the safety latch off. The distinction between security and thuggery was lost. We paid our small tribute and continued along.

The oil terminal did not look dramatic—just four circular storage tanks in the middle of a field with a nest of pipes emerging from the ground, an air-conditioned office, and a security fence around the perimeter. It was a little piece of the West in the middle of Georgia. Scott Bates, a friendly technician from Los Angeles, wearing a construction helmet, assured me that the alarms go off if the groundwater holds more than ten parts per million of oil in it, though the soil for miles around the enclosure is environmentally ruined. The handful of expatriates who ran the facility had their own electrical generator, purified drinking water, and on-site living quarters. Bates showed me the 22-inch-diameter green pipe that ran underground from Baku, in Azerbaijan, 515 miles to the east on the Caspian shore. At the moment, that pipe carried the equivalent of 105,000 barrels daily from the Caspian oil fields to a nearby offshore loading buoy, where the first tanker to ship Caspian oil to the United States had left Supsa on May 16, 1999, the day before my visit. Bates took me to a small computer room. "Three to five of us are all it takes to operate the terminal at any one time," Bates told me. "You can do it all from that desktop."

That computer and the 22-inch pipe it controls represent what the West might be willing to fight a major war over in the future. I remember visiting an airstrip in the 1980s in Berbera, Somalia, whose strategic position had provided the United States with an incentive to challenge the Soviet Union in several proxy wars in the Horn of Africa, wars that I had covered. It was a single runway with a small office and foldout beds where a few American technicians passed the time reading back issues of *Sports Illustrated*. That is all it was. Of course, strategy was about what such things did and represented. The Baku–Supsa pipeline provided a reliable way to export Central Asian oil through Georgia and Azerbaijan to the West without going through Russia. Thus, for the first time in their history, these lands could have access to the West directly by way of the Black Sea and the Bosporus. While 105,000 barrels daily wasn't much, the Baku-Supsa pipeline was the start of a Caspian oil transshipment network expected to exceed a million barrels daily by 2010. My route from Georgia to Azerbaijan and across the Caspian to Central Asia followed exactly this new Silk Road of oil.

On my last morning in Batumi, I turned on my shortwave radio to listen to the BBC World Service News. The top story was the election of Ehud Barak as Israel's new prime minister. Barak promised to seek a historic peace settlement with Syria, which experts said could leave the door open for a U.S.-Iranian rapprochement. That scared some of the Georgians I met, who worried that Western companies might rather ship Caspian oil south through Iran than west through Georgia. The Near East was interconnected as never before, and what was good news for some places was not necessarily good news for others.

※ ※

My journey eastward across Georgia from Batumi to Tbilisi took nearly seven hours in a crowded minibus filled with cigarette smoke and loud Western rap music. It was raining, and our shoes were muddy. As we left Ajaria, some scruffy-looking militiamen pulled us over; their pants didn't fit, and the zippers were missing. The driver argued with them for a few minutes. Suddenly, the driver's assistant became impatient. He stormed out of the van and strutted over to the militia post, where he slapped a packet of Georgian money into one of the soldiers' hands. We were off. The Georgian police were both a mafia and a social welfare system for themselves. Nobody really minded paying them bribes, because it was commonly assumed that their uniformed presence helped in some way to prevent another outbreak of civil war.

The road east was cluttered with pigs, mules, chickens, cows, and children selling gum to the drivers of passing cars, which were battered and reeked of diesel fumes. From the minibus's window, I saw village streets filled with women, dressed either in black or in print housedresses, trundling along carrying bags toward grim apartment blocks; men clad in worn tracksuits stood around idly smoking. The distempered walls, broken fences, and rusted, deserted factories spoke of economic decay. All the roads were full of potholes, and almost every structure was made either of undressed cement or of corrugated iron. Periodically, the militia pulled us over to a "customs station," where they accused the driver of a small infraction, and we got off with a bribe.

The minibus driver did his best to make us comfortable. He handed out candies and played a Drew Barrymore video on a small monitor beside him. We passed through lush fields, deep canyons, wooded valleys, stormy seas of mountains half hidden in mist, and across wide rivers that cut through gravel beds and soft red soil. The thick, rain-soaked grass was like velvet. How magnificent this fertile, majestic land must have appeared to the first Russian adventurers plodding south across the monotonous Ukrainian steppe! It was easy to understand the maniacal tenacity with which Russia has attempted to retain the Caucasus. Medieval churches stood like fortresses above rocky crags. Shepherd women dressed in flowing robes and carrying wooden staffs looked less primitive than the apartment blocks from the Khrushchev era.

East of Gori—the town where Stalin was born, and to which I would return—the road became smoother as we neared Tbilisi. I began to see BMWs and other expensive cars, modern gas stations, cafés sporting new red-and-white umbrellas with Coca-Cola logos: I was slowly entering an outpost of the West.

I left the minibus at a chaotic, noisy lot outside of town and took a taxi to the home of Reuters correspondent Lawrence Sheets. My first impression of Tbilisi that night was of a Balkan town, historically suggestive and with a heartrending rusticity. Leafy birch and horse-chestnut trees shaded the park where Cossacks had slaughtered striking Georgian workers a century ago near the theological institute where the young Stalin had studied for the Orthodox priesthood. Passing the park, my taxi climbed steep and narrow tree-lined cobblestone streets, some webbed over with tram wires. As in the Communist-era Balkans, there were few streetlights.

Over a dinner of heavy food and rich wine in a small, underground restaurant as intimate as the surrounding alleys, Sheets, who had covered all the Caucasus wars in the 1990s, told me that during the past winter there had been only four hours of electricity a day, and to keep from freezing, he had had his fireplace going constantly. I learned later that the electricity shortages were the result of corruption and dirty politics. Local distributors had been selling Georgia's electric power to Turkey in return for hard currency. And as if that weren't enough, kerosene suppliers were both bribing them to cut power so the population would be more dependent on kerosene and refusing to let Armenia export its electric power to Georgia. So despite $100 million in foreign aid, there was less electricity in the peaceful winter of 1998–1999 than in the winter of 1994–1995, when the civil war was winding down. In Georgia's barter economy, the companies that repaired the electric grids bought rights to sell the electricity to whom they wanted: to Turks, for instance. Corruption here was less a moral shortcoming than a survival mechanism by a people living in poverty and dominated for centuries by outsiders.

In Sheets's house the next morning, I woke to the sound of arias from the conservatory across the street. Walking downhill to Tbilisi's main thoroughfare, Rustaveli Prospekt (named for a twelfth-century Georgian poet, Shota Rustaveli), I saw flower stands, dark-haired women in black dresses, and green hills in the distance: Because of Tbilisi's medieval compactness, the countryside is always close by.

Rustaveli Prospekt was a late-nineteenth-century architectural confection, with touches of Budapest, Ljubljana, and Prague. There was a neo-Moorish opera house and city hall, a Renaissance gymnasium in happy pastel shades, a neo-Baroque theater, another building in Empire style, with caryatids, and another that was neo-Classical and painted a fabulous pink. The statues of two nineteenth-century poets, Ilia Chavchavadze and Akaki Tsereteli, stood sentinel near the two symbols of former Russian rule: the nineteenth-century viceroys' palace in delicate Empire style with dressed stone—the symbol of a bourgeois mentality that oversaw the emergence of modern European institutions—and, next to it, the vulgar, gray-brown brutalism of the mid-twentieth-century Soviet-era parliament.

At the end of Rustaveli Prospekt I turned downhill toward the Kura River, flowing east from the mountains of Turkey, and entered the oldest part of the city. Tbilisi, from the Georgian *tbili* meaning "warm"— a reference to the hot sulfur springs by the river—was founded in A.D. 458 by the Georgian king Vakhtang Gorgaslani. Marco Polo, passing through here, found it a "handsome city."[17] Byzantines, Arabs, Persians, Mongols, Seljuks, Ottomans, and North Caucasian tribes all destroyed or looted it: Each time, Tbilisi was rebuilt. Though the city center around Rustaveli Prospekt looks European, in past epochs Tbilisi looked wholly Oriental. The architecture of the old city tells the exotic story: a Persian caravansary topped by Russian domes; a Turkish bath; a Shi'ite mosque with dazzling faience, like a transplant from Isfahan; the yellow-and-white Art Nouveau residence of the former Russian patriarchate near a quiet park lined with linden trees; and towering above everything, the Persian fortress that King Vakhtang occupied in the mid-fifth century. By the river stood the mustard-colored Sioni Cathedral, which I entered for the noon mass.

Named after Mount Zion in Jerusalem, Sioni was founded sometime in the late sixth or early seventh century by a Georgian prince, but was destroyed and looted often—by Tamerlane among others. Inside, amid the monumental gray stone illuminated by shafts of sunlight, the frescoes were so faded as to be almost invisible. The cathedral was packed with people singing ethereal hymns, the musical equivalent of incense. The women wore mud-colored head shawls and had the faces of harem beauties. Herodotus suggests that every place touched by classical Greece was civilized, and here, that same ancient Greek style (not Saint Paul's Christianity) was responsible for Eastern Orthodoxy's sensuous radiance. This church service was a window into pagan antiquity.

But it was more than ancient Greece that I felt here. Assyrian monks had spread Christianity throughout Georgia following Saint Nino's conversion of the royal family, and in Georgian churches you saw an eclectic mixture of Assyrian, Hittite, Persian, Scythian, Greek, and other styles. In the eleventh-century Cathedral of Sveti-tskhoveli (The Life-Giving Column), north of Tbilisi, amid dark rugs and burning candelabra, were icons and frescoes of a savage Christ that I knew from Serbian and Ethiopian Orthodox churches. This was the Eastern faith, which is not about rationality but magic.

At the Samtavro Monastery a few miles from Sveti-tskhoveli, a nun showed me where the Russians—like the Moslem Turks—had covered all the Georgian frescoes under whitewash. The style of Russian Orthodoxy is imperial—whitewashed walls, to highlight the material accumulation of icons, censers, and silver chandeliers—whereas the Georgian church, with its primitive and austere frescoes, is a fighting church, a peasants' church, whose aim is sheer preservation. The nuns at Samtavro were shrouded in black, like Iranian women. They showed me an icon of King Mirian and Queen Nana, the royal couple who converted to Christianity in the fourth century and who are buried here. The royal faces were pious and stern. I thought of the dangerous certainty of the icon painter and sensed the insecurity of an old ethnic nation surrounded by enemies. Here, as in Romania, people offered you Oriental coffee while they talked of their Europeanness. And, as in Romania, their insistence was all the more poignant because they were partially right.

22

FOSSIL NATIONS

The message from Tbilisi's intellectuals about Georgia's future was grim and well argued. But the very erudition of their monologues, along with the return to normal life after the civil war that I had observed in Tbilisi's cobblestone streets, made Georgia's capital seem at times a credible, precious little outpost of Europe.

On a narrow street in Tbilisi I entered a dilapidated house with exposed mortar and peeling walls and one of those awful eaten-away Soviet-era hallways. A door opened and Zaal Kikodze, an archaeologist specializing in the Stone Age, invited me inside. Old books crammed every inch of wall space. Kikodze, with his wiry, ashen beard, wore a dark woollen work shirt. I asked him what Georgian history says about Georgia's future. He said, "Such questions are best discussed over cheese and wine."

We ate and drank a bit. Then he began in earnest.

"We, the Armenians, the Romanians, and others want to swim in a pure river. But the water we want to swim in has already passed to the ocean. You can't be a pure nation anymore, like the French and Germans used to be. At the stage of technology we have reached, nations work only if they float in the larger world. And what you have in this part of the world are fossilized nations, dead societies that have yet to revive. There are a group of young reformers in our parliament, educated in the West. But Georgians only want heroes. These reformers have never killed, they don't drink two liters of wine every evening, they don't fight, they have no mustaches or daggers, so they can't be heroes!

"And we will never be able to rely on the United States or NATO. We are too far from Europe, too close to Russia. NATO will not bomb for weeks to save Georgians from ethnic cleansing in Abkhazia the way it bombed to save Albanians in Kosovo." Kikodze told me that many of the American and European NGOs—aid workers from "non-governmental organizations"—in Georgia had a trait in common with the early Marxists: "They don't realize that their ideas about improving society are abstractions that float above culture and history. And when they are absorbed by a culture, any culture, their ideas are changed or subverted."

Kikodze criticized the Soviet Union but defended Russia. "The Russians built up Tbilisi in the nineteenth century as the capital of Transcaucasia. On this street, where I have lived since 1958, there used to be Kurds, Armenians, Jews, Russians, and others. It was a golden age. We thought nationalism did not exist. Then it destroyed us. The Jews left for Israel; the Armenians, for Armenia; the Russians, for Russia; and so on. And now we are losing the Russian language, which is a disaster for us. English is still only for a rarefied elite, while the loss of Russian cuts the average Georgian off from the outside world. All our books of learning, our encyclopedias on art, literature, history, science, are in Russian. Young Georgians can no longer communicate with Armenians and Ossetians. There is a new illiteracy that is promoting ethnic separation."

Americans, I thought, are triumphant about the collapse of the Soviet Union. But throughout the Caucasus and beyond, I experienced firsthand how the Soviet collapse, while a blessing in the long run, has meanwhile ruined millions of real lives. Communism, however disastrous, was still a system that provided pensions, schooling, social peace, and physical security for a multitude of people who often had no recollection of anything better. The collapse of that system has left a chaotic void that, so far, has made life here much worse.

※ ※

"Georgians are a very old tribal entity, but we have no identity as a modern state. We are a quasi-state," said Alexander Rondeli, the head of a research institute connected to the Georgian Ministry of Foreign Affairs. Rondeli, the doyen of Georgian intellectuals, was fifty-seven but looked older. With his grave and sardonic voice, his large physique, striking white hair, and thick black eyebrows, Rondeli was like the magisterial voice of history itself, issuing up from the ground, wise and ironic, laden with a vast accumulation of knowledge and memories.

"All nations often get what they deserve," Rondeli told me with a slight smile, "so to see what kind of government Georgia will have in the future, it is merely a matter of dissecting our national character. We are nominally Christian, but really we are superstitious atheists. We know how to survive but not how to improve. Our church is pagan, politicized, part of the national resistance, and thus unable to move forward." This was exactly what Romanians and Bulgarians had told me about their Orthodox churches.

"Remember," Rondeli went on, "we had seventy-four years of political-cultural-economic emasculation under the Soviet Union; three generations of Georgians were destroyed. The West concentrates on the crimes of Hitler, but the Nazis ruled for only twelve years."

Rondeli was bursting with stories. As we talked, we moved to a restaurant that served homemade wine, and he continued for hours: "My mother's family, all educated people, were shot in the purges of 1937. You see, Stalin would never have been promoted in a democratic society—he would have ended his life as a marginal criminal. In the 1930s, when Stalin arrived at the Tbilisi railway station for an official visit as the emperor of Russia, it was the first time in years that he saw his mother. You know what he said to her? 'Are you still a whore?' I know people who were there. They heard it.

"My father," Rondeli continued, "had a friend, a prominent actor, Spartak Bargashvili, whom Stalin invited once to the Kremlin. Spartak sat with Stalin late into the night, drinking vodka and speaking in Georgian. Spartak wanted to leave, but Stalin wouldn't let him. Finally Spartak left. At the door, Stalin said, 'Come live with me here. I have no one to talk to.' Stalin, Spartak had told me, was looking at him with the eyes of a child.

"Let me tell you another story." Rondeli's voice and expression had now lost all trace of wit and irony, so that his manner was merely sad. "I knew this old Georgian who as a young boy had lived at a collective farm in the 1930s. There had been an election at the farm, and the man nominated to run the farm was not very good and everyone knew it, but of course no one said anything. But my friend spoke up from the back of the hall: 'You know, this man is not qualified.' There was some small rumbling, and an older fellow sitting nearby said gently, 'Come with me, young lad.' My friend went with the man. The man asked to see his identity card. The card showed that my friend was seventeen. The man quickly took a pencil and changed the seven to an eight, because you couldn't imprison someone under eighteen, according to the *law*," Rondeli said the word sarcastically. "This older fellow was with the NKVD. My friend spent the next ten years in a labor camp in north-central Siberia—from the age of seventeen to twenty-seven." Rondeli snapped his fingers and said, "Like that, ten years—that's how those things happened.

"Well, my friend was tough and he survived. His job was to drive the cart each evening that transported the bodies to the common grave. They weren't always dead—nobody was careful about these things—but it didn't matter, since the cold and the dirt would kill them soon enough. Anyway, one night, after his work detail, my friend was lying in his bunk singing a tune in Georgian. Suddenly, amid the howls of the wind, he heard a voice crying faintly in Georgian, 'Help me, help me.' This startled my friend, because he hadn't heard Georgian spoken in a long time. He went out to investigate. One of the bodies was still alive. It was another Georgian, who heard my friend singing and called for help. My friend dug him up—the grave hadn't been completely covered—and he managed to save the man. Years later, after they were both released, they met in Batumi, where the fellow insisted that my friend come and meet his family. They spent days drinking and honoring my friend. Both my friend and this other fellow died a few years later, still relatively young. The years in Siberia had done something to their health. You multiply this story by fourteen, twenty, or thirty million, you will have an idea what Stalin was able to accomplish." Across the table from me, Rondeli raised his thick eyebrows.

Like everyone else in Georgia, Rondeli was obsessed with Russia. In words similar to the archaeologist Kikodze, he told me: "After Kosovo, the West will not intervene east of the Carpathians. Kosovo was a difficult and lucky victory for NATO, so we in the Caucasus know that we are alone against the Kremlin." NATO's air war against the Serbs in Kosovo coincided with my journey through the Caucasus. People here seemed to have two related reactions to it. They were much too impressed with the bold, naked display of Western power to be concerned over the Clinton administration's clumsy diplomacy and planning for the operation. But they also felt that the ten weeks of NATO bombing would never be replicated in the Caucasus, no matter what atrocities the Russians or anyone else perpetrated here.

Another Georgian intellectual described the Russians to me "as Scythians, still unformed, unsettled, who in the twentieth century rediscovered the art of laying waste whole tracts of territory." Along with the hatred of communism that often spilled over into hatred of Russians went a dislike of Armenians, "usurers who ruined Georgian families, who are now allied with Russia against Georgia and Azerbaijan."

"The Armenians are always claiming that they are the best, that they are fighting with nothing, even while Russia supports them."

"I don't like Armenians. The Azeris are nicer people."

"The only good-looking Armenian is Cher."

Listening to Georgians talk about Armenians gave me the chilling sensation of what Old World anti-Semitism must have been like.

※ ※

Yet in Tbilisi I felt hope. Its economy had been declining by double digits in the first half of the 1990s, but since 1996 it had been growing by double digits.[1] Traffic had doubled within a year. A city that in the mid-1990s had few cars now had downtown traffic jams. Art galleries had opened. New apartment buildings were rising near the parliament, in an area that had been destroyed by the civil war. Tbilisi in the late 1990s seemed like Beirut in the early 1990s, when rising property values indicated that confidence had returned.

The intellectuals viewed these developments skeptically, because they knew how Georgia had experienced one revival after another, only to be crushed by Turkey, Persia, or Russia, as in the 1920s, when the West withdrew and the Bolsheviks rebuilt the Russian empire. Yet while history follows familiar patterns, precise repetitions are rare.

For instance, there was Mikheil Saakashvili, and what he might portend.

Saakashvili, thirty, was the majority leader in parliament, the head of the Citizens Union party founded by President Shevardnadze. The westernized Saakashvili—he had a law degree from Columbia University—was among the reformers that, the archaeologist Kikodze had lamented, were not heroes because they had not killed and did not drink enough. I met Saakashvili, a tall man with stringy black hair and a dark suit, at his office in parliament at ten at night, working. He was not naive, as I had feared, but cagily analytical. He had an ego—favorable articles about him covered the walls—and his manner was slightly sleazy: useful survival traits.

Saakashvili disagreed that Georgia was doomed because NATO would never bomb here. "Sometimes very little is needed to survive," he told me. "We don't need thirty thousand NATO troops or weeks of bombing—just small, highly specialized security forces from the West to protect our president from assassination, to monitor our borders, to protect the new oil pipeline. If Washington pays attention and gives us advance warning and technical help, we may manage." Saakashvili spoke smoothly, as if he had used these same phrases before, but he made sense.

"Unemployment and other statistics are meaningless, because a huge black market helps Georgia survive.[2] . . . because Georgians have always been corrupt and cynical, with mafias an old tradition, there is not a strong Communist opposition in parliament as in Russia. This helps. . . . Ultimately, a loose federal state is unavoidable, in order to make peace with Abkhazia and South Ossetia."

Saakashvili and Georgia's feisty parliament were the work of one man, Shevardnadze.

※ ※

During my stay in Tbilisi, it was announced that yet another plot—the nineteenth—to assassinate Shevardnadze had been uncovered. The next morning, Shevardnadze called a press conference. The president calmly told the gathered journalists that the latest plot was more than a planned assassination attempt against him—it involved a military coup "to remove the entire leadership," including cabinet members and parliamentarians. Of the nineteen reported conspiracies, at least two had been full-fledged assassination attempts: a gun-and-grenade attack, and a car bombing. When we started to ask questions, Shevardnadze required a hearing aid: The car bomb had damaged his ear.

"The chieftain of this new plot is located abroad, in Russia," Shevardnadze told us. It was nothing new. With Georgia gradually stabilizing; with democracy, however tenuous and corrupt, beginning to take hold; and with the country becoming a strategic corridor for Western oil companies, killing Shevardnadze, who was bringing Georgia closer to the West, was the only game the Russians could still play here. For the Russians, a buffer state like Georgia that could serve as a listening post into the Moslem world was vital. No Western diplomats I met had any doubt that Russia was behind the assassination attempts.

Shevardnadze, seventy-one, was a burly man with white curly hair and, normally, a ruddy complexion. But now he was haggard and exhausted, and it was clear that helping to run the world as Soviet foreign minister had been a lot easier for him than running Georgia. His voice was deep and gruff, but he was patient, as though he were conducting a fireside chat with us—twenty local reporters and myself. Unlike in Moscow, none of the reporters here wore ties, and quite a few wore jeans and disheveled shirts. Nor were they overly polite. One reporter asked the president why he was blaming the Russians when the CIA was known to have ordered assassination attempts on Castro. This former Politburo member, used to limousines with the curtains drawn, symbolizing the power he had wielded in a vast tyrannical state, did not lose his temper at this. He smiled and enjoyed the exchange. In his own way, Shevardnadze had become a democrat. At his side was his media adviser, known to be a loyal mediocrity. In Shevardnadze's position, having loyal people around you was more important than having talented ones. Shevardnadze had a simple strategy: personal physical survival. If he survived a few more years without dying or being killed—enough time, perhaps, for more political stabilization, more reforms, more institution-building—then his personal survival, or that of his successor, might no longer be synonymous with the survival of the state itself.

Shevardnadze was careful not always to confront the Russians but to make deals with them, too. He kept dishonest men in power, and he had many lines of communication open to old friends in Moscow. George Washington had fought the British by retreating until they got tired of the war and left. Shevardnadze's strategy was similar.

Eduard Amvrosiyevich Shevardnadze was one of three famous Georgians in twentieth-century world history. The other two were Stalin and Stalin's feared secret police chief, Lavrenti Beria, a bespectacled man who combined the roles of Himmler and Eichmann in Stalin's death machine. There are many similarities between Shevardnadze and these two great criminals. They too were manipulators, able to take advantage of any situation; they both betrayed their best friends as they rose to power. None of the three was truly educated, but all were talented: Each man had the strong intuition of a good hunting dog, who could sniff the essence of every idea and situation and adapt it to his needs. A local publisher, Zaza Gachechiladze, showed me a Georgian translation of Machiavelli's *The Prince* and exclaimed, "Shevardnadze did not have to read this—he had it in his genes. For example, after one assassination attempt, everyone expected Shevardnadze to fire his interior minister. But he didn't. What could be more useful than an interior minister who has been politically discredited, so that he cannot plot against you, because he is now totally dependent on your goodwill! Shevardnadze now runs the police directly through this man."

Morality is a funny thing. In the 1970s and early 1980s, it seemed that Gamsakhurdia—the intellectual who had translated Shakespeare—had been a moral man while Shevardnadze, the Communist hack, was an immoral one. But Shevardnadze, the Machiavellian hunting dog, had sniffed out the rot in the system he was a part of, and, along with his allies Mikhail Gorbachev and Alexander Yakovlev, tried to reform it for the sake of their own survival. They failed and the Soviet Union collapsed. The peaceful dissolution of the Soviet Union, perhaps the single most significant event of the twentieth century, owes almost as much to Shevardnadze as to Gorbachev. Meanwhile, Shevardnadze's survival game continued in Georgia, where the lessons of *The Prince* were the surest path to democratization.

But how long could Shevardnadze survive? The Kremlin had an imperial mentality, but Washington did not. America's diplomats sounded practically fatalistic: "It's their game in the end. They've got to reform the tax system, the police, to end corruption, and so on." Of course, corruption constituted the most corrosive afterimage of communism, but for that very reason it would continue at high levels long after Shevardnadze's death. The West could not just fold its hands and hope that in a few years Georgian society would unlearn the bad lessons of not only decades but centuries. "We'll be walking along the edge of a razor blade until enough oil is flowing through here to give the West the selfish interest it needs to fight for us. Russia will do everything to destabilize Georgia before that happens," Revaz Adamia, the Parliament's head of the defense committee, told me.

❦ ❦

The slow-moving train from Tbilisi westward to Gori, Stalin's birthplace, took two hours. The ticket cost the equivalent of 70 cents. The carriage, with peeling walls, rusted luggage racks, broken ceiling lights, and hard wooden seats, was stuffed with people lugging burlap sacks and wearing dark, smelly clothes. Old women went through the aisles selling biscuits, gray-striped socks, plastic slippers, and cigarettes. Gori stood on the sloping grasslands along the Kura River, in sight of the snow-capped granite pinnacles of the High Caucasus, the main spine of the mountains that separate the Russian Federation from the Transcaucasian republics of Georgia, Armenia, and Azerbaijan. Gori was a town of five thousand when Iosif Dzugashvili (Stalin) was born on December 21, 1879, a short while before this railway was built. In 1999 its population was almost seventy thousand.

The architecture of Gori's train station symbolized the violence of the Soviet system: massive cement walls and undressed stone at sharp angles. The area was deserted except for swarms of flies and a few old women outside selling beets, scallions, and dusty bottles of beer. The columned waiting room inside was decorated with cheap plywood and also deserted, except for a woman dressed in rags who was talking to herself and swatting away the flies. A large, yellowing statue of Stalin, scroll in hand like a prophet, watched over the bleakness of the room.

Behind the station, I found ramshackle huts with tin roofs, a single beggar, a dead puppy, mounds of garbage, some hideous Khrushchev-era apartment blocks, and absurdly wide boulevards nearly empty of traffic and pedestrians. On a hill in the distance was a fortress besieged by Pompey in 65 B.C., and rebuilt by Persians and Turks in medieval times. I walked along a boulevard that soon opened out into an immense square, dominated by a three-story-high statue of Stalin. The entire square was empty except for two men fixing a car.

I was hungry, and found what seemed to be the only café downtown. It looked like the dining room of a small prison. I inquired about the cheese pies behind the counter. "They're two days old," the woman told me. "What about the other cakes?" I asked. "You must ask the other woman," she replied. I settled for Turkish coffee and watery ice cream. The napkins were strips of rough toilet paper.

Stalin had been born across the street, in a small wooden hut that was now enclosed within a pompous Greco-Italianate pavilion, built in 1939. I entered and saw the room where he was born and lived till he was four years old. The family's coarse blankets and wooden table were on display. From the tiny porch, I looked out over a vast promenade. There were weeds everywhere.

Beside the pavilion was a palatial structure that housed the Stalin Museum. A middle-age woman with a flashlight and a pointer led me through the succession of dark, freezing rooms: There was no electricity in town at the moment. Between massive ceremonial urns were large black-and-white photos that showed Stalin in all stages of his life. There were also pictures of smiling peasants on tractors and other images of socialist happiness. In one glass case was a bureaucratic document that Stalin had filled out. I remembered Stalin's infamous dictum that "paper will put up with anything that is written on it."[3]

"I see no photos of Trotsky, Bukharin, and Zinoviev," I remarked.

"They were not significant in the Revolution," the woman told me calmly.

"Tell me," I asked her. "What do people in Gori really think of Stalin?"

"Why, people here love Stalin!" she exclaimed, surprised at my question. "If we still had Stalin's iron discipline, we wouldn't have crime and disorder. Chaos will never lead to a positive result. The Communists built bridges and other things. What has the new government done for us?" This explained the survival of the huge statue I had seen earlier.

In a café on Tbilisi's Rustaveli Prospekt several days later, I met Yasha Djugashvili, Stalin's great-grandson. "Stalin is a business for them," he told me casually, referring to Gori's citizens. "What else do they have? Stalin was the only one in town who made it big. Gori reflects the collapse of living standards in Georgia since the late 1980s. It represents all the people who are not able to compete in a cruel economy or who were not positioned to make quick wealth when the system collapsed. Now we have a new wealthy class that doesn't care about culture, science, or anything except money and pleasure, and spends too much at the new casinos and on fancy cars, while the rest of the population is unprotected, exposed. Stalin represents nostalgia for those who can imagine nothing better than the security of the Communist era."

"In other words," I said, "if Gori ever develops economically, the Stalin Museum will probably close and people will be embarrassed by it."

Djugashvili, in his late twenties, agreed. He looked shockingly like his great-grandfather, I thought. But I quickly forgot about his looks, and even his ancestry. With his fluent English and intelligence, Djugashvili represented something more important: the smattering of highly educated young Georgians with decent values, who will probably emigrate if the pace of development and institution-building here doesn't speed up.

❧ ❧

I left Gori for South Ossetia, a region of north-central Georgia where a nasty little war was fought in the early 1990s, a war that to the outside world was incomprehensible and forgettable, while to those involved nothing less than the universe itself was at stake.

Among the Ossetes, who speak a language akin to Persian, there are both Moslems and Orthodox Christians. Their religious heterogeneity helped keep them neutral in czarist Russia's campaigns against the purely Moslem peoples of the Caucasus, such as the Chechens, Ingush,

Dagestanis, and so on. Thus, they emerged as a somewhat convenient ally to the atheistic Soviet Union. The Ossetes also boasted a strategic position, straddling both the north and south slopes of the High Caucasus, halfway between the Black and Caspian Seas. Lenin and Stalin adopted the Ossetes as a favored people: They were provided with an autonomous republic on the northern slopes of the High Caucasus and an autonomous region within the Soviet Republic of Georgia, on the southern slopes. After the Soviet Union collapsed, North Ossetia became the site of an ethnic war between the Ossetes and the Ingush, their neighbors, whom Stalin had deported from North Ossetia in 1944 and who returned in the late 1950s only to find the best land taken by Ossetes. The Northern Ossetes, helped by Russia, won a military victory and expelled thousands of Ingush civilians in 1992. At the same time, South Ossetia declared its intention to leave Georgia and join North Ossetia in a new "Greater Ossetia." This led to a war in which about thirty thousand ethnic Georgians (a third of South Ossetia's population) were expelled.

The border between Georgia and South Ossetia was marked by militia posts, which ignored my rented car. South Ossetia proved to be a lower circle of hell than provincial Georgia. Its site, adjacent to the snow-blanketed High Caucasus, was damp and cold even in May. The potholes were deeper and more numerous here than in Georgia, and the outskirts of Tskhinvali, the South Ossetian capital, were a panorama of weedy lots, muddy streets, garbage mounds, shell-pocked houses, and destitute people. I left the car and searched for a café. The only one I found was inside a warehouse, and it resembled a soup kitchen for the homeless. The only customer, I ordered Turkish coffee. On Stalin Street, a principal thoroughfare, the breeze-block tenements were decorated with pergolas made of rusted poles and camouflage netting. The sidewalks were broken, and dangling electric wires were ever-present. Among the women, I saw many brave attempts at Western fashions and makeup, applied no doubt in badly lit, leaky bathrooms. For a traveler, everything is relative: Compared to Tskhinvali, rural Georgia was like Tuscany.

Yet Tskhinvali's markets were bursting with goods: fruit from South America, American cigarettes, Russian beer and caviar, and a wide variety of luxury liquors and toiletry items from Western Europe. I even found a pair of designer jeans that fit me, for which I paid $8. Outside of town I found large, muddy lots, where Georgians, arriving in caravans of cars, came to buy pure grain alcohol, diesel fuel, and cigarettes in large quantities. U.S. dollars, Russian rubles, and Georgian lari were all accepted.

South Ossetia's was a kiosk economy, like Georgia's other breakaway provinces, Abkhazia and Ajaria. These places survived on smuggling and narcotics traffic. Here was another way that Russia undermined Georgia—by flooding it with untaxed fuel and other goods through Abkhazia and South Ossetia. In Tskhinvali, as in Gori, everyone I met (students, tradespeople, pensioners) revered Stalin. They talked about how much better life had been in the Soviet era, when a 120-ruble monthly pension had meaning. Nobody I met had much hope, and they all spoke generously about the past. When I mentioned that a reunion with Georgia would likely mean an improved economy for South Ossetia, no one seemed interested. They wanted union only with North Ossetia, which was currently embroiled in Russia's chaos. Politics here was not about rationality as the West conceives it but about manipulating the irrational. As I had found in the Balkans, in the Caucasus one could be optimistic in the capital cities, but in the provinces one confronted the hardest truths.

23

FROM TBILISI

TO BAKU

Heavy rains from the previous night had turned the rippling highlands southeast of Tbilisi a bright green with a dusting of red poppies. Even so, the lushness of western and central Georgia was absent here, and the landscape soon evoked the bone-dryness of Anatolia. I was still following the path of the new underground oil pipeline eastward. After an hour of driving, I reached the border post with Azerbaijan, marked by a photo of Shevardnadze clasping hands with the Azeri president, Heydar Aliyev. Like Alexander's generals, who carved up his empire after his death, these two ex-Politburo members had each taken a piece of the former Soviet Union. However, while Shevardnadze belonged to the reformist Gorbachev-era Politburo, Aliyev had been a Brezhnev-era man, whom Gorbachev expelled from the Politburo for his corrupt ways. The difference between them explains a lot about the difference between Georgia and Azerbaijan.

Despite the horde of slovenly officials doing nothing, nobody asked me for a bribe. This was a border between two poor countries, not between a poor one and a richer one, where prosperous people could be ripped off. In a moment my passport was stamped and I had, effortlessly, entered Azerbaijan.

The difference between Turkey and Georgia was less cultural than political: It was the difference between a free-market society and a society recovering from civil war and seventy-four years of communism.

But the border I had just crossed represented an authentic civilizational divide—between Orthodox Christianity and Turkic Islam—and a subtle political fault line, too.

The road immediately deteriorated, and the kiosks alongside it were rustier and more run-down. There were few cars. Tiny donkeys lugged massive bundles of wheat in old carts that wended their way through the potholes. The corrugated-iron roofs were more weathered here than in Georgia, and often had large gaps. The grinding Soviet brutality was more apparent as the landscape turned browner and drier, as dry riverbeds replaced the magnificent rivers of Georgia. The cool thunderstorm of the night before in Tbilisi seemed a distant memory now. By the road, I saw two men squatting on their haunches as they talked and smoked. It was a common sight throughout the Moslem world and much of Asia, where men were comfortable in such a position, but during the past few weeks in Georgia I hadn't seen it. From where I was now, Georgia seemed European.

I saw dark-skinned shepherds with flat caps, as I had in Turkey, working with hoes and pitchforks. Sheep, donkeys, cows, and even large turtles crossed the road. I passed a village on the last day of school, where the children were parading in uniforms with their diplomas. The parents, in their best clothes, walked awkwardly, like peasants. Men held one another's hands and fingered prayer beads. The women stumbled on their high heels. I felt as if I were back in Turkey—but a Turkey of the 1940s. A young man in a flat cap was selling scarves. As I passed him, he waved the scarves at me in a slow and syrupy movement that for some reason conjured up all the grace of Islamic civilization.

I had last visited Azerbaijan in 1993, when it was in a state of chaos and collapse. Since then, the news from Azerbaijan reported the country's oil boom. I expected to see dramatic development. But, except for a few new mosques and gas stations along the pipeline route, Azerbaijan looked even poorer than I remembered it.

To the south, the snow-covered mountains rose sharply. These were the mountains that led into Armenia and the ethnic-Armenian enclave of Nagorno-Karabakh, officially part of Azerbaijan but taken by Armenia in a war in the early 1990s. By midafternoon I reached

Gandzha, Azerbaijan's second-largest city, with a population of three hundred thousand. I was traveling with Nata, my new translator, whom I had met in Tbilisi and who spoke Russian and Azeri. She thought I was crazy to stop in Gandzha. "There is nothing in Gandzha—it's a dump," she said. That's also what journalist Thomas Goltz had written in his comprehensive account of the country, *Azerbaijan Diary*. And that's why I decided to stop here. Gandzha was journalistic terra incognita. Yet history had shown how important Gandzha could be. In May 1918, with the Russian empire dissolving in a civil war between Bolsheviks and pro-czarist Whites, soldiers in Gandzha declared an independent republic. With the help of a Turkish army that had just crossed the border, they marched on Baku, where the Azerbaijan Democratic Republic was born, only to be overrun by the resurgent Bolsheviks in 1920. Then in June 1993, a militia leader in Gandzha, Surat Husseinov, revolted against the local government garrison. This sparked a chain of events that led to the overthrow of newly independent Azerbaijan's democratically elected government and the appointment of Heydar Aliyev as dictator.

※ ※

The first thing I saw in Gandzha were the usual hideous apartment blocks, their windows broken and filthy. Then came quiet, dusty streets with a lone hotel, whose vast, empty lobby led to grim hallways and forlorn rooms: Mine had a broken television and a poster of a bowl of cherries that hung askew. There was no hot water, and the toilet seat was broken.

Across the street was the old Communist party headquarters, a brown-concrete structure about the length of a football field, with a billboard-size poster of Aliyev facing an immense square. Under the colorful new umbrellas with Coca-Cola and Marlboro logos that shaded the café tables, the square was filled with people, and it seemed a happy place. Men predominated, sipping tea, twirling prayer beads, playing backgammon, and listening to Turkish music. The waiters, too, were all male—many of them boys. In Georgia women were everywhere; here, they were not. The tea (*chai*) was freshly brewed and better than in Georgia. But, unlike in Georgia, there was no wine to be had. No one spoke Russian. Everyone spoke Azeri.

I ordered Cokes and kebabs for Nata and me, and then approached the nearby mosque, took my shoes off, and entered. The interior was marked by machine-made carpets and peeling paint, yet it was filled with men and boys, who, I noticed, did not all know the Arabic prayers. But this is how observance begins—by simply doing it, however incorrectly. The mosque, like the square with the men quietly sipping *chai,* was a real Islamic space.

"What are we going to do?" Nata asked me.

It was a good question. Gandzha didn't offer much choice. "Let's talk to that guy," I said, pointing to a young man with a crew cut, who was wearing a leather vest over his pajama shirt. "He looks interesting."

"All right," said Nata. We walked over to introduce ourselves.

"I'm visiting from the USA," I began, with Nata translating for the young man. "I haven't been in Azerbaijan for six years. What's happening here? Are the Turks still gaining influence? What's the economy like?"

He exploded: "Yes, there's more and more Turkish influence and less Russian, but we're still slaves. In Baku they hate Gandzhavis. They're afraid of us. They know how rebellious we are. We are like a Kosovo inside the beast of Yugoslavia. Islam is growing here. All the young men like me are without jobs. Life is much worse now than under the Soviets."

The young man's friend, no less angry, joined the conversation: "Yes, economic development and more Islam is what we need. Aliyev is no good. Politics is only for dirty people in Baku. We don't want politics or nationalism. We are Moslems. We want to be like Europe, not like Baku."

A policeman was standing nearby, but the two young men didn't seem to care. "Can I take out a notebook?" I asked them. They shrugged. I began to write in their presence. The policeman, unshaven and with an ill-fitting uniform, paid no attention.

The two young men then began complaining about the "Nakhichevansi mafia" that ran Baku under both Aliyev and the democratic regime before him. Nakhichevan was a cartographic anomaly: an isolated fragment of Azerbaijan off to the southwest—surrounded by Armenia, Iran, and Turkey. Because Nakhichevan's inhabitants lived in close proximity to the Christian Armenians, they had developed a

strong and organized sense of Moslem clan loyalty. Though Nakhichevan and Gandzha were both part of Azerbaijan, these two young
men talked as if Nakhichevan were the enemy. In fact, they never mentioned the words *Azeri* or *Azerbaijan* at all. They talked only of *Islam,
Baku,* and *Gandzha.* Here in Gandzha, the nation was weak and the police were weak, but regional identity was strong. At the same time, pan-
national yearnings in the form of Islam and Western pop culture were
growing. It was hard to imagine a more politically unstable combination.

Azerbaijan had always been a marchland, conquered by Alexander
the Great and fought over by Turkey and Persia for centuries. As with
Georgia, Russia entered the fray here relatively late, occupying the area
briefly in the 1720s and 1730s and then returning in the nineteenth century. The local Azeris, who knew little political unity until the twentieth
century, speak a Turkic language much like modern Turkish, but they
are Shi'ite, like most Iranians. Most Azeris live not in Azerbaijan but to
the south, in northwestern Iran.[1] Until the early twentieth century, the
Azeris were considered "Tartars" by their neighbors, and responded to
questions about themselves by mentioning their family, their clan, and
their religion—but rarely their national group. Georgia has a 2,500-
year-old alphabet all its own. Azerbaijan, by contrast, changed its alphabet three times over the course of the twentieth century: from
Arabic to Latin in the 1920s; from Latin to Cyrillic in the 1930s; and
back to Latin in the 1990s.

The inability of the Azeris to congeal into a defined nation may be
why the Armenians could destroy them in the war over Karabakh. The
Armenians, with their own language and 1,500-year-old alphabet—and
with the memory of brilliant ancient and medieval kingdoms and the
Turkish genocide always before them—had a fine sense of who they
were. The Armenians, everyone in the Caucasus knew, were never
going to give up Karabakh in negotiations. No one gives up what has
been captured in battle when the area is occupied overwhelmingly by
one's own ethnic group and the rest of the population has been violently expelled, with barely a murmur from the Great Powers or the
global media.

Nata and I said good-bye to the two young men and left the square.

We had no plan as we walked other than to look for other people to chat with.

Gandzha, founded in the fifth or sixth century A.D, may have got its name from the Arabic *dzhanzar,* meaning "treasury" or "harvest store." Throughout its history, Persians, Arabs, Mongols, and Seljuk Turks leveled or captured it; but in the eighteenth century, Gandzha became an independent khanate. In the Soviet period through 1990, Gandzha was known as Kirovabad, after Sergey Mironovich Kirov, the Russian revolutionary who helped secure Transcaucasia for Stalin.[2] But by 1999 Russian influence was fading fast. We passed a new Turkish *pastane,* a sweets shop like those in rural Anatolia but that here seemed modern. I spotted a grocery with Turkish and Azeri flags outside and a glossy photo of Manhattan inside. It turned out to be a Turkish-Azeri joint venture. I found other stores selling sports shoes and compact disks, also owned or partly owned by Turks. It wasn't so much Turkish culture that Azeris were attracted to but global culture, which, because of its language and proximity, Turkey was in the best position to offer. I noticed an awning with a picture of the Great Mosque in Mecca. It identified an office where locals could sign up to make the annual Moslem pilgrimage, the *haj.* It had opened after the Soviet Union collapsed. Later, we found a market selling refrigerators from Belarus, electric mixers from France, cell phones from Asia, and fresh fruit from Iran, Israel, and Greek Cyprus, priced in U.S. dollars. A kilo of mandarins cost $3, about the same price as in New York City. I also saw quite a few BMWs and sports utility vehicles. Gandzha was like Batumi, a sprinkle of globalization with criminal overtones over a carcass of Soviet-era poverty. There may be no crueler kind of capitalism than the post-Communist variety.

But we also found quiet streets with lovely brickwork and tulip-shaped archways, what seemed an original confection of Seljuk, Armenian, and Persian influences. We were admiring a beautiful courtyard when a group of middle-aged men invited us to sit with them and drink *chai* at a nearby café. They asked me where I was from and what I knew about Gandzha. When it was apparent that I knew nothing about the medieval poet Nezami Ganjavi, one man ran to his home and returned with a book of Nezami's poetry for me to look at.

Nezami Ganjavi (Nezami "of Gandzha"), I soon learned, was born in 1141 and died in 1209. He spent his entire life in Gandzha, during a golden period of weakening Seljuk power and before the Mongol invasion. At the time, Gandzha was virtually independent, and a form of enlightened multiculturalism reigned. Persian has historically been a fine medium for sensuous poetry, and Nezami's *Khamsa* poems are rated among the greatest in the Persian language, along with Firdausi's *Shah Nameh* and the poems of Hafiz. Nezami Ganjavi, as the name implied, was associated with Gandzha, not with Azerbaijan, which didn't exist then. He didn't write in Azeri, and for these men he was a local hero, not a national one.

"Life is miserable," one of the men told me, slapping his hands angrily. "We have electricity, water, and gas only a few hours a day, even though in Baku they have all this money from oil and natural gas. Baku is like a separate republic from us."

Another man broke in, his arm slicing the air: "Where are our pensions? Our pensions should be worth twenty dollars. Now they are worth three dollars! The money never leaves Baku. Baku is rich, with all of its oil! We were better off under Moscow. We don't want those Nakhichevansis Aliyev and Elcibey." [Ebulfez Elcibey was the democratically elected president whom Aliyev toppled.]

A big, burly man with a gray mustache and a tight-fitting shirt with an Adidas logo said: "I killed forty-two Armenians in the fighting in Karabakh—it's only an hour from here. Where is my reward?"

"The only real democracy we had in Gandzha was under Brezhnev," one of the men explained, "because then we lived well and had good pensions." Another told me: "The German army advanced as far as North Ossetia in World War Two. Had the Germans conquered Baku, we would all be better off. Look how well they live in Germany!" But another disagreed: "Stalin was a real man. He gave us a good living standard compared to now." When I mentioned the NATO bombing of Serbia, which was occurring during my visit, they all approved. "NATO is strong—it's a real power," one man said. The others nodded. Though they were doubtful that the West would intervene militarily here for any reason. Among such people, dropping bombs on a city the size of Belgrade gave the West credibility. It was the kind of aggression that locals had seen often through their history and could respect.

The attitudes of these men were typical of the politics I found throughout the Near East, an attitude that was morally neutral compared to that in the West and that saw politics in terms of physical power and living standards, as might have been expected with people living on the edge.

That day, I heard repeated variations on the theme of Gandzha versus Baku. Georgia was a weak quasi-state, but compared to Gandzha, the Georgian state seemed very strong.

※ ※

The next morning, I attended the mass at the local Russian Orthodox church. In the Middle Ages, Gandzha, though Islamized, was also a center of Christianity, and through much of the twentieth century, it had a sizable community of Armenian Orthodox and Russian Orthodox Christians. Now, only a handful of old people were left in the Christian community, since the Russians and Armenians had fled with the collapse of the Soviet Union. The old Russian women conducted the mass themselves, without a priest. Some supported themselves with canes, hunched over almost until their heads were beneath their shoulders. Once again, I experienced the rapture of Christian Orthodoxy—the chants, the crackling beeswax, and the smoldering censers replicated the pagan mysteries. Once these old women die, ethnic and religious apartheid here will be complete.

Baku lay due east of Gandzha, across a flat stretch of nearly 250 miles. At first, the snow-capped peaks of Karabakh drew closer, and vineyards and rolling vales of fir trees appeared. But soon the dusty, weedy plain resumed, the mountains receded, and we spent hours crossing a biscuit-brown, alkaline tableland, populated by sheep, cattle, and a few beautiful horses. Two policemen pulled us over. One leaned inside the car and placed his hand on the steering wheel. He had been drinking. "Oh, you are coming from Georgia," he said. "Maybe you have a nice present for us—some cigarettes or some of that nice mineral water," referring to Borzhomi, a well-known Georgian brand.

"But we have committed no infraction," Nata said to him.

The policeman shrugged and wouldn't take his hand off the wheel until we gave him a little tip. Here the corruption was more blatant than in Georgia: They didn't go through the pretense of fining you for a "violation."

We passed Yevlakh, a battered, destitute town, poorer-looking than almost any I had seen in Georgia, but with a new mosque and gas station. The dreary landscape was broken only by the occasional irrigation canal filled with carp. The police pulled us over again for another bribe. They had no guns—only nightsticks made of cheap wood, with frayed rope at the ends. The landscape became more brutal, a desert of silt and black volcanic hills. Then over a low ridge—it appeared just like that, without the warning of a fresh breeze—was the Caspian Sea, a milky-green chemical color at this time of the afternoon. Driving north along the coast toward Baku, I still saw no sign of development. We stopped at a cinder-block stall that offered only fly-covered fish to eat. As we reached the outskirts of the Azerbaijani capital, I saw children playing in the shade of rusted shacks. The water offshore was cluttered with old drilling platforms from the Soviet era. Closer to town, there was a forest of cranes and oil derricks, also Soviet, like giant insects on the oily sand.

Then, after a few turns of the car, the big change happened.

24

IMPERIAL COLLISIONS

When I last visited Baku in spring 1993, the only place to get a Coke was in the "dollar bar" of the Hotel Azerbaijani, the best hotel in town at the time—though, with broken lightbulbs and filthy rooms, it was no better than the hotel where I had just stayed in Gandzha. Credit cards were unheard of in 1993; so were foreign restaurants or simple amenities such as mineral water and decent phone service. Shops were few and depressing. There were three or four good restaurants serving local specialties, such as caviar, grilled meats, and stuffed vegetables. That was it.

Now, six years later, it was as though a strange new skin had been placed over the decayed downtown. There were new hotels, foreign restaurants, and nightclubs amid ranks of stage-lit marble storefronts. Nineteenth-century buildings had been sandblasted and restored, and tinted-Plexiglas ones built. I saw thousands of new cars and taxis; flashy signs advertised cell-phone and courier services and quick-service Laundromats; groceries and convenience stores offered an array of Western products; and satellite dishes were everywhere. In 1993, it was the conventional wisdom among foreigners that the Azeris could not adapt to a service economy. Now, even the worst restaurants and stores from that era had improved their service as Azeris copied what the foreigners were doing. From the perspective of downtown, it was as if Baku's 1.7 million inhabitants had recovered from slow motion.

On a lonely pedestrian square where I used to go for bad coffee and stale cake in 1993 were an Irish pub, a Cajun bar, an Iranian-owned cinema complex showing first-run American films, a supermarket, and splashy Italian- and French-designer boutiques. Within the surrounding streets were the only ATM machines between Turkey and China at this latitude, dispensing both Azerbaijani manats and U.S. dollars.

And this was *after* the 1998 "bust": the drop in world oil prices that year, the initial failure to find new Caspian oil fields, the oil-company mergers that saw local layoffs, and the Russian financial collapse, all of which caused the price of apartments in Baku to drop 50 percent and the number of *expats* (foreign workers) to drop by over 10 percent. "In 1997, Baku was a boom town. By early 1999 it had returned to being a backwater," an Iranian oil speculator told me. It all depended upon your terms of comparison. Mine were the bad old days of 1993.

Herodotus wrote that "there is room for anything in the course of time," but the conversion of Baku from a dimly exotic place-name to the crossroads of international energy commerce had taken almost no time at all. Only war is a faster locomotive than oil for change in the Third World. There are businessmen who follow negotiations between oil companies and host countries and specialize in transporting boutiques and theme restaurants to the most underdeveloped places to service *expat* workers and the local nouveaux riches.

The first night in Baku, I had dinner at an expensive piano bar. The piano was painted bright yellow; the walls were black, with tooled steel trimmings. The tables were decorated with handmade models of luxury cars. Later, I went to the Irish pub with a dark-wood decor that offered stouts and meat pies. Both places were filled with graying *expats* and attractive young Azeri women, drawn to these balding and drunken men by money and foreign passports. The women's smiles were pasted on, but they were not prostitutes. They were probably trying to leave Azerbaijan through marriage. Big oil, it would become clear to me, had not stabilized this country at all. It had merely raised the stakes for the next march on the capital by another rebellious militia from a place like Gandzha.

From what I learned over the next two weeks, I was left with the queasy apprehension that what Vietnam was to the 1960s and 1970s, what Lebanon and Afghanistan were to the 1980s, and what the Balkans were to the 1990s, the Caspian region might be to the first decade of the new century: an explosive region that draws in the Great Powers.

When I left the pub, a group of beggars trailed me like a swarm of bees.

§§ §§

The crowd strolling the seashore the next morning revealed what had changed and what had not. People looked slightly better dressed than in 1993. Here and there, I saw a man with a cell phone clipped to his belt. Otherwise, it was very much a Soviet-era scene: vendors with old Polaroids taking photos of children next to old and dusty stuffed animals, amusement-park rides that badly needed repairs and paint, old scales that measured your weight, miserable women in scarves and smocks dragging garbage crates roped to their waists, and countless beggars. People bought greasy sausages and watery ice cream, and occasionally splurged on a can of Coke or Fanta for the children, though they usually purchased the cheaper, locally produced soft drinks. Money had trickled down to the populace when the oil companies began hiring locals in the mid-1990s, but the majority of Bakuvians were little better off than before.

Here, unlike in Gandzha, the signs were in Russian. Baku had for decades been the capital of a major Soviet republic, whereas Gandzha had remained a Turkic backwater that, because it was near a military base, remained off-limits to all but the indigenous population. The suspicion of the Gandzhavis toward the Bakuvians, therefore, had a linguistic-cultural dimension that was a product of the twentieth century.

What was most Russian about Baku was hard to define, a unique, exotic quality that may arise from the encounter between Europe and Inner Asia, what made John Gunther call attention to "Moscow's illimitable sheer strangeness."[1] For example, dinner with an Azeri couple in a local restaurant would have been forgettable if not for the washroom, where I walked through the door marked TOILET and found a plush anteroom featuring red velvet and a large, gold-framed portrait of

Stalin. Beside it, a beautiful couple—they looked like ballet dancers—were noisily embracing, paying no attention to the people walking through. From an adjoining chamber, I could hear other men and women similarly groaning. Next to the couple, sitting on a stool, was an old woman with a mustache, who badgered me and others for tips.

In Baku, as in so many other places on my journey east since leaving Budapest, I rediscovered a little piece of Europe after I was sure that I had left it:

This wasn't the first oil boom here but the second. It was the soldiers of Alexander the Great who first discovered methane gas leaking from the sandy soil and saw the shrines built by Zoroastrian fire worshipers around the "eternal flames." Following the discovery of oil for commercial use in the nineteenth century, the Baku region became, by the turn of the twentieth century, the world's largest producer and exporter of oil, the Persian Gulf of an earlier age, where Alfred Nobel, Calouste Gulbenkian, and others made their fortunes. In Baku's old city, with its twelfth-century Persian walls, I found the dream palaces, with friezes and gargoyles, erected by these oil barons a hundred years ago. Oil had been a locomotive for development then, too. In these mansions, I gaped at the Baroque hallways, ceremonial staircases, and Italian frescoes of nude men and women that were forbidden to the wealthy Moslem owners and therefore "twice sweet," according to a local historian. Then as now, oil was transported from Baku to the Batumi area, only back then it traveled via a railroad completed in 1883 with Rothschild money.

"To be a Bakuvian at the turn of the twentieth century meant to be part of a cosmopolitan city-state of its own," the historian Fuad Akhundov told me. In 1913, for example, out of a population of 214,000, only a third were Azeri Turks; another third were Russians; about 20 percent, Armenians; and the rest, Jews, Germans, and Poles. As recently as 1988, there were over 200,000 Armenians in Baku, making this capital of Turkic Azerbaijan one of the largest Armenian cities in the world. But in response to anti-Armenian pogroms in nearby Sumgait, the Armenian population of Azerbaijan fled between 1988 and 1991, and the names of Armenian revolutionaries were erased from the local Lenin Museum. Armenians' apartments were seized by Azeris, who in turn rented them out for thousands of dollars per month to *expat* oil workers.

The end of multiethnic civilization was not the only divide between the first oil boom and the second. Now the architectural pattern was generically global. The splashy new marble-fronted boutiques reminded me of suburban Kansas City and Los Angeles. On an evening stroll, I saw a stream of well-dressed Azeri men and women shopping at these stores with the same hard, acquisitive looks that the nouveaux riches have the world over, but this version of global materialism was purely oligarchical.

"In the late nineteenth century," Akhundov told me, "people would point to this mansion and say, 'That is Ramanov's house,' and to that mansion and say, 'That is Tagiev's house.' Now nobody advertises who owns what. Everything is bought by front men because of the semi-criminal way that business is done. Now when they build a mansion, they build the high guardwalls first, so that nobody sees what is going on inside."

I met another Azeri, a former oil company official, soon after I arrived. He put it this way: "During the so-called era of Soviet stagnation, we were actually happy, because we all survived on a dream, the dream of democracy. Then we got it and it was a disaster. Now we are doomed to *live,* to just go on existing with this banal authoritarian regime that provides stability and which will soon sell off the assets of the state to its cronies through 'privatization.' "

Democratic Azerbaijan when I visited there in the early 1990s was a nightmare, with roadblocks downtown manned by drunken soldiers shaking you down for cigarettes, with such administrative chaos that the phone in the president's own office often didn't work, where no oil contracts were signed, and where tens of thousands were being killed and hundreds of thousands made refugees in Karabakh because freedom both here and in Armenia had stoked nationalistic passions. It was the same problem that I had encountered in Romania: The only people with the skills to wrest control from chaos and to run a bureaucracy were the old Communists, but of course they opposed reform.

Here, as the militia rebellion spread from Gandzha to Baku in June 1993, there was no other choice but to call in Heydar Aliyev, the ex-KGB general, ex-Party boss of Azerbaijan, Brezhnev Polit-buro man, and "master manipulator with the crocodile smile." Aliyev arranged a cease-fire with Armenia. He dismantled downtown road-blocks. And to show everyone who was boss, he established a person-ality cult, displaying his likeness in every public place. Whenever he traveled, the entire government saw him off at the airport: a far cry from Shevardnadze's Georgia. Most important, he gave the oil compa-nies what they wanted: the equivalent of offshore agreements, with guaranteed tax schedules.

But while Aliyev had produced order out of chaos, he had done nothing to transform order into civility. After six years in power, he had established virtually no institutions. Aliyev still ran everything. Seventy-six years old and in bad health, he was now trying to orchestrate the succession of his son, Ilham, to power. In Georgia, the parliament had meaning; in Azerbaijan, it had none. In Georgia, corruption was bad enough, but in Azerbaijan—which had $30 billion in oil contracts—corruption was reaching Nigerian and Indonesian levels.

I had put up at a friend's apartment in a good section of Baku, where I went without water for twenty-four hours. Large parts of the city would soon be uninhabitable unless the urban water system was re-built, which the government had made no plans to do. Water and gas shortages were symbolic of a general collapse of living standards here since 1993, according to the U.N. Development Report. Food con-sumption per person in Azerbaijan had dropped by a third in recent years, while food costs as a percentage of household expenses had increased fourfold.[2] Meanwhile, the new luxury Hyatt and Europa hotels—both of which had plenty of water—were packed with Ameri-can, European, and Asian businesspeople in town for the annual oil show.

Every major world oil company, in addition to dozens of engineer-ing, accounting, law, and public relations firms, was here, represented by a flashy booth. Giant photos of Aliyev covered the walls of the ex-hibition hall. During a speech by one of Aliyev's cronies, I tried to leave the building for another appointment, but the Azeri security detail had barricaded all the doors of the sports complex where the show was being held. I complained to a Western oil company official, who told me: "The Azeris are dreadful—hopelessly intransigent, I know. But we have interests here."

The theme of the exhibition was the "New Silk Road," the planned vector of power that would connect Europe with the Far East through oil and gas pipelines and railway and trucking routes. The proposed route went from Budapest to Bucharest to Istanbul, Ankara, Supsa, Tbilisi, Baku, and on to Turkmenbashi and Ashgabat, in Turkmenistan, and finally to Kazakhstan, China, and Japan. The pulsing lights on the display maps conjured a vision of general prosperity, though I knew that the reality in places along the way was otherwise. A century ago, Alfred Nobel held the concession for the northern, Russian part of the Black Sea, while Standard Oil had the southern part. The question now was which consortiums would control which geographical regions—in cooperation with which dictators—as the social vacuum that had followed the collapse of the Communist empire was gradually, imperceptibly being filled by nontraditional corporate empires. Gibbon wrote that the mantle of Roman imperialism protected immature states from themselves. I knew from my travels that much of the territory through which this New Silk Road passed was no less immaturely governed; but now there was no Rome to guarantee tranquility.

Do the oil companies know what they are getting into? Unocal, an oil company whose gas stations dot the southwestern United States, sought to build a pipeline in the mid-1990s to move natural gas from Turkmenistan southeastward through Afghanistan to a Pakistani port on the Indian Ocean. Unocal thought that economics would help Afghanistan's fundamentalist Taliban regime see reason. It assumed a Western notion of materialistic self-interest where none existed, and in 1999 finally closed its office in Turkmenistan.

Geostrategic poker dominated this oil show. Though the Caspian region's proven oil reserves comprised only 3 percent of the world's total, there could be much more, in addition to large amounts of natural gas.[3] The Soviet Union had lacked the technology to develop the Caspian's deep-water (below 600 feet) oil and gas reserves, but now every major Western oil firm and seventeen consortia were in Baku. Two proposed pipeline routes were battling for ascendancy. The American and Turkish governments were lobbying the oil industry to construct a 1,080-mile pipeline from Baku through Georgia to the Turkish Mediterranean port of Ceyhan, near Antioch. Indeed, in November 1999, at a sumit in Istanbul, President Clinton signed an agreement of intent to build the Baku–Ceyhan pipeline. But the companies were cautious, and were hardly ready to pump the 500,000 barrels daily required to justify such a pipeline. In addition, the Turkish route went through mountainous and politically unstable Kurdish country, while the hydraulics of pumping oil up through the mountains were enormous. A more direct and cheaper route for Caspian oil was south through Iran. Moreover, almost every oilman with experience in both Iran and the former Soviet Union knew that the Iranians were less corrupt, more efficient, and easier to deal with. Though no one would say so publicly, the oil companies were delaying a decision on the Turkish pipeline until the United States normalized relations with Iran, a possibility given Iran's gradual move toward democratization.

Given enough time for deep-water exploration, both pipelines— through Turkey and Iran—would probably be constructed, and Baku would be the origin of each.

Igor Effimoff, the American who ran the Caspian operation for Houston-based Pennzoil, told me that "the U.S. effectively went to war in 1991 over two million barrels of oil pumped daily out of Kuwait. Well, that's what we'll be producing around the Caspian Sea in a worst-case scenario: I'm talking about what has already been discovered and can be profitably extracted. You can ballpark it easily," he said. "At a minimum, we'll be pumping four million barrels daily from the Caspian in, say, five to seven years. That's another North Sea, or another Iran. The big question is, Can the government in Baku handle all the money that's going to pour in here, because you haven't seen anything yet."

At the sports complex, the Azeri security detail finally opened the doors, and I left to see a "knowledgeable foreign resident," who didn't want to be identified, even remotely. This is what he told me:

"Azerbaijan's national budget is $550 million. That's nothing! Most of us own shares in mutual funds that are worth more. And what are they pumping now from Baku to Supsa—105,000 barrels a day? That's also nothing. Keep in mind that Azeri oil is very high quality, with a low sulfur content. It took years to hit real quantities in Saudi Arabia and the North Sea. So this is barely the beginning—if it doesn't all go up in smoke. The new wealth that you see around here—the restaurants, the boutiques, the new supermarkets—it's all from speculation and signing bonuses. There is still very little oil pumped from Azerbaijan. Nobody knows who got that bonus money [that the oil companies handed out to Azeris when the contracts were signed]. It's all secret. Much of it could be abroad by now.

"The new apartments, the fancy stores," he said. "They're built by Turkish contractors. Who do you think is building the new sports and apartment complex at the Hyatt Regency, including indoor and outdoor pools, a disco, restaurants, cafés, you name it—the Turks! The intention is that in a few years, the entire downtown will move from the harbor up the hill to the Hyatt. That's Baku's next reincarnation. The Turks are importing everything, even the cement. The only thing Azeri about it is the water they mix the cement with. Yet it's all being built on nothing. The government here may not exist in a few years. Nobody expects Ilham [Aliyev's son] to consolidate control after his father dies."

"But how stable was Saudi Arabia in the early days, when oil was first found there?" I asked.

"Saudi Arabia," this knowledgeable foreigner told me in a calm voice, "had three advantages that Azerbaijan lacks: It had a royal family with a predictable line of succession; it had no pretensions to democracy; and it was in a relatively nice neighborhood." Saudi Arabia, he explained, was surrounded by the Red Sea and desert and faraway regimes occupied with their own struggles. Azerbaijan, on the other hand, has a long northern border with Russia in Dagestan, which could be the next Chechnya. Russia would see a strategic victory in exploding the plans of Western oil companies here, since that would lead to a collapse of Western influence. Then, to the west, are Karabakh and Armenia, where Russia has bases, and on the southern border, Iran. "Do you realize how crazy it drives the Iranians to see this Shi'ite country to the north of them bursting with vodka, pornography, and Israeli visitors, and with irredentist dreams on Iranian Azerbaijan?"

Then he said: "The Iranians have built five hundred new schools and mosques in Azerbaijan. Those new mosques you saw when you drove from Gandzha are the only functioning institutions outside of Baku, and Aliyev didn't build them. He doesn't care about his own people. The Iranians built them. There are thousands of Azeris in schools in Iran. The Iranians are smart. They've conceded downtown Baku to the Turks and the Western oil companies; they are working on the rest of the country. It's a long-term strategy. The Turks have a shorter-term one: infiltrating the army with hundreds of Turkish officers, while bringing Azeri officers to Turkey for training. When Aliyev dies, the Turks could try to promote one of the democratic opposition figures here as a figurehead for a military regime. The businesspeople promoting the Baku–Ceyhan pipeline would like that."

This was only one of several potential scenarios in a country where the government lacked legitimacy, and all were plausible. It made me realize once again that the U.S. could assuage many of its problems in the Middle East through a rapprochement with Iran. Next, I went to see the democratic opposition.

※ ※

In Georgia I had many memorable late-night conversations in cellars, drinking homemade red wine. The Azeris consumed much vodka in private, but in public this was very much a traditional Moslem society, where you often met people over *chai* or Fanta at a plastic table in a sunlit square. But what made my conversations with Azerbaijan's democrats memorable was their half-baked "incompleteness," like Dostoyevskian monologues.[4]

Shahin Hajiyev was the deputy chief of the Turan News Agency and among the most lucid of the oppositionists with whom I spoke. His description of the Aliyev regime was hard to argue with. "You cannot open a business here without a bribe to the police and the government, meaning a bribe to Aliyev's relatives." Hajiyev decried "this café business" of some government ministers, and confirmed that the Iranians were active not only outside Baku but also in the poorer outlying neighborhoods of the capital—those most affected by water shortages. "The Iranians have an opportunity here," he explained. "We're both Shi'ite. There is a moral vacuum in Azerbaijan following the fall of communism. And the level of our political culture is low compared to theirs."

Then he told me that "you cannot compare the drawbacks" of Ebulfez Elcibey's earlier government with Aliyev's "because Aliyev's is not democratic." If democracy were restored, he said, "you would see development in the whole country, not just in Baku. The people here will fight for the democrats, while Aliyev has only businessmen on his side."

I didn't believe this. War and chaos had defined Elcibey's rule in the early 1990s. Why should democracy lead to development when it hadn't done so before? And were Azeris really on the side of the democrats? The men I had met in Gandzha wanted better pensions and salaries and would support whoever delivered them—whether a Hitler or a Brezhnev, they had told me. When I mentioned this to Hajiyev, he simply continued to talk about Aliyev's corruption.

Gunduz Tahirli edited an opposition newspaper with a circulation of ten thousand. The walls of his office were bare except for a clothes hanger dangling from a heating pipe. Unlike the oil company offices, there was no air-conditioning and flies were everywhere. The screen saver on his computer was a shot of Leonardo DiCaprio and Kate Winslet embracing in *Titanic.* He was young and pale and smoked Marlboros incessantly. "I still trust the old dissidents like Elcibey," he told me. "All popular movements will lead to positive change. Elcibey could govern again, and we do have a constitutional process."

I asked him about a certain Rasul Guliev, whom people had been telling me about. Guliev was an Azeri businessman, living in the U.S., who had been exiled by Aliyev and who had been crafty enough to run a private oil trade during Soviet times, from which he had amassed a fortune. "People here have faith in Guliev," Tahirli admitted, "because he is a good businessman." "Could Guliev rule Azerbaijan in the future?" I asked. Tahirli said it was possible. He mentioned that the oil companies wanted stability at any cost and that they were Azerbaijan's best guarantee for security.

But could someone like Elcibey, whose regime had brought chaos, now work with the oil companies to bring stability? Tahirli offered only foggy phrases when I challenged him.

Bakhtiyar Vahabzada, born in 1925, was Azerbaijan's most prominent poet, the modern successor to Nezami Ganjavi. Dressed in a work shirt and warm-up pants, he was gripping his stomach with an ice pack in his stifling apartment when I met him. He apologized for his illness, and I apologized for bothering him. He was handsome, with a sculpted face, olive complexion, and full head of white hair. He exuded warmth.

"I hope we will never be influenced by Russia again," he told me. "We are oppressed by Russia and Iran. Whenever I say 'I am free' in Russian, it means that I am really not free. Who are these Russians? *They* don't even know who they are! Nezami was Azeri even if he wrote in Persian, but whoever writes in Russian is not a real Azeri. . . . The Iranian people want us to lose our identity and speak Persian. There are twenty-five million Azeris in Iran, where there is total repression of Azeri culture. Iran favors Armenia, even though it is Christian, because the Iranians know that if the day comes when we Azeris are truly free, we will free all the Azeris in Iran."

Vahabzada had spent his creative life in the darkness of Soviet oppression. His hatred of Russia was based on a life experience that I could not dismiss. Nevertheless, his nationalism was dangerous and ill informed. Azeris were not nearly as repressed in Iran as he claimed. Many members of the Iranian elite, including cabinet members, were Azeris. Even the supreme leader, Ayatollah Sayyed Ali Khamenei, is said to be part Azeri. Iran was a multiethnic empire in which Persians barely dominated. The relationship between ethnic Azeris and Persians in Iran is highly complex, but Vahabzada's feelings, I learned, were typical of the democratic opposition here.

I had last seen Ebulfez Elcibey in his presidential office in April 1993. Now I found him living in a noisy tenement on the outskirts of Baku. Sweat seemed to drip from the walls of his clammy apartment. Children played in the hallways, where all the wires had been torn out of the circuit box. "Next time we meet, I'll be back in the presidential office," he told me. I didn't discount it. When I had met Elcibey in 1993, Heydar Aliyev had been living in similarly miserable circumstances in Nakhichevan.

Still, the fall from power must have been particularly hard on Elcibey. The presidency of the new democracy had been the culmination of a life of dissidence. In the 1970s and 1980s, Elcibey was Azerbaijan's Gamsakhurdia, a professor who had served years at hard labor for leading a nationalist revival and for changing his name from Aliyev to a Turkic one, Elcibey (meaning "chief ambassador"), to symbolize his break from Russian customs. When I had interviewed him as president, he appeared bewildered by his administrative responsibility. Now sixty-one, with the same neatly clipped silver beard, he could hardly restrain his anger as he spoke to me. He seemed distant, disembodied, even crazed. He had deep circles under his eyes. He smoked Camels and offered me raisins and *chai*.

"These stupid new buildings and restaurants downtown mean nothing. I feel no change," he told me. "This foreign investment is nothing but a benefit to Aliyev's relatives. This is the work of a dictator who is making nice surroundings for himself to show off to the foreigners. Instead of stupid restaurants, why isn't there a new academy or a hospital? Yes, we had some problems when we were in power, but Aliyev has created chaos. He has let the foreign forces into Azerbaijan. He signed oil contracts to satisfy his clients. America wants oil. 'Please, here you are, take it,' he says. Russia wants this, and Iran that, and Aliyev gives all."

Elcibey went on in this vein, banging his hand on the table. "We have our strict principles. We demand protection for Azeris in Iran. This is our strategy. Our orientation is totally European. Iran is against our Latin alphabet. We must develop democratic institutions and work to liberate southern Azerbaijan, which is now held by Iran. Liberalization in Iran will eventually lead to its collapse, then Azeris will get their liberty. I am against all imperialisms. . . ."

It was irresponsible of Elcibey to encourage Azeri nationalism across the border in Iran, but irresponsible people can also be prophetic. From my own visits to Iran, I knew that the fracturing of Iran and the reunification of northern and southern Azerbaijan were things that worried the Iranians. When Iranian president Mohammed Khatami tempered his encouragement of democracy with a warning against anarchy, it was the Azeri issue he partly had in mind.

In the taxi returning from Elcibey's tenement, I saw a huge Marlboro advertisement covering the side of a Khrushchev-era apartment house. The collapse of communism in the Caucasus had evidently created a greater opportunity for big tobacco than for liberal democracy.

Isa Gambar, the head of the Musavat (Equality) party, was the only opposition figure who seemed to me to make sense. Musavat had historical legitimacy. It had been founded in 1911 by Mamed Amin Rasulzade, who took advantage of the power vacuum created by the collapse of czarist Russia to establish the short-lived Democratic Republic of Azerbaijan. Before Elcibey's election, Gambar had been Azerbaijan's acting president. In a hot, fetid office, and surrounded by well-dressed men wearing gold watches who seemed to worship him, the rumpled Gambar spoke in slow, syrupy cadences. He spoke about tax and judicial reforms, and about a peace treaty with Armenia if only Russia would withdraw from its Armenian military bases. "There are many parallels with the post–World War One era," he told me. "Armenia was waging war against us and we had a military agreement with Georgia, while Russia and the West were competing in the Caucasus for oil. The difference is that then the West was fighting Turkey, while now Turkey and the West are allies, and the West is closer to us because of the postindustrial revolution—computers, airplanes . . . Maybe this time we can remain independent."

※ ※

I met another "knowledgeable foreigner," an avuncular man with an old-fashioned, rather subtle Kiplingesque aura about him that appealed to me. When I made the usual disclaimers about the conversation being "off the record" and so forth, he raised his hand and lifted his eyebrows to stop me. Gentlemen can trust each other, he seemed to say.

"The West faces a stark moral dilemma here," he began, his voice tired and sad. "On the one hand we have this regime, which, aside from the agreements with oil companies, offers a hostile business environment. 'Sanctity of contract' is something they can't even spell. The only issue is who pays the judges, the police—well, you know . . . The human-rights situation is beyond the pale. The ICRC [International Committee for the Red Cross] can't even get permission to visit the prisons, where TB is rampant. They harass the families of dissidents. Outside Baku, if you want to use an unemployment figure, you might as well say 100 percent. Meanwhile, there are massive imports of exotic fruits, luxury cars, and flowers, but not one profitable manufacturing firm outside the oil industry. You've got a kleptocracy at the top that is bringing the country to its knees.

"On the other hand," he emphasized, "Aliyev is the only one who can deliver the institutions, the independent judiciary, the civil-service reforms that we need before this wall of oil money pours over us in a few years." He handed me charts showing that while the oil boom had begun more slowly than expected in Azerbaijan, even without dramatic new discoveries there could soon be a huge increase in revenues. "Forget a benign Guliev oligarchy. It would not be benign at all. Elcibey is the mad professor. Ilham [Aliyev's son] is hopeless. The other democrats," he said in exasperation, "well, you just don't institute these kinds of fundamental reforms from scratch without formidable power. In a place like this, only a dictator can start the process.

"You see," he continued in a pleading tone, "the police are corrupt and ruthless. But what can you do about that? You train them, you expose them to the values of the West, you pay them more and encourage an esprit de corps. It's no good just banging on the table and criticizing the Azeris to get their house in order, to respect human rights. But could you imagine the furor in Western capitals if we gave money to the police here? It's easy to pontificate from Europe or America, but those of us in the trenches in places like this are forced to be pragmatists."

I had seen enough to sympathize with his dilemma. Torture and chauvinistic policies in Turkey have often been greater under democratic governments than under military ones, in part because the generals are better able to control the lower ranks in far-off detention centers than are the civilian politicians.

"What if Aliyev dies tomorrow?" I asked.

"If he dies tomorrow," said the knowledgeable foreigner, shaking his head and punching a closed fist against his palm, "it would be the Turks up against the Russians. The Turks would try to unite a few key figures in the government and the military before the Russians tried to destabilize Baku." The Iranians, he implied, would not be players here for a few more years yet.

Baku, I thought, was a place where Turks, Russians, and Iranians are all at home without a translator, yet because of so many changes in alphabets and street names, people are constantly disoriented. This was a real collision zone. The first battle of the Cold War had not been in Berlin but in southern Azerbaijan in 1946, when the West forced Stalin to stop supporting a puppet regime there run from Baku, leading to its collapse as Iranian forces reconquered the area. The next major battle of the new era could begin here, too.

In 1918, the British vowed to protect Baku, Batumi, the railroad between them, and their own oil interests, but they withdrew from the region as chaos spiraled and Russian forces—this time Bolshevik—positioned themselves to reconquer what their czarist predecessors had lost only a few years before. If the ground again collapses under our feet here—if Vladimir Putin, for example, consolidates Russia as a new and aggressive autocracy—what will the West do?

❦ ❦

Before leaving Azerbaijan I took a taxi to Sumgait, the country's third-largest city, twenty-five miles north of Baku on the Caspian. The Soviets had made Sumgait the center of Azerbaijan's heavy industry, where detergents, pesticides, chlorine, superphosphates, and lindane, the Soviet equivalent of Agent Orange, were produced. Downtown Sumgait was a row of decrepit housing blocks, with iron stalls lining the streets, filled with badly dressed people. The smell of chemicals was everywhere. Along the beach I saw rusted, abandoned ships, broken glass, and rotting elevated pipes pumping sewage into the sea. Nevertheless, I also spotted a pair of lovers embracing on the sand and two old men looking at a photograph. Families strolled by, enjoying the pale sun. At a café, a waiter scrubbed clean my ashtray and filled it with sucking candies. The human spirit seemed to me indomitable.

We drove next to a cemetery in the industrial zone, passing an apocalyptic scene of devastation. My lungs ached and my eyes burned from the stench of chlorine filling the desert of brownish silt, littered with factory skeletons. In a field of bramble and broken bottles I saw a clutter of black stones identifying small dirt mounds—the graves of children who had died of birth defects from the industrial pollution. "Now that the factories have closed, there is less illness, but we have no work," lamented a man with a white skullcap, fingering prayer beads.

As we left the cemetery, I saw long cinder-block walls encircling the abandoned factories. The construction was primitive, haphazard, as though these walls were the product of prehistory, before the term *civilization* meant anything. The cinder blocks had been laid unevenly. Nobody cared, and nothing had meaning. I was reminded of the story that Alexander Rondeli had told me in Georgia about the stacks of bodies dumped at dusk in Siberia. "All of us," Rondeli had said, "Georgians, Azeris, Armenians, have this heavy weight from the past attached to our legs. We can only move forward while looking back."

25

BY BOAT TO

TARTARY

There was no schedule for the freighters that sailed eastward on the Caspian from Baku to Turkmenbashi, in Turkmenistan. Some friends told me they had waited three days at the docks. With my duffel bag, I approached the massive stone port building whose windy hall was empty except for a tea stand. I walked around to the side of the building and found a little office, where a woman sat knitting and a policeman swaggered about. He was thickset, with black hair, a black mustache, and a puffy, sunburned face. Handcuffs dangled from his belt. He asked me what I wanted. Was there a ship that evening to Turkmenbashi? I asked.

"Yes, we have cargo, so there will be a boat tonight."

"How much is a cabin?" I asked.

He looked hard at me, and said scornfully, "You give me forty-five dollars and I'll give you a receipt to show the steward, then you'll pay him a little something for your cabin."

"If I pay you money, I want a ticket."

"If you don't pay me forty-five dollars, you don't get on the boat. I'm giving you a discount." He smiled, turning aside to spit on the cement floor. I gave him two twenty-dollar bills. "Five more dollars," he said, rubbing his fingers. I had no change, and gave him another $20. He smiled again as he put all three bills in his pocket. The woman stopped knitting and wrote me a receipt. "Go have tea for a few hours. I'll tell you when the boat is ready," he said.

"Where's my fifteen dollars in change?" I asked.

He smiled and spit again, looking at me as though I were an idiot. He held his palms out empty. We had a staring match. Finally, he gave me some Azerbaijani manats, but less than fifteen dollars' worth.

Outside the port building, I found a table by the water's edge and nursed my tea for two and a half hours, looking at the container cranes and listening to the lapping waves. Then I took a short taxi ride to the ship after the policeman told me the boat was ready. I got through the customs and passport checks, and at the top of the gangplank, several women, grimy with dirt, barked at me. They were crew members offering to sell their bunk beds for a few dollars. For $25 I secured a cabin. The mattress was wet, the stained sheets riddled with holes. The electric sockets had been ripped from the walls, and somebody's old slippers were on the floor. Pornographic photos cluttered the sun-beaten walls. A crew member came to take some clothes from the closet and use the toilet. It was his cabin. There were no private cabins on this ship.

The ship typified the poverty and squalor of the former Soviet Union in more concentrated form, foul with oil and peeling, grayish-green lead paint. The passengers were a tableau of grotesques: men in dark, soiled pajamalike garments and the women in old nightgowns and housedresses, carrying shopping bags full of evil-smelling food: They were far from ugly. Many had beautiful faces, with deerlike Tartar eyes. Their expressions hinted at a wealth of stories.[1]

Railway cars rolled aboard on tracks that led directly into the ship. At last the cargo doors hissed shut, and several hours after I had boarded, the smokestack released a cloud of black fumes. The deck vibrated and we pulled out to sea. I leaned over the stern railing as the sun set and Baku melted into the darkness.

I remained on deck until late, the sea blackening around me as the ship sputtered eastward toward the invisible boundary between Azerbaijan and Turkmenistan—between the Caucasus and Central Asia. The Caspian, fed by three major rivers from the north—the Volga, the Ural, and the Terek—and several smaller ones from the west, is the world's largest inland sea, larger in area than Japan. Called the world's greatest salt lake, it is 750 miles long and 200 miles wide. In earlier geologic times, it was linked via the Sea of Azov, the Black Sea, and the

Mediterranean to the ocean. The changes it has seen in area and depth make it of great interest to scientists studying local geology and climate, though, for the next few years, the only Caspian mystery likely to interest most people is the extent of the oil deposits here. Some estimates say that as much as 200 billion barrels of oil—the deposits of Iran and Iraq combined—might lie hidden beneath the seabed.[2] But the amount likely to be pumped will be considerably less, as I had learned at the oil show.

Finally, I descended toward my cabin. In the corridor, I met a man, better dressed than the others, who asked if I wanted to share a meal with him and his friends. The dining room was small and grim, the dark plywood walls lined with old calendars. A few Formica tables covered with vinyl cloths stood before a television that played a bootleg out-of-focus action video. Aslan, the fellow with whom I shared dinner, looked around fifty, with gray hair and a handsome, tough face. He told me that he and his friends were Azeris whose families had been deported to Kazakhstan in the 1930s by Stalin. "Not many were murdered, so the deportation of hundreds of thousands was forgotten by everyone, because compared to other things Stalin did, it wasn't so bad."[3] Aslan was a small-time trader who brought meat and other products from Azerbaijan to Kyrgyzstan, where he lived. Over beer, vodka, and boiled chicken, he and his friends lamented perestroika, which, they said, had brought chaos. They complained about trade barriers between the former Soviet republics that didn't exist before 1991, and praised Uzbekistan's authoritarian leader, Islam Karimov, for providing a better business climate than the other republics. "To you," Aslan told me, "perestroika and the end of communism were good and a dictator like Karimov bad, but we have to survive. For us, it's the opposite."

Pleasantly drunk, I wandered back to my cabin, but the mosquitoes wouldn't let me sleep. Near dawn I fell asleep for an hour or two, then awoke to the spare, abstract shoreline of what the Sassanid Persians in the third century A.D. called Turkestan and what the Elizabethans later called Tartary. But the coast was farther away than it seemed, and the ship was slow. Over a breakfast of *chai* and biscuits that I had brought from Baku, Turkmenbashi gradually came into focus, a cluster of rust-ing cranes and whitish hutments against a line of cliffs the clay color of death. As the boat turned and eased into the dock—the water an unreal jade green—I realized how much warmer the eastern shore of the Caspian was than the western one. I had been told again and again that the journey would take twelve hours. But despite calm seas, it had taken sixteen, not counting the three hours on deck before departure. (In Herodotus's time, the crossing took nearly eight days.) The way people defined literal truth said much about a culture, I thought.

It was midday now. The passengers were ordered to line up in the hot sun, in near-100-degree temperature, before a peeling white gate at the end of the dock, where a lone policeman checked our passports. He allowed only Turkmen nationals through and gruffly told the handful of foreigners to wait. This was a change, I thought. In poor countries, particularly in Africa, it had been my experience that the harshest treatment was often reserved for the locals.

At last I was let through to a booth, where my visa was closely inspected and stamped. Then I entered a bare shed, where a hot wind blew through windowless gaps. In the middle of the shed was a metal table, where another policeman motioned with his hand for me to empty the contents of my duffel bag. He went through everything meticulously, seizing on the Pepto-Bismol tablets and demanding to know if they were illegal narcotics. When he found my pocket flashlight, his expression turned wild as he stared at me with his jet-black eyes. Then he unscrewed it, letting the 1.5-volt batteries fall to the dirt floor. I picked up the batteries, screwed the flashlight back together, and turned it on to show him there was no danger. Everything—the shed, the landscape, the policeman's expression—suggested utter desolation. In Georgia and Azerbaijan, encounters with the police were transactions: "You are here on some business, and so we will make business from you," their expressions had always said. I felt no fear, because I knew it was merely a matter of money. But I sensed a frightening deficiency of emotion in this policeman, and avoided his eyes.

I repacked my bag and slipped away into a crowd of clawing taxi drivers.

26

NEW KHANATES

I had arrived at an even lower level of existence than when I left Turkey and entered Georgia, or when I left Georgia for Azerbaijan. It wasn't so much that the poverty was worse but that I felt an imprisoning desolation. The drivers and money changers were like starving animals. The women, who shuffled about in plastic slippers and grimy housedresses, wore blank, sleepwalking expressions. The whole crowd dissolved into insignificance amid the unshaded vastness of this desert port, locked deep within the land mass of Asia.

A knowing sympathy showed through the streetwise mask of the first driver who grabbed me. He was an Azeri named Telman. His dusty, oily, squeaking Moskvich did not so much move as lurch. On the way into town, I saw dromedaries on the stubbly desert hills. A few minutes later we passed through Turkmenbashi, sleepy and deserted, as if it were drugged by the heat. Traditional Russian houses, with tin gabled roofs and naive Baroque facades in light pastels, lined clean streets. I saw a mosque with fabulous brickwork in geometric patterns, then a tulip-shaped archway with columns of a gaudy nomadic design, and a pair of women crossing the road in flowing, gold-braided robes and colorful scarves. Suddenly I was exhilarated.

I also saw garish, billboard-size pictures of a stocky, black-haired man with the proprietary smile of a casino manager. There were empty squares with gilded statues of him, seated on a throne. He was Saparmurad Niyazov, the president of Turkmenistan, who had renamed himself Saparmurad Turkmenbashi ("Chief of the Turkmens") and in 1993 renamed this town, which the Russians had called Krasnovodsk, Turkmenbashi, in honor of himself. The gold statues were crude and looked hollow inside, like props for an old Hollywood epic. Here and there, I saw signs that read HALK, WATAN, TURKMENBASHI, in Latin script, the Turkmen equivalent of *Ein Volk, ein Reich, ein Führer.*

Telman didn't stop the car, but continued north along the sea, where we passed a line of cinder-block shacks resting on stilts in the bleached desert. "They are vacation dachas," he told me. Then we passed blocks of cheap flats that had no playground, or even a tree. Telman called this a "very desirable" new "microdistrict" for local refinery workers. A half hour later we reached a small hotel by the water, where *expat* oilmen stayed. Telman wanted only $3 for the ride. I told him to wait while I checked in. The two government channels on the television in my hotel room showed the president smiling as he strode down a red carpet in a white dinner jacket, with women in traditional Turkmen dress throwing flowers at him. I turned the set back on five minutes later and saw the same scene. The station logo in the upper-right-hand corner of the screen was a profile of Turkmenbashi. I asked Telman to take me back to town to explore.

The train station caught my eye, and I asked Telman to wait as I went inside to check the departure schedules. The architecture featured white-and-black Mamluk masonry topped by Russian church domes painted a fabulous orange. I was admiring the arabesques in the ticket hall when an unshaven policeman approached. His uniform was filthy. With no gun or even a club, he looked destitute. He demanded my passport and examined it suspiciously. "What are you looking for? You shouldn't walk around without permission," he told me. "I'm just a tourist," I said politely.

Telman stopped next at the market, a large open-air shed lined with rows of produce. I saw turbaned men with white beards and women with robes that exploded in color. There were Kazakhs—who looked Chinese—and Russians, Uzbeks, Azeris, Turks, Iranians, Greeks, Armenians, and, of course, Turkmens. Someone told me that people of fifty-five nationalities inhabit Turkmenbashi. As Central Asia's only sea link to European Russia, this quiet former garrison town is a regional gateway and melting pot.

※ ※

The Russians first arrived in Turkmenbashi in 1717. Led by Prince Alexander Bekovich, they set up a base, then marched five hundred miles northeast across the desert, intending to capture the wealthy Uzbek khanate of Khiva. But the expedition failed, and Prince Bekovich was hacked to death, while the khan himself looked on.[1] The Russians didn't return here until 1869, when they built a fort called Krasnovodsk (Red Water), named for the color of the sea and the inlets at dusk. In 1880, Czar Alexander II sent General Mikhail Dmitriyevich Skobelev to Krasnovodsk to continue the Russian conquest of Central Asia. Skobelev, a hero of the 1877–78 Russo-Turkish War, which freed Bulgaria from Ottoman rule, was a man with a chilling expression, short hair, a long, carefully shaped beard, and a reputation for cruelty. Considering the mission, he was a good choice.

By then the czars had conquered much of Central Asia as far as Afghanistan—that chaotic buffer between the expanding Russian empire and British India. But St. Petersburg's hold on these sprawling deserts was tenuous, and it still had to master the various Turkoman (Turkmen) tribes. In the tenth and eleventh centuries, these Turkmens—descendants of the "Black Sheep" and "White Sheep" Tartars, whose language is similar to Turkish and Azeri—had begun migrating here from the Altai region of Mongolia, nearly two thousand miles to the northeast of the Caspian. For centuries thereafter, nomadic Turkmens terrorized the farming areas of Persia and Afghanistan, as well as caravans along the Silk Route: raping, looting, and taking many slaves, whom they traded with the Arabs and the khans of Khiva and Bukhara, in present-day Uzbekistan.[2] Whenever Persia mounted an expedition northward, the Turkmens fled into the wastes of the Kara Kum Desert. But while they were good raiders, the Turkmens, steeped in their tradition of clans, were never able to form a state of their own, and in 1741 the Persian king Nadir Shah subdued them. Then, in 1813, the Russians broke Persia's hold on Central Asia and began erecting forts in the desert to attack the Turkmens, who responded with guerrilla raids, killing and enslaving Russian civilians. It was a replica of a war that was going on at the same time between white settlers and native inhabitants in the American West.

When General Skobelev arrived here in 1880, a million Turkmens were living in tents scattered throughout the Kara Kum (Black Sand) Desert and the adjoining Kizyl Kum (Red Sand) Desert to the north. Seven years previously, the Russian general Konstantin Petrovich Kaufmann had moved against the Yomut tribe of Turkmens near Khiva, the Uzbek oasis in the Kizyl Kum. The Yomuts fought house to house, and Russian retribution was vicious. "This expedition does not spare either sex or age," Kaufmann told his officers. "Kill all of them."[3] With the defeat of the Yomut Turkmens, the Russians next had to defeat the Tekke Turkmens, the most ferocious of the Turkmen groups that inhabited "Transcaspia": the tract of desert east of the Caspian and Krasnovodsk in the Kara Kum. Defeating the Tekkes was Skobelev's mission.

His army set out from the Caspian in the summer of 1880, marching through a desert where temperatures reached as high as 172 degrees Fahrenheit[4] and subduing Tekke oases along the way. In early January 1881 the Russians invested the mud walls of the Tekke stronghold of Geok-Tepe, three hundred miles southeast of Krasnovodsk. Ten thousand Tekke Turkmen warriors and forty thousand of their family members stayed inside. Skobelev had seven thousand infantry and cavalry. Fighting continued for three weeks. The stubborn Tekkes refused to evacuate their women and children. Finally, on January 24, Skobelev's troops completed a tunnel underneath Geok-Tepe's walls and exploded a ton of gunpowder at the far end, which they followed with artillery barrages. Hand-to-hand fighting ensued, until Skobelev had slaughtered almost the whole male population, killing eight thousand Tekke Turkmens while sustaining less than a thousand Russian dead and wounded.[5]

The Russian conquest of Turkestan was now nearly complete. A colonial administration was established, and by the end of the nineteenth century, the Russian-built Transcaspian Railway linked Krasnovodsk with Bukhara, a meandering distance of 750 miles through the desert. Russian settlers came to this poorest patch of the empire, introducing the *karakul* (black rose) sheep and cotton farming to the Turkmens.

Then the first leader ever to unite the various Turkmen tribes emerged: Mohammed Qurban Junaid Khan, an Islamic cleric of the Yomut tribe, who, in 1916, ejected the czarist forces and turned his men on the Bolsheviks. The Reds had conquered the Caucasus by 1920, but Turkmens continued to attack Red Army camps through 1927, when Junaid Khan finally retreated into Persia and Afghanistan, where he died a natural death in 1938. Stalin had not, and would not, encounter a tougher enemy.

The Soviets changed the Turkmen alphabet from Arabic to Cyrillic and sealed the borders with Iran and Afghanistan to prevent the locals' contact with Turkmens south of here. Then Stalin began wave after wave of purges and executions, interspersed with the resettlement in the new Soviet Republic of Turkmenistan of Russians and other deportees from all over the Soviet Union. Almost all educated Turkmens were annihilated. When Turkmenistan became independent in 1991, its people inherited both a void and a deep suspicion of foreigners. No other formerly Soviet republic had a higher unemployment rate, a higher infant mortality rate, or a lower literacy rate.[6]

❦ ❦

With only 2.5 percent of the land arable and a population of just 4 million, Turkmenistan was less a country than an expanse of desert with underground wealth: In addition to oil, it had the world's fourth-largest natural-gas reserves. In the nineteenth century, the Russians competed with the British for this desert, a contest known as the Great Game. In the contemporary version of this competition, Russia, Iran, China, and the West (as represented by major oil companies) are vying for oil and gas pipelines.

I had found in Tel Aviv that the Israelis were also active here. Indeed, President "Turkmenbashi" had hired an Israeli investment firm, the Merhav Group, to represent the Turkmen government in some of its major energy projects. "The Turkmens simply have no qualified people in their own bureaucracy to do it," a Western businessman told me, "so in their mind, they've subcontracted the responsibility to 'clever Jews' to protect their interests."

There were two oil refineries in the port of Turkmenbashi. The old, inefficient one, still in operation—its gas flares visible for miles—had been built by the Soviets in 1942, when the Wehrmacht's thrust into the Caucasus forced Stalin to relocate his oil production to the far side of the Caspian. The new one, a gleaming pageant of silver tanks and towering pipe configurations, was under construction by Japanese and Turkish contractors, with French and German managers and consultants. A handful of Israelis oversaw the entire $1.5 billion operation.

David Sima was the Israeli site manager for the new refinery. His small office, in a forlorn courtyard, was decorated with a map of Israel and little Israeli flags. In late middle age, with receding gray hair and glasses, he had an informal and unpretentious manner that reminded me of kibbutzniks I knew.

"Because of the new refinery," Sima began in thick Hebrew-accented English, "Turkmenbashi's oil production will rise from four million to nine million tons per year by 2010." But the really big change, he said, is that the new plant would produce oil and a range of petroleum by-products all up to the latest Western environmental standards, including low-lead, low-sulfur, high-octane gasoline. "We are also constructing separate facilities for the production of bitumen, home heating oil, and various lubricants. The refinery we're building for this country is state-of-the-art." This state-of-the-art oil refinery was to be an important node in the pipeline network exporting Turkmenistan's energy products west beneath the Caspian to the Caucasus and Turkey's Mediterranean coast; south to Iran and the Persian Gulf; and east through Uzbekistan and Kazakhstan to China and Japan.

"It's a quiet, peaceful country," Sima continued offhandedly, "with a regime that controls everything with a very strong hand—for good and for bad. When the Russians left, they took everything. There is no cultural life. When the police harass you here, remember that only two generations ago these people were all nomads." They have no urban experience, he meant to say. Thus, anyone they don't know makes them suspicious.

The Israelis were taking a big risk here. But one never knows the future in a place like this, and the oil industry is about taking huge risks: If one project succeeds, the profits more than make up for those that fail.

Because of the heat, the trains ran only at night, so I asked Telman if he could drive me to Ashgabat, Turkmenistan's capital, 375 miles southeast through the Kara Kum Desert. He wanted a better car for the seven-hour journey, and drove through town for five minutes to meet a friend, whose car he borrowed. With so many people here jobless and having nothing to do, borrowing someone's car on the spot in return for money was easy.

Before leaving town, Telman and I shared a lunch of grilled meat at a new Turkish-run restaurant. The television had a satellite hookup. While we ate, I watched an Istanbul talk show. A woman in a black scarf and sunglasses was explaining to the host about Islam. The show was interrupted by a slick advertisement for a Turkish washing machine. In another corner of the restaurant I noticed a plastic clock, a Koranic inscription, and a trite photo of the Swiss Alps, the same photo I had seen often in the poor and sweltering Third World. The *expat* oilmen from Turkey at the next table looked neat and comfortable in their khakis. My soft drink was cold and the table was clean. Compared to what was outside, this was like being back in the West.

I smelled hot tar as we left the Caspian behind and entered an ashen wasteland of alkaline silt fringed by distant lunar cliffs. Small groups of Kazakh girls in colorful dresses were selling camel's milk in old soda bottles by the roadside: They had migrated with their families from Kazakhstan into the western reaches of the Kara Kum. There were almost no other cars on the road. The police posts we passed looked abandoned, their rusted roofs rattling in the wind. But as we traveled southeastward, deeper into Transcaspia—the region east of the Caspian—the first of many hundreds of camels that I would see in the next few hours appeared, walking in single file along the narrow asphalt highway. In the thick haze, their massive, swaying bodies were reduced to the thinness of a ruler as we drove directly behind them. The road paralleled the Transcaspian Railway and the Kara Kum Canal: two monuments to Russian colonialism. The railway had been completed during the reign of the reactionary Czar Alexander III, linking the region as the British railways linked India. The Khrushchev-era canal was the longest irrigation ditch in the world, stretching for nearly seven hundred miles, from the Caspian to the Oxus (Amu Darya) River, in northeastern Turkmenistan. By diverting water from the Oxus that would normally have replenished the Aral Sea, the canal has created an environmental disaster—drying up the Aral to serve a useless cotton monoculture. A reactionary czar had proven less destructive to Central Asia than a liberalizing Bolshevik like Khrushchev.

Iron-and-cinder-block houses bleached white with dust announced the town of Nebit Dag, where a smiling Uzbek girl in a ramshackle hut sold me a container of warm mineral water. Though Turkmens account for three quarters of the population, they are a rural people. The towns are occupied by Russians, Uzbeks, Armenians, and Azeri tradesmen. In the center of Nebit Dag I encountered for the first time a large group of Turkmens: old men with wispy beards, shaggy woollen hats called *telpek*s, and inscrutable expressions. They were sitting by an elevated hot water pipe and a new apartment block with satellite dishes sprouting from the rooftops.

Beyond Nebit Dag, the sand became finer still and the landscape utterly flat, like an endless brown beach without a sea. It was late afternoon and about 100 degrees when our borrowed car broke down. The problem was a failed spark plug. We fiddled with it for a while, until a car pulled over and the driver fixed it for us. Though we were strangers, we shook hands and the males embraced, the custom throughout Central Asia. The desert continued to transform itself, becoming like hardened cigarette ash, stained white with salt in places and speckled with innumerable sheep, statuesque camels, and patches of vegetation. There was nothing man-made in sight, as if communism, with its brute concrete forms, had never existed here and the czars' governors still ruled from beneath a gabled roof nearby. Crossing this desert in an old automobile gave me respect for the sheer persistence and determination of Skobelev's troops, who had crossed it on foot and horseback for nothing more than the glory of empire.

A mountain range appeared off to my right, in the south. At first it was just another line of heartless gray dunes. But as the hills swept higher, they became a fabulously intricate tea-colored carpet, unfurling steeply and majestically in delicate, bony creases. This was the Kopet

Dag—literally, Lots of Mountains—rising 11,000 feet and forming the border between Turkmenistan and Iran—between the hazy and flat, featureless wastes of Central Asia to the north and the dramatic mountains and plateaus of the Middle East to the south.

In the early evening we stopped at Geok-Tepe, the Turkmen stronghold invested by Skobelev. Here President Saparmurad "Turkmenbashi" had erected a $40 million mosque, which he called the Geok-Tepe Mosque of Saparmurad Haji, in honor of his pilgrimage to Mecca. The ex-Communist boss of Turkmenistan had thus performed the supreme ritual of Islam and memorialized both it and the site of the Turkmens' last stand against the Russians, a retroactive symbol of national identity by way of his own personality cult.

The mosque—built by a French construction firm—was monstrous, like a white marble refrigerator. The arches were pseudo-Islamic, like those of a Southern California shopping mall. The prayer service had ended and about a dozen leathery Turkmen ancients, with wiry white beards, woollen hats, and flowing robes, gathered in the courtyard as I entered. A few boys about six or seven years old were with them, lined up for the prayer in which Moslems symbolically wash their hands and faces in purification. One of the boys turned his head to look at me, but the old man beside him quickly cupped the boy's head with his large hands and turned it back. These old Turkmens looked like the sword-bearing tribesmen who had held out for three weeks against Skobelev by burying earthen jugs in the ground to keep their drinking water cool. Rather than be swallowed by the vast courtyard, they seemed to assume its proportions.

We drove eastward into the night and arrived in Ashgabat in less than an hour. Eventually, Telman lost his way. Eventually, we found the first-class hotel where I had decided to stay. We embraced and said good-bye in the darkness, our clothes layered in filmy grit, and I entered a brightly lit marble lobby crowded with well-dressed foreign businessmen speaking English. The reception desk had the first credit-card stickers I had seen since Baku and was staffed by elegant Russian women, one of whom told me I couldn't have a room because I had not made a reservation.

"Do you have rooms available?" I asked.

"Yes," she replied.

"Then why can't I have one?"

"Because I see no reservation on file."

I pestered, begged, and soon prevailed. It was characteristic of Turkmenbashi's bureaucratic regime, like a blanket in which everyone was entangled. In the hotel dining room, the foreign businessmen sat alone, slugging back vodka as they stared at the walls in boredom and frustration.

❦ ❦

No other republic capital of the former Soviet Union lies as far south as the Turkmen capital of Ashgabat (Persian for "lovely setting"), only a few miles from the Iranian border at the foot of the Kopet Dag Range. The morning heat left me weak in the knees as I walked along a wide, unshaded boulevard lined with intimidating new buildings—a presidential palace, a congress center, luxury hotels, a casino, office suites— combining Stalinist grandiosity with the dazzling ceramic patterns, domes, and archways of the Moslem Near East. These Islamic-Stalinist structures were made of expensive stone and marble. Sliding gates and tinted two-way mirrors on some of the buildings combined the security fetish of the new global elite with Soviet oppressiveness, merging corporate power with Interior Ministry brutality.

Human beings were dwarfed amid such grandiosity. At the edges of the empty, treeless boulevards, pedestrians in polyester and the traditional velvety robes and skullcaps of Central Asia shuffled in single file beside cheap wooden stalls, which created a narrow strip of shade. Elsewhere there were large parks and a vast grid pattern of hushed streets with single-story Russian provincial houses, their scabby facades melting in the heat. As I watched a band of shirtless boys run through a dirty fountain, a disheveled policeman came up and asked me not for my passport but for the time. Ashgabat, sleepy and colonial, reminded me of a British-built cantonment in India. No other place I had been was more suggestive of imperial Russia's thrust southward toward the Indian Ocean than this steamy town of 450,000—more pleasant, despite the heat and architecture, than Tashkent, the Uzbek capital, and Almaty, the Kazakh one, with their neither-nor junkiness, million-plus populations, and higher crime rates.

On the northern fringe of Alexander's domain, the Ashgabat region was the heart of the Parthian empire from the second century B.C. to the first century A.D., as well as that of the Seljuk Turks from the eleventh to the thirteenth century, when the Mongols sacked it. Only in 1881 did it recover from its desolation, when the Russians built a fortified settlement here, following Skobelev's conquest. In October 1948, Ashgabat suffered a major earthquake that destroyed the entire city, including schools, hospitals, theaters, shops, municipal buildings, and the colonnaded railway station. Two thirds of Ashgabat's population—110,000 people—died. The new city that the Soviets built over the ruins was transparently colonial in style. Since the early 1990s, it has been studded with the monuments of Turkmenbashi's megalomania: so Stalinist and so much like the cities of the ancient tyrants of nearby Persia, Babylonia, and Assyria.

The towering "Arch of Neutrality," a marble-and-gilt edifice, with glass elevators crawling up the sides, rose over a downtown plaza, giving it a theme-park aura. Atop the arch was a gold-plated statue of Turkmenbashi which rotated so that he always faced the sun. Beside the arch was the "Sacred Bull": a gargantuan statue of a gilded bull resting on a marble plinth. The bull was shaking a globe that rested on its shoulders. In Turkmen lore, the shuddering bull is the symbol of an earthquake. Standing before the bull was a woman holding a gilded child to the sun. The woman was Turkmenbashi's mother, who was killed in the 1948 earthquake; the child, Turkmenbashi. Smaller gold-and-marble monuments to the president dotted the edges of the plaza.

There was, too, the Turkmenbashi National Museum, which rose above the city in the foothills of the Kopet Dag: a colossal palace of marble and dressed stone that resembled Ceauşescu's one-thousand room "House of the Republic" in Bucharest, fanning out into an immense, Vatican-size courtyard, with tall columns crowned by five-headed golden eagles and winged horses. In the entrance hall, under massive ceilings, were large maps of the proposed gas pipeline and the new Turkmen currency, the manat, with the president's picture on bills of every denomination. I walked through rooms filled with archaeological relics and photos of folkloric dance troupes. Emblazoned on the wall were Turkmenbashi's words:

> . . . There is no place on our native land where there wasn't bloodshed. The Turkmens' ancestors lived on this land and defended this

land. We must defend the land sodden with the blood of our ancestors as an apple of an eye and must know how valuable it is.

In other words, the oil and natural gas were a national patrimony to be
protected and exploited by Turkmenbashi, who, in his own person,
symbolized this old-new nation. As in Azerbaijan, the money that
had poured in here represented only contract bonuses and advance
payments for exploration—and had been spent here on fascist-style
monuments—while the "real wall of money" had yet to arrive. The
Arch of Neutrality, the Sacred Bull, the museum, the presidential
palace, the congress center, the Geok-Tepe Mosque, and other edifices
such as the "Pyramid of Independence" and the Olympic-size sports
complex cost roughly $600 million: a staggering sum for a country with
an insolvent central bank, no middle class, ten-dollar-a-month pensions, and a mostly jobless workforce.

The president called his foreign policy "positive neutrality," which
in practice meant isolationism reflecting the xenophobia and suspicion
of his nomadic forebears. Visa restrictions made it hard even for citizens of other former Soviet republics to visit, while Turkmenistan's
own people faced vast bureaucratic obstacles if they wished to travel.
Few foreign journalists and aid workers were allowed in; cell phones
were rare, because the usage fee was deliberately high. "Positive neutrality" also meant playing one power and company off against the
other. Everyone—the Israelis, the Iranians, the oil companies, etc.—
were working on projects here, busily massaging Turkmenbashi's ego.
Turkmenistan was the only country where Israelis and Iranians worked
on related oil and construction projects. The president reportedly kept
$1.2 billion in private European bank accounts for "national security."
The big questions asked by foreigners in Ashgabat were the same
as those asked in Baku: With the overwhelming portion of oil and gas
revenues still to come, what would all the money be used for? What
would the president do with it?

"The experiences of early childhood really are determining," a foreign
resident of Ashgabat explained to me. "The president's father was
killed in World War Two. His mother died in the 1948 earthquake,

when he was eight. He grew up in an orphanage. His personality cult is a childish desire for the attention he never got as a boy. The president *is* the golden child, like the one in the statue. He lives in an imaginary world. He has no personal life. His wife is in Moscow. His children are also abroad. It is unclear if he has anyone close to him that he loves."

It was truly a strange dictatorship. The police went unarmed. The only executions were those of fifty criminals, in 1993. There were no identifiable dissidents: The kind of dissent that focuses on universal values such as human rights requires urbanity, and the Turkmens were a nomadic, tribal people, who still wore traditional costumes and didn't know the names of streets, perhaps because knowing street names requires an abstract and impersonal knowledge that is not based on habit. The people I met who knew one street from another were usually Russian hotel clerks, Armenian cabdrivers, Azeri merchants, and so on— the urbanized foreigners. Outrage against the regime was muted. When I asked why, I got a one-word answer: "Tajikistan." Tajikistan was another former Soviet republic in Central Asia that had collapsed into violent anarchy, by some counts split among twelve different warlordships. Turkmenistan was prone to similar disintegration, and everyone here knew it. Turkmenistan was not even a "fossil nation" like Georgia. Four-fifths desert, Turkmenistan had a history of nothing but clans of nomadic raiders: the Tekke in the center (to which Turkmenbashi and his ministers belonged), the Ersry in the southeast, and the Yomut in the north and west. "The current stagnation is still better than chaos," a diplomat told me.

Stagnation there certainly was. The Kara Kum Canal was silting up, threatening the country's water supply. Compulsory education had been reduced. No money was being spent on infrastructure; houses and roads everywhere were collapsing. If someone opened a small business, a swarm of tax collectors descended, demanding bribes and permits. Turkmenbashi was re-creating his own idealized version of a Soviet republic. Ashgabat was suffused with Brezhnevian gloom: no crowds, traffic jams, or street life. But there were new casinos and nightclubs filled with foreign oilmen and Russian women, the latter presumably seeking passports through marriage to leave the country.

I heard a typical story about a local family. The daughter had a degree in history but no job and was living with her grandmother. Because the grandmother's trifling pension wasn't nearly enough to survive on, the two women raised roses to sell and were bartering their furniture for food and other necessities.

※ ※

Compared to Turkmenistan, Aliyev's "banal authoritarianism" in Azerbaijan appeared enlightened. At least in Baku there was an opposition with whom I could meet. Here there was only the airless, pulverizing desert heat; diplomats and businessmen who wouldn't talk freely even in their own offices; and an official at one of the government ministries who kept plying me with green tea and apologizing that since the head of his department was unavailable, he couldn't arrange interviews for me on his own. The ministry building was unguarded. Anyone could walk into the offices, where little work seemed to be getting done. When I got back to my hotel room, the phone rang. It was the same official, asking me to return to the ministry to answer some questions: "We need to know always where you will be—for your own protection, of course." I was reminded of Romania and Bulgaria in the 1970s and 1980s.

I could have answered his silly questions over the phone, but it was clear that he wanted an opportunity to see me again, to sip tea and chat. Like the other officials in the ministry, this man was ethnic Turkmen: The minorities had been squeezed out of government service. He had straight black hair, coal-colored eyes, semi-Asiatic features, and a slow, graceful manner. In the close, clammy heat of his gloomy office, he told me that "with communism over, we are back to our Oriental traditions. Clans and families are all we have left. The family is so strong," he emphasized. "That's why there are so few beggars here despite the poverty.

"But my son is learning capitalism," he said, his face brightening. "Every morning he shines my shoes and asks for a thousand manats [ten cents]. Then he washes my car and asks for five thousand. But the older ones are ruined. They cannot change. And the pace of life has become so fast in Ashgabat, too fast, because of the foreigners. There is so much traffic now, too much . . ." Everything is relative, I thought.

Through this official, I met an "artist," who wore a wristwatch with Turkmenbashi's picture on it and told me about Turkmenbashi's generosity to the artistic community. When I asked about his own art, though, he had little to say, as if all self-assertion had been crushed under Turkmenbashi's personality cult.

"We are rediscovering our Turkmenness," the artist told me. "*Independence* is a deep word. It means the rise of national culture, not the rise of the individual. In Soviet times, the borders with our Turkmen brothers in Iran and Afghanistan were closed. Now we are sending official delegations of Turkmen art students to show the Turkmens in Iran how we are one big nation whose borders reach beyond Turkmenistan."

In other words, the anti-Iranian irredentism that I had found in Azerbaijan existed here, too. Ruslan Muradov, a blunt-spoken ethnic Turkmen whom I had met through a foreign friend and who was the head of a government department for the restoration of historical monuments, admitted that it was based on cultural insecurity. "Concerning who the Turkmens are," he told me, "there is a great gap between historical and literary fact and what the government here declares. Local scholars know the truth, but they still must recite other 'facts' that are sometimes nonsense—like that the Turkmens are the source of everything, that the Turkmens discovered America, for example. The truth is that because the Turkmens were nomadic, we were always in close contact with other cultures: Hellenistic, Parthian, Iranian. So it is impossible to know what, exactly, is Turkmen about us and what is not. Look outside the window," he said, pointing. "You see the Kopet Dag Mountains, which guard the farming and urban civilization of Iran." Iran had a strong monarchical tradition, he said. The ayatollahs constituted an organized, evolved, and impressive autocracy compared to Turkmenistan's. Democracy was possible in Iran because Iranian society was already sophisticated and developed. "But the Turkmens never knew any kind of government. This is the homeland of classical anarchy."

Historically, monarchies have filled the vacuum as a relatively stable and benign form of tyranny in regions where there was no middle class to staff democratic institutions. In Central Asia, where the middle classes still don't exist, medieval khans such as Turkmenbashi have returned following the collapse of communism.

Teheran's Islamic fundamentalism terrified the Turkmens and thus Iran's influence was limited here. But a future democratic Iran would culturally overwhelm this khanate, whose ruler was depleting the social fabric, making it even harder for Turkmens to defend themselves against the far more populous and dynamic neighbor to the south.

※ ※

"You cannot imagine how much we lost with the end of the Soviet Union," my middle-aged friend Anna, a singer, told me with tears in her eyes. Anna's family was originally from the Caucasus. Her father was Armenian; her mother, Azeri Turk. Her parents had moved to Turkmenistan for their jobs. Like intermarriage between Serbs and Croats in Tito's Yugoslavia, none of this was unusual in a multiethnic empire. "We were so rich," Anna went on in anguish. "There were good communal relations; we had an orderly framework of government. Perestroika was paradise, really, a bit of freedom without the anarchy that came later. You should have seen Ashgabat then. We were a real cosmopolitan city—with theater, ballet. Now it's ninety percent Turkmen; it's suffocating." An empire had collapsed, and all that remained were blood loyalties.

Anna and I were walking through one of Ashgabat's vacant lots, filled with rusty metal and the omnipresent smell of oil. A rose growing in the dirt made her smile, and she walked over to admire it. In such a landscape, you must learn to extract pleasure from small things.

On my last evening in Ashgabat, Anna took me to a singing session, where in the miserable heat of a schoolroom, a group of men and women took out their guitars and played music set to the poems of Pushkin and other Russian writers: even in Central Asia, Europe had still not completely vanished. The high voices, reminiscent of Moscow and St. Petersburg, rang out sad and sentimental in this subtropical setting as I glimpsed the mountains of Iran through the windows. The singers were Russian, Armenian, Azeri Turk, and Georgian—all longing for a lost empire, like the last British *expat*s in India. "This is a Soviet tradition begun around campfires in the 1950s," Anna explained. "Not everything Soviet was bad, you know."

Of course, it's hard to deny that the destruction of the Soviet Union was a good thing. But ever since I had crossed into Georgia from

Turkey, I found people whose lives had been ruined by it. Many of these people insisted that they were "European" and felt they did not deserve to be abandoned to chaos and uncivil regimes simply because of geography. I understood their agony. But I also knew that remaking this part of the world—even with the incentive provided by energy pipelines—would take both the resolve of a missionary and a sheer appetite for power that the West could probably never muster, especially given the difficulties it was having in the relatively nearby and less challenging Balkans.

27

A HERODOTEAN LANDSCAPE

In June, there was not a blade of grass to disturb the baked-yellow mathematical purity of Nyssa, the 2,300-year-old Parthian capital located a few miles outside Ashgabat. The Parthians were nomads who repelled Alexander's Greek armies. Under kings Mithradates and Artabanus they secured an empire stretching from Mesopotamia, in the west, to the Indus Valley, in the east, including the Iranian Plateau and adjacent parts of Central Asia. The Parthian empire was feudal and decentralized, somewhat like Russia's now. It made use of art, architecture, and administrative practices inherited from the Greeks. What was Parthian was often Greek, just as what was Turkmen was still, after two millennia, Parthian—as I had seen from the gaudy carpets, the clanging jewelry, and the headdresses sold in dusty local bazaars, with their magenta colors and primitive, geometric motifs.

Nyssa was a series of disintegrating sand castles at the foot of the bare roller-coaster updrifts of the Kopet-Dag. The smooth clay landscape could have been shaped by a potter. The naked hills, the honeycomb of ruins with lizard-filled pits, the dry heat and emptiness, the fact that I was alone and that Iran beckoned—it all made a perfect backdrop for bridging the gap between ancient history and now.

Through much of history, the trade routes had been more or less constant—an east-to-west network for the transport of spices, silks, precious stones, and, lately, oil and natural gas through protected underground pipelines, from as far east as China and Kazakhstan to the Mediterranean. The Parthian empire had been a trading one (like any new empire likely to emerge here). The flat wastes posed no geographical impediment to conquest by a resurgent Russia, or Iran or another power. But the flat landscape also encouraged anarchy, because there were no natural borders and no focus of urban settlement, only scattered oases with competing clans. This was true not only of Turkmenistan but also of neighboring Uzbekistan and Kazakhstan, whose regimes, though less absurd than Turkmenbashi's, were run by formerly Soviet, Brezhnev-style bosses, whose sterile dictatorships kept their countries from fracturing along ethnic and religious lines.[1]

Anarchy in some form or other, as I had seen, was almost everywhere in the Near East. Thus far in my journey I had found vibrant institutions only in Turkey, Israel, and, to a lesser degree, in Jordan. Even in Romania and Bulgaria, the countryside was anarchic, while the situation in the Caucasus was much worse. Syria was like Brezhnev's Soviet Union: instability kept at bay by a stultifying sectarian tyranny. Meanwhile, democracy—which offered the best hope for building and sustaining vibrant institutions—was facing serious obstacles when one considered Romania's seamy coffeehouse politics; Bulgaria's corruption; Lebanon's company-run state; and the various power vacuums in the Caucasus. History shows that only states with the unity and strength to preserve themselves remain sovereign, and I had seen few of those in my travels. The rest would likely be absorbed into some new imperium—unless they disintegrated to the point where nobody cared. Herodotus had recorded cycles of autocracy, freedom, chaos, and autocracy once again. The Medes, for example, shook off Assyria's asphyxiating yoke, and eventually all the peoples of Assyria's empire won their independence. "But it was not to last," writes Herodotus, "and they became once more subject to autocratic government." Freedom and democracy certainly make for the strongest states, but with so little to build upon in this part of the world, civil society will likely be introduced only by force and Machiavellian tactics, as in Shevardnadze's Georgia. Even so, the chances of success were not great.

Fundamentally, little had changed in regional politics since Herodotus and Thucydides. For Herodotus, the fault zones had been ethnic and cultural. Greeks, Persians, Scythians, and others fought each other

over territory in ancient times, just as Georgians, Abkhazians, Ossetians, Azeris, and Armenians fought each other over territory in the
1990s. Thucydides later reduced Herodotus' chronicle of cultural clash
to the steely confines of power politics. Indeed, the Near East remains
a cauldron of pure self-interest.

My visit to Turkmenistan was still not concluded, but in the clear air
and silence of this archaeological site outside Ashgabat, I couldn't help
but think about what I had found in my travels. I remembered Zarqa,
that noisy urban sprawl north of Amman, Jordan—with its hordes of
unemployed teenagers, typical of Jordan's population—where the future of the Near East might truly be written. Arab-Israeli reconciliation
might be irrelevant as economic and demographic forces in the Arab
world cause central authority to give way to more unwieldy oligarchies,
composed of self-interested politicians and middle-level officers, themselves under pressure from the young urban poor and dynamic middle
classes. The end of bipolar Arab-Israeli conflict and the birth of new,
more complex systems of strife might even lead to the collapse of fragile states like Syria and Jordan. Classical geography might reassert itself
as new Silk Roads—from Antioch south to Tel Aviv; from Central Asia
west through the Caucasus to the Mediterranean; and from Baku south
to the Persian Gulf—hum with commerce even as instability reigns
close by. It would be like ancient times, when this now-silent Parthian
capital was alive with traders.

But it was globalization that concerned me most as I prowled the
ruins of this once-great cosmopolitan city. In many quarters of the
West, free markets are seen as a solution in and of themselves. But from
Romania to Turkmenistan, I had seen how a wave of unrestrained capitalism, along with the absence of institutions and social safety nets—
particularly in the ex-Communist world—had opened dangerous gaps
between a rapacious new oligarchal class and the working poor. The
new rich were building high stone barricades equipped with electronic
sensors—whether around villas in Romania and Bulgaria, around new
private communities in Lebanon, or around office suites in Ashgabat. It
was a siege mentality that, here and there, might foreshadow revolutionary upheaval. Few places I had visited appeared stable.

With an Armenian driver who had offered me a good rate, I left Ashgabat a few days later for ancient Merv, 250 miles to the east. We drove through a brown, featureless emptiness, followed by a scrub plain marked by distempered factory walls lashed by gray silt. Always, there was the signature of formerly Soviet Central Asia: a camel grazing by an elevated hot water pipe, its fiberglass insulation flaking off. The roads were bad, the gasoline bad enough to make the car stall, and coffee nonexistent. In the middle of this dustbowl were these fantastic billboards, recently erected: HALK, WATAN, TURKMENBASHI.

After several hours we reached the new, Soviet-built town of Merv, which reminded me of Sumgait without the chlorine and pesticide pollution. The Intourist Hotel was a dead zone. The temperature outside was over 100 degrees, and the air-conditioning was broken. The clerk lay half asleep, sweating on a couch. The restaurant walls were cinder blocks spray-painted pink. The waitresses, Russian and Turkmen—old, overweight, and with paralyzed expressions—were smoking and drinking vodka at a corner table, the food half eaten on their plates. The heat and sight of the food convinced me to skip lunch. The green tea we ordered came in wide bowls without handles. Sweating, we waited for the tea to cool.

Ancient Merv lay a little farther to the east. Beside a hodgepodge of asbestos-roofed shacks and abandoned, rusted vehicles, we came upon a long, curving line of crumbling walls sculpted by the wind. Sand and dust were indistinguishable; a gust of wind washed both into my eyes. "A garbage heap," my driver said, sneering, baffled that I wanted to come here, to what the medieval Seljuk Turks had called the Queen of the World.

Called Margiana by the Persians, Merv was vanquished and rebuilt by Alexander in the fourth century B.C. Later, the Parthians made a great city here, and so did the Persians again. In the early Middle Ages, Merv was a melting pot of creeds, including Christians, Buddhists, and Zoroastrians. Then came centuries of Arab rule, followed by that of the Seljuk Turks. By the eleventh and twelfth centuries, Seljuk Merv was the urban masterpiece of the Silk Road and the second city of the Islamic world after Baghdad, filled with palaces, libraries, and gardens.

Then in 1221, Merv became an early symbol of mass murder. Tuluy, the most brutal of Genghis Khan's sons, accepted the city's peaceful surrender, then ordered each of his soldiers to decapitate at least three hundred civilians. With swords and axes, the Mongol army killed several times more victims than the 225,000 killed by atomic bombs in Hiroshima and Nagasaki.[2] Merv did not regain a degree of prominence until 1884, when its occupation by a czarist army completed the Russian conquest of Transcaspia begun by Skobelev. Because the road from Merv through Afghanistan to India was unimpeded by mountain ranges, the Russian move stirred a long bout of "Mervousness" on the part of the British government. Great Britain and Russia nearly went to war over Merv—of all things!—averted only by a treaty in 1887 that delineated the borders of nearby Afghanistan.

But strategy concerns itself with military and economic significance, not cultural or architectural splendor, so what armies fight for is often a dump in the middle of nowhere. Now, because of the natural-gas fields near here, this area is again worth a war.

Tuluy's Mongols hadn't destroyed quite everything. We drove another mile over the piecrust plain toward a magnificent building with a barrel dome thirty-eight meters high, which stood on an upward slope, as if between earth and sky. The mausoleum of the Seljuk sultan Sanjar, who died in 1157, had a cubelike mystical quality typical of Central Asian architecture: It would not have been out of place in a science-fiction movie. The turquoise tiles had peeled away from the dome, revealing fabulous brickwork. Guarding this structure of Rodinesque strength and proportions was a leathery-faced Turkmen elder with a fur hat and a sublime smile.

"This is a holy place that influences your fortune," he told me. "Here you will find freedom and energy." He was a simple man, full of such clichés. But what were my own conclusions after almost four thousand miles of travel if not clichés, too? I was now halfway between Herat (to the south, in Afghanistan) and Bukhara (to the north, in Uzbekistan), the farthest point east I would go in my journey, and what had I learned? That power and self-interest would shape the immediate future, at least in this part of the world.

I sat down inside the tomb and let my body cool in the shade of its three-foot-thick walls, tasting the salt on my lips. The eerie cries of pigeons in the dome brought to mind the slaughter that had occurred here. My eyes lighted on a brilliant blue faience shard: a fragment from the Mongol destruction. I imagined thousands of people waiting over many days to be dispatched methodically by knives and axes. As I looked through a doorway at the moonscape of loose dirt, I thought of the ruined Seljuk masterpiece where I was sitting as a memorial to victims of a mass murder that, only because it happened so long ago in what seems now like a storybook setting, did not affect me. I thought, too, of the lonely Jewish cemetery in the Romanian town of Sărmaşu that I had seen near the start of my journey: a memorial to a more recent slaughter that did roil my emotions. Would that cemetery affect a visitor as deeply hundreds of years from now?

Close by was another twelfth-century Seljuk mausoleum, whose thick walls and deep foundation had helped save it from Tuluy Khan's destruction. A tree draped with colorful rags—pagan fertility offerings—graced this Moslem holy place. Inside, next to the burial slab, was what looked like a Parthian altar with Hellenistic geometric designs. How wonderful the mixture! I thought. Amid the dust and semidarkness, I groaned at Turkmenbashi's attempt to re-create a monochrome Turkmen identity that, in fact, had never existed. Rudolf Fischer had told me at the start of my travels to be "cosmopolitan." Was there a better moral response to what I had seen? The fact that national characteristics were undeniable did not mean that they would always be so. The fact that the Near East was a battleground of power politics did not mean that power politics could not make a positive difference. It was the impermanence of bad governments that gave me hope.

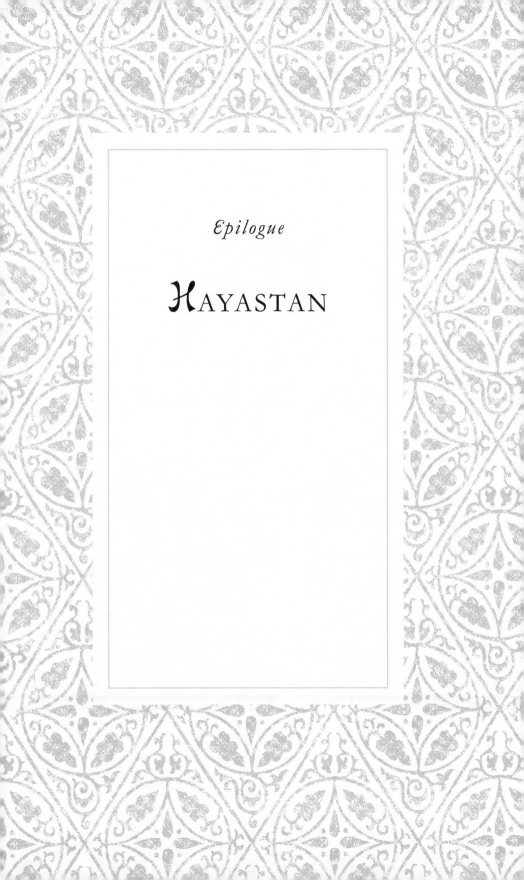

Epilogue

HAYASTAN

28

EARTH, FIRE, WATER

The Armenian capital of Yerevan sits under the spell of Mount Ararat, soaring 16,874 feet over the surrounding plain; a giant smoky-blue pyramid capped by a craggy head of silvery-white snow. On many days, the summit emerges from a platform of clouds halfway up the sky, like a new universe in formation. The name Ararat is from the Armenian root for "life" and "creation," *ara*. Mount Ararat is Armenia's national symbol, appearing on maps and banners and in paintings. Ararat is where Noah's Ark is supposed to have come to rest. In nearby Echmiadzin, the Armenian Vatican, where sits the "Catholicos of All Armenians," a shard of stone said to be petrified wood from the Ark is embedded in a silver-plated icon. Armenians choose to think they are the first people who settled the earth after the Deluge.

From the unfinished cement balcony of my hotel room, Mount Ararat looks close enough to touch—a pure and dreamlike vision of heaven that humbles the ramshackle iron roofs and barracks-style apartment blocks of Yerevan. But Ararat is unreachable. It lies beyond the border with Armenia's historic enemy, Turkey. The border between the two countries is sealed with barbed wire. In the words of an Armenian poem:

> *We have already seen the other side of the moon.*
> *But when will we see the other side of Ararat?[1]*

Ararat's power as a mythic symbol is intensified by its location in Turkey. Ararat calls forth the forbidden land—the lost part of historic Armenia encompassing much of present-day Turkey and the site of the 1915 genocide, when a crumbling Turkish regime starved, exiled, and killed over a million Armenians. Whenever they look toward the southwestern horizon at the awe-inspiring mountain, the inhabitants of Yerevan are reminded of ancient and medieval glory, and of twentieth-century mass murder.

Armenia is the quintessential Near Eastern nation: conquered, territorially mutilated, yet existing in one form or another in the Near Eastern heartland for 2,600 years, mentioned in ancient Persian inscriptions and in the accounts of Herodotus and Strabo. Armenians trace their roots to Hayk, son of Torgom, the great-grandson of Japheth, a son of Noah himself. While their rivals the Medes and Hittites disappeared, the Armenians remained intact as an Indo-European people with their own language, akin to Persian. In the first century B.C., under Tigran the Great, Hayastan (what Armenians call Armenia) stretched from the Caspian Sea in the east to central Turkey in the west, incorporating much of the Caucasus, part of Iran, and all of Syria. In A.D. 301, Armenians became the first people to embrace Christianity as a state religion; today, Orthodox Armenia represents the southeastern edge of Christendom in Eurasia.[2] In 405, the scholar Mesrop Mashtots invented the Armenian alphabet, still in use today. (When I remarked to a friend in Yerevan that the Armenian alphabet looked vaguely similar to the Georgian one, she shrieked: "Nonsense. There is a joke that when the Georgians needed an alphabet, they asked Mashtots, who took the macaroni he was eating and threw it against the wall. The patterns it made became the Georgian alphabet.")

Armenia soon became engulfed by the Roman and Byzantine empires. But when the Arab caliphate fell into decline in the ninth and tenth centuries, Armenia rose again as a great independent kingdom under the Bagratid dynasty, with its capital at Ani, in present-day Turkey. In the eleventh century, the Seljuk Turk chieftain Alp Arslan overran Ani, Kars, and the other Armenian fortresses, destroying over ten thousand illuminated manuscripts, copied and painted at Armenian monasteries.[3] Independent Armenia survived in the form of baronies but eventually fell under the rule of Turks, Persians, and, later, the Russian czars and commissars. It is the Russian part which forms today's independent state.

Now squeezed between Turkey to the west, Iran to the south, Azerbaijan to the east, and Georgia to the north—with its lost, far-flung territories lying in all directions—this newly independent former Soviet republic straddles the Caucasus and the Near Eastern desert to the south. Like Israel, Armenia is a small country—its population is only 3.5 million—surrounded on three sides by historical enemies (the Anatolian Turks, the Azeri Turks, and the Georgians), but it boasts a dynamic merchant tradition and a wealthy diaspora. Beirut, Damascus, Aleppo, Jerusalem, Teheran, and Istanbul all have influential Armenian communities. Jews and Armenians also share the legacy of genocide. The Nazis' World War II slaughter of the Jews was inspired partly by that of the Armenians in World War I. "Who today remembers the extermination of the Armenians?" Hitler remarked in 1939.

I had come to Armenia because I wanted to see *the other side*. Throughout Turkey, Georgia, and Azerbaijan, I had heard people crudely, matter-of-factly curse the Armenians. The Armenians have been despised in these countries the way the Israelis and Jews have been in much of the Arab world, compared with "lice" and "fleas" sucking the blood from native peoples. I had come to Armenia to look again at the issue of national character, for here was a distinctly identifiable people and a country that was more ethnically homogeneous than most others in the region: While Jews comprise 83 percent of Israel's population, Armenians make up 93 percent of Armenia's. (Armenia used to be multiethnic, but with the collapse of the Soviet Union, hundreds of thousands of ethnic Azeris fled to Azerbaijan and abroad, while a similar number of ethnic Armenians fled Azerbaijan.)

Finally, I had come here to end my journey where it began: in the Balkans. Of course, Armenia is not exactly in the Balkans, situated as it is at the opposite end of Turkey from Bulgaria and Greece. However, along with Greece, Bulgaria, Macedonia, and Serbia, Armenia was central to the tangle of nationality problems arising from the death of the Ottoman empire, a headache that bedeviled European statesmen at the turn of the twentieth century and that collectively was known as the "Eastern question." It was the national movements of the late-nineteenth-century Balkans that had inspired Armenian revolutionaries seeking freedom from both the Turkish sultans and the Russian czars.

But there was a crucial difference between the revolt of the Greeks and the Slavs against the Turks in the Balkans and the Armenian revolt against the Turks in eastern Anatolia. The Balkans lay within the Ottoman empire but outside Turkey itself, so only imperial control was at issue; while in eastern Anatolia, Turkish and Armenian communities fought over the same soil. That is partly why—in the shadow of Mount Ararat—traditional ethnic killing first acquired a comprehensive and bureaucratic dimension.

From Merv I had returned to Ashgabat and then home to the United States. Shortly thereafter, I flew to Armenia. My fellow passengers cried and cheered as the plane touched down before dawn in Yerevan. They were Armenians from the diaspora visiting their ethnic homeland, many for the first time. In few countries—Israel being one—have I seen such emotion when a plane lands.

At the airport, there were no bothersome forms to fill out or bribes to pay. Travelers had told me that efficiency and honesty also prevailed at Armenia's land frontier with Georgia. The cabdriver who took me to Yerevan was well groomed, and charged a reasonable price. The roads throughout much of Armenia, as I would see, were better than in Georgia or Azerbaijan. Nor would I encounter any slovenly militiamen demanding bribes. In these and other ways, Armenia was more of a functioning country than others in the Caucasus. In 1998, it carried out a smooth democratic succession when President Levon Ter-Petrosian was replaced by Robert Kocharian.

But behind the scenes, the election had been less than democratic. Real power rested with the prime minister, Vazgen Sarkisian, who controlled the military and security forces. Sarkisian had played a major role in Armenia's successful war in the early 1990s against Azerbaijan in the disputed region of Nagorno-Karabakh, where Armenian troops brutally expelled the Azeri Turk minority. In fact, the new president hand-picked by Sarkisian, Robert Kocharian, was not even an Armenian citizen; he was an ethnic Armenian from Nagorno-Karabakh. Armenia was very much a quasi–military security state with a wafer-thin democratic facade: a multiparty system that masked a one-party dictatorship in which the opposition was intimidated and bribed. "We have only national forces in Armenia, not democratic or universal ones," Mikael Danielyan, the local chairman of the Helsinki Association, a human-rights group, told me.

Still, by the standards of the region, Armenia's political system wasn't bad. An easy presidential transition in Georgia after Shevardnadze, in Azerbaijan after Aliyev, or in Iraq after Saddam Hussein is difficult to imagine. Armenia works, I told myself. There is no absurd personality cult in Armenia as there is in Syria, Azerbaijan, or Turkmenistan; nor does the very existence of the state depend on one man, as in Georgia. Armenia is the only state in the Caucasus—and one of the few I had encountered anywhere in my travels—whose cohesiveness I thought could be taken for granted. "We are united," a local friend told me upon my arrival. "We are ruled by one mafia, not several competing ones."

But my friend and I were insufficiently skeptical. A few days after I left the country, in late October 1999, gunmen entered the Parliament and killed Prime Minister Sarkisian and seven other members of the government before surrendering to authorities. The gunmen were angry about corruption and the government's plan to compromise with Azerbaijan over Nagorno-Karabakh. If this could happen in Armenia, I shuddered for the future of Georgia and Azerbaijan, whose systems were more fragile and whose countrysides were in worse disarray. The entire region was a house of cards.

At a bar over a cup of Turkish coffee (which the bartender insisted on calling Armenian coffee), another Armenian friend shrugged and said cynically: "Government officials here talk about nationalism, but all they care about is making money for themselves. Karabakh, democracy, oil pipelines—these are not things that the population thinks about. People here think only about survival, for themselves and their families." As in most places I had seen on my journey, the local inhabitants were subjects, not citizens. I looked around the bar and saw burly men whose counterparts I had seen throughout in the Balkans and the Caucasus: men dressed in black, with unshaven faces, cigarettes stuck behind their ears, and reeking of expensive cologne. They ordered drinks worth more than a monthly pension and were being served by shy and submissive waitresses barely out of their teens, who were dressed like hookers or circus performers. Here, too, the rich got richer; the poor, poorer. The underlying fear I sensed from my conversations was not that the Turks or another historical enemy would invade but that the most talented people would leave the country for the West. Nothing was produced locally for export, and much of the hard currency fled abroad.

After Bucharest, Sofia, and Tbilisi, Yerevan looked all too familiar: birches and aspens in the spectral darkness of early morning lining intimate streets with dull brown pseudo–Baroque and Art Nouveau buildings, interspersed with corrugated-iron stalls, all fanning out from a grandiose plaza, the legacy of Soviet rule. Later on, men in threadbare clothes laid out transistor-radio parts on the pavement for sale. Others opened foldout tables on which they would play backgammon, while old women in shawls arranged bread and jars of pickles and homemade preserves. Yerevan had a landlocked, provincial air. Armenian merchants had built many of the stately buildings I had seen in Tbilisi and Baku—leaving them for the Georgians and Azeris to enjoy—but since historic Armenia included many cities now inside Turkey, Yerevan had never truly developed until the twentieth century. As elsewhere in the ex-Communist world, the dreary panorama was brightened by the gilt and expensive marble of new casinos and the bright red Marlboro logo on umbrellas, creating café life where none had existed.

As in Tbilisi and Bucharest, the square mile or so of downtown was filled by a mock-Italian class of well-dressed men and women with intelligent, aggressive expressions and sharp-featured beauty. As in Israel, I could tell that this was a country of talented people competing and intriguing among themselves on a claustrophobic playing field. But beyond downtown lingered the same type of urbanized peasantry I had seen in other ex-Communist cities.

❧ ❧

The Armenian Genocide Memorial stands on a plateau overlooking Yerevan, in the same splendid isolation as the Yad Vashem Holocaust Memorial outside Jerusalem. It consists of a forty-four-meter-high dark-granite needle and twelve inward-leaning basalt slabs forming an open tent over an eternal flame, with a museum and offices located underground. The Armenian Genocide, like the Jewish Holocaust, was an event that grew—rather than diminished—in significance over the decades, to the point where it became a collective memory of mythic proportions.[4] The Jews created an identity for the Holocaust, as the Armenians did for the massacres at the hands of the Turks, as blacks did for slavery. Partly because the Armenian Genocide was harder than the Holocaust to isolate from the other violence of a world war, the term *genocide* is relatively new, applied retrospectively decades later.

Because the genocide occurred in the Turkish part of Armenia rather than in the Russian part, where the current Armenian state is located, its memory has always resonated more in the diaspora with its communities of survivors than in Yerevan itself—especially since any discussion of the genocide in Soviet Armenia was discouraged by Moscow, fearful as it was of a nationalist revival. Nevertheless, in 1965, there was a major demonstration here on the fiftieth anniversary of the massacres. This prompted Leonid Brezhnev to make a canny decision. He recognized that a sharpening of hostilities between NATO-member Turkey and a Soviet republic on Turkey's eastern border would benefit the Kremlin at a time when enthusiasm for the Cold War was waning; it would also allow the local population in a strategic and relatively prosperous Soviet republic to express its rage. This is why Brezhnev ordered the construction of the Genocide Monument in Yerevan. Completed by two Armenian architects in 1967, it is a Soviet-style edifice of brutish socialist realism, indistinguishable from many of the war memorials I had seen throughout the former Warsaw Pact nations, with weeds growing between the cracks of poorly laid stones.

Recognizing the genocide was one thing; actively encouraging its memory was another. "The Soviets used the genocide as a political weapon against Turkey but did not teach it in Armenian schools," Laurenti Barsegian, the Genocide Museum director, told me over glasses of cognac and "Armenian coffee" at ten in the morning. What had really ignited the collective memory of the genocide was the terrorist campaign against Turkish diplomats in the 1980s, organized by Beirut-based Armenians. "Killing Turkish diplomats was wrong, for they are just as human as we are," the museum director declared, "but, ironically, it worked. The genocide became more widely known."

Then came Mikhail Gorbachev's glasnost, and, with it, the explosion of ethnic nationalism in Nagorno-Karabakh and the rest of the Caucasus. "The enemy in Karabakh was not the Azeri Turks but our own past," Mikayel Hambardzumyan, a young local reformer, explained to me. "The genocide had given Armenians a nationalism built on defeat and masochism, like the Serbs and Shi'ites," he said, "but now the victory in Karabakh has changed that. It has made our nationalism healthier." I noticed that some Armenian war dead from Karabakh were buried at the Genocide Monument, merging formally the crime committed against the Armenian nation at the beginning of the twentieth century with the ugly revenge exacted at its end.

Because the memory of the genocide had always burned deeper in the diaspora, Karabakh became the diaspora's war as much as Yerevan's, with money and volunteers coming from Armenian communities around the world. "Karabakh—much more than independence from the Soviet Union—unified Armenia with the diaspora," Aris Khazian, a geographer and intellectual, told me.

From the office of the director, I entered the museum, commissioned by post–Soviet Armenia's first president, Levon Ter-Petrosian, and opened in April 1995, on the eightieth anniversary of the genocide, completing the memorial complex begun by the Soviets on the fiftieth anniversary. The official anniversary of the genocide is April 24, the night in 1915 when the Turkish authorities arrested the political, intellectual, and religious leaders of the Armenian community in Istanbul and deported them to the Anatolian interior, where all were savagely murdered.

In the museum's somber basalt interior, I faced a wall-size map, made of stone, showing all the Armenian settlements of eastern Anatolia: Trabzon, Van, Erzurum, Diyarbekir, Bitlis, Sivas, and so on: 2,133,190 Armenian inhabitants, 1,996 Armenian schools, and 2,925 churches. I had traveled often through these now Turkish cities, where, except for the occasional ruin of a church turned into a pigsty that I had seen outside Trabzon, every trace of Armenian civilization has been erased. Nor do the Turkish authorities acknowledge that Armenians once lived on their soil. The Germans could concede their crime against the Jews because postwar Germany was forced to adopt the values and institutions of the Western allies and because the Jews had been a minority with no territorial claim—unlike the Armenians, whose very existence threatens Turkey's right to sovereignty over eastern Anatolia. In the Near East, where states built on a single tribal identity occupy formerly mixed areas, to acknowledge crimes against a whole people is to put your own dominion in doubt.

Passing through the dimly lit hallway, seeing grainy old photos of beheaded Armenians that the Turks had lined up on shelves, naked bodies stacked on hillsides and in trenches, and corpses swinging a few inches off the ground from makeshift gallows, I reflected on the trail of events that sparked such barbarism. I realized then that the Turkish atrocities against the Armenians—more than the Nazi Holocaust—are the appropriate analogy for recent events in Bosnia, Kosovo, Rwanda, and East Timor, among other places. Hitler had no territorial motive for his industrialized racial killing. Indeed, the focus on killing the Jews may have distracted his war machine from fighting his real strategic enemy, the Russians. But eastern Anatolia in 1915—like Bosnia, Kosovo, and Rwanda—was a battlefield upon which two peoples fought over the same soil, with one in a strong enough position to destroy the other. The Armenian Genocide—like the humanitarian disasters of the 1990s—was mass slaughter arising from ethnic conflict over territory. Thus, what happened in eastern Anatolia is politically and morally a more complicated event than the Holocaust. Because the early twenty-first century may see more such humanitarian emergencies, the Armenian Genocide will grow in significance.

The Armenian Genocide occurred during World War I, when Ottoman Turkey was allied with Germany against czarist Russia and the Western allies. While an Allied fleet was bombarding the Dardanelles in western Turkey, eastern Turkey was open to Russian attack. At the same time, Armenians in eastern Turkey (Anatolia) were deserting the Moslem Turkish army and joining their fellow Orthodox Christians on the Russian side, and Armenians farther to the east in the Caucasus were organizing anti-Turkish militias. A brutal competition for land in eastern Anatolia made relations among the Turkish, Armenian, and Kurdish inhabitants even worse, with Armenian villagers refusing to pay taxes to the Kurdish tribesmen who controlled the area on behalf of the Ottoman Turkish authorities.[5] The Turks, in effect, subcontracted the slaughter of the Armenians to the Kurds, whose irregulars, the Hamidieh, murdered the Armenians. In many Anatolian villages, the absence of Turkish authority was worse than its presence.

According to Ronald Grigor Suny, the Alex Manoogian Professor of Modern Armenian History at the University of Michigan: "Political disorder . . . led to chaos. . . . A state of war existed between the Muslims and the Armenians as the government abdicated its responsibilities."[6] Nevertheless, the various local massacres suggested a deliberate policy crafted in Istanbul. The museum displays a document issued by Talaat Pasha, a leading Turkish official, ordering the elimination—by whatever means necessary—of Armenians from Ottoman lands. Thus, 600,000 to 1.5 million people were murdered and exiled—people who had inhabited Anatolia for a thousand years before the Turks arrived. "In my apartment I have the key to my grandfather's house in Erzurum, in western Armenia, a house I can never enter because it is now in Turkey," an Armenian friend in Yerevan told me.

While specific individuals in the highest reaches of the Turkish government ordered the killings, it is also true that imperial authority was disintegrating, causing mayhem in distant reaches of the empire given over to ethnic hatred—a hatred aggravated by competition for scarce land and other resources. The Armenian Genocide was one aspect of an unwieldy, multiethnic empire's re-formation into smaller, uniethnic states. The same ingredients have been at work in our own time: in the Balkans, the Caucasus, the Indonesian archipelago, and other places where large-scale human rights abuses have occurred. The collapse of empires and the desire for ethnic self-determination and regional independence are a messy, bloody business. When central authority dissolves, custom and superstition often take over: something I was keenly aware of when I visited a monastery outside Yerevan.

꽃 ꚙ

Driving east for an hour from Yerevan to the Gegard Cave monastery, I was profoundly moved by the spare solemnity of the Armenian landscape, whose iron-gray mountains, with their wind-tortured shapes, are an ideograph of the pitiless history of the Near East, dominated by marauding armies and earthquakes while peace treaties have merely formalized temporary stalemates on the ground. I drove higher into these alkaline and immense updrifts, where the mountains of Anatolia, Iran, and the Lesser Caucasus converge, and descended into a green valley, tinged with the russets and tawny golds of autumn, and arrived at the Gegard monastery. *Gegard* means "spear" in Armenian, a reference to the spear with which a Roman soldier pierced Jesus on the cross, kept here as a relic. The cave monastery had been carved out of the rock in the early fourth century, soon after Gregory the Illuminator converted Armenia to Christianity. It took its present, expanded form in the thirteenth century, when, with the help of the Georgian queen Tamara, this part of Armenia freed itself from Seljuk Turkish rule.

I left my car and walked uphill to the monastery, along a path where old women sold flowers, ceremonial cakes, and necklaces strung with small fruits. It was Sunday, and these impoverished people were dressed in their best clothes. Men and boys stopped to throw stones into a sacred niche for good luck. An old man played a flute. Branches were draped with colorful cloth, the same fertility offering I had noticed at Merv, in Turkmenistan. I passed a series of *khatchkar*s, elaborately carved crosses in the side of the canyon, a pre-Christian tradition revived in medieval times. By the side of the road I noticed a slab flowing with blood, where two young men were methodically cutting the throats of sheep under the direction of an old woman in black. There was no café, only spring water from the rock. Here, I thought, were hard, overpowering essences. I entered the church.

The gray walls were blackened from candle smoke and incense, and adorned with a single icon of the Virgin. In an adjoining room was the altar, a simple black plinth on which a candle sat, flanked by a geometric Hellenistic design cut in the rock. Water that was revered as holy trickled from the black walls of the church onto the ground, where worshipers young and old washed their faces. In Georgian churches, patriotic frescoes lined the walls. In Armenian churches, the only images were the shadows of flickering candles on the blackened stone. Religion here was reduced to its basic properties: earth, fire, water.

There were few images of Christ, and only the single icon; an ancient cult was holding out—Hayastan—against Islam. At the end of the twentieth century, passion and mystery ruled. The black plinth with its yellow candle was no different from a pagan altar in a two-thousand-year-old sun temple I had seen at Garni, a few miles away.

"Amid the flames and dark walls you become part of the mystery. Here you are not distracted or oppressed by art," a deacon in black robes told me. "Don't talk to me anymore," he said. "Just observe!"

In many of the places I had visited, national and religious myths were powerful stuff, however manipulated by self-interested politicians they might be. Compassion often didn't reach beyond the extended family and ethnic group. And while individuals were more tangible than the national groups to which they belonged, it did not mean that national character was an illusion, especially in wartime. That is why phrases like *democracy building* and *civil institutions* seem abstract except to the local intellectuals, whom Western diplomats and journalists quote in their reports. But are they abstract? Perhaps not. This scene before my eyes was primitive. I could easily imagine these people being cruel to their adversaries. But the fact that stability and civility are even harder to achieve in the Caucasus than in the Balkans—and harder to achieve in the Balkans than in Central Europe—does not mean that a variety of choices, good and bad, does not exist here. Of course, countries are not empty slates full of possibilities: history, culture, and geography really do set limits as to what can be achieved. But bold statesmanship operates near the limits of what is possible, not far from them.

The cave monastery cut out of the rock from which holy water trickled also revealed the awesome effect of nature on human beings—something I'd been thinking about because of the earthquakes that had struck both Istanbul and Athens within weeks of each other in 1999, shortly before my trip to Armenia. The earthquakes had catalyzed talk of reconciliation between Greeks and Turks, their divisions suddenly obliterated by truly monumental forces that had nothing to do with ideology.

※ ※

Gyumri, known as Leninakan in Soviet times, lay two hours northwest of Yerevan, through a gaunt, nut-brown plateau beneath the snowy sawtooth formations of Mount Aragats, 13,497 feet high. Gyumri is a vast shantytown that used to be a city. On December 7, 1988, a major earthquake struck the area. Because the Soviet-style apartment blocks were of even worse quality than those next door in Turkey, some estimates put the death toll as high as fifty-five thousand. The Gorbachev government had promised to rebuild Gyumri within three years, but in 1991 the Soviet Union collapsed. The few reconstructed buildings I saw were financed by the Armenian diaspora.

Gyumri looked like a Caribbean slum transported to a freezing sandpaper tableland, where the trees had been cut down for firewood. Windows were sealed with rocks in place of glass. People lived in what they called "wagons," which resembled shipping containers constructed from sheet metal. Some families lived in scrubbed-out oil drums that still smelled faintly of oil. It was October but already cold here. The wagons were so damp that it was colder inside people's houses than outside, where at least there was sunlight. Inside these makeshift dwellings without electricity, and with the walls black from cooking stoves, I experienced a darkness and squalor of a kind that I had never encountered before.

"We all became stones. We still ask, 'Where is the way out?' " mumbled Arakadi Grigorian, an artist with a neat white beard. Like the other men and women I met who had lost wives and husbands, he told me that he had lived alone in an iron wagon ever since his wife was killed in the earthquake. "We start from zero. The landscape—everything—is frozen, without color. We have lost our relatives, books, photographs, all the material possessions of memory." He went on: "The late 1980s and 1990s have been a terrible time in history. We have relived the equivalent of World War Two and the siege of Leningrad—the destruction of our city, the collapse of the Soviet Union, and the war in Karabakh. What I experienced as a little boy, I have suffered as an old man: little to eat, little to wear, and unburied bodies in the streets. Once again, we make bicycles with our hands. We live in iron doghouses and need to create a bourgeoisie as your country began doing in the 1830s. Yes, I can be optimistic about my children, but about the government, never."

People in Gyumri told me that they felt sorry for the victims of the Turkish earthquake the previous summer. Here, too, natural forces had dissolved animosities. But looking at the desperate, ill-clothed people in the darkened wagons at the onset of winter, I could not be optimistic about whatever political system might emerge from such despair. People here would follow anyone who filled their bellies and gave them work.

※ ※

The Near Eastern ethnic dispute over land in Nagorno-Karabakh hastened the breakup of the Soviet Union. When the Bolsheviks took control of the Caucasus in the early 1920s, they made Nagorno-Karabakh an autonomous region within Turkic Azerbaijan. At the time, Karabakh's population of 131,500 was nearly 95 percent ethnic Armenian. By the time Gorbachev came to power, the ethnic-Armenian part of the population had fallen to 75 percent and Armenians feared that in Karabakh, Armenians would one day be a minority as they were in Nakhichevan, another lost part of historic Armenia surrounded by Armenia and Iran yet now part of Azerbaijan. In Nakhichevan, the ethnic-Armenian share of the population had also fallen dramatically.

This whole muddle of territories in the southern Caucasus represents the illogic of borders and attempts to force pure ethnic identities on places where ethnicity is complex. In ancient and medieval times, much of this area was settled by the Caucasian Albanians (no relation to the Balkan Albanians). Over time, some of these people were converted to Christianity and merged with the Armenians, while others converted to Islam following the arrival of the Seljuk Turks.[7] The Azeri inhabitants of Nakhichevan—including Azeri president Heidar Aliyev and ex-president Ebulfez Elcibey—may, in fact, be closely related to the Armenians, though they would never admit it. But however false these divisions may be, they are real in the minds of the inhabitants. So in 1988, after Gorbachev initiated glasnost and perestroika, Armenians in Yerevan demonstrated for the unification of Nagorno-Karabakh with Armenia at the same time that Azeri authorities began a crackdown on ethnic Armenians in the disputed enclave. Continued demonstrations in Yerevan led to anti-Armenian pogroms in the Azeri industrial city of Sumgait, where ethnic Armenians were killed by Azeri mobs.

Gorbachev sent Soviet troops to Karabakh to impose direct rule, but ethnic violence continued. Azerbaijan then blockaded ethnic-Armenian communities in Karabakh. Armenia responded by declaring Karabakh part of a unified Greater Armenia. Following the collapse of the Soviet Union in 1991, full-scale war erupted between Armenia and Azerbaijan in Karabakh: a war that ended in 1994, after Armenian forces had driven all the Azeris out of Karabakh and annexed adjacent areas of Azerbaijan, so that Armenia and Karabakh were now joined, even if the outside world did not officially recognize it. No issue demonstrated so brutally as Karabakh the extent to which the Soviet system was a facade.

Nagorno-Karabakh lies east and slightly south of Armenia proper. The drive there from Yerevan took six hours through a maze of naked canyons and mountains the dark-red color of lava. I stopped at a dilapidated caravansary for a breakfast of tea, honey, homemade cheese, and a glass of vodka. Later, a tableland of rich black soil rippled upward to snow-dusted granite fastnesses as I approached the heart of the Lesser Caucasus and Armenia's international border with Azerbaijan. Here the road split, one branch turning south to Iran, the other east to Karabakh.

Getting from Armenia to Karabakh means crossing a former piece of Azerbaijan called the Lachin Corridor, which Armenian troops captured in May 1992, looting and slaughtering civilians as the local ethnic-Kurdish population fled.[8] Except for a police post, where I registered the car, I met no border formalities, no sign that this area (which international maps labeled part of Azerbaijan) lay outside Armenia. In fact, Armenia's presence was established by a new road financed by diaspora Armenians, built to Western standards, with guardrails and night reflectors that looped precipitously down the side of one gorge and up the other. It was part of a longer highway connecting Goris, the town just west of Lachin, with Stepanakert, the capital of Karabakh. The road cost $10.1 million, raised in telethons held in Los Angeles in 1996 and 1997 by Armenian-Americans, an example of how, in an interconnected world, a wealthy diaspora can be more important for a country's survival than oil, which Azerbaijan has in abundance.

At the time of my visit, the Armenian diaspora was gearing up to raise an additional $25 million to build a one-hundred-mile-long, north-south highway linking all the main towns of Karabakh, which would connect at Stepanakert with the east-west highway through the Lachin Corridor. This road system, like the one the Israelis had built through the West Bank, would guarantee Armenia strategic control over Karabakh regardless of the symbolic concessions made at the peace table. Armenian foreign minister Vartan Oskanian had told me in Yerevan that his country was creating facts on the ground in Karabakh while also pursuing a diplomatic strategy.

Upon crossing from the Lachin Corridor into Nagorno-Karabakh, I showed my visa to an official, who wrote down my passport number. The visa had cost $27 in Yerevan at the "Consulate of the Republic of Nagorno-Karabakh," a country nobody recognized—not even Armenia, which effectively ran Karabakh as a fiefdom from Yerevan while hosting this phony consulate. "What is Karabakh's real legal status here?" I had asked Mikael Danielyan, of the Helsinki Association in Yerevan. "It's a good question," he answered. "I myself can't figure it out." The messiness and vagueness of the map of the Caucasus, with anarchic places such as Nakhichevan and Nagorno-Karabakh stranded in the middle of other states, rather than an aberration to be clarified by diplomats, might be a bellwether for the entire Near East as sovereignty itself becomes too subtle for the confines of standard maps.

Nagorno-Karabakh means "Mountainous Black Garden," and indeed, as you enter Karabakh, the landscape softens beneath mountainsides bearded with dark evergreens. Shushi, the first town I came upon, seemed the archetypal landscape of ethnic cleansing: a semideserted ruin of gutted streets, demolished buildings and mosques, an expensively reconstructed Armenian church, and an eerie silence, in which I could hear the rattle of autumn leaves. Both the Armenian and Azeri graveyards had been destroyed; broken headstones lay scattered on the ground beneath lovely mountain vistas. Breaking headstones is not like scrawling graffiti: It is hard labor, requiring real passion.

From Shushi, the Azeris had shelled Karabakh's capital of Stepanakert in the valley below with GRAD missiles, forcing Stepanakert's ethnic-Armenian population underground. When the Armenians captured Shushi in the spring of 1992, they took revenge. The Azeri population here fled. Now the Armenians are busy creating facts on the ground. The earth-movers worked throughout the day finishing the highway to Stepanakert. The Karabakh Armenians are a classic, firmly rooted peasantry, living off the land while they reside in ghastly apartment blocks, growing vegetables on cement balconies, confounding the plans of diplomats with the help of rich relations abroad. There was a hard-to-define obscenity about the glistening produce in the marketplace—pomegranates, raisins, olives, grapes, eggplants—given the violence against innocent civilians that had occurred here. People's expressions were implacable. Poor people hate each other more passionately than rich people do, I thought, perhaps because they fear they will remain an underclass if they do not dominate others.[9] There may be no solution to ethnic nationalism, only sedation of it through gradual economic growth.

One café was open, fly-blown, with a single table and a linoleum floor. A woman with badly applied makeup served me a Coke. Some schoolgirls wandered in for soft drinks. After they left, a man approached and sat down. He was the owner of the café—stockily built, balding, with a black mustache. Smoking a Bond cigarette, he grieved over the war. The town, he told me, was dead. There were no jobs, no real economy; none of the refugees had returned. In Soviet times there had been restaurants, hotels, factories, a radio station, and so on. I had heard this lament many times before.

"What's your name?" I asked him.

"Ramik Atayan," he said.

"Do you want a settlement with the Azeris?"

"You never concede anything that you have taken in war," he responded. "This land is sacred, because it was taken with our blood. We are part of Armenia now." He began talking about how as a boy in a heavily Azeri school he was discriminated against because he was Armenian. "On one level, we all got along; on another, there were these tensions."

I asked a theoretical question—the same one that Western diplomats had been asking their Armenian counterparts for years. "How about a deal where the Armenians keep everything here and remain in political control but the Azeris are allowed to fly a few symbolic flags to assert a face-saving sovereignty?"

He answered: "When we can fly flags over Trabzon, Van, Kars, and all the other places we lost in western Armenia, then the Azeris can fly flags over Karabakh."

※ ※

Gogol observes that writers are happy when they focus on characters who "manifest the lofty dignity of man," while grim is the path of writers who focus on characters who are "boring, disgusting, shocking in their mournful reality.... For contemporary judgment," he explains, "does not recognize that equally wondrous are the glasses that observe the sun and those that look at the movements of inconspicuous insects...."[10]

I would have preferred not to end my Near Eastern odyssey in Shushi, with that conversation, but that is where it ended. My encounters in Stepanakert, Karabakh's capital, were variations of what this café owner had told me. I had begun my journey with the lofty and dignified Rudolf Fischer. Along the way, I had met others who yearned for civil society, such as Prince Hassan of Jordan and Farid el-Khazen, the young and earnest professor at the American University of Beirut. Yet through the former Soviet Union, more pessimistic characters and scenes predominated. That was not an accident, just as my last conversation here in Shushi was not accidental but a reflection of the human landscape after seven decades of communism.

The response to this picture should not be denial or fatalism. But I am afraid that calls in Western capitals for "democracy"—while branding as "evil" those who do not comply—is an evasion, not a policy. Holding an election is easy. But because the "state," as Burckhardt says, "is a work of art," building one from scratch requires guile, force, and years of toil.[11] And, in many of the places through which I had traveled, the state is being created from scratch. Fragile states, as I had been told in Romania and in many places thereafter, will copy whatever system is dominant: Nazism, communism, criminal oligarchy, or liberal democracy. The only way to ensure that the latter triumphs is not to force elections on societies ill prepared for them but to project economic and military power regionally, through pipelines and defense agreements. If our weight is felt, our values may follow. But if we only lecture sanctimoniously, new empires that arise in the Near East will not reflect our values. The human landscape is grim, but great powers throughout history faced grim landscapes and were not deterred from pursuing their goals.

Is it in our self-interest to battle chaos and absolutism in the Near East? It is in the Balkans, because they are near Central Europe, and a natural area for the expansion of the West's zone of influence and prosperity. Elsewhere, our interests depend on whether an overriding necessity is at stake. Otherwise, it is hard to imagine a Western government sending troops to, say, Syria, Georgia, or Azerbaijan were they to disintegrate. Only oil pumped in large quantities will represent enough of an interest for us to intervene. But here is where elite military units and more powerful intelligence services are needed to provide us with more options. As Mikheil Saakashvili, the reformist parliamentarian in Tbilisi, told me, Georgia does not need thousands of NATO troops, just early warning to prevent assassinations, special forces to help monitor the borders, and so on.

Nothing is *written,* or determined in advance. Bulgaria, for example, where organized crime was rampant at the time of my visit, is in the midst of vanquishing the mafia-style groupings. However rotten the attitudes on the street may be, enlightened leaders—democrats and autocrats both—can always compromise, as the late King Hussein did, and as Armenian and Azeri rulers might yet do. But weak democracies dominated by criminal groups and rank populism will find it difficult to make peace. Politicians with flimsy majorities, cornered by public opinion and irresponsible media in poor and angry countries, are unlikely to compromise their nationalistic principles. It was two democratic rulers, Levon Ter-Petrosian in Armenia and Ebulfez Elcibey in Azerbaijan, who led their countries deeper into war over Karabakh in the early 1990s. While there is no hatred so ingrained that it cannot be sedated by prosperity (as Nazi hunter Simon Wiesenthal once told me), the building of a middle class from a nation of peasants requires strong and wily leadership more than it may require elections.

Democracy may prosper in Central Europe, the Southern Cone of South America, and elsewhere, but in much of the Near East in the first decade of the twenty-first century, democracy will, unfortunately, be beside the point. The fundamental issue will be the survival of the states themselves—by whatever means. The battle over Caspian pipelines, the coming conflict between Iran and Azerbaijan, the resurgence of Russia under a quasi-autocracy, instability in post-Assad Syria, chaos in Georgia, and stagnation in rural Romania and Bulgaria—if those two countries are left out of NATO—such might be tomorrow's headlines. Confronting them will require Western leaders who understand power and the use of it—leaders who know when to intervene, and do so without illusions.

ACKNOWLEDGMENTS

Jason Epstein, my editor at Random House, William Whitworth and Cullen Murphy at *The Atlantic Monthly,* and my literary agent, Carl D. Brandt, worked assiduously to provide me the early backing I needed to research and write this book, while Joy de Menil at Random House was a strong advocate and editorial adviser. Other editors whom I need to thank are Martha Schwartz and Veronica Windholz at Random House and Michael Kelly, Corby Kummer, Chris Berdik, Avril Cornel, Toby Lester, Amy Meeker, Yvonne Rolzhausen, Martha Spaulding, and Barbara Wallraff at *The Atlantic.* In the final stages of this project, I received financial support from the New America Foundation in Washington, D.C. I thank its board of directors, especially Ted Halstead and James Fallows.

Overseas, a group of foreign correspondents unrolled a magic carpet for me of cheap places to stay and wonderful contacts. Stephen Kinzer, the Istanbul bureau chief of *The New York Times,* showered me with hospitality and insights. Thomas Goltz, author of the most underrated and unsung work of foreign correspondency of the 1990s, *Azerbaijan Diary,* was equally generous. In Bucharest, Anatol Lieven gave me a roof over my head and pummeled me with material about the Balkans and the Caucasus. Then there were the fine company and generosity of Lawrence Sheets, the press viceroy of the Caucasus, as he is known, who did everything and went everywhere in a decade of war but did not get the credit that correspondents in the Balkans did, because the Caucasus were just too far afield. In Israel, Edit Bornstein, the office manager of *The New York Times* in Jerusalem, and the archaeologist Avner Goren also provided accommodations free of charge. There was, too, John Dimitri Panitza of the Free and Democratic Bulgaria Foundation—doing in Bulgaria what George Soros is doing throughout the former Eastern Europe—who provided remarkable assistance.

Christopher Klein, a young and talented foreign service officer, helped in a number of ways in Turkmenistan. Then there were my translators and occasional travel companions, insightful people all: Lilia Babayeva, Eka Khvedelidze, Mariana Lenkova, Nata Talakvadze, and Natasha Tarasova.

Others who provided various kinds of generous help include Fouad Ajami, Fuad Akhundov, Antoine and Sam Akl, Ambassador Ken Alowitz, Maka Antidze, Deniz Aral, Khalid Askerov, Major Charles von Bebber, Ambassador Avis Bohlen, Mehmet Bugac, Georgi Danailov, Chris Dell, Tom Devine, Craig Dicker, Ambassador Edward Djerejian, Helena Finn, Zaza Gachechiladze, Jane Geniesse, Nilufer Gole, Elias Haddad, Professor Michael Handel, Dick Hoagland, Ioana Ieronim, Susan Jacobs, Marwan Kassem, Ian Kelly, Craig Kennedy, Judith Kipper, Michael Krause, Samir Lahoud, Ernest Latham, Murray and Lonnie Levin, Bernard Lewis, Alan Luxenberg, David Makovsky, Maia Mania, Ambassador Steve Mann, Judith Miller, Yehuda Mirsky, Jamil Mroue, Professor Williamson Murray, Lima Nabeel, Corneliu Nicolescu, Ayse Ozakinci, Gizem Ozkulahci, Ambassador Mark Parris, Robert Parsons, Semadar Perry, Daniel Pipes, Allen Pizzey, Hugh Pope, Tom Prondus, Vasile Puscas, Ahmed Rashid, Alexander Rondeli, Ambassador Jim Rosapepe, Ayman Safadi, Tudor Şeulean, Harvey Sicherman, Carl Siebentritt, Victoria Sloan, Mihai Statulescu, Amjad Tadros, Gebran Tueni, John Waterbury, Laurie Weitzenkorn, Mary Ann and Ben Whitten, Selina Williams, and General Anthony C. Zinni.

My wife, Maria Cabral, and son, Michael Kaplan, put up with my long absences, for which I thank them dearly.

Finally, I would like to say a word about guidebooks. Lately, there has been talk of journalism as literature. Well, the same might be said for some guidebooks. When you come down to it, most policy works about countries are too abstract for practical use. But nothing is as insightful as a comprehensive guidebook. Correspondents I know rely on them, but few of us like to admit it. The best one I encountered in this project was Roger Rosen's *The Georgian Republic,* published by Odyssey.

NOTES

AUTHOR'S NOTE

1. Quoted in John Keegan's *Six Armies in Normandy* (London: Jonathan Cape, 1982).

1.   RUDOLF FISCHER, COSMOPOLITAN

1. Fischer's knowledge of the Balkans can indeed be compared with Burton's knowledge of India, Arabia, and Africa. In the introduction to his Balkan travel classic *Between the Woods and the Water: The Middle Danube to the Iron Gates* (London: John Murray, 1986), Patrick Leigh Fermor writes, "My debt to Rudolf Fischer is beyond reckoning. His omniscient range of knowledge" has been a "constant delight and stimulus . . ."

2. See Fischer's article "The Shriving of a Penitent Central European" (Cluj-Napoca, Romania: *Transylvanian Review*, Summer 1997).

3. Fischer refers to *The Merry Widow*, a Viennese operetta written in 1905 by the Hungarian composer Franz Lehár.

4. See Robert Strausz-Hupe's *Geopolitics: The Struggle for Space and Power* (New York: G. P. Putnam's Sons, 1942).

5. For more background, see Gusztav Molnar's "The Geopolitics of NATO Enlargement" (Budapest: *The Hungarian Quarterly*, Summer 1997).

6. See John Lukacs's *Budapest 1900: A Historical Portrait of a City and Its Culture* (New York: Weidenfeld & Nicolson, 1988) and Henry Kissinger's *A World Restored: Metternich, Castlereagh and the Problems of Peace 1812–1822* (Boston: Houghton Mifflin, 1954). Kissinger, particularly, offers a critique of the 1848 revolutions, which, as he intimates, while espousing universal principles, were in fact based on ethnic nationalism.

7. Many cities and towns in Transylvania have traditionally been known by three names—Romanian, Hungarian, and German—because of the historical ethnic mix of peo-

ple living in the region. Kolozsvár is the Hungarian name for the city of Cluj (now known as Cluj-Napoca), Romania, which has also been called Clausenburg. Sármás is the Hungarian name for the village known as Sărmaşu in Romanian.

8. See Randolph L. Braham's *The Politics of Genocide: The Holocaust in Hungary,* Volume 2 (New York: Columbia University Press, 1981) for an account of these events. Hungarian units swept into Transylvania in a last-ditch attempt against a combined Soviet-Romanian onslaught. The killings at Sărmaşu were not the work of the Hungarian fascist group the Arrow Cross but rather of ultrarightist officers in the regular army. The day of the massacre, the army unit in Sărmaşu was under the command of Captain László Lancz.

9. The translation was provided by Tudor Şeulean, a Romanian friend who accompanied me.

2. HEADING EAST

1. Source for the energy statistics: Geoffrey Kemp's and Robert E. Harkavy's *Strategic Geography and the Changing Middle East* (Washington, D.C.: Carnegie Endowment for International Peace and the Brookings Institution Press, 1997).

2. The phrase "seismograph of Europe" is from Kissinger's *A World Restored.* "Tartary" is the Elizabethan word for the mainly Turkic areas of western Central Asia, which is also known as Turkestan.

3. The most lucid explanation of the complicated origins of the Hungarians I have come across is not in a historical or academic text but in a cookbook: George Lang's *Cuisine of Hungary* (New York: Random House, 1971).

4. See Volume 4 of Edward Gibbon's *The Decline and Fall of the Roman Empire* (New York: Everyman's Library, 1910).

5. Roughly speaking, Pannonia overlaps with western Hungary, Upper Moesia with Serbia, and Dacia with Romania.

6. Source for all statistics: European Association for Comparative Economic Studies in Budapest.

3. THE WIDENING CHASM

1. Herodotus' reference is to a northern Thracian people called the *Getae*—the Greek word for what the Romans called the Dacians, who are the forerunners of the modern Romanians.

2. Romanians'—and particularly Iancu's—violent resistance against the Hungarians illustrates how the noble goals of the 1848 democratic uprisings descended sometimes into mere interethnic warfare. See Kurt W. Treptow's *A History of Romania* (Iaşi, Romania: The Center for Romanian Studies, 1996).

3. Today, the province of Moldavia, Romania (known as "Moldova" in Romanian), shares a border with the independent (formerly Soviet) republic of Moldova, to the east.

4. Ceauşescu, combining extreme Romanian nationalism with Stalinism, made life miserable for the Saxons. In the 1980s, he allowed the German government to buy exit

visas for them at exorbitant prices in hard currency. See chapter 10 of *Balkan Ghosts: A Journey Through History* (New York: St. Martin's, 1993).

4. THIRD WORLD EUROPE

1. Source: European Bank for Reconstruction and Development.

2. About three quarters, or more, of Romanians are Eastern Orthodox Christians. (The *World Almanac* says 70 percent; the Romanian Orthodox Church claims 87 percent.) Minorities include Roman Catholics, Greek Uniates, Protestants of various denominations, and Jews.

3. See Traugott Tamm's *Über den Ursprung der Rumänen* ("About the Origin of the Romanians") (Bonn, 1891). This passage is quoted in English by D. Mitrany in his essay "Rumania: Her History and Politics," included in *The Balkans: A History of Bulgaria, Serbia, Greece, Rumania, and Turkey*, by Nevill Forbes, Arnold J. Toynbee, D. Mitrany, and D. G. Hogarth (Oxford: Clarendon, 1915).

4. Confirming this, Father Iustin Marchis, a reform-minded cleric at the Stavropoleos Church in Bucharest, told me: "Eastern Orthodoxy puts one's relationship with God ahead of one's relationship with the community."

5. BALKAN REALISTS

1. See Brucan's *The Wasted Generation* (Boulder, Colorado: Westview Press, 1993).

2. Trans-Dniestria lies east of Moldavia and Bessarabia, in the Ukraine. Here the Romanian army murdered 185,000 Jews in late 1941 and early 1942. See my book *Balkan Ghosts*.

3. This was a common emotion. Milovan Djilas, a Yugoslav partisan leader during World War II, wrote that Stalin "got right to the heart of a matter with lightning speed and in such a way that little or nothing was left to discuss and resolve. Stalin was decisive." See Djilas's *Fall of the New Class: A History of Communism's Self-Destruction* (New York: Knopf, 1998), and *Conversations with Stalin* (New York: Harcourt, Brace and World, 1962).

6. PIVOT STATE

1. See Codrescu's *Armata Română* in *Revolutia din Decembrie 1989* ("The Romanian Army in the Revolution of December 1989") (Bucharest: Editura Militara, 1994).

2. Reverend László Tökes, the ethnic-Hungarian pastor of the Calvinist Reformed Church in Timişoara, had been preaching against Ceauşescu's repression of Hungarians. The regime's attempt to send Tökes into internal exile sparked riots, which spread to Bucharest and ended ten days later with the execution of the Ceauşescus.

3. See Sulzberger's *A Long Row of Candles: Memoirs and Diaries, 1934–1954* (Toronto: Macmillan, 1969).

4. Greece and Serbia are both Eastern Orthodox nations and traditional allies against

the Moslem Turks. For a review of Greek foreign policy toward the former Yugoslavia, see Nicholas X. Rizopoulos's "Pride, Prejudice, and Myopia," *World Policy Journal,* Fall 1993.

5. See Huntington's "The Clash of Civilizations?" *Foreign Affairs,* Summer, 1993.

6. See Robert Chase's, Emily Hill's, and Paul Kennedy's *The Pivotal States: A New Framework for U.S. Policy in the Developing World* (New York: Norton, 1999).

7. "CIVILIZATIONAL CHOICE"

1. See especially Canetti's *Crowds and Power* (London: Victor Gollancz, 1962).

2. See also Krassimir Kanev's *Ethnicity and Nationalism in East-Central Europe and the Balkans* (Hanover, New Hampshire: Dartmouth University Press, 1998).

3. The Partnership for Peace was one of several organizations initiated by NATO and the European Union to provide quasi-European status for countries seeking to join the Western alliance network.

4. The official figure is 312,000. Most experts, though, put the figure at 500,000. Ilona Tomova, in *The Gypsies: In the Transition Period,* published by the International Center for Minority Studies in Sofia in 1995, cited a Ministry of Interior survey indicating a Gypsy population as high as 600,000. Statistics and other information about Gypsies in Bulgaria are partly based on an interview with Antonina Zhelyazkova, president of the International Center for Minority Studies in Sofia, which receives support from the Soros foundation.

8. WRESTLERS VERSUS DEMOCRATS

1. See Jovo Nikolov's "Organized Crime in Bulgaria," *East European Constitutional Review,* Fall 1997.

2. The English edition is called *Fascism* (Sofia, Bulgaria: Zlatorog, 1997).

3. Zhelev was Bulgaria's president from 1990 through early 1997, one of the longest-serving leaders of post-Communist Eastern Europe, along with Vaclav Havel of the Czech Republic and Árpád Goncz of Hungary.

9. THE LEGACY OF ORTHODOXY

1. Galina Sabeva, Reuters, Internet (Sofia), November 6, 1997.

2. Nicolas Berdyaev, *The Origin of Russian Communism,* translated by R. M. French (Ann Arbor: University of Michigan Press, [1937] 1960).

3. See Michael Radu's "The Burden of Eastern Orthodoxy," *Orbis,* Spring, 1998.

4. Moslems here include both the Turkish minority and the Pomaks, Bulgarians who converted to Islam during the Turkish occupation and who live mainly in the Rhodope Mountains.

10. "TO THE CITY"

1. Edward Gibbon. *The Decline and Fall of the Roman Empire,* [1776–1787] Volume IV (New York: Everyman's Library, 1910).

11. THE "DEEP STATE"

1. Quoted in Lord Kinross's *The Ottoman Centuries: The Rise and Fall of the Turkish Empire* (New York: Quill, 1977).

2. See Paul B. Henze's "Turkey: Toward the Twenty-First Century (Santa Monica, California: the Rand Corporation, 1992).

3. Three quarters of Turkish officers are from lower-middle-class backgrounds. It is thought that the petit-bourgeois character of the Turkish military is what accounts for its benign influence on politics. See Mehmet Ali Birand's *Shirts of Steel: An Anatomy of the Turkish Armed Forces,* Foreword by William Hale, translated from the Turkish by Saliha Paker and Ruth Christie (London: I. B. Tauris & Co., 1991).

4. See Daniel Pipes's "A New Axis: The Emerging Turkish-Israeli Entente" in the Winter 1997–98 issue of *The National Interest* (Washington) for a substantive account of the accords.

12. THE "CORPSE IN ARMOUR"

1. In fact, the Kurds are the world's largest nation without a state.

2. Statements by the Turkish prime minister, generals, and other officials were all reported in the Turkish press during my stay. Quotes by intelligence specialists are based on off-the-record interviews I conducted.

3. The October 6, 1998, speech was reported in the *Turkish Daily News.*

4. Öcalan's expulsion from Damascus was reported by the media. The Kurdish leader's subsequent wanderings led him to Italy, where he was arrested on November 13, 1998. PKK training bases in the Syrian-controlled Bekaa Valley of Lebanon were also reportedly closed.

5. See Nicole and Hugh Pope's *Turkey Unveiled: A History of Modern Turkey* (Woodstock, New York: Overlook Press, 1998).

6. See Arnold J. Toynbee's *A Study of History* (Oxford: Oxford University Press, [1939] 1946).

7. Toynbee's source is Xenophon's *Anabasis,* known in English as *The Persian Expedition,* the memoir of the Greek general's 401 B.C. retreat from Persia through Anatolia to the Black Sea. It is now published by Penguin (1984).

8. See Georges Roux's *Ancient Iraq* (London: George Allen & Unwin, 1964).

9. It was in the Museum of Anatolian Civilizations that Atatürk had lain in state for years after his death in 1938, before a mausoleum was built for him outside Ankara.

13. THE NEW CALIPHATE

1. See Olivier Roy's *The Failure of Political Islam,* translated by Carol Volk (Cambridge, Mass.: Harvard University Press, 1994).

2. Ibid.

3. In 1926, Atatürk yielded the contested Mosul province, dominated by ethnic Turks and Kurds, to the British. It later became part of Iraq. For a complete description of the negotiations, see Lord Kinross's *Atatürk: The Rebirth of a Nation* (London: Weidenfeld and Nicolson, 1964).

4. Indeed, Turkish rule over Islam can be said to have started even earlier, in A.D. 861, when Turkish soldier-slaves called Mamluks assassinated Al-Mu'tasim, heir to the caliph Al-Mutawakkil in Baghdad, making the Mamluks the power brokers throughout the Middle East.

5. See Daniel Pipes's *Greater Syria: The History of an Ambition* (New York: Oxford University Press, 1990).

6. I wrote briefly about Antioch (Antakya) in *The Ends of the Earth* (New York: Vintage, [1996] 1997).

14. THE SACRED AND THE PROFANE

1. I learned about Syria's economy from briefings in Damascus, Beirut, and Amman and from printed reports, including "Syria's Economy: The Party's Over," *The Economist,* January 17, 1998.

2. Eblaite is a Semitic dialect discovered in the 1970s by Italian epigraphers in the course of their excavation of Tel Mardikh, thirty-four miles south of Aleppo, containing the remains of the ancient city of Ebla. The excavation is mired in controversy, basically because the Syrian authorities are uncomfortable with results that indicate Eblaite's close relationship to ancient Hebrew.

3. See the World Bank's *World Development Report 1997* (New York: Oxford University Press).

4. See "As Christians Vanish From Their Cradle," *The Economist,* July 18, 1998.

5. For example, on March 16, 1993, Öcalan announced a cease-fire in his war against Turkey to the world press at Bar Elias, in the Bekaa Valley. In addition to the news reports, see Nicole and Hugh Pope's *Turkey Unveiled.* There is a large photo of combat training at the PKK camp in the Syrian-controlled Bekaa in Susan Meiselas's *Kurdistan: In the Shadow of History* (New York: Random House, 1998) (Photo by Ed Kashi, *National Geographic*).

6. Some of this history is reprised from my book *The Arabists: The Romance of an American Elite* (New York: Free Press, 1993).

7. The best account of Syrian politics in this period is Patrick Seale's *The Struggle for Syria: A Study of Post-War Arab Politics 1945–1958* (Oxford, England: Oxford University Press, 1965).

8. See Seale's *The Struggle for Syria.*

9. See Pipes's *Greater Syria.*

10. See Roy's *The Failure of Political Islam.*

11. See Roy, in addition to Bernard Lewis's *The Middle East: A Brief History of the Last 2,000 Years* (New York: Simon & Schuster, 1995).

12. See Gibbon's *Decline and Fall of the Roman Empire,* Volume 4.

13. Freya Stark, *East Is West* (London: John Murray, 1945).

14. Ibid.

15. Associated Press, "To Dismay of Scholars, Syrians Use 'Dead Cities,' " *The New York Times,* September 6, 1998.

16. *Mesopotamia* is Greek for "between the rivers," a reference to the fertile land between the Tigris and Euphrates, in the heart of present-day Iraq.

17. See Gibbon's *Decline and Fall of the Roman Empire,* Volume 1.

18. The source is *The Historia Augusta,* the section written by Flavius Vopiscus (quoted in Gibbon).

19. The massacre occurred on June 27, 1980, the day after a failed assassination attempt on Assad. See Patrick Seale's *Assad: The Struggle for the Middle East* (London: I. B. Tauris, 1988). Human-rights groups regularly mentioned the Tadmor prison in Palmyra as one of Syria's worst.

15. THE CORPORATE SATELLITE

1. Lebanese presidents Bashir Gemayal and René Mouawwad were killed in 1982 and 1989, respectively. Prime Minister Rashid Karami was killed in 1987. Communal leaders and notables who were killed included Druze chieftain Kamal Jumblatt in 1977, Mufti Hasan Khaled in 1989, and Christian militia leader Dany Chamoun in 1990.

2. Imam Musa al-Sadr disappeared in Libya in 1978, killed, presumably, by the Sunni leader there, Muammar Gaddafi. See Fouad Ajami's *The Vanished Imam: Musa al Sadr and the Shia of Lebanon* (Ithaca, New York: Cornell University Press, 1986).

3. The Lebanese women who work as maids in hotels by the Sea of Galilee are relatives of soldiers in the South Lebanese Army, a group supported by Israel in the area of Lebanon it occupies. Whatever the politics, in poverty-stricken South Lebanon, an Israeli work permit is considered a "perk."

4. The magazine was the October 1998 issue of *Lebanon Opportunities.* The poverty figure is from "The Mapping of Living Conditions in Lebanon," a United Nations Development Programme study. Concerning the widening gulf between rich and poor, Lebanon is not unique. Gated communities and luxury flats are proliferating in Egypt, where a third of the population lives in homes with dirt floors, according to an October 27, 1998, Associated Press article by Anthony Shadid.

5. See my book *The Arabists* for a brief history of the AUB.

6. For a description of how and why secular Arab nationalism failed, see Fouad Ajami's *The Dream Palace of the Arabs: A Generation's Odyssey* (New York: Pantheon, 1998).

7. See Ajami's *The Vanished Imam.* Also see Robert Fisk's *Pity the Nation: The Abduction of Lebanon* (New York: Simon & Schuster, 1990).

8. See Ajami's *The Vanished Imam.* Crown prince Hassan bin Talal of Jordan takes up this theme, too, in his remarks to me in a later chapter.

9. In his political-science classic *The Ruling Class,* Gaetano Mosca distinguishes "feu-

dal" from "bureaucratic" states. By "feudal," Mosca meant "that type of political organization in which all the executive functions of society—the economic, the judicial, the administrative, the military—are exercised simultaneously by the same individuals, while at the same time the state is made up of small social aggregates," each of which is self-sufficient. Lebanon and Syria, controlled by a handful of men in Damascus, yet at the same time an assemblage of regionally based religious communities (Maronite, Druze, Sunni, Shia, Alawite . . .) satisfy Mosca's definition of feudalism. They may have bureaucracies, but they are by no means bureaucratic states, built on laws and institutions, with stability and predictability. The same is true for many other Arab states.

10. The editorial ran October 8, 1998.

11. See Warren Singh-Bartlett's "Deconstructing Beirut," The *Daily Star,* Beirut, October 22, 1998.

12. Niccolò Machiavelli, *Discourses on Livy,* translated by Julia Conaway Bondanella and Peter Bondanella (New York: Oxford University Press, 1997).

13. See Fisk's *Pity the Nation.*

14. Ibid.

15. Photos of Dany Chamoun and his family were on display in Deir al-Qamar. The younger Chamoun, the leader of the Maronite "Tiger" militia, was murdered with his wife and children in 1990, when the Syrians consolidated their hold on Lebanon. Many blame the killing on Assad.

16. See Stark's *East Is West.*

17. For an overview of Tyre's history, I used, among other works, Ali Khalil Badawi's *Tyre and Its Region* (Beirut: Ezzedine Printing).

18. Herodotus, *The Histories,* translated by Aubrey de Selincourt (Middlesex, England: Penguin Books, 1954).

16. THE CARAVAN STATE

1. See Machiavelli's *Discourses on Livy.*

2. See Seale's *The Struggle for Syria.*

3. See Roy's *The Failure of Political Islam.*

4. See Mosca's *The Ruling Class.*

5. T. E. Lawrence, *Seven Pillars of Wisdom: A Triumph* (London: Jonathan Cape, [1926] 1935).

6. Ibid.

7. Demographic and economic figures on Jordan come from interviews with Jordanian experts—including the economist and writer Fahed Fanek—and published reports.

8. See the 1998 report on living conditions in Jordan by the Norwegian Fafo Institute for Applied Sciences.

9. These statistics were compiled from the Central Intelligence Agency, among other sources, by Professor Michael Handel of the U.S. Naval War College.

10. Christians made up 2 to 4 percent of the populations of Jordan, the West Bank, Gaza, and Iraq; 10 percent of Syria; and 30 to 40 percent of Lebanon, according to *The Economist,* July 18, 1998.

11.   See Roy's *The Failure of Political Islam.*

12.   See Ira M. Lapidus's "The Middle East's Discomfiting Continuities," *Orbis,* Fall 1998.

13.   Indeed, Hassan, too much of an intellectual, perhaps, lacked the steady temperament of the late king's eldest son, whose career had been in the military.

17.   CROSSING THE JORDAN

1.   Muhammed Asad, *The Road to Mecca* (New York: Simon & Schuster 1954).

18.   SEPPHORIS AND THE RENEWAL OF JUDAISM

1.   *Babylonian Talmud,* Megillah 7:1. The Babylonian Talmud is a version of the Talmud composed by Jewish scholars in Babylon in the fifth and sixth centuries A.D.

2.   See Bernard Lewis's *The Middle East: A Brief History of the Last 2,000 Years* (New York: Simon & Schuster, 1995). Lewis notes that whereas the Middle East has seen one civilization and language displace another—with many disappearing from history—the ancient cultures and languages of both India and China have, to the contrary, continuously evolved.

3.   My summary of Sepphoris's history comes mainly from the following sources: *Sepphoris in Galilee: Crosscurrents of Culture,* edited by Rebecca Martin Nagy, Carol L. Meyers, Eric M. Meyers, and Zeev Weiss (Raleigh, N.C.: North Carolina Museum of Art, 1996); "Sepphoris, the Well-Remembered City," Stuart S. Miller, *Biblical Archaeologist,* June 1992; and *Zippori,* Ehud Netzer and Zeev Weiss (Jerusalem: Israel Exploration Society, 1994). I have also met with Israeli historians and read the material available at the site itself.

4.   Josephus Flavius, *Antiquities of the Jews,* translated by William Whiston (Edinburgh, Scotland: William P. Nimmo, 1867).

5.   Josephus Flavius, *Life,* translated by William Whiston (Edinburgh, Scotland: William P. Nimmo, 1867).

6.   Scholars passionately debate these points.

7.   Sources: *Palestinian Talmud:* Kila'yim 9, 32b; Ketubot 12, 35a. See Miller article in *Biblical Archaeologist.*

8.   See Netzer's and Weiss's *Zippori,* in footnote 3.

9.   Josephus Flavius, *The Jewish War,* translated by G. A. Williamson (Middlesex, England: Penguin, 1959). Amos Elon comments on the negative characteristics of the first-century Jewish zealots in *The Israelis: Founders and Sons* (New York: Holt Rinehart and Winston, 1971).

19.   THROBBING HEART OF THE MIDDLE EAST

1.   A Jordanian associate of Assad made such a comparison with Alexander the Great to *New York Times* correspondent Judith Miller. See her book *God Has Ninety-Nine Names: Reporting from a Militant Middle East* (New York: Simon & Schuster, 1996).

2. See Lewis's *The Middle East: A Brief History of the Last 2,000 Years,* and Mosca's *The Ruling Class.*

3. Economic statistics in this chapter are from numerous published sources. Eliyahu Kanovsky has written intelligently about the Israeli economy (see his "Marketing the 'New Middle East,'" *Commentary,* April 1997.) *New York Times* columnist Thomas Friedman has also written often on this subject.

20. TO TURKEY'S NORTHEASTERN BORDER

1. See national security analyst Ralph Peter's description of extreme nationalism and fundamentalism in *Fighting for the Future* (Mechanicsburg, Pennsylvania: Stackpole Books, 1999).

2. See *Black Sea* by Neal Ascherson (New York, Hill and Wang, 1995) for a worthwhile description of Trabzon and Greek civilization around these shores.

21. STALIN'S BEAUTIFUL HOMELAND

1. See Bertram D. Wolfe's *Three Who Made a Revolution: A Biographical History* (New York: Dial, 1948).

2. Ibid.

3. Memoirs of Soso Iremashvili, quoted by Wolfe.

4. Leon Trotsky, *Stalin: An Appraisal,* translated by Charles Malamuth. See Roger Rosen's *The Georgian Republic* (Kent, England: The Guidebook Company and Hodder and Stoughton, 1991).

5. L. Mellaart, "The Earliest Settlements in Western Asia from the Ninth to the End of the Fifth Millennium, B.C.," *The Cambridge Ancient History,* Volume 1 (Cambridge, England: Cambridge University Press, 1970–75).

6. *The Geography of Strabo,* translated by Horace Leonard Jones (New York: Loeb Classical Library, 1928). See also Ascherson's *Black Sea.*

7. See Paul B. Henze's "Conflict in the Caucasus: Background, Problems, and Prospects for Mitigation." Unpublished.

8. See Rosen's *The Georgian Republic.*

9. My summary of Georgian history is based largely on a definitive work by Ronald Grigor Suny, *The Making of the Georgian Nation* (Bloomington, Indiana: Indiana University Press, 1988 and 1994).

10. See N. Adontz, *Armenia in the Period of Justinian: The Political Conditions Based on the Naxarar System* (Lisbon: Louvain, 1970).

11. See Wolfe's *Three Who Made a Revolution.*

12. See my book *Balkan Ghosts: A Journey Through History* (New York: St. Martin's, 1993).

13. See Elisabeth Fuller's "Geopolitics and the Gamsakhurdia Factor," a paper delivered at an academic conference in Phoenix, November 1992. See also Suny's *The Making of the Georgian Nation.*

14. It was a Georgian-speaking BBC reporter, Robert Parsons, who first compared Gamsakhurdia with Macbeth in his article "A Georgian Tragedy," in the October 23, 1991, issue of *Soviet Analyst.*

15. See Suny's *The Making of the Georgian Nation.*

16. Anatol Lieven, "*Qu'est-ce qu'une nation?* Scholarly Debate and the Realities of Eastern Europe," *The National Interest,* Fall 1997.

17. See *The Travels of Marco Polo.*

22. FOSSIL NATIONS

1. Source: The United Nations Development Programme.

2. According to the United Nations, Georgia's unemployment rate had risen from 15.7 percent in 1989 to 38.2 percent in 1995; since then, statistics have been unavailable.

3. See Wolfe's *Three Who Made a Revolution.*

23. FROM TBILISI TO BAKU

1. For more details see my book *The Ends of the Earth: A Journey at the Dawn of the 21st Century* (New York: Random House, 1996).

2. Kirov went on to become a popular party leader in Leningrad. His assassination sparked the Great Purge of 1934–1938. But in 1956, Khrushchev strongly suggested that Stalin himself had planned Kirov's assassination.

24. IMPERIAL COLLISIONS

1. John Gunther, *Twelve Cities* (New York: Harper & Row, 1967).

2. Sources: the Central Intelligence Agency and the Commonwealth of Independent States' Statistical Yearbook. See also Martha Brill Olcott's "The Caspian's False Promise," *Foreign Policy,* Summer 1998.

3. See "Unlocking the Assets: Energy and the Future of Central Asia and the Caucasus" (Houston: Baker Institute, Rice University, April 1998); and "Central Asia and Xinjiang, China: Emerging Energy, Economic and Ethnic Tensions," by James P. Dorian, Brett Wigdortz, and Dru Gladney, Society for Central Asian Studies, 1997.

4. See Richard Pevear's introduction to the 1993 edition of Fyodor Dostoyevsky's *Crime and Punishment* (New York: Vintage, 1993).

25. BY BOAT TO TARTARY

1. I use the word *grotesques* in the same way that Sherwood Anderson did in his novel *Winesburg, Ohio* (New York: Viking, [1919] 1958). Anderson writes: "The grotesques were not all horrible. Some were amusing, some almost beautiful . . ."

2. See Robert Cullen, "The Rise and Fall of the Caspian Sea," *National Geographic,* May 1999.

3. Nevertheless, the collectivization of peasants in Azerbaijan in 1930, for example, met with brutal repression, with troops firing indiscriminately at civilians and thousands escaping into Iran. See Robert Conquest's *The Harvest of Sorrow: Soviet Collectivization and the Terror-Famine* (New York: Oxford University Press, 1986). See also Isaac Deutscher's *Stalin* (New York: Oxford University Press, 1949).

26. NEW KHANATES

1. For the best general history of the colonial wars in Central Asia, see Peter Hopkirk's *The Great Game: The Struggle for Empire in Central Asia* (New York: Kodansha, [1990] 1992).

2. See Ahmed Rashid's *The Resurgence of Central Asia: Islam or Nationalism* (Atlantic Highlands, New Jersey: Zed, 1994). This is the sharpest book on the historical background and the present conditions of the successor states to the Soviet Union in Central Asia.

3. See both Rashid's *The Resurgence of Central Asia* and M. Saray's "Russo-Turkmen Relations up to 1874," *Central Asia Survey,* vol. 3, number 4.

4. See Kathleen Hopkirk's *Central Asia: A Traveller's Companion* (London: John Murray, 1994).

5. See Peter Hopkirk's *The Great Game.*

6. See Rashid's *The Resurgence of Central Asia.*

27. A HERODOTEAN LANDSCAPE

1. I reported on Uzbekistan and Kazakhstan in *The Ends of the Earth.*

2. See Geoffrey Moorhouse's *On the Other Side: A Journey Through Soviet Central Asia* (New York: Henry Holt, 1990).

28. EARTH, FIRE, WATER

1. This poem was read in public by Iasha Bablian in Nagorno-Karabakh in March 1975. See Ronald Grigor Suny's *Looking Toward Ararat: Armenia in Modern History* (Bloomington, Indiana: Indiana University Press, 1993).

2. The Orthodox Church in Armenia is officially called the Armenian Apostolic Church. It broke from the rest of the Orthodox world in A.D. 506, at the Council of Dvin, when it rejected the ruling of the earlier Council of Chalcedon (A.D. 451) that Christ had two natures (man and god). The Armenians, thus, are Orthodox Monophysites, believing Christ has only one nature, that of god. The Coptic Churches of Ethiopia and Egypt and the Syrian Jacobites are also Monophysites.

3. See G. W. Abgarian's *The Matenadaran* (Yerevan, Armenia: Armenia State Publishing House, 1962).

4. See Peter Novick's *The Holocaust in American Life* (Boston: Houghton Mifflin, 1999).

5. See Suny's *Looking Toward Ararat.*

6. Ibid.

7. Ibid.

8. See Thomas Goltz's *Azerbaijan Diary* (Armonk, New York: M. E. Sharpe, 1998).

9. See Karl W. Deutsch's "Are Our Models of Nationalism Western and Provincial?" unpublished lecture, Harvard University, November 1980.

10. Nikolai Gogol, *Dead Souls* [1842], translated by Richard Pevear and Larissa Volokhonsky (New York: Vintage, 1996).

11. See Jacob Burckhardt's *The Civilization of the Renaissance in Italy* [1860], translated from German by S.G.C. Middlemore, 1878 (New York: Random House, 1878, 1954).

INDEX

ABOUT THE AUTHOR

ROBERT D. KAPLAN is a correspondent for *The Atlantic Monthly* and the bestselling author of seven previous books on travel and foreign affairs, translated into many languages, including *Balkan Ghosts, The Arabists, The Ends of the Earth,* and *The Coming Anarchy.* He is a senior fellow at the New America Foundation. He lives with his wife and son in western Massachusetts.

ABOUT THE TYPE

This book was set in Garamond, a typeface designed by the French printer Jean Jannon. It is styled after Garamond's original models. The face is dignified, and is light but without fragile lines. The italic is modeled after a font of Granjon, which was probably cut in the middle of the sixteenth century.